Data Communications

Uyless Black Series on Computer Communications

Subscription information to BYTE Magazine:
Call 1-800-257-9402 or write Circulation Dept.,
One Phoenix Mill Lane, Peterborough, NH 03458.

Data Communications

Larry Hughes

Department of Mathematics and Computing Science
Saint Mary's University
Halifax, Nova Scotia

McGraw-Hill, Inc.

New York   St. Louis   San Francisco   Auckland   Bogotá
Caracas   Hamburg   Lisbon   London   Madrid
Mexico   Milan   Montreal   New Delhi   Paris
San Juan   São Paulo   Singapore
Sydney   Tokyo   Toronto

Library of Congress Cataloging-in-Publication Data

Hughes, Larry.
    Data communications / Larry Hughes.
      p. cm. — (Uyless Black series on computer communications)
    Includes bibliographical references and index.
    ISBN 0-07-909872-X
    1. Computer networks. 2. Data transmission systems.
  3. Communications software. I. Title. II. Series.
  TK5105.5.H84   1992
  004.6—dc20   91-32418
                                              CIP

1 2 3 4 5 6 7 8 9 0 DOC/DOC 9 7 6 5 4 3 2 1

ISBN 0-07-909872-X

The sponsoring editor for this book was Neil Levine.

Printed and bound by R. R. Donnelley & Sons Company.

To all the trees that went into making this book.

Contents

Preface

A fundamental concept characteristic of computing science (from the basic electronic circuit, through programming languages, to user applications) is *input-processing-output*. One aspect of computing science that exhibits the principle of input-processing-output, but that is often overlooked and taken for granted, is *communications*. Communications have always been an integral part of the development of computers and computing science: from von Neumann's original architecture through the early timesharing systems of the 1960s, to the growing array of computer networks that exist today.

As with most aspects of computing science, communications can be discussed in terms of different levels or *layers*. At the highest level is the user who wants to transfer information from one location to another (whether a file from a computer on one side of the world to the user's local computer or simply a character from a terminal to a central computer), while at the lowest level is information, in the form of bits, moving between computers. The term *data communications* is usually applied to the "lower layers" of a communication; that is, those layers that are responsible for the transfer of the information (i.e., the data) to the intended destination(s). Since most users are well removed from the intricacies of the system supporting the communication, the lower layers may only become an issue should the system fail. For example, to the user of a remote database, communications become important if the communication system fails. However, to the person maintaining the communication system, the contents of the information should be irrelevant; what is important is the reliable transfer of the information.

Although traditionally an engineering discipline, data communications is rapidly becoming of interest to professional programmers as well as to many university and college computing science programs for a wide variety of reasons, including:

- growing demand for computers to support different types of communication
- development and reliance upon communication software
- expanding use of computer networks

With the appropriate facilities, data communications can be taught in a practical, hands-on manner. Ideally, students should have access to equipment that supports a number of different networks and permits experimenting with as many different aspects of data communications as possible. However, much of the equipment needed to teach data communications is prohibitively expensive, even when used with low-cost personal computers such as the ubiquitous PC. For example, the costs associated with an Ethernet card for a single PC can range anywhere from $200 to $1600; additional expenses may be incurred since many local area networks require further specialized hardware and software to manage the network. If a number of different types of networks are to be taught, the costs escalate rapidly.

Fortunately, it *is* possible to teach data communications using the minimum of equipment, while at the same time allowing students to gain a practical understanding of the subject. For example, this book, with its software, covers the major areas of data communications in a practical manner using the PC— the only additional expense being a second serial port (if the machine is not already equipped with one). The software, known as *Commkit*, has been designed to permit anyone with access to at least two PCs to gain experience with the concepts associated with point-to-point communications, network analysis tools, modems, store-and-forward wide area networks, bus and ring local area networks, gateways, and a version of UNIX sockets.

Commkit has been designed to be as unobtrusive as possible, thereby allowing the reader to concentrate on communication issues, rather than on the operating system or the hardware. The software, written entirely in Turbo C, supports message passing between low-level interrupt handlers, background processes, and a foreground process.

The book is organized in a structured fashion, beginning with an examination of the methods by which communications can take place between two computers separated by distances of less than 50 meters. Once limited-distance, point-to-point communications have been thoroughly examined, techniques for handling longer distance communications and larger volume data transfers are presented: the telephone system, and wide area networks. Having presented the principles of networks and synchronous protocols, the book then considers local area network communications. Finally, mechanisms to support communications between computers on separate networks are introduced. The various topics covered in the book are all examined using the Commkit software to highlight the issues surrounding specific areas of data communications. Both executables and source are supplied on the Commkit diskette for all of the topics examined.

The book is divided into five parts.

Part 1 introduces the reader to data communications and the Commkit software. In Chapter 1, the basic concepts and terminology associated with communications in general and data communications, in particular, are covered. The material presented in this chapter is used throughout the remainder of the text. This chapter concludes, as do all subsequent ones, with a series of exercises covering the material presented in the chapter.

The Commkit software, its operation, and the interaction between Commkit and the PC's hardware is described in Chapter 2. A detailed discussion of Commkit, its design, and internal structure is presented by examining interprocess communication using Commkit.

The type of communication that most readers of this book will encounter involves the transmission of information between pairs of objects (such as a PC connected to a central computer). In Part 2, *point-to-point communications* (i.e., communications between pairs of objects) are examined. Once the terminology and concepts associated with point-to-point communications are understood, nearly all other types of communication can be explained.

Point-to-point communications are introduced in Chapter 3 using the asynchronous communication hardware available on all PCs. The chapter presents a detailed examination of how asynchronous communications are achieved. Commkit's point-to-point telephone utility that supports communications between pairs of PCs is given as a detailed case study of asynchronous communications.

Some of the different standards and methods of physically supporting a communication are introduced in Chapter 4. Standards examined include RS-232; while twisted pair and coaxial cable are among the media considered.

One of the biggest headaches in the detection and correction of errors in a communication system is trying to determine what is actually being sent across the communication channel between the communicating devices. This is true in the commercial world as well as in a course on data communications. To assist in error detection and correction, as well as to monitor what is taking place on the communication channel, commercial tools known as *line analysers* are available. Since commercial line analysers can be extremely expensive, Commkit is supplied with a software line analyser. Both Commkit's and existing commercial line analysers are discussed in Chapter 5.

Part 3 moves away from communications consisting solely of single-byte transmission between pairs of computers to the transfer of large volumes of information consisting of hundreds or thousands of bytes across a network of computers. A number of topics are covered including: sending large volumes of information with the minimum of overheads; file transfer; using the telephone system to support data communications; maximizing channel utilization; and utilizing networks of computers to handle data communications.

Chapter 6 examines techniques for sending information that minimize the overheads associated with asynchronous communications by reducing the amount of control information sent, while simultaneously improving the reliability of the data transfer. Commkit is supplied with one such data transfer protocol, which is examined in detail, showing how large volume transfer can be supported while also handling the detection and correction of errors.

The transfer of large volumes of information is typified by copying files between machines. In Chapter 7, file access using Commkit is described and a reliable file transfer protocol is designed. The resulting file transfer protocol is implemented atop the reliable large-volume transfer protocol examined in the previous chapter.

How the telephone system handles communications over longer distances is considered in Chapter 8. Different methods of representing information in the telephone system are discussed in detail. RS-232-C, originally introduced in Chapter 4, is covered in depth to help explain how computers can access the telephone network. Commkit's modem software is discussed and illustrates how access to the telephone network can be achieved.

Chapter 9 is the first of two chapters which consider methods of reducing the overheads associated with using a telephone for communications. This chapter examines how a single channel can be shared or *multiplexed* amongst an number of communicating devices. An example of multiplexing is presented using Commkit's statistical multiplexing software.

The first four chapters of Part 3 serve as the basis for the introduction to wide area networks, which are examined in Chapter 10. Several existing wide area networks are discussed and the concepts associated with them are applied using the Commkit store-and-forward network.

Part 4 moves away from the "traditional" areas of data communications into local area networks, examining two of the best known local area networks topologies: the bus and the ring. In Chapter 11, bus local area networks are discussed in light of existing commercial local area networks such as the Ethernet. The bus network emulator supplied with the Commkit software is examined and illustrates many of the issues associated with bus local area networks.

Chapter 12 builds upon the material covered in the previous chapter to explain ring networks and how they operate. The chapter initially considers the token bus and then progresses into ring local area networks. The concepts associated with ring local area networks are presented in a detailed examination of the Commkit token ring network.

Part 5 considers internetworking, a methodology that allows machines on different, potentially dissimilar, networks to communicate. Two major internetworking issues are examined in detail: the layering of systems and the interconnection of networks. Layering concepts are presented in Chapter 13 using Commkit's version of UNIX sockets, known as sockettes. Sockettes are part of a layered architecture that presents a network independent addressing structure and function atop any of the Commkit networks discussed in Parts 3 and 4. Chapter 14 examines some of the problems associated with interconnecting networks. The chapter includes examples of existing internetworking standards, some of which are illustrated using the Commkit bridge software.

Four appendices are also included. The first, for those readers unfamiliar with the language, is a brief introduction to C. A detailed description of how to run and test Commkit, is given in the second appendix. The third appendix contains a listing of several well-known character codes including ASCII and EBCDIC. The last appendix includes suggested modifications to the software that permit the support of single port operations.

NOTATION

Unless otherwise indicated, all notation in the book conforms to the following formats:

- All software is written in C; source code examples found in the book are displayed in a `typewriter font`. MS-DOS commands are also shown in a `typewriter font`.

- Control characters such as *ETX* and *STX* are shown in *slanted font*.
- Keyboard input to Commkit is highlighted using SMALL CAPITALS.

ACKNOWLEDGEMENTS

In writing a textbook, an author always benefits from the experience of others; *Data Communications* is no exception. Accordingly, I must thank the following people for their helpful suggestions on both the book and the Commkit software: Liz Leboffe of St. John Fisher College, Greg Baur of Western Kentucky University, Doug MacGillivary of Bell Canada, and to the many students who have taken my courses in data communications using Commkit.

Finally, I must thank Sandy Scott, the one person who always knew that the book and the software would be written. Her constant support and encouragement made this book possible.

Larry Hughes

Data Communications

Background

After the American Revolution, the one major seaport on the eastern coast of North America to which the British Navy had access was Halifax. Since the British did not want to lose the rest of their North American colonies, it was imperative that the port of Halifax be defended. Accordingly, a form of an "early warning system" was installed, which consisted of a series of forts stretching from the Atlantic Ocean to the port of Halifax. These forts could relay information about a ship sighted off the coast to the Citadel (a fortress) in Halifax in about 15 minutes:

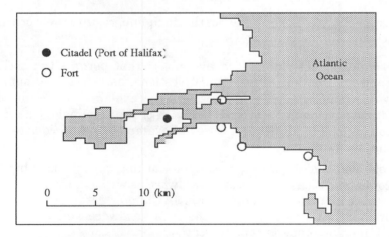

Flags were used to communicate between the forts. Whenever a ship was spotted off the coast, this information was encoded as a unique sequence of flags and then passed from one fort to the next until it reached the Citadel. If the officers in the Citadel were to react to the information, it was important that the encoded information was sent and received correctly by each fort along the coast. For example, the results could have been disastrous if a fort identified a ship as a neutral man-of-war only to have the information corrupted, indicating a French man-of-war. Similarly, if an Admiral's ship was identified, but fog caused the information to be read as "the incoming ship is a scow"; the Admiral might not have been too pleased with the welcome he received.

This seemingly simple example illustrates all of the major issues surrounding data communications:

- information must be *encoded* before it can be *transmitted*. The sailors watching for incoming ships had to decide among themselves the type of ship sighted, and then translate that information into a set of flags.

- *rules* must be in place to ensure that any information sent is received correctly. At a minimum, both the transmitter and receiver must agree upon the same method of translating the encoded information. In eighteenth-century Halifax, all of the forts would be required to use the same flags and interpret them in the same way.

- *detected* errors must initiate an agreed upon set of procedures to follow, which allow the errors to be *corrected*. If errors are permitted to propagate through the system (or, for example, up the chain of command from the officers in the forts to those in the Citadel), the information is of no value and cannot be used or acted upon safely.

- mechanisms must be available to ensure that both the transmitter and receiver remain *synchronized* (or *in-step*). Should the communicating parties lose synchronization, information may be lost. This may have disastrous results (for example, an enemy warship might enter the harbor undetected).

All technical subjects, regardless of the discipline, require their practitioners to understand and be familiar with:

- the *terminology* associated with the subject that permits the exchange of ideas and information. Data communications, as a technical subject, has its own terminology, most of which can be explained in terms of everyday activities. Chapter 1 introduces much of the terminology used in data communications by utilizing a series of examples and by considering how humans communicate.

- the *tools* available for working with (or learning about) the subject. Since data communications incorporates hardware as well as software, it is important to have an understanding of both. In Chapter 2, the Commkit software is examined in terms of some of the PC's hardware and the methods by which Commkit supports communications.

1

Basic Concepts and Terminology

1.1 INTRODUCTION

Communications, whether among humans, animals, or computers, involve the *transfer of information*. Considering that people have developed computers, it should not be surprising that many of the problems that the designers of data communication systems face are, in many respects, similar to those encountered by people communicating on a day-to-day basis. For example, some potential problem areas occur:

- When two people want to talk some agreement must be made to ensure that the person talking eventually stops and the other person has a chance to respond.

- If a person misses part of what was said in a conversation, mechanisms should exist that allow the lost information to be repeated.

- When a person finishes speaking, it is often considered polite (and sometimes necessary) to ask whether what has been said was heard and comprehended.

In this chapter, some of the general terms and concepts associated with communications are introduced. In all cases, everyday examples are used to reinforce the ideas.

1.2 ENTITIES

Communications, unless otherwise stated, are assumed to be between pairs of objects, often called *entities*. The transfer of information occurs across a *channel* (sometimes referred to as a *line*), and can occur over any *medium*, including air, copper wire, or optical fibers. At any moment, an entity can be:

- a *transmitter*, that is, it sends information.
- a *receiver*, that is, it receives information.
- a transmitter *and* a receiver; that is, it can both transmit and receive information simultaneously.

There are three broad categories that describe the type of communication that can take place between entities:

1. A communication in which one entity is the transmitter and the other is the receiver is defined as a *simplex* communication. A simplex communication channel permits the information to flow in one direction only: from the transmitter to the receiver (Figure 1.1). (In Figure 1.1 and subsequent illustrations, T denotes the transmitting entity and R denotes the receiving entity.)

Figure 1.1   Simplex communication

   Examples of simplex communications are often somewhat contrived, but one (common?) example is a programmer talking to a terminal; for as much as the programmer talks, the terminal doesn't respond (and the program doesn't improve either).

2. A communication that permits either entity to transmit, but not simultaneously, is known as a *half-duplex* communication. A typical half-duplex communication involves one entity transmitting its information, while the other receives. The roles are then reversed, and the entity that was originally receiving is now transmitting (while the original transmitter is now receiving). The reversing of roles is known as *line turnaround* (see Figure 1.2).

   An example of a half-duplex communication is a "tin-can telephone" consisting of two tin cans connected by a piece of string. At any point in time, only one person can speak (i.e., transmit) while the other listens (i.e., receives). Line turnaround requires the transmitter to inform the receiver that there is no more information to be transmitted and that the receiver can now transmit.

   A half-duplex communication channel can be used in a simplex fashion if one entity does not relinquish the channel and continues to transmit indefinitely.

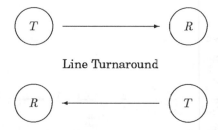

Figure 1.2   Half-duplex communication

3. A communication that permits either entity to transmit and receive simultaneously is known as a *full-duplex* communication. Full-duplex communications are generally used when both entities have large volumes of data to send or when the transmitter wants to determine if the information sent has been received correctly, without having to perform a line turnaround (Figure 1.3).

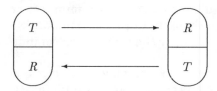

Figure 1.3   Full-duplex communication

Examples of full-duplex communications include (a) sending mail (a person might send a letter to a friend and receive one from the same friend "at the same time"), and (b) talking to someone (both people might attempt to talk at the same time).

Full-duplex communications can be realized in a number of ways. If a single channel is used in a full-duplex communication, each entity is allocated a distinct part of the channel. For example, one entity may transmit on frequency X and receive on frequency Y, while the other entity would transmit on frequency Y and receive on frequency X (Figure 1.4).

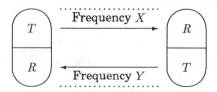

Figure 1.4   Full-duplex communications through frequency sharing

It is possible to make a full-duplex communication channel out of a pair of simplex channels or a pair of half-duplex channels. In these situations, each entity transmits on one channel and receives on the other (see Figure 1.5).

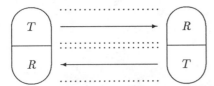

Figure 1.5   Full-duplex communication using half-duplex channels

A full-duplex communication channel can be used in a half-duplex or simplex fashion by forcing the entities to follow certain rules. For example, stopping one of the entities from transmitting would ensure that the channel was used in a simplex fashion.

In a communication involving humans, it is obvious who the entities are—the people involved in the communication. However, in a communication involving computers, it is not so easy to determine the entities, since an entity may be the application processes (i.e., the software requiring the communication), the support software (i.e., the software supporting the communication requirements of the application processes, perhaps needing the communication facilities offered by the underlying hardware), or the processors (computers) themselves.

For example, a communication between two processes may involve one or more processors. In the single processor case, only the processor's communication software is necessary. However, if the processes reside on separate interconnected processors, both communication software and hardware is needed.

The structuring of software so that one level uses the services of an adjacent, lower level is known as *layering*. Layering will be discussed further in subsequent chapters.

1.3   PROTOCOLS

At the beginning of this chapter, a number of examples of communications between humans were presented. These examples illustrated the need for a set of rules to ensure that the communication would proceed in spite of problems such as people attempting to speak simultaneously and information being misunderstood or missed entirely.

Other communicating entities, such as computers or processes, also require rules or *protocols* to ensure that the communication can proceed. Protocols are intended to control both the communication between the stations as well as to define certain characteristics about the communication. Regardless of what they are, all entities participating in the communication must agree on the protocol or the communication may fail. For example, if a protocol states that the communicating entities must transmit in a half-duplex fashion, the communication will probably fail if the entities are connected by a single simplex communication channel.

Broadly speaking, any communication protocol can be discussed in terms of the following:

Coding of information: how the information is represented between the various entities.

Control: how the communication is controlled by the entities involved in the communication.

Error checking and recovery: how the entities ensure that the information is sent and received correctly.

Channel utilization: how efficiently the channel is used by the communicating entities.

Synchronization and timing: how the entities remain "in-step" during the progress of a communication.

Transparency: how the mechanisms supporting the communication are hidden from the entities.

1.3.1   Coding of information

For a communication to take place, both the transmitting and receiving entities must agree upon a common language, written or verbal. For example, for a person in England to carry on a conversation with a person in France, requires that either the person in England know how to speak French, or the person in France know how to speak English, or that both agree to speak a third language.

Although there is no universal *standard* for the coding of information in computers, all manufacturers agree upon the *value* and structure of the *bit*: a single cell having the value of zero or one. Bits can be grouped into four-bit quantities known as *nibbles*, and 3-bit quantities known as *bytes* (Figure 1.6).

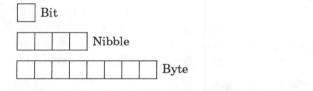

Figure 1.6   Sample bit combinations

The description of the byte data structure depends entirely upon the manufacturer, although some standards do exist (see following list). For example, some manufacturers label bytes from 1 to 8, while others label bytes from 0 to 7. Similarly, the labelling may run in ascending order from right to left (i.e., the right-most bit being 0, and the left-most, 7), while other systems use descending order from right to left (i.e., the right-most bit being 7, and the left-most bit, 0).

The value and interpretation of the byte depends, once again, on the manufacturer. If bytes are considered to be *unsigned*, their possible values are 0 through 255, however, if they are *signed*, the range of values is -128 through +127.

Bytes are also used to represent *characters*. The two most common character codes used by computer manufacturers are:

1. **EBCDIC** (Extended Binary Coded Decimal Interchange Code) a code made popular by IBM in their large mainframe computers in the 1960s, and

2. **ASCII** (American Standard Code for Information Interchange) an alternate standard adopted by almost all non-IBM computer manufacturers; now it is so widespread that even IBM uses it for their PCs.

Appendix C contains character code tables for the 5-bit Baudot code, 7-bit ASCII, and 8-bit EBCDIC.

Not all bytes are intended to represent textual, printable characters; some bytes are used to convey control information such as line feed, carriage return, and form feed. For example, in the table of 7-bit ASCII bytes (see Appendix C.2), the first two columns contain *control characters*, while the remaining six columns (with the exception of DEL at the bottom right of the table), are used to represent printable, or *graphic*, characters.

Although most communications usually occur at the bit or byte level, applications may deal with other data structures that comprise of groupings of bytes. Depending upon the manufacturer, a *word* may be a 16-bit (two-byte) or a 32-bit (four-byte) data structure. Floating-point numbers, consisting of a fractional part (the *mantissa*) and an *exponent*, may be stored and interpreted in a variety of ways, depending upon the precision offered by the manufacturer and the number of bits available to represent the number (floating-point numbers can be 32-bit, 64-bit, or even 128-bit quantities). Fixed-point, or **binary coded decimal (BCD)**, numbers can be stored in one of several different ways, two of which are:

Zoned decimal format has each digit in the BCD number occupying a single byte, the left-most nibble, the *zone nibble*, contains 1111, while the right-most contains the digit (one of 0000 through 1001). The sign (one of 1100, positive; 1101, negative; or 1111, unsigned, assumed positive) is stored in the left-most nibble of the low-order digit. For example, −218 would be stored as:

1111 0010	1111 0001	1101 1000

Packed decimal format removes the zone nibble from each byte and stores each digit in adjacent nibbles. The sign nibble is the same as for zoned decimal but is stored in the right-most nibble of the first byte. In packed decimal, −218 would be stored as follows:

0010 0001	1000 1101

How information is represented on different computers is an important issue in data communications because unless the entities involved in the communication can agree upon how the information is coded, there can be no meaningful exchange of information. For example, if a file of ASCII information is transmitted to an EBCDIC computer, unless some form of translation is made available (i.e., the ASCII bytes are translated into EBCDIC or the EBCDIC computer can interpret ASCII), the information received by the EBCDIC computer may be meaningless.

To make matters even more confusing, although two manufacturers may agree upon the character code, the internal organization or *byte ordering* of the computer's memory may differ from machine to machine. For example, the string ABCDEF is stored as shown in Figure 1.7 in an Intel 80x86 processor.

```
15          8 7          0
+-----------+-----------+
|     B     |     A     |
+-----------+-----------+
|     D     |     C     |
+-----------+-----------+
|     F     |     E     |
+-----------+-----------+
```

Figure 1.7   Intel 80x86 byte ordering

However, the same string, ABCDEF is stored in a Motorola 68000 processor with a different byte ordering (but still ASCII). See Figure 1.8.

```
15          8 7          0
+-----------+-----------+
|     A     |     B     |
+-----------+-----------+
|     C     |     D     |
+-----------+-----------+
|     E     |     F     |
+-----------+-----------+
```

Figure 1.8   Motorola 68000 byte ordering

If data is transmitted between an Intel and a Motorola processor as a series of 8-bit ASCII bytes, the hardware ensures that each byte is read from and written to memory in its proper order. However, if the information is sent as a series of 16-bit words, the receiving processor will receive the bytes in the reverse order. Similar problems can occur when attempting to transmit 16-bit integers as pairs of bytes. In situations such as these, a common byte ordering must be agreed upon. This is discussed in more detail in Chapter 13.

1.3.2 Control

When two people talk, there are many techniques and cues that are used to signal whether the information has been understood, if the information should be repeated, and when the other person can speak. These signals are not usually part of the information that is being conveyed, but the signals are necessary to allow the communication to continue. For example, if you want to gain someone's attention, you might preface what you're about to say to them with their name; however, the person's name has no bearing on the actual information that you want to convey. Other types of control information exist, as well: in order to determine if the receiver has actually received (and understood) the information, the speaker may end what has been said with a question, expecting the receiver to respond to it. The additional information that is used to control the communication is known as *control information*. To distinguish between the information being transmitted and the control information, the noncontrol information is often referred to as a *message*. The extra information required to ensure that the communication can continue is known as an *overhead*.

Although control information does impose an overhead on all messages sent in a communication, the overhead is intended to ensure that the communication can proceed and that the message is received correctly. In a communication between two (computing) entities, messages are rarely, if ever, sent without some type of control information. The message, plus the control information, is sent in a *frame* or a *packet* (Figure 1.9).

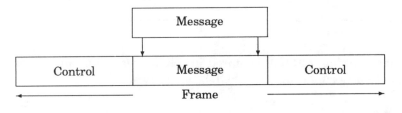

Figure 1.9   Message-Frame relationship

Both frames and packets must conform to a standard agreed upon by all entities in the communication.

What is transmitted as control information depends, in part, upon the protocol being used. At a minimum, the control information should signal the receiver when a message is about to begin and when the message has ended. In situations where there may be many entities that could accept a message, the control information could contain a *destination identifier* which identifies the intended destination entity. A *source identifier* is usually included to permit the destination entity to determine the transmitter of the message.

As an analogy, the frame can be considered an envelop into which the message, a letter, is placed. The destination address is the address on the front of the envelop and the source address is the return address.

Some protocols may require that responses be generated at certain intervals during a communication. These responses, which are also a form of control information, must be distinguishable from the information within the frame, otherwise it will be impossible for the entity receiving the frame to determine whether it is a message or control information.

1.3.3   Error Checking and Recovery

During a communication an entity may not receive the incoming message correctly. At this point it is necessary for the receiving entity to indicate to the transmitting entity that the message was not received correctly. For example, when two people are speaking, if one person does not understand what is being said or misses what is being said because of some form of interference (such as a loud noise), the speaker may be asked to repeat what has just been said.

When a message is damaged or lost because of a *fault* on the communication channel, an *error* is said to have occurred. If a communication is to be reliable, the entities involved in the communication should be checking each message for errors; and if an error is detected, an agreed upon procedure whereby the damaged or lost message can be recovered should be activated.

Errors can occur on the communication channel connecting computers through any one of a variety of faults, including:

Signal Attenuation. As a signal is transmitted through a medium, it must overcome resistances in the medium and, as such, may become weakened to the point that it is no longer possible to determine the meaning of the signal. For example, consider the problems involved in trying to determine what someone is saying if they stand several hundred meters away and talk in a whisper.

Signal attenuation can be overcome by either boosting the initial signal strength (i.e., getting the person to talk louder) or including amplifiers in the communication channel. There is a trade-off here: the signal cannot be boosted to the point where it is unintelligible or distorted to the receiver (consider the effect of someone yelling in your ear).

Noise. Changes in signal strength due to external interference or anomalies within the communication medium are known as *noise.* There are a number of different categories of noise:

- *white* (or *thermal*) noise, is a background interference caused by the motion of electrons in the communication medium due to temperature. Unless the communication can take place at a temperature of absolute zero, the interference associated with thermal noise cannot be eliminated.
- *intermodulation noise* occurs when a number of communications share the same channel (as in a full-duplex communication, see Section 1.2) and one frequency interferes with another. For example, if a station's transmission hardware is faulty, it may produce signals at the wrong frequency, causing intermodulation noise (Figure 1.10).

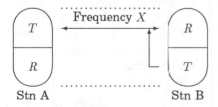

Figure 1.10   An example of intermodulation noise

In the example shown in Figure 1.10, station B is to transmit signals at frequency Y, but instead, signals are produced at frequency X, thereby interfering with the transmission from station A, also transmitting at frequency X.

- signals that are sent electronically across wires can be subject to *electromagnetic interference* or *impulse noise* caused by events such as lightning or power surges.

In addition to the previous examples, a communication can be curtailed if the transmission medium is physically destroyed (for example, in a fire).

The recovery from an error typically involves the *retransmission* of the message; that is, the transmitter begins retransmitting from the first message that the receiver missed. In many protocols, there is a limit to the number of times the transmitter will retransmit the same message. Should this limit be exceeded, the transmission is terminated because the flow of information approaches zero as the entire communication is taken up with retransmissions of the same message and the receiver is not obtaining any useful information.

Similarly, recovery from an error may make it necessary to have mechanisms to ensure that both entities can remain *in-step* with each other and that the transmitter does not flood the receiver with too much information. For example, during a conversation, the person speaking (the transmitter) often watches the person listening for cues to indicate that what has been said is understood. If the speaker is talking too fast, the person listening may request that the speaker slow down. This is known as *flow control*.

Computers can also use flow control to limit the amount of information flowing across a channel. For example, simple terminal-host communications often use the control characters X-OFF and X-ON for flow control. A person typing X-OFF (CTRL-S) will cause the transmitting host to stop sending, thereby allowing the person to read what is on the terminal's screen, and typing X-ON (CTRL-Q) restarts the output. More advanced protocols use various control sequences to achieve the same effect.

Frames (or packets) sent from a source to a destination can be lost or damaged either through faults on the communication channel or because the destination entity loses frames due to processing overheads. The fact that frames can be lost or damaged means that the protocol should support mechanisms that permit the destination to determine if the incoming frame is in error or out-of-sequence (implying that a frame has been lost), such as:

- out-of-sequence frames can be identified if each frame is sent with additional control information known as a *sequence number*. For example, if each frame is sent with a unique number and both the source and destination agree upon the numbering scheme (typically a series of increasing numbers: 0, 1, 2, and so on), then if frames 0, 1, and 2 are transmitted, but only 0 and 2 are received, the destination "knows" that frame 1 must have been lost.
- both the source and the destination must use the same algorithms for determining the next sequence number and agree upon the layout of the control information within the frame.

Once an error has been detected by the destination, it is standard practice to attempt to recover from it. A typical recovery entails the destination sending some form of error indication to the source; the source then may transmit the message again (see Figure 1.11).

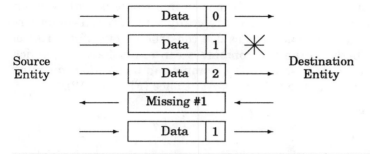

Figure 1.11   Retransmission due to message loss

Although the mechanism for recovery may seem simple enough, there are other problems that can occur, including:

- How does the protocol handle the situation in which the error indication message is lost?

- What procedures should be taken if the message sent from the source is always received in error?

Techniques for overcoming these and other problems will be discussed in subsequent chapters.

1.3.4 Channel Utilization

In a communication, the information flowing between the entities must utilize some type of communication channel. There are many different media that can be used as a communication channel; for example, when two people talk on a telephone, the communication channel is the telephone system. Ideally, communication channels should be used as efficiently as possible, maximizing the amount of information passing from one entity to the other. The amount of useful information that flows between the transmitter and the receiver is known as *throughput*.

As an example of channel utilization and throughput, consider the delivery of letters to your house by a letter carrier. The channel is the person carrying the letters. The letter carrier could deliver one letter at a time, rushing back and forth between the post office and your house (clearly an example of poor channel utilization and throughput). On the other hand, as an example of efficient channel utilization, the letter carrier could deliver all your letters to your house once, thereby minimizing the number of trips required and consequently maximizing throughput.

Throughput can be maximized in a number of ways. For example, in a frame the ratio of control information to message should be as low as possible. That is, the number of bytes of control information should be much less than the number of bytes of message. If this is not the case the channel is carrying more control information than useful information. Throughput can also be enhanced by increasing the speed of the channel (that is, the number of bits, or bytes, that are sent in a given period of time).

A third technique involves *how* the information in a frame is sent between the communicating entities. Information is typically sent between computers as a stream of bytes (for example, frames are constructed out of a series of bytes). The channel between the two computers can either be *serial*, which means that one bit at a time is sent; or the channel can be *parallel*, meaning that all eight bits making up the byte are sent at once (Figure 1.12).

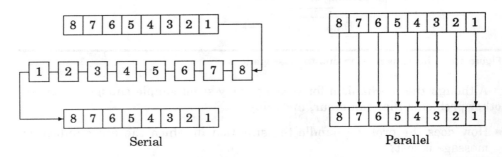

Serial   Parallel

Figure 1.12   Serial transmission (single channel) vs. parallel transmission (multiple channel)

The obvious advantage of sending bytes in parallel channels is that it is eight times quicker than sending them serially. The trade-off is the cost of setting up a communication channel consisting of one path (for serial), or eight paths (for parallel): eight times as many connections and paths are needed for parallel. One usually finds parallel connections *within* the computer or between closely coupled computers; however, over distances of more than a few meters, most communications are serial.

Within the computer, bytes are moved in parallel channels. Before a byte can be transmitted serially, it must be converted from parallel to serial using a hardware *parallel-to-serial converter*. Similarly, the stream of serial bits must be assembled into a (parallel) byte using a *serial-to-parallel converter*.

1.3.5   Synchronization and Timing

In any communication, certain steps must occur before others. For example, in a telephone conversation, before the conversation can take place, one person must dial the telephone number of the other person, and before the person being called can answer the telephone, the telephone must ring. Once the called person answers the telephone, the conversation can proceed.

Protocols often require the entities involved in a communication to be in-step or *synchronized*. That is, one event occurs which is followed by another. Continuing with the telephone analogy, once the communication has been established, synchronization is maintained, typically with one person making a series of statements, to which the other responds. At the end of the telephone conversation, both parties agree that the conversation is over and hang up.

Synchronization in a computer can occur at any number of levels. Two communicating processes must exchange synchronization information (such as sequence numbers, as discussed in Section 1.3.3), to ensure that no messages are lost. Synchronization is achieved by the use of an external timing device, typically a clock.

At lower layers, synchronization must be maintained by the communicating computers at the frame, byte, and bit levels. Since the computers are operating independently, the receiver must "know" when the next bit is to arrive. This can be achieved by having each computer maintain a clock that is *in sync* with the other computer's clock. For example, at each "tick" of its clock, the transmitter sends a bit; while at each "tick" of the receiver's clock, a bit is read from the channel.

The term *synchronous communication* is applied to those communication systems that can send a stream of bytes with only periodic timing information (typically attached to the start of the frame). The term *asynchronous communication* is applied to those communication systems that require each transmitted byte to be prefixed with timing information.

Communicating entities can also use timing to ensure that the communication is still in progress. For example, if an entity does not receive a response to a message within a given time period, the entity can take action to determine the cause of the inactivity. The inactivity could be due to a variety of reasons, including a break in the communication channel (giving the false impression that the other computer is inactive), or the other computer may have crashed (thereby halting any communication activities on the channel). Many protocols require special frames to be sent periodically; these allow each entity involved in the communication to determine that the other entities are still active.

Examples of synchronization and timing will appear throughout the remainder of the book.

1.3.6 Transparency

In any communication, the underlying facilities supporting the communication should be *transparent* to the entities involved in the communication. For example, when using the telephone, the people involved in the communication should not be concerned with the details of how the telephone system actually places the call.

The same arguments can be applied to entities within a computer communication system, for similar reasons:

- Application programmers should not be concerned with the "hows" and "whys" of the underlying communication system, as long as the facilities exist to get information from one machine to another. For example, the channel could be serial (or parallel), or the bytes could be sent synchronously or asynchronously: these issues should be transparent to the programmer (and to the application).

- It can become very difficult to transfer the software to another computer using a different communication system if an application is written for a specific communication system. Therefore, by layering the software and making the underlying layers transparent to the application software, it should be possible to transfer the software to another computer as long as the *interface* between the application and the lower layers is the same for both systems.

The term transparency can also be applied to the type of information that is transmitted. A *transparent frame* is one that can contain all possible characters (both control and noncontrol characters) as part of its message; while a *nontransparent frame* is one that can only contain noncontrol characters (i.e., printable characters only).

1.4   DATA TERMINAL EQUIPMENT

In its simplest form, a computer can be considered to be a device that, when given *input*, *processes* it, and produces *output*. If a computer is to communicate with other computers, it also requires some type of *connection*. A computer that serves as a point of collection, use, or transfer of data, is referred to as **Data Terminal Equipment (DTE)**. A DTE is depicted diagramatically in Figure 1.13.

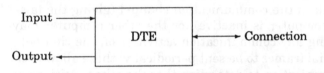

Figure 1.13   A DTE and its basic components

Examples of DTEs include terminals, point-of-sale terminals, line printers, and computers.

1.4.1   Input

To the vast majority of people who use computers, input takes place through the keyboard. Most keyboards are equipped with more than the standard typewriter QWERTY keys; for example, function and cursor control keys are also available.

Over the past decade, a variety of specialized input tools have been developed, including optical scanners, to interpret the bar codes associated with items such as supermarket goods; voice-to-digital units, to allow people to talk to the computer rather than type; magnetic strip decoders, to read the magnetic material found on the back of most charge cards; and pointing tools such as the mouse and trackball, to allow a user to select an object on the screen.

Although most DTEs support either ASCII or EBCDIC internally, input to the DTE need not be either. The PC keyboard is an example of an input device which produces its own character code which must be converted to another character code (typically ASCII), before being processed. Similarly, a voice input device may produce 8-bit data values, but an individual byte probably has no direct equivalent in either ASCII or EBCDIC.

1.4.2 Output

For the most part, DTE output is visual; originally output was textual, either on hardcopy (paper) or softcopy (*cathode ray tube* or *CRT*). Today, output can be a bit-mapped image including *icons* (still-pictures on the screen), *facsimile* (fax documents), and animation. Monochrome CRTs are being superseded by color and *liquid crystal display* (*LCD*) terminals.

It is worth noting that a DTE need not be associated with input. For example, a line printer (a DTE) produces output and is connected to a computer; however, the line printer need not support input.

Similarly, not all output need be printable text. Consider the following examples:

- Both ASCII and EBCDIC support control characters that can be used to control the output text stream. For example, certain escape sequences are intended as control signals to the DTE rather than for the user.

- Some DTEs support voice output for tasks that require people to listen rather than read. For example, voice output is necessary for people with sight disabilities.

- Output can be an *action* such as unlocking a door after a person has typed the password associated with the lock. That is, the DTE's output is used to control an external device.

1.4.3 Connections

By definition, a DTE must have at least one connection to another computer (a DTE), otherwise communication cannot be achieved. Connections are typically physical, consisting of insulated wires or glass (optical fiber cable). In longer distance communications, the DTEs need not be connected physically. For example, information can be passed through the air via microwave communications, or through space via satellite communications.

It is worth noting that although some DTEs do not support input and output directly, input and output can occur across the connection. For example, some highly specialized computers do not communicate with humans directly. Instead, all input and output is passed to the specialized computer from an external processor: humans communicate with the specialized machine via the external processor. In this situation, the specialized computer does support input and output, but only through the connection.

1.4.4 More DTE Terminology

Typically the most common type of DTE interaction that users experience involves a terminal connected to a remote host (both the terminal and the host are examples of DTEs). Terminals usually operate in one of two modes:

Block mode. A block mode terminal is one in which the information entered at the terminal by the user is not sent to the remote DTE until the terminal receives an explicit signal from the user. Examples of block mode terminals include airline reservation systems in which information is accepted from a client and verified before being sent to the remote host for processing. Block mode terminals are typically CRTs.

Character mode.   Character mode terminals accept single characters entered by the user and forward them to the remote host. In some situations, the character mode terminal will buffer one line of characters before sending it to the remote host.

The characters entered by a user can be displayed from either the local *or* the remote DTE:

- A *remote echo* occurs when a character is entered at the user's local DTE and the remote DTE is responsible for outputing the character. The local DTE accepts the character and transmits the character to the remote DTE; the remote DTE performs whatever processing is required on the character and returns the character to the local DTE for output (Figure 1.14).

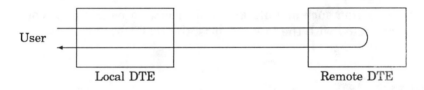

Figure 1.14 Remote echo

Remote echoing is often used in applications such as screen editors, that do not expect the user to end each command with a delimiter such as a carriage return. Remote echoing is sometimes referred to as *echoplexing*.

- A *local echo* occurs when the user's local DTE is responsible for echoing each character entered by the user. The local DTE is still responsible for forwarding each character to the remote DTE (data sent from the remote DTE is displayed on the user's local DTE). This is illustrated in Figure 1.15.

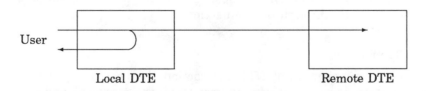

Figure 1.15 Local echo

Local echo is often used by block mode terminals; when the user types ENTER, the information is transmitted to the remote DTE.

1.5 SUMMARY

This chapter has introduced some of the terminology and concepts associated with data communications. There are a couple of points that should be kept in mind when dealing with data communications:

- almost all aspects of data communications have a "human parallel"; should you ever become stuck trying to unravel a problem in data communications, think of it in "human" terms.
- the only means by which society functions is through rules: the same is true with data communications. Protocol standards exist to be adhered to, otherwise there is no guarantee that the implementation or any applications that use the implementation will succeed.

1.6 EXERCISES

1. Classify the following communications as either simplex, half-duplex, or full-duplex:

    a) two polite people talking   b) two angry people yelling
    c) a message sent by pigeon   d) a politician speaking
    e) television functioning   f) a message sent by smoke-signals

    Do all answers fit "neatly" into a single category? What can be said about the amount of information passing through the communication channel?

2. Assuming that most, if not all, human speech falls into the half-duplex category, identify some gestures and phrases that people use to indicate that they have finished talking (i.e., the point at which the line can be turned around).

3. Describe the steps required to convert information stored in parallel to serial. Consider the hardware required for such an operation.

4. Repeat the previous question, but convert the byte from serial to parallel.

5. Does X-OFF (CTRL-S) and X-ON (CTRL-Q) work on your computer? What happens if you type CTRL-S then a command, and finally CTRL-Q?

6. What character codes (i.e., ASCII or EBCDIC) are used on the computer to which you have access? Try implementing the following C program to display the computer's different characters:

```
#include <stdio.h>

main()
{
unsigned char ch;

for(ch = 0; ch < 256; ch+-)
    printf("%d %c\n", ch, ch);
}
```

Now, explain why the above program runs forever, printing the characters and their numeric equivalents.

7. In certain situations a file containing ASCII characters (such as a program or electronic mail) may be sent to a machine that only supports EBCDIC characters. Similarly, EBCDIC files may be sent to ASCII machines. When the file arrives at the destination, it is necessary to convert the file contents to the character code of the destination machine.

   Write a conversion program that will take a file (in either ASCII or EBCDIC) and convert it to the "other" character set (i.e., EBCDIC or ASCII). Ideally, your program should operate as follows:

   ```
   C:\> convert DIR in-file out-file
   ```

   The option DIR should indicate the direction (either EA, EBCDIC to ASCII, or AE, ASCII to EBCDIC).

   To examine the contents of an EBCDIC out-file, use your system's dump utility. Create a dummy EBCDIC file by generating a file of all 256 possible byte values. If a character does not map directly into an ASCII (or EBCDIC) character, replace the character with a question mark.

8. Every character typed by a user is displayed *twice* by a DTE. Explain what is happening and how to correct it.

9. A DTE doesn't display anything that is typed by a user, but the remote DTE responds when a carriage return is pressed. Explain what is happening and how to correct it.

Commkit

2.1 INTRODUCTION

Before a computer can communicate with a user or another computer, it requires:

- hardware to support the communication and
- software to control the communication

This chapter examines some of the hardware supplied with a typical PC and considers the software required to control the hardware. The chapter then introduces Commkit, a software tool that supports the development of practical data communications software. An example of an application that uses some of the PC's hardware and Commkit is also presented.

2.2 THE 80x86 HARDWARE

The 80x86 is the generic name given to those microprocessors developed by Intel and those supplied with personal computers such as the IBM PC and its clones. The x signifies the generation:

nothing (8086)   the "original" 80x86 processor (there were earlier versions, such as the 8080 and 8008, but they are not of concern here)

'1' (80186)   an enhanced version of the 8086, with several new instructions

'2' (80286)	a faster, more powerful version of the 8086 with enhancements for memory management and multitasking
'3' (80386)	a still more powerful version of the 80286 with additional instructions for 32-bit arithmetic and bit manipulation
'4' (80486)	a faster version of the 80386 with built-in floating-point hardware.

All versions are upwardly compatible, meaning that software developed for an earlier version of the processor should be able to run on a later one. Other generations of the 80x86 have either been announced or are in the planning stages.

Although recent versions of the 80x86 (such as the 80386) are more powerful than earlier ones (such as the 8086), the mechanisms allowing the external hardware (or *devices*) to be accessed have essentially remained unchanged to allow the upward compatibility of software.

2.2.1   80x86 Devices

Information is supplied to and received from the 80x86 through devices such as the keyboard, screen, disk, light pen, serial port, and mouse. Although there seems to be a limitless supply of possible devices that can be attached to a PC, the standard PC configuration generally allows only eight to be attached: typically, the clock, keyboard, hard disk, floppy disk, printer, and two serial communication interfaces (the eighth device is system specific).

Devices are not accessed directly (as, for example, memory is); instead, the 80x86 accesses a device through one or more *ports*. To ensure that the PC can distinguish between them, all devices are assigned one or more unique *port numbers*. Although only eight devices can be attached at any one time, there are some 2^{16} possible ports available on the PC. The number of ports associated with a device depends, in part, upon the number of functions the device performs. For example, the clock is associated with four ports, while the keyboard uses two.

Ports can be accessed through software using two "low-level" instructions. The in instruction allows a port to be read, while a port can be written to using the out instruction. The in instruction accepts a port number and returns the value (a byte) associated with that port, while the out instruction requires both a port number and the byte to be written to the device. The high-level Turbo C counterparts of these instructions are:

```
unsigned char inportb(int portid)
```
   returns an 8-bit byte associated with port portid

```
void outportb(int portid, unsigned char value)
```
   writes an 8-bit quantity (value) to the port portid

```
void outport(int portid, int value)
```
   writes a 16-bit word (value) to the port portid and port portid + 1

The types of operation (i.e., reading or writing) that can be performed on a port depend upon the functions of the device that the port supports. For example, some ports, such as the input buffer associated with the keyboard (port number 0x60), are to be read; while others, such as the clock command register (port number 0x43), used for programming the clock are for writing. Finally, some ports can be both written to and read from. For example, the keyboard status register (port number 0x61) can be read (to obtain the status of the keyboard) and written (to signal the keyboard that the supplied character has been accepted).

Of the eight "standard" devices that can be supported by a PC, only two are of direct interest at this moment: the keyboard and clock, because they are both used by the Commkit software.

The keyboard   The keyboard is an input device that allows a user to supply information to the processor in alphanumeric format. The number of keys on the keyboard and their layout depends upon the type of PC and the keyboard's manufacturer.

Although the 80x86 uses the ASCII character code, the PC keyboard does *not* generate ASCII characters; instead, each character on the keyboard is associated with a one-byte *scan code*. The scan code is returned to the processor via port 0x60.

IBM has defined a scan code for each key. To remain compatible with the IBM PC, keyboards built by other manufacturers must generate scan codes that correspond to those found on the IBM PC, regardless of where the keys are placed on their keyboard). For example, the Escape key (ESC) generates scan code 0x01, while the delete key (DEL) generates scan code 0x53. Since the value of the scan codes do not correspond to a specific character code (such as ASCII or EBCDIC), the scan code must be translated into the character code required by the application. The translation is done by the software within the processor mapping the scan code into the equivalent character code character, typically using a translation (or mapping) table as shown in Figure 2.1.

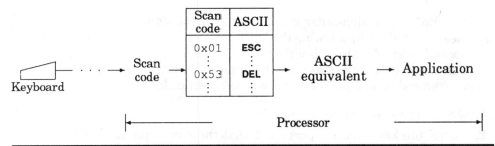

Figure 2.1   Keyboard scan code to ASCII translation

The processor is signalled *twice* whenever a key is touched: once when the key is pressed (generating the *make scan code*), and once when the key is released (generating the *break scan code*). Regardless of whether the scan code is a make or a break, the lower seven bits of the scan code identify the key. The eighth bit is cleared by the keyboard to indicate a make and is set to signal a break. For example, the make scan code for the delete key (generated when the DEL key is pressed) is 0x53, while the break scan code (generated when the DEL key is released) is 0xD3 (Figure 2.2).

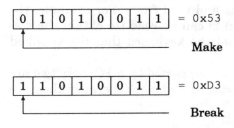

Figure 2.2   The make and break scan codes for DEL

The keyboard can generate 127 different scan codes (with values 1 through 127). Scan code 0x00 is reserved to allow the keyboard to expand to more than 127 characters. Keys outside the 127 character range are sent as *two* scan codes, 0x00 and the scan code of the key. If the keyboard is equipped with an "auto-repeat" feature (that is, when a key is held down, the keyboard eventually starts to repeat the character), the keyboard sends each character as a make, then as a break, eliminating the need for the user to continuously press and release the same key. The keyboard is also equipped with a 16-byte buffer for storing scan codes until they are read by the processor.

The keyboard software obtains the scan code by reading port 0x60. It must then signal the keyboard that the character has been read; this is a seemingly convoluted process involving the following steps:

1. Read port 0x61 to obtain the keyboard status

2. Write port 0x61 with the keyboard status or'ed with 0x80

3. Write port 0x61 with the original keyboard status

The "flip" of the high-order keyboard status bit signals that the scan code has been read, thereby allowing the keyboard to remove the scan code from the keyboard buffer. An algorithm that converts all scan codes into a single case (i.e., all upper or all lowercase) can be implemented by ignoring any incoming make scan codes, and processing the break scan codes only:

1. Obtain the scan code from port 0x60.

2. Signal the keyboard via port 0x61 that the scan code has been obtained.

3. If the scan code is a "break":

    a) Convert the scan code into a character, ideally using a mapping table that consists of the ASCII characters associated with the different scan codes. The scan code is used as a subscript into the mapping table.

    b) Process the character.

This algorithm is limited in that it supports a single case and does not permit control characters. Fortunately, the make/break cycle allows a program to determine which keys have been pressed and the order in which they have been pressed, thereby permitting the keyboard software to distinguish between sequences such as A-SHIFT, SHIFT-A, or even SHIFT (release) A. For example, the key designated A on the keyboard can generate one of a number of ASCII values, depending upon what other keys that have been pressed before and how the software interprets the sequence of keys being pressed. (Note that the keyboard distinguishes between left and right SHIFTs and that CTRL is an abbreviation of CONTROL.) See Table 2.1.

TABLE 2.1   Keystroke Interpretation

First key	Second key	Third key	Result	ASCII value
A			a	0x61
SHIFT LEFT	A		A	0x41
SHIFT RIGHT	A		A	0x41
CTRL	A		☺	0x01
ALTMODE	A		β	0xE1
ALTMODE	SHIFT	A	⊥	0xC1
CTRL	ALTMODE	A	ü	0x81

If multiple keys are pressed (for example, to obtain a capital letter, a control character, or a special sequence such as CTRL-ALT-DEL), the keyboard software must maintain state information about these keys since the scan codes are supplied to the processor one at a time. At a mimimum, the keyboard software should be able to "remember" whether the CTRL, ALTMODE, LEFT SHIFT, and RIGHT SHIFT keys have been pressed. The state of any of these keys can be maintained as a Boolean condition (a key is either pressed or it isn't), with the initial state of each key being FALSE. Whenever one of these keys is pressed (i.e., the make scan code), the state can change to TRUE, and when the key is released (i.e., the break scan code), the state can change to FALSE.

This also means that two mapping tables are required, one for unshifted characters and the other for shifted characters. There is not necessarily a one-to-one correspondence between the tables (for example, a to A), since some unshifted characters do not have a shifted equivalent (such as 1 and !).

ASCII control characters are those less than 0x20 (space) and can be obtained by and'ing the character with 0x1F. Similarly, altmode characters are those greater than 0x7F (DEL) and are generated by or'ing the character with 0x80.

The clock   The clock (or more correctly, the 8253 timer chip) is used to supply the PC with a regular, periodic *clock pulse* that can be used to control various actions. The 8253 has *three* independent timing channels that are used by the PC as shown in Table 2.2.

Of the three channels, channel 0 can be used by programs (such as MS-DOS and Commkit) as a mechanism to control hardware and software access to the PC. Channel 1 *must* not be changed, since this can result in the loss of the contents of the PC's memory. Channel 2 is not used by Commkit.

TABLE 2.2   Clock Channels and Functions

Channel	Function
0	System timing and counting
1	Memory refresh (via DMA controller)
2	PC speaker (for sound effects)

Internally, the 8253 has a 1.19318 MHz clock which supplies each timing channel with 1,193,180 clock pulses each second. Since most applications do not require this accuracy of timing, each channel is associated with a programmable 16-bit counter that can be decremented by the timer chip every clock pulse. When the counter reaches zero, the application can be informed. As an example, assume that an application requires the clock to signal the processor 1000 times a second (in other words, once a millisecond). The counter must be initialized to a value that will reach zero after one millisecond has passed. Dividing the clock speed of 1,193,180 by 1000 gives 1,193; setting the counter to 1,193 results in the counter reaching zero after approximately one millisecond.

The 8253 clock is associated with four ports. Ports 0x40, 0x41, and 0x42 are known as the *clock counter registers* and are used to supply the initial clock values to channels 0, 1, and 2, respectively. The *clock command register*, port 0x43, allows the programmer to specify how a clock is to be used, as well as how the clock is to be initialized. For example, once a clock's counter reaches zero, the clock can be programmed to load itself with the original counter value (stored in the *clock latch*) and repeat the cycle. Alternately, it can be programmed to stop at zero (this is known as *single-shot mode*). Similarly, the value loaded into the clock latch (through the clock counter register) can be the full 16 bits (obtained by writing the low-order and then the high-order byte to the clock counter register), or simply half of the clock value (i.e., either the low-order or the high-order byte).

2.2.2   Accessing Devices

Although a device can be accessed through one or more of its ports at any time, it is not always advisable to do so. For example, the keyboard register can be read, regardless of whether or not the user has typed a character. Accessing a device before it is ready can result in the duplication of information (reading the serial communication interface more than once before a new character has arrived will result in a copy of the original character being returned), or the loss of information (writing to the serial communication interface before the last character has been sent can result in the new character overwriting the previous character). To avoid situations in which data is lost or duplicated, most devices are able to signal their status to the processor. Typically, the status indicates whether the device has information for the processor or is ready to accept more information. The status of the device can be obtained either by the processor *polling* the device or by having the device *interrupt* the processor.

Device polling   The state of a device is obtained by reading one or more ports associated with the device. For example, it is possible to configure the clock so that it counts down to zero and stops. By polling the port associated with the clock, a program can determine whether the clock has reached zero.

Device polling is a simple and sometimes convenient mechanism whereby a program can determine the status of a device. Software for device polling is typically written as a loop known as a *polling loop*:

```
for(;;)
{
    if (device1_ready()) service_device_1();
    if (device2_ready()) service_device_2();
}
```

There are, however, at least two drawbacks to using device polling: (1) The processor performs no useful function other than polling, and (2) the data can be lost if a device happens to generate data faster than it takes the processor to execute the polling loop. For example, consider the following polling loop:

```
for(;;)
{
    if (device1_ready()) then service_device_1();
    if (device2_ready()) then service_device_2();
    if (device3_ready()) then service_device_3();
    if (device4_ready()) then service_device_4();
}
```

If device1 supplies data faster than it takes the processor to check each device in the polling loop, there is a possibility that data from device1 could be lost. A common trick that can be employed to overcome this problem is to poll the fast device more than once in the polling loop.

Interrupts Ideally the processor should only access a device when the device needs to be serviced or when the device has information to supply to the processor; thereby permitting the processor to perform tasks other than device polling (for example, a user can type information at a keyboard while other information is being written to a disk). Most processors, including the 80x86, allow devices to signal or *interrupt* the processor when a condition has been reached, thereby overcoming the limitations associated with device polling. For example, instead of the software polling a disk to determine if a block of data has been written, the disk itself can inform the software that the data has been written.

When a device interrupts the processor, a number of things occur. First, the task currently being run by the processor is suspended while the processor handles the interrupt. Second, a procedure known as an *interrupt handler* (or *interrupt service routine*) must be activated. The interrupt handler is responsible for servicing the interrupt (that is, determining why the interrupt occurred and what to do about it). Third, the suspended task must be resumed once the interrupt handler is finished.

In the case of the 80x86, when an interrupt occurs, the task currently executing is suspended by pushing the instruction counter and the status flag on the stack, thereby permitting control to be returned to the task once the interrupt has been serviced. To ensure that no further interrupts will occur during the handling of the first interrupt, the 80x86 disables interrupts. If other interrupts occur, they are blocked until the processor either explicitly enables interrupts or resumes execution of the interrupted task.

Each device is associated with a unique *interrupt number* that the processor obtains when the interrupt occurs. The interrupt number is used as an index to the list of *interrupt vectors* stored in segment zero. Each interrupt vector contains the address of the interrupt handler associated with the device (see Table 2.3). (Note that there is no obvious relationship between the ports associated with a device and the device's interrupt number.)

TABLE 2.3   80x86 Device Interrupt Vectors

Interrupt number	Interrupt vector location	Device
0x08	0x20 - 0x23	Clock
0x09	0x24 - 0x27	Keyboard
0x0A	0x28 - 0x2B	Reserved
0x0B	0x2C - 0x2F	Serial port
0x0C	0x30 - 0x33	Serial port
0x0D	0x34 - 0x37	Hard disk
0x0E	0x38 - 0x3B	Floppy disk
0x0F	0x3C - 0x3F	Printer

When a device causes an interrupt, the instruction counter is assigned the value of the device's interrupt vector. Control is then passed to the interrupt handler. Once the interrupt has been serviced, the stack is popped, restoring the original task's instruction counter and status flag. Interrupts are reenabled because the interrupt enable bit is set in the status flag.

Although the 80x86 is designed to handle up to eight external devices, there is only a single interrupt line connecting the processor to the outside world. This means that without some form of additional hardware, at most one external device can be connected to the 80x86. Fortunately, hardware such as the Intel 8259 Interrupt Controller has been designed to share the single interrupt line between eight different devices (Figure 2.3).

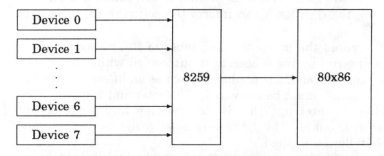

Figure 2.3   8259 interrupt controller

This means that instead of directly interrupting the processor, a device first signals the 8259, which then interrupts the 80x86 using the single interrupt line. The 80x86 determines which device is interrupting by obtaining the device's number from the 8259. The 80x86 uses the device number to access the list of interrupt vectors that indicates which interrupt handler should be activated.

The 8259 permits the programmer to select those devices that are to interrupt the 80x86 by writing a one-byte *interrupt mask* to the 8259. Each bit in the mask corresponds to one of the eight devices. Device priority is indicated from right to left, with the clock having the highest priority and the printer, the lowest (Figure 2.4).

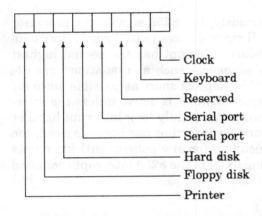

Clock
Keyboard
Reserved
Serial port
Serial port
Hard disk
Floppy disk
Printer

Figure 2.4   8259 interrupt mask

A bit value of one in the interrupt mask indicates that any interrupts coming from the device are to be ignored, while a bit value of zero means that the device is allowed to interrupt the 80x86. For example, to permit clock, keyboard, and printer interrupts, the interrupt mask would be set to 0x7C (Figure 2.5).

The 8259 interrupt mask is accessed through port 0x21, the *interrupt mask register*. Figure 2.5 could be implemented as follows:

```
#define INT_MASK    0x21
#define CLKENA      0xFE    /* Clock enable:    11111110 */
#define KEYENA      0xFD    /* Keyboard enable: 11111101 */
#define PRTENA      0x7F    /* Printer enable:  01111111 */

init_8259()
{
        outportb(INT_MASK, CLKENA & KEYENA & PRTENA);
}
```

For each device that is selected, there must be a corresponding interrupt handler and the interrupt vector associated with the device must contain the

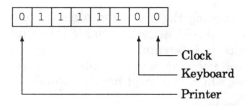

Figure 2.5   8259 interrupt mask allowing clock, keyboard, and printer interrupts

entry point of the interrupt handler. Results are unpredictable if either the interrupt handler is missing or the interrupt vector contains an invalid entry point, since control will be passed to a location that does not service the interrupt.

If several interrupts occur simultaneously, the 8259 signals the processor with the highest priority interrupt. All other devices (with lower priority interrupts) are kept waiting. The keyboard interrupt has the second highest device priority to ensure that special sequences such as CTRL-ALT-DEL are not blocked. The interrupt handler should be kept as short as possible since *all* interrupts are blocked while the interrupt handler is active unless the interrupt handler explicitly enables interrupts. An unduly long interrupt handler can result in interrupts being lost. Once the interrupt has been serviced, the 8259 must be informed so that any pending (or any subsequent) interrupts can be signalled. This is done by writing 0x20 to the 8259 interrupt command register (port number 0x20).

2.3   THE COMMKIT SOFTWARE

By itself, the hardware described in the previous section performs no useful function without software controlling it. For example, simply pressing a key on the keyboard does not mean that the character will appear on the screen; software is required to read the scan code from the keyboard, convert the scan code into a character, and then display the character on the screen.

Few computer users have the time or the patience to write their own software to control the underlying hardware; instead, they rely upon software written by other people who know the hardware. This software, sometimes referred to as an *operating system*, *kernel*, or *monitor* is intended to hide the idiosyncracies of the hardware by offering a common, well-defined interface to the user. Examples of operating systems include MS-DOS, UNIX, and VMS.

In addition to hiding the hardware, many operating systems support the pseudo-concurrent execution of a number of different tasks referred to as *processes*. Depending upon the operating system, a process may be associated with all the actions invoked by a user (as in VMS, where a single process is used for all actions such as editing a file and compiling a program), or each action invoked by the user may result in a new entity (as in UNIX, where the user's process spawns separate child processes to perform actions, such as editing or compiling). In operating systems that support multiple processes,

it is often both necessary and useful to allow the transfer of information between processes. For example, the output of one process may be the input
to another. Operating systems that allow processes to communicate are said
to support *interprocess communication (IPC)*. Interprocess communication is
an extremely useful feature, and it is also a cornerstone in many aspects of
computing science, including data communications, distributed systems, and
object-oriented programming.

One method of implementing interprocess communication is to use messages. A *message* is simply a data structure that is passed between the communicating processes. As in any other communication, all entities involved
in the communication must agree to a common protocol covering items such
as the the format of the message and the required control information. The
underlying operating system is responsible for ultimately controlling the communication and supplying the message to the intended destination process.
A typical cycle (Figure 2.6) involves a process sending a *request message* to
a second process; the second process replies with a *response message* to the
original request.

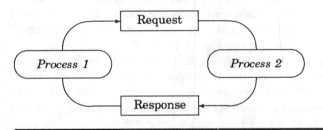

Figure 2.6   Request-response cycle

Although MS-DOS supports neither the concurrent execution of processes
nor interprocess communication, it does run on the PC and many powerful
tools have been written for MS-DOS. To facilitate the teaching of data communications in an MS-DOS environment, it is necessary to either modify MS-
DOS or develop a teaching tool that can be invoked by the user. It is possible
to modify MS-DOS; however, without a detailed description of the internals
of MS-DOS, a course in data communications can degenerate into a painful
exercise in debugging, with little time left over for communications. The approach adopted in this book is to keep MS-DOS and its tools intact, but to
use a stand-alone program known as *Commkit* to help teach data communications.

Commkit is a small, event-driven monitor which supports multiple processes
and message passing. A Commkit executable program is like any other MS-
DOS executable program in that the program is invoked by typing its name
after the DOS prompt. Once executing, Commkit controls the PC and allows the various processes to function and communicate. When the Commkit
software has finished executing, control is returned to MS-DOS.

2.3.1 Overview of Commkit

Structurally, a Commkit program can be represented as a series of layers, each performing a specific function, built atop the PC's hardware as shown in Figure 2.7.

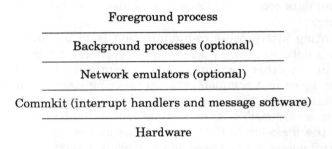

Figure 2.7   The structure of a Commkit program

The Commkit software is supplied on a diskette containing about 40 files. The various files consist of message-handling routines, network emulators, interrupt handlers, and a number of different processes illustrating different aspects of data communications. All of the software, with the exception of about ten lines of in-line assembler, is written in Turbo C.

A Commkit executable program is made by linking one or more modules containing a foreground process with the Commkit interrupt handlers and message-handling software. When necessary, modules containing additional processes (known as background processes) or modules containing network emulators, can be included to make an executable program.

All entities (i.e., foreground and background processes, network emulators, and interrupt handlers) communicate via messages using two communication primitives: `send()` and `recv()`. Each entity is associated with a unique process identifier, a message queue, an entry point known to Commkit, and a series of procedures implementing the process. For two entities to communicate, the source entity (i.e., the originator of the message), sends the message to the destination entity by calling `send()` with the destination entity's identifier and the message. The message remains on the destination entity's message queue until the destination entity accesses the message by calling `recv()`.

Every Commkit executable program requires a mainline procedure (i.e., the entry point from MS-DOS), called `main()`. Commkit must be initialized before it can be used. This is done in the mainline with a call to `initialize()` (defined in `commkit.c`). `Initialize()` sets up the message queues, interrupt handlers, and various support routines. Upon completion, control is returned to the mainline. Once initialized, any background processes are "registered" with Commkit. Finally, control is passed to the foreground process. Execution continues until control is returned from the foreground to the mainline, at which point `rtn_to_dos()` is called, restoring the interrupt vectors to what MS-DOS expects them to be.

Although the basic message-handling paradigm is true for all entities, there are minor variations which warrant an examination of each type of entity supported by Commkit.

2.3.2   The Foreground Process

The foreground process is simply an algorithm implemented in C that is called by the mainline. The Commkit software (consisting of the foreground process, any background processes, and the interrupt handlers) will continue to run until a condition is reached that causes the foreground process to return to the mainline, at which point Commkit is terminated and control is returned to MS-DOS.

The basic structure of the foreground process is a large loop that is terminated when some condition is reached (for example, the user typing CTRL-C). Within the loop is a call to recv() which allows the process to receive messages from other entities:

```
void foreground_process()
{
int running = TRUE;

while (running)
{
    recv( /* recv() parameters */ );

    /* Some condition is reached... */
    running = FALSE;
}
}
```

The foreground process is interruptable by any of the interrupt handlers (interrupts are transparent to the foreground process). Control remains with the foreground process until it attempts to receive a message. If a message is available, it is returned immediately to the foreground process; otherwise the process is blocked and any background processes with pending messages are allowed to execute. As soon as a message arrives for the foreground process, control (and the message) returns to the foreground process.

The foreground process is associated with the process identifier APPLICATION; all messages sent with a destination of APPLICATION are placed on the foreground process's queue. There is only one foreground process.

2.3.3   Background Processes

A background process, like the foreground process, consists of an algorithm implemented in C; however, background processes differ from the foreground process in a number of ways:

1. There can be any number of background processes (from zero on up), whereas there can only be a single foreground process.

2. Background processes are only executed when the foreground process is idle (i.e., waiting for a message) and a message is available for a background process.

3. Background processes must be *registered* with Commkit before they can receive messages. Each background process is registered separately with a call to `register_background()` (found in `commkit.c`):

```
void register_background(int proc_id, void (*proc_name)());
```

4. Background processes should not contain software that waits for multiple messages or implements infinite loops. Failure to observe this can result in Commkit losing all of its message buffers as messages go unread.

5. The entry point (i.e., procedure) associated with a background process must be declared as type `void`.

Since control is only to remain with a background process for the time it takes to handle a single message, the following points must be considered when writing a background process:

- Local variables, if used, are undefined upon entry to the process.

- Static variables allow values to be kept while the process is inactive.

- Global variables should be avoided when storing values between calls to a background process. Global variables can be changed by other routines. For example, since interrupts can occur at any time (i.e., clock or keyboard), it is possible that the value of a global variable can change while a background process is executing, potentially leading to unpredictable results.

Five background process identifiers are defined in `general.h`: BACK-GROUND_1, BACKGROUND_2, BACKGROUND_3, BACKGROUND_4, and BACK-GROUND_5; more can be added if needed. However, if more are required, the global constant TOTPROCS (also defined in `general.h`) must be increased to reflect the total number of processes and interrupt handlers.

If control remains in a background process (for example, an infinite loop is entered), execution can be terminated by typing CTRL-ALT-DEL, which causes the keyboard interrupt handler (described in Section 2.3.4) to call `rtn_to_dos()`.

2.3.4 Interrupt Handlers

Commkit supports five different external devices (the keyboard, clock, two serial interfaces, and the parallel-port interface), each of which is associated with an interrupt handler. The software associated with each interrupt handler can be found in `commkit.c`. An interrupt handler is associated with a process identifier, which means that the interrupt handler can both send and receive messages. The process identifiers are as outlined in Table 2.4 (defined in `general.h`).

Of the five external devices supported by Commkit, only two are considered here: the keyboard and the clock. However, before examining the interrupt handlers, the available support software is discussed.

TABLE 2.4 Interrupt Process Identifiers

Identifier	Interrupt handler
KEYIH	Keyboard
CLKIH	Clock
SP1IH	Serial port 1
SP2IH	Serial port 2
PPIH	Parallel port

Support software   Writing an interrupt handler in Turbo C is fairly straight-forward because of the extensions to the language that permit control over 80x86 interrupts. The Turbo C extensions used by Commkit are:

void interrupt. The void interrupt type can be associated with either a variable or a C function. A variable of this type can hold the 32-bit address (segment and offset) of an interrupt handler. A void interrupt function causes the compiler to generate the necessary instructions to save all registers on the stack upon entry to the function. It is assumed that the function will be called when an interrupt occurs, which will require the saving of the registers. Conversely, upon exit from the function, the compiler generates the code to restore the registers (by popping them from the stack). Instead of ending the function with an ret (return from subroutine), the compiler generates an iret (return from interrupt).

For example, the keyboard interrupt handler entry point could be declared as follows:

```
void interrupt kb_ih()
{
/* Statements to handle keyboard interrupt */
}
```

setvect(). The Setvect() function stores the address of an interrupt handler (which must be declared to be of type void interrupt) in the specified interrupt vector. For example, the code needed to store the address of kb_ih() (the keyboard interrupt handler) in interrupt vector location 9 (the keyboard interrupt vector) is:

```
setvect(9, kb_ih);
```

getvect(). The getvect() function returns a copy of the 32-bit interrupt address stored in a specific interrupt vector. For example, the code to get a copy of the original clock handler's address stored in interrupt vector 8 and to store it in the variable old_clock (declared to be of type void interrupt), would be:

```
{
void interrupt (*old_clock)();

old_clock = getvect(8);
}
```

The variable `old_clock` could be restored using `setvect()`:

```
setvect(8, old_clock);
```

In addition to the interrupt support facilities supplied by Turbo C, two additional functions have been written to allow control over interrupts:

unsigned `clear()`. The `Clear()` function disables 80x86 interrupts by clearing the interrupt enabled bit in the flags register, with the result that the 80x86 can no longer be interrupted. The value of the flags register is saved and returned by `clear()` to the calling function. `Clear()` is used rather than Turbo C's `disable()`, because `disable()` clears the interrupts but does not retain the original state of the processor.

void `restore(unsigned flags)`. The `restore()` function restores the 80x86 to the state indicated by the value in `flags`. `Flags` is obtained by calling function `clear()`.

Since these functions contain in-line assembler, they are kept in a separate file, `intrpt.c`, and the Commkit diskette is supplied with an assembled version, `intrpt.obj`.

Interrupt handler-process communication   Since different applications of Commkit may require the messages generated by the interrupt handlers to be sent to different processes, the application software is expected to determine the destination of any interrupt handler data. Accordingly, all interrupt handlers call the external function `low_level()` upon completion of their interrupt, thereby allowing the application to decide on the final destination of, for example, a character read from the keyboard. The major benefit of this approach is that it minimizes the need to modify `commkit.c`, thereby reducing the amount of recompiling necessary as well as decreasing the likelihood of making unexpected changes to `commkit.c`.

All Commkit applications must support an entry point to `low_level()`:

```
void low_level(int device, int code, unsigned char data)
```

where:

device   The process identifer of the device associated with the call to `low_level()` (one of KEYIH, CLKIH, SP1IH, SP2IH, or PPIH).

code   The cause of the call to `low_level()`, one of:

  0   Indicates that the field is to be ignored.
  RECVDONE   Indicates that a data available interrupt has occurred (serial and parallel ports only).
  XMITDONE   Indicates that the Transmit Holding Register is empty (serial ports only).
  MODEMSTATUS   Indicates that a modem status change has occurred (serial ports only).

MSG_AVAIL   Indicates that a message has been received from a process for interrupt handler specified in device. The message can be retrieved using recv().

data   The data, if any, associated with the call to low_level().

The keyboard interrupt handler   The keyboard interrupt handler is an implementation of the algorithm discussed in Section 2.2.1, converting keyboard scan codes into their equivalent ASCII characters.

Since keys can be pressed in various combinations, the keyboard interrupt handler maintains global-state variables for the keys listed in Table 2.5.

TABLE 2.5   Keyboard Global-state Variables

Variable	Purpose
left_shift	State of **LEFT SHIFT** key
right_shift	State of **RIGHT SHIFT** key
caps_lock	State of **CAPS LOCK** key
alt	State of **ALTMODE** key
ctrl	State of **CTRL** key
num_lock	State of **NUM LOCK** key

These state variables are all initialized to FALSE, indicating that the key has not been pressed. Once pressed, the value changes to TRUE, returning to FALSE when the key is released. By maintaining this state information, it is possible to determine the various keys being pressed by the user. For example, CTRL-ALT-DEL can be detected if the variables ctrl and alt are TRUE, and the character just assembled from the keyboard is DEL.

The keyboard interrupt handler software consists of three procedures:

keyboard_init(). The keyboard initialization software—responsible for initializing all keyboard state variables to FALSE.

kb_ih(). The keyboard interrupt entry point—called whenever a keyboard interrupt (i.e., make or break) occurs. The address of kb_ih() is stored in interrupt vector 0x09 (memory locations 0x24 through 0x27). Kb_ih() passes control to keyboard_handler().

keyboard_handler(). The keyboard interrupt processing software—called from kb_ih() whenever a keyboard interrupt occurs. The keyboard handler uses the aforementioned state variables and two mapping tables (shifted and unshifted) to convert the scan code into the equivalent ASCII character and store it in the variable ascii.

Once the character has been generated, the keyboard_handler() calls low_level() with the character ascii for forwarding to the appropriate process. If the combination of keys signal CTRL-ALT-DEL, execution is halted by the keyboard_handler() calling rtn_to_dos().

The clock interrupt handler   The Commkit clock interrupt handler uses the 8253 timer chip (described in Section 2.2.1) to supply timing signals to applications.

The clock initialization software does not change the clock counter value already defined by MS-DOS, for the following reasons:

- The system clock is updated each time a clock interrupt occurs in many versions of MS-DOS,

- The floppy disk software uses the clock interrupt to determine when to switch off the disk motor. If the clock interrupt is blocked (i.e., the original clock interrupt handler is not called), once the motor starts it cannot be stopped (fun, but hard on the disk).

When a clock interrupt occurs, control is first passed to clk_ih() and then to clock_handler(). Clock_handler() then calls low_level(), with an indication that a clock interrupt has occurred. The clock "ticks" HZ times a second, allowing low_level() to forward timing signals to various processes every 1/HZ seconds or perhaps to count interrupts and then to send a message after HZ interrupts have occurred (i.e., once a second).

Once the clock interrupt has been processed, control is *not* passed back to the previously executing process. Instead, the stack is modified to appear as if an interrupt has just occurred (the flags are pushed onto the stack), and the *original* MS-DOS clock interrupt handler is then called. This "faked" interrupt is achieved by the following two lines of Turbo assembler in procedure dos_call(), called from clock_handler() (dos_call() is found in intrpt.c):

```
asm pushf
asm call dword ptr DGROUP:old_clock
```

Note that the result of the pushf and the call is a stack frame that "looks like" an interrupt stack frame. The return address is the location in dos_call() after the call. This mechanism, whereby the Commkit application services the software associated with the interrupt and then calls MS-DOS, is known as *chaining*.

Turbo C does not compile the two lines of code displayed previously; instead, the entire file, intrpt.c, is supplied to the Turbo Assembler for assembling into the object file intrpt.obj. Since Commkit is supplied with intrpt.obj, it is not necessary to purchase Turbo Assembler; however, if intrpt.obj is lost, it *will* be necessary to purchase the assembler!

Once the MS-DOS clock interrupt handler has finished, the registers are restored to their original values and control is returned to clk_ih(). Since clk_ih() is declared to be of type interrupt, the stack contains the register values associated with the process that was running when the clock interrupt occurred: these registers are restored and control is returned to the original process.

Initializing and restoring interrupt vectors When any Commkit module begins execution, the interrupt vectors are, not surprisingly, associated with MS-DOS interrupt handlers. While the module executes, the keyboard, clock, and serial port interrupt handlers must refer to the Commkit interrupt handlers.

When Commkit terminates, the interrupt vectors must be restored to the original MS-DOS interrupt handlers.

Procedure initialize() (found in commkit.c) is responsible for saving the MS-DOS interrupt vectors in five global variables: old_clock, old_kb, old_sp1, old_sp2, and old_pp. These vectors, all of type interrupt, are obtained using getvect(). Upon termination, procedure rtn_to_dos() (in commkit.c) restores the five interrupt vectors using setvect().

2.3.5 Message Handling

Commkit permits any entity (i.e., a foreground process, a background process, or an interrupt handler) to communicate with any other entity by sending messages. All processes are message driven; that is, a process is idle until it is sent a message, at which point it is activated. Entities send messages using the send() primitive and receive messages using the recv() primitive.

Since an entity may be sent a message while it is processing an earlier message, all pending messages are queued until they can be received by the entity. Each Commkit entity is associated with its own message queue (Figure 2.8).

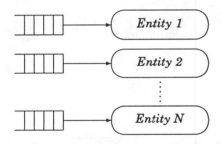

Figure 2.8 Commkit entities and their message queues

The message handling software can determine the intended destination of a message since each message is sent with the process identifier of the destination entity. There is a one-to-one relationship between the entity, its queue, and its identifier number.

A message is any data structure having a maximum size of 128 bytes. When an entity sends a message, Commkit copies the contents of the data structure into the first available buffer taken from the queue qe (the contents of the message are ignored). The buffer is then kept on the queue associated with the destination entity. When an entity requests a message, Commkit checks the entity's queue. If the queue is not empty, the contents of the first buffer on the queue are copied into the message structure supplied by the destination entity. (An entity can determine the size of a data structure using the sizeof compiler directive.) Once read, the buffer is then returned to qe, the list of available buffers.

Since Commkit is responsible for supplying the message to the correct destination, information must be maintained in addition to the message itself:

- Information specific to the message—its size (`size`), and the identifier of the sending entity (`source`) is kept in the structure `queue_entry` (defined in `commkit.h`):

*next	source	size	msg

Since there can be many messages waiting to be read by the entity, all queue entries associated with an entity are linked together through the field `next`.

- Since there are many entities and each has its own list of messages, Commkit maintains a table `queue`, in which each entry corresponds to the list of messages waiting to be received by an entity (the identifier is used as a subscript to access an entity's queue). An entry in the table `queue` consists of two pointers: (1) `head`, which points to the entity's first pending message; and (2) `tail`, a pointer to the last message in the entity's list of pending messages. In addition, each queue entry has a field `count` which indicates the number of pending messages waiting to be received by the entity.

In the Figure 2.9, three messages are pending for entity number 7: the first is a single-byte `S` sent from entity 3; the second is a 10-byte message sent from entity 9; and the third, a 2-byte integer (with value 0) from entity 1 (`head` points to the first available message, while `tail` points to the last message in the list).

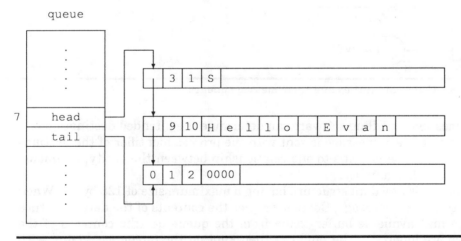

Figure 2.9   Message queue and pending message structure

A second set of data structures are maintained to handle messages intended for background processes. `Num_back` is a global count used by Commkit to indicate the number of background processes. Initially, `num_back` is zero; however, as each background process is registered using `register_back-ground()`, `num_back` is incremented. In addition, the array `back_list` contains the list of background process identifiers and entry points for each background process. This list is used in do_other_tasks() to determine which background process has a pending message and, if a message is available, the address of the procedure (i.e., the process entry point).

The send primitive   The send primitive allows an entity to send a message to another entity. The transmitting entity must specify the intended destination's identifier, the message, and the size of the message. The send software stores the message on the queue associated with the supplied destination identifier.

The format of the send primitive is as follows:

```
send(int src, int dst, char *msg, int size)
```

where:

src   the identifier of the transmitting (i.e., source) entity.

dst   the identifier of the intended destination entity.

*msg   the address of the message to be transmitted to the destination entity. The address is specified by prefixing the data structure with an &. The message is stored on the queue associated with the destination entity (as indicated by the dst identifier).

size   the size of the message msg.

For example, the procedure for the foreground process APPLICATION to send a 64-byte message to the background process BACKGROUND_1, could be written as follows:

```
void write_msg(msg)
char *msg;
{
     send(APPLICATION, BACKGROUND_1, msg, 64);
}
```

A one-byte message sent from the clock interrupt handler (via low_level()) to a background process BACKGROUND_3 could be written as:

```
void low_level(int device, int action, char data)
{
   if (device == CLKIH)
     send(CLKIH, BACKGROUND_3, &data, 1);
}
```

The receive primitive   The receive primitive allows an entity to receive a message sent from another entity. The receiving entity specifies the maximum number of bytes that it is willing to accept as well as supplying the address of the buffer into which the message should be copied. The number of bytes that the receive primitive copies into the message buffer is the *smaller* of either the size of the message (as specified by the source), or the number of bytes that can be accepted by the destination.

The format of the receive primitive is:

```
int recv(int *src, int dst, char *msg, int size)
```

where:

*src	the identifier of the entity that sent the message; returned by the receive primitive software. The identifier can be returned since the address of src is supplied (using &).
dst	the identifier of the receiving entity. The receive primitive software uses this identifier to determine from which queue to remove the message.
*msg	the address of a data structure where the message is to be stored. The address is specifed using &.
size	the size (in bytes) of the message. The entity must specify the *maximum* size the data structure can accept. The receive software checks the size associated with the message and chooses the *smaller* of the two sizes.

The number of bytes copied into the message buffer is returned by the recv() function.

As an example, consider the following code fragment which allows the foreground process, APPLICATION, to receive a message from any other source entity:

```
{
int src;
char data;

if (recv(&src, APPLICATION, &data, 1) == 1)
    /* Code to handle a one-byte message */
}
```

In some situations, an entity might be required to wait for messages from a number of different entities. If the entities send messages of different sizes, the receiving entity must specify the *largest* message size possible, to ensure that no data is lost when receiving a message. For example, in the following code fragment, the process BACKGROUND_1 can accept messages of nine bytes in length from process BACKGROUND_2 and one-byte messages from process APPLICATION:

```
{
int src;
char msg[9];

recv(&src, BACKGROUND_1, &msg, 9);

switch (src)
{
case BACKGROUND_2:
```

```
    /* Data in msg[0] through msg[8] */
    break;
case APPLICATION:
    /* Data in msg[0] */
    break;
default:
    message(0, 0, INVERSE, "Bad message in BACKGROUND_1");
}


}
```

The message handling software Interprocess communication via messages in Commkit involves not only the transmitting and receiving entities, but at least two other procedures: send() and recv(). For example, if process 1 sends a message to process 2, the following sequence of events occurs.

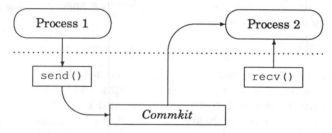

When an entity (i.e., a process or an interrupt handler) sends a message, the send() procedure is invoked. Send() takes a copy of the message and appends it to the message queue of the destination. What happens next depends upon the type of destination:

Foreground. If a message is available on the foreground process's queue when the foreground process executes a recv(), the message is returned immediately. However, if the foreground process's queue is empty, the foreground process is suspended and control passes from recv() to do_other_tasks(). Do_other_tasks() performs other tasks until a message becomes available for the foreground process. When a message is placed on the foreground process's queue, control returns to recv() which copies the data from the queue into the foreground process's message and execution resumes with the foreground process.

Background. The background process is activated when the foreground process is suspended and a message is available for the background process. The background process is called from do_other_tasks(). Do_other_tasks() obtains the process identifier and the entry point from the array back_list. The background process will continue to be called as long as messages exist for it and the foreground process is suspended.

The background process should have a call to recv() so that the pending message is read immediately. If the background process fails to perform a recv(), it will continue to be called since its message queue is never emptied!

Interrupt Handler. A message arriving for an interrupt handler results in a call to `low_level()` from `send()` with a code of `MSG_AVAIL`. If the interrupt handler can accept the message, it is expected to perform a `recv()`; otherwise the call is ignored (presumably the message is received at a later time).

2.3.6 Support Routines

In addition to the transmission and reception of messages, there are a number of functions offered by Commkit that can be used for support purposes such as screen output, numeric conversion, and screen clearing. These routines are intended for use by the interrupt handlers, although they can be used by either the foreground or background processes. The routines are found in `commkit.c`:

- To display a single `character` on the screen at a specific `line` and `column`, the `display()` procedure is used:

```
display(int line, int column, char character, char attributes)
```

The `attributes` indicate how `character` is to be displayed. Attribute values defined in `devices.h` include `NORMAL` (white on black), `INVERSE` (black on white), and `BLINK` (flashing on and off). Note that the `BLINK` attribute must be or'ed with another attribute in order to function. For example, the following code displays the upper case letters of the alphabet across the middle of the screen (line 12, columns 27 through 52) with attributes blink and inverse set for each letter:

```
void display_example()
{
int i;
char ch;

i = 27;
for(ch = 'A'; ch <= 'Z'; ch++)
    display(12, i++, ch, INVERSE | BLINK);
}
```

- To display a `string` with certain `attributes` starting at a specific `line` and `column` the `message()` procedure is used:

```
void message(int line, int column, int attributes, char *string)
```

`String` must be null terminated (`'\0'`). The same attributes apply to `message()` as to `display()`. The following example shows how a string can be displayed in the upper left-hand corner of the screen:

```
void message_example()
{
message(0, 0, NORMAL, "Press ENTER to continue");
}
```

The previous string is null terminated since, by default, C appends the null character to the end of any text string (i.e., a string enclosed in double quotes).

- To convert a 16-bit quantity (such as an integer) to a five-byte string procedure int2hex() is used:

```
void int2hex(int number, char *string)
```

String must be at least five bytes long to ensure sufficient storage exists for four hex digits *and* a null character ('\0'). Int2hex() is usually used in conjunction with message(). The following example shows how a the contents of the variable data can be displayed:

```
void hexoutput(int data)
{
char mask[5];

int2hex(data, mask);

message(10, 0, INVERSE, "Data: ");
message(10, 7, INVERSE, mask);
}
```

- To move the cursor to a specific location on the screen, procedure move_ cursor() is used:

```
void move_cursor(int newx, int newy)
```

For example, to move the cursor to the center of the screen (x: 12, y: 40):

```
move_cursor(12, 40);
```

This routine does not work on all PCs, apparently because of differences between various video cards.

- To dump the message queues at any time call:

```
dump_queues(int line)
```

Each queue entry is a pointer to a message (maximum 128 bytes). Dump_ queues() displays the queue entries associated with each entity (i.e., process or interrupt handler) as a pair of bytes, starting on the specified line of the screen. The first byte displayed (in inverse video) is the identifier of the entity to which the messages are destined. Subsequent bytes are displayed in pairs: the first indicating the source of the message (in normal video), and the second containing the first byte of the message (in inverse video).

To save space, empty queues are not displayed.

- To clear portions of the screen, use:

```
void clear_scr(int xup, int xlo, int yup, int ylo)
```

The screen is cleared between points xup, yup and xlo, ylo. The following code fragment shows how the lower half of the screen (lines 12 through 25) can be cleared:

```
clear_scr(12, 25, 0, 79);
```

2.3.7 Co-existing with MS-DOS

Unlike many applications that run in an MS-DOS environment, Commkit controls a number of the PC's interrupts. Control over these interrupts is necessary in order to understand how hardware and software interact to support data communications. There are two exceptions to this: (1) the MS-DOS and BIOS disk-access software are still permitted to function (since there is no single standard of disk supplied with the PC); and (2) clock interrupts are chained from Commkit to MS-DOS.

When an interrupt occurs that passes control to MS-DOS, MS-DOS changes two sets of registers: the 32-bit stack pointer (consisting of a 16-bit segment and a 16-bit offset register pair) and the 16-bit data-segment register, to point to those segments specific to MS-DOS. Most, if not all, MS-DOS interrupt handlers enable interrupts soon after entry into the interrupt handler. Upon completion of the interrupt, the original stack pointer and data-segment registers are restored and control returns to the interrupted procedure.

Although control passes to the correct Commkit interrupt handler should an interrupt occur from a device controlled by Commkit when an MS-DOS interrupt handler is active (remember, the code segment-offset is taken from the interrupt vector), there are two important points that must be taken into consideration:

- The data-segment register will be pointing to the data segment associated with MS-DOS, not Commkit.

- The MS-DOS stack may not be large enough to accommodate the stack requirements of the Commkit interrupt handler—*possibly* resulting in stack overflow and the destruction of part of the MS-DOS data area.

Fortunately, part of the problem is already solved: when an interrupt occurs, the data segment register is pushed onto the stack (thereby saving the MS-DOS data segment register value) and Turbo C assigns Commkit's data segment to the data segment register. When the interrupt handler has finished, the data segment register is popped from the stack, thereby restoring the register to MS-DOS's data segment.

To overcome the potential stack problems, the following algorithm is implemented in each interrupt handler:

1. Upon entry to the interrupt handler, save the old stack segment and stack offset registers.

2. Set the stack segment and stack offset to the local stack associated with the interrupt handler.

3. Perform the task required to service the interrupt.

4. Restore the old stack segment and stack offset, thereby permitting control to return to the interrupted software.

Changing the stack pointer requires access to the 80x86 stack segment register and the stack offset register; both of which are available to Turbo C as the pseudo registers _SS (stack segment) and _SP (stack offset). (The pseudo registers are mapped into the actual registers by the compiler; they are declared unsigned int.) Saving and restoring the stack pointer is achieved by:

```
void interrupt sample_ih()
{
/* Saving... */
old_ss = _SS;
old_sp = _SP;
...
/* Restoring... */
_SS = old_ss;
_SP = old_sp;
}
```

The variables old_ss and old_sp cannot be declared as variables local to the interrupt handler, since they will be stored on the stack set up upon entry (i.e., the original stack). If the stack-pointer registers (i.e., _SS and _SP) are subsequently changed, old_ss and old_sp will no longer refer to their locations on the original stack. This means that the original stack-pointer will be lost. Therefore, old_ss and old_sp must be declared as globals.

Fortunately, changing the stack-pointer registers is a straightforward operation, simply setting the register to a globally stored array (i.e., in the interrupt handler's data segment):

```
char lcl_stk[256];

void interrupt sample_ih()
{
/* Old _SS and _SP saved */

_SS = _DS;
_SP = (unsigned int) &lcl_stk[255];

/* Old _SS and _SP restored */
}
```

The stack segment pseudo register, _SS, is assigned the value of the data segment pseudo register, _DS, thereby ensuring that the segment is that of lcl_stk. The stack-offset pseudo register, _SP, is then assigned the address of the last location in the stack (since stacks operate from high to low memory).

Each Commkit interrupt handler has its own stack, declared of type stack (defined in commkit.h and used in commkit.c):

```
struct stack
{
unsigned int ss;
unsigned int sp;
char stk[256];
};
```

2.3.8 Miscellaneous

In addition to the previous discussion on Commkit, all modules require the following header files to permit compilation to proceed:

```
#include "general.h"
#include "ascii.h"
#include "devices.h"
```

The header file general.h contains a list of common directives; ascii.h is the ASCII character set, and devices.h contains the definitions of various device ports.

The module containing the mainline should also have an external definition of register_background() if background processes are to be used:

```
extern void register_background(int proc_id, void (*proc_name()));
```

2.4 INTERPROCESS COMMUNICATION USING COMMKIT

To illustrate how Commkit supports interprocess communication, consider the following problem:

Problem 2.1 Write a program that will allow a user to enter data from a PC's keyboard and display it on the PC's screen. Simultaneously, the time elapsed since the program started execution should be displayed as hh:mm:ss in the upper left-hand corner of the screen. When the user attempts to type beyond the last line of the screen, the screen should be cleared and the cycle should continue. A CTRL-C entered by the user should terminate the program, returning to MS-DOS.

2.4.1 Design Considerations

Commkit.c is supplied with software that handles clock interrupts, keyboard interrupts, and screen character output. However, software must be written that meets the other criteria in Problem 2.1, notably clearing the screen, watching for CTRL-C, and formatting the clock information into hours, minutes, and seconds.

Instead of writing a single process that handles all of these functions, the problem is divided into three separate tasks to illustrate how Commkit supports interprocess communication.

1. a process to examine each character that is entered by the user to determine whether it is a CTRL-C

2. a process to accept a 1-second timing signal from the clock and update the current time

3. a process to display the clock information and the keyboard input on the screen

Figure 2.10 illustrates the different paths that the information can take.

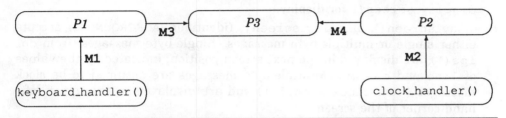

Figure 2.10 Information flow for Problem 2.1

where:

P1	A process that accepts characters from the keyboard_handler(), scans for CTRL-C, and forwards all other characters to *P3*.
P2	A process that accepts timing signals from the clock_handler() and converts them into a data structure consisting of hours, minutes, and seconds. The data structure is then forwarded to *P3*.
P3	A process that displays individual characters (from *P1*) or character strings (from *P2*). This process is also responsible for clearing the screen should printing an individual character cause it to go off screen.
M1	A character sent in a message from the keyboard_handler() to *P1*.
M2	A one-second timing signal message sent from the clock_handler() to *P2*.
M3	A character (other than CTRL-C) sent in a message from *P1* to *P3*.
M4	The current-time string (expressed as hh:mm:ss), sent from *P2* to *P3*.

2.4.2 Implementation

An example of an implementation of Problem 2.1 is available as the file ipc.c on the Commkit distribution diskette. The file consists of three processes (one foreground and two background processes):

do_ipc(). Do_ipc() is the foreground process (identifier APPLICATION); it accepts single-byte messages sent from the keyboard handler (identifier KEYIH). When a CTRL-C (*ETX*) is detected, do_ipc() terminates, returning to the mainline (and eventually MS-DOS). All other characters are sent to process display_screen() (identifier BACKGROUND_2).

clock_signal(). Clock_signal() is a background process (identifier BACK-GROUND_1) that receives timing-signal messages once every second from the clock interrupt handler, clock_handler(). Upon receipt of the message, the number of seconds is increased, the number of minutes are increased (if seconds exceed 59), and the number of hours are increased (if minutes exceed 59). The current hours, minutes, and seconds are then stored as a string of characters in the structure tod and sent to process display_screen() for display.

display_screen(). Display_screen() (identifier BACKGROUND_2), accepts either single or multiple-byte messages. Single-byte messages (from do_ipc()), are displayed in the next screen position, indicated by the values of line and column. Multiple-byte messages are assumed to be clock messages (from clock_signal()) and are displayed in the upper left-hand corner of the screen.

Two static variables are maintained by display_screen(). Column indicates the present horizontal character position and line contains the current line number. When column exceeds 79 or a carriage return is detected, column is set to zero and the line number is incremented. When line exceeds the screen length, the screen is cleared and the next character is displayed at the top of the screen.

Before the program can be run, the background processes must be registered and the low-level software must be written:

- the background processes are registered with Commkit in the mainline of ipc.c:

```
register_background(BACKGROUND_1, clock_signal);
register_background(BACKGROUND_2, display_screen);
```

- the Commkit interrupt handlers use low_level() to communicate with the foreground and background processes. In ipc.c, low_level() is called from either the clock handler (clock_handler()) or the keyboard handler (keyboard_handler()). Characters from the keyboard are sent immediately as messages to the foreground process. One-second timing signals are sent to the background process associated with identifier BACKGROUND_1 after HZ interrupts have occurred; the static variable sec_count keeps track of the number of clock interrupts that make up one second.

2.4.3 A Software Walk-through

Internally, the steps taken to display a character entered on the screen are as follows:

1. The keyboard_handler() receives a series of interrupts indicating that a key has been pressed and released. Once the value of the character has been determined and stored in the variable ascii, the keyboard_handler() calls low_level(), which sends the character to APPLICATION:

```
send(KEYIH, APPLICATION, &data, 1);
```

2. The keyboard character is kept on the queue APPLICATION until the foreground process performs a recv() with identifier APPLICATION.

3. When the foreground process do_ipc() performs a recv(), the next available character from queue APPLICATION is returned:

```
recv(&src, APPLICATION, &ch, 1)
```

The received byte, ch, is then checked. If ch is an *ETX*, control is returned to MS-DOS; otherwise the byte is sent to process BACKGROUND_2:

```
send(APPLICATION, BACKGROUND_1, &ch, 1);
```

Do_ipc() then executes another recv(), waiting for its next message.

Clock interrupts follow a similar path from the clock_handler(), via low_level(), to clock_signal(). However, unlike the keyboard interrupts, clock interrupts occur on a regular (one-second) basis, signalling that the current hours, minutes, and seconds are to be converted into a string of the format hh:mm:ss. The string is then sent to display_screen() which is responsible for displaying it. Note that since clock_signal() is a background process (identifier BACKGROUND_1), it is only executed when the foreground process is suspended.

Process display_screen() is activated whenever a message is detected on queue BACKGROUND_2 and the foreground process is suspended. When called, display_screen() reads the message into a 10-byte buffer using recv():

```
recv(&src, BACKGROUND_2, &msg, 10);
```

There are two possible sizes of message that display_screen() can receive: a single-byte character sent from do_ipc() and a time string sent from clock_signal(). Although clock_signal() can distinguish between the messages by the message's source identifier, it uses the message size instead; single characters are displayed directly in the next available screen position, while strings are displayed in the upper left-hand corner of the screen.

The message flow between the interrupt handlers and the processes can be illustrated as in Figure 2.11.

2.5 COMPILING COMMKIT

The Commkit software is written in Turbo C using the Turbo C extensions for handling interrupts and in-line assembler. As mentioned in Appendix A, the make utility ensures that only those modules that have been changed are actually recompiled and linked.

All modules can be compiled and linked without the use of Turbo Assembler. (There is an exception to this rule: all in-line assembly is in a single module, intrpt.c; as long as neither intrpt.obj nor intrpt.c are modified, Turbo Assembler is not required.)

Assuming that changes have been made to ipc.c, the creation of the new ipc.exe executable is made by typing:

```
C:\> make ipc.exe
```

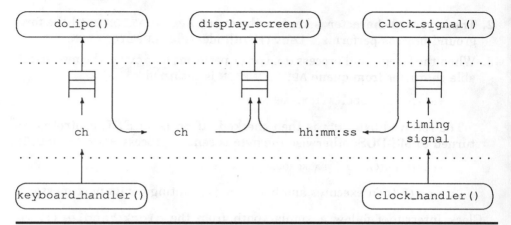

Figure 2.11   Message flow for interprocess communication example

Make will detect that ipc.c is "younger" than ipc.obj and proceed to compile ipc.c into a new object module using the options -ms (small model) and -c (create an object file only). All of the necessary include files are accessed by the compiler. The Turbo linker, tlink, is then invoked because make detects that ipc.obj is "younger" than ipc.exe. The linker links ipc.obj, commkit.obj, intrpt.obj, as well as the small model libraries to form ipc.exe.

To run the compiled program, simply type:

```
C:\> ipc
```

At this point, the screen will be cleared and the elapsed time since the start of execution will appear in the upper left of the screen. Whenever a character is typed, it will appear on the screen. Lines can be terminated explicitly, by using carriage returns, or implicitly, by filling the line (i.e., 80 characters have been typed on a line); in either case, output is started on the next line. If the screen is full, the next character entered will cause the screen to clear and the character will be placed in the first column on the line under the elapsed time.

2.5.1 When Things Go Wrong

Programs, on occasion, don't do what the programmer expects them to do; requiring the programmer to halt the program's execution. Any Commkit program can be aborted by typing CTRL-ALT-DEL; this is *not* the MS-DOS reboot, it is simply a signal to Commkit to restore the original interrupt vectors and return control to MS-DOS. All of the user-level processes supplied with Commkit can also be stopped using CTRL-C.

Software errors can be traced by placing display(), message(), or printf() procedure calls throughout the code. Since printf() is not recursive, only display() and message() should be used inside the interrupt handlers. The dump_queues() procedure can also be used, although usually as a last resort.

A process can send a message to any other process, and as such there are two possible results:

1. If a message is sent to the foreground process, a background process, or an interrupt handler, the destination process will eventually be called; or

2. If a message is sent to a non-existent process, send() will fail, returning a value of −1.

Should the destination process or interrupt handler not read its queue whenever a message becomes available, Commkit can run out of message space. If this occurs, the message queues are dumped and control is returned to MS-DOS via rtn_to_dos().

2.6 SUMMARY

This chapter has introduced the tools that will be used throughout the remainder of the book: the PC and Commkit.

The PC devices are all interrupt driven and are controlled by the Commkit software. Interrupts are converted into messages that are sent from the interrupt handlers (by calling low_level()) to processes.

Commkit supports two types of processes in addition to the interrupt handlers: foreground and background processes. There is one foreground process, associated with identifier APPLICATION; while there can be zero or more background processes, each with their own unique identifiers.

Messages are sent using the send() primitive and received using the recv() primitive. The intended destination of a message is indicated by the destination identifier specified by the transmitting process.

Finally, it is worth noting that communications within the DTE itself are subject to protocols. For example, when receiving a character from the keyboard, certain rules must be followed in order to receive and accept the character. Similarly, when one is using the interprocess communication primitives, rules must be followed if the data being sent is to be received and processed correctly.

2.7 EXERCISES

1. Commkit maps the keyboard scan codes into an equivalent set of ASCII characters. Use ipc to experiment with the various key combinations (i.e., CTRL, ALTMODE, and SHIFT) to determine which characters are displayed when various keys are pressed.

2. Does the "digital" clock displayed in the upper left-hand corner of the screen keep accurate time when ipc is running? Devise a method to determine the accuracy of the clock.

3. Is the accuracy of the clock affected by the typing of characters when ipc is running? Explain.

4. Explain what the following foreground process displays and whether the data displayed ever changes. What process supplies the initial input? You may assume that Commkit is functioning correctly and that the foreground process receives all keyboard input.

```
void do_fun()
{
int src;
char ch;

while (TRUE)
{
    recv(&src, APPLICATION, &ch, 1);
    display(12, 40, ch, NORMAL);
    send(src, APPLICATION, &ch, 1);
}
}
```

This question leads to some interesting problems; you might try implementing the process to see what actually happens.

5. It is often useful to know what a program does when it crashes. Modify ipc.c so that the foreground process do_ipc() never reads the messages that are sent to it. What happens when ipc is run and characters are entered at the keyboard? Continue typing for about 30 seconds. What happens now? Why doesn't CTRL-C cause Commkit to return to MS-DOS? Does the clock signal appear in the upper left-hand corner? Explain. If the suspense gets too great, CTRL-ALT-DEL will return control to MS-DOS.

6. Add character deletion to ipc.c using backspace to indicate the deletion of the character.

7. Modify ipc.c so that the user can treat the screen as an edit buffer, using the up, down, left, and right arrows to move throughout the text.

8. Modify ipc.c so that the user can enter the current time of day. When a special character (such as CTRL-A) is entered, this should signal do_ipc() that a new value for the time of day is about to be supplied. The next eight characters (in the format hh/mm/ss) can be treated as the new time. Remember that KEYIH supplies one character at a time.

9. Rewrite dump_queues() so that complete messages will be displayed.

10. Add another background process to ipc.c that takes the output from do_ipc() and changes the case on each letter before forwarding the character to display_screen(). The information flow should be as illustrated in Figure 2.12.

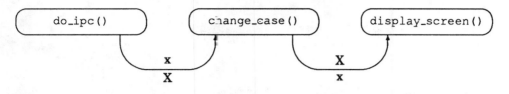

Figure 2.12 The change-case process

The new process (change_case() in Figure 2.12), should receive any message sent to queue BACKGROUND_3. Once the case has been changed, the character should be forwarded to queue BACKGROUND_2.

2

Point-to-point Communications

Most computer communications occur between pairs of DTEs. For example, one widespread application of computer communications involves the transfer of information from an individual's terminal to a remote computer. This type of communication is commonly known as an *asynchronous point-to-point* communication.

In Chapter 3, asynchronous point-to-point communications are discussed with regard to:

- the general concepts and terminology associated with asynchronous communications
- the hardware required to support asynchronous communications (illustrated using the PC's asynchronous hardware)
- the Commkit software that controls the asynchronous hardware.

Communications between DTEs cannot occur without some form of connection. Chapter 4 examines some of the different types of media and standards that are available to support communications between pairs (or groups) of DTEs.

Data communication software, as with any other type of application software, may be subject to errors in design or implementation. Software "debugging" techniques, such as inserting printf() statements within the code in order to display values, often lead to further problems. The time taken to display values may result in the loss of data from the communications channel. Instead, tools are needed to permit the "eavesdropping" of the traffic on the channel. In Chapter 5, techniques for analysing the contents of the communications channel are examined and a Commkit tool for channel monitoring is presented.

2

Point to Point Communications

3

Asynchronous Communications

3.1 INTRODUCTION

An *asynchronous communication* is one that can occur without regard to time. Asynchronous communications are typified by terminal-host communications in which the user can periodically send data from the terminal to the host at random, unpredictable intervals. Due to the widespread popularity and availability of asynchronous communications (for example, the PC is equipped with at least one asynchronous communications adapter), this chapter examines asynchronous communications in detail.

3.2 GENERAL CONCEPTS

In Chapter 1, information within a DTE was shown to be stored in *binary* form. For example, the ASCII letter S is represented by the 7-bit binary pattern:

```
101 0011
```

When information is transmitted on the channel between DTEs, it is not sent as a letter (such as S), but rather in a form that can be easily manipulated by the DTEs. Since the information is already stored in binary form within the DTE, data is, not surprisingly, transmitted as a series of 0s and 1s. For example, the transmission of the letter S can be represented pictorially as in Figure 3.1.

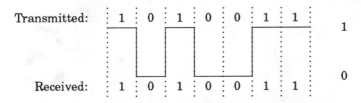

Figure 3.1   Transmission and reception of the letter S

When data is transferred between DTEs, it is usually done serially, since it is cheaper to use one wire instead of the seven or eight wires (depending upon the number of bits in the byte) that would be required in a parallel transmission. The right-most (low-order) bit is sent first, followed by the remaining bits while working from right to left.

It is generally accepted that a transmitted '1' is called a *mark*, while a transmitted '0' is called a *space*. These terms come from the days of telegraphy when a '1' on the communication channel was represented by a flow of current, which resulted in the equipment making a "mark" on the receiver's output device (a moving strip of paper), while the lack of current left a "space" on the paper.

The receiving DTE must read the data bits from the communication channel at the same rate at which they are being transmitted, otherwise a loss of information will occur. For example, Figure 3.2 depicts what might result in sending the byte S if it is received at twice the rate of transmission.

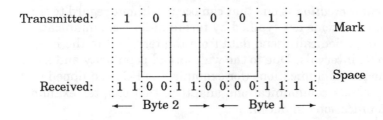

Figure 3.2   Result of receiving at twice the transmission rate

The receiver receives *two* bytes instead of one.

Similarly, if the transmitter is transmitting faster than the receiver can accept, there may also be a loss of information. In Figure 3.3, the transmitter is sending data at twice the rate it is being received (the letter S is sent once again).

The receiver receives only four bits rather than the seven that make up the byte. The value of the third bit could be either a mark (1) or a space (0), depending upon the exact moment the channel was sampled. Channel sampling is discussed in greater detail in Section 3.3.2.

As the previous examples illustrate, in any communication, both the transmitting and receiving DTE must agree to a single, common channel speed known as the *line speed*.

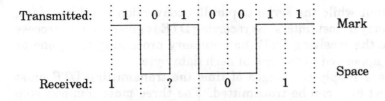

Figure 3.3 Result of receiving at half the transmission rate

Asynchronous line speeds can be expressed in terms of *bits per second (bps)* and typically range from 50 bps to 9600 bps. Some commonly used line speeds are 300 bps, 1200 bps, 2400 bps, and 9600 bps. As well as agreeing upon the line speed, both DTEs must concur upon the number of bits in a byte. This is usually a choice between 7-bit and 8-bit, as these are the most common character code widths.

Since the channel can only be in one of two states, mark or space, when there is nothing to transmit, the channel must always be left in one of these states. All DTEs, when they are not transmitting, leave the channel in the mark state.

This then raises another issue: if the channel idles in the mark state, how does the receiving DTE determine where the first data bit occurs? In the worst case, if a DTE transmits the binary pattern 1111111, the receiving DTE will not be able to distinguish between the marks representing the idle channel and the marks representing the data!

The solution to this problem is to have the first bit sent as a nondata space. That is, before the first data bit is sent, the channel changes state from mark to space. After the space, the bits making up the byte are transmitted. Therefore, when transmitting the byte S, one finds the condition given in Figure 3.4.

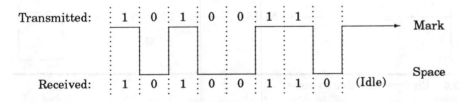

Figure 3.4 The initial mark-to-space transition denotes the start of transmission

The first bit, indicating the start of data, is called the *start bit*. The start bit signals the receiving DTE that a data byte is about to follow. The width of the start bit is the same as each of the data bits (that is, it takes the same length of time to send the start bit as it does to send a data bit). Upon receipt of the start bit, the two DTEs are *synchronized* for the length of time it takes to send the data byte.

Once a data byte is received, the receiving DTE must process it. Processing the character is not an instantaneous operation; at a minimum, the receiving DTE must convert the incoming serial data byte into a parallel byte for storing. This is known as a *serial-to-parallel conversion*). If the transmitting DTE continues to transmit while the serial-to-parallel conversion is taking place, one or more bytes may be lost unless the receiving DTE is given time to process each byte. To give the receiving DTE the necessary processing time, one or more *stop bits* are appended to the end of each data byte.

The stop bit(s) are simply the length of time the transmitting DTE must wait before the next byte can be transmitted. The three most common stop bit times are: 1 bit, $1\frac{1}{2}$ bits, and 2 bits.

In Figure 3.5, the byte S is transmitted with a start bit, and two stop bits.

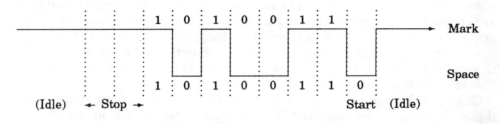

Figure 3.5   The letter S sent with a start bit and two stop bits

The start and stop bits are said to *frame* the transmitted data byte.

3.2.1   Errors

On occasion, one or more of the bits in the transmission may be changed from a 1 to a 0 (or vice versa) due to noise, typically some form of electromagnetic interference, (see Chapter 1) or other interference on the channel (Figure 3.6).

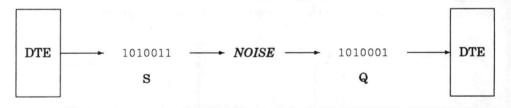

Figure 3.6   Bit inversion due to noise

In Figure 3.6, the byte S is changed into the byte Q because of noise on the line (the second bit is inverted from a 1 to a 0). Even with the start and stop framing bits, the receiving DTE has no way of determining from the information received whether the byte is correct or not. A mechanism is needed whereby the receiving DTE can detect that an error has occurred in the transmission of the information.

One possible error detection technique is to transmit each byte *twice* and to have the receiver examine both bytes. If the bytes are different, the receiver has detected an error (but cannot determine which byte is the correct one). Interestingly enough, if both bytes are the same, the receiver still has no indication of whether the bytes are correct, since the same error might have occurred to both bytes and resulted in the same bit pattern.

Retransmitting the entire byte presents another problem: Using the channel to send each byte twice means that only half as much information is being transmitted. A much less costly form of *error detection* can be achieved by summing the bits and determining whether the sum is *odd* or *even*. The result of the sum, odd or even, can be represented as a single bit and transmitted within the frame. This extra bit is known as the *parity bit* and is transmitted after the last data bit and before the stop bit(s) (the byte S is transmitted again). See Figure 3.7.

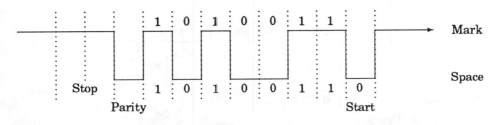

Figure 3.7   The parity bit follows last data bit and precedes stop bit(s)

The two best known types of parity are:

Odd parity. The sum of all the bits, including the parity bit, is *odd*. For example, if the byte S (bit pattern 1010011) is transmitted, the parity bit has a value of 1, since the sum of the data bits is even (there are *four* data bits set to 1), but the total must be odd (Figure 3.8).

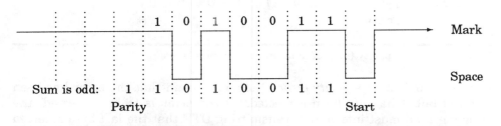

Figure 3.8   Odd parity (sum of data and parity bits is odd)

However, if the byte L (bit pattern 1001100) is transmitted, the parity bit has a value of 0, since the sum of the data bits is already odd (there are *three* data bits set to 1). See Figure 3.9.

Even parity. The sum of all the bits, including the parity bit, is *even*. For example, if the byte S is transmitted, the parity bit would have a value of 0, since the sum of the data bits is already even (Figure 3.10).
  If the byte L (bit pattern 1001100) is transmitted, the parity bit would have a value of 1, since the sum of the data bits is odd, but the total must be even (Figure 3.11).

The receiving DTE can detect an error when the sum of the bits (data plus parity) is wrong (i.e., odd instead of even, or even instead of odd). This type

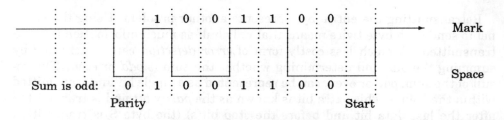

Figure 3.9   Odd parity (sum of data and parity bits is odd)

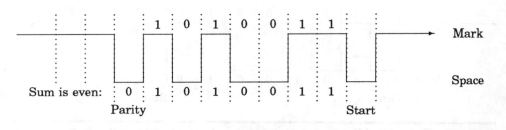

Figure 3.10   Even parity (sum of data and parity bits is even)

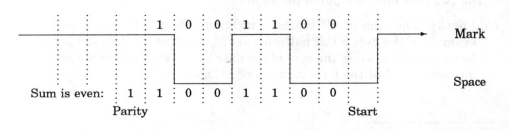

Figure 3.11   Even parity (sum of data and parity bits is even)

of error is known as a *parity error*. Note once again that the error has been detected but it has not been corrected. If the error is to be corrected, the receiving DTE must inform the transmitting DTE that the last byte received was in error.

If the receiving DTE is to detect the parity error, it must support the same parity the transmitting DTE is using (i.e., both must be odd, or both must be even). Failure to observe this will result in all bytes being flagged as having parity errors. As an example, consider the transmission of the byte S with even parity, where there are a total of four bits set to 1 (the parity bit is therefore zero). If the transmitted byte is received by a DTE expecting odd parity, the byte will be received in error, because an even number of bits are set.

Now, if interference occurs on the connection between the two DTEs, the receiving DTE can *detect* the error; however, the error cannot be *corrected* since it is not possible to determine which bit(s) are in error. In Figure 3.12, the byte S is transmitted with odd parity, but noise changes the second bit from a 1 to a 0.

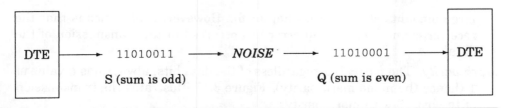

Figure 3.12 Error detection using parity bit

Upon receipt of the byte **Q**, the receiver can immediately determine that the data was not received correctly because the parity is wrong (the sum of the bits is *even* when it should be *odd*).

Does parity error detection still work if the parity bit is changed? Yes, since parity error detection works by summing all the bits, data *and* parity (Figure 3.13).

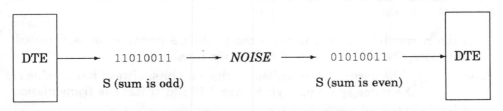

Figure 3.13 Error detection using parity bit (parity bit inverted)

Although the byte S that is received is valid, the parity is incorrect, indicating that an error has occurred somewhere in the transmission.

Parity error detection does not work in all cases, as illustrated by Figure 3.14, in which the byte S is affected by noise which inverts bits 2 and 3, producing the byte U (bit pattern 1010101); odd parity is being used.

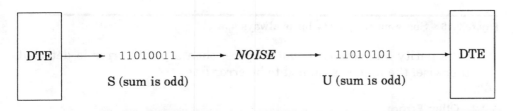

Figure 3.14 Failure of parity bit to detect an error

The sum of the bits is *still* odd, which means that the error goes undetected since the parity is correct. Parity checking (odd or even) is not foolproof: it can only detect *odd* numbers of errors.

In addition to odd and even parity, many asynchronous systems also support the following parities (in all cases, the start and stop bits are still sent):

No parity. The parity bit is neither generated nor transmitted. This reduces the number of bits in the frame, which can be useful when transferring large amounts of data (see Chapter 6). However, it also means that the receiver cannot detect if an error has occurred in the transmission of the data.

Mark parity. The parity bit, regardless of the data bits, always has a value of 1 (hence the name mark parity). Figure 3.15 illustrates the transmission of the byte S with mark parity.

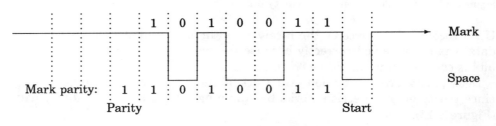

Figure 3.15   Mark parity (parity bit is always mark)

If the parity bit received is *not* a mark, then a parity error is detected; otherwise, the byte is assumed to be error free.

Space parity. The parity bit, regardless of the data bits, always has a value of 0 (hence the name space parity). Figure 3.16 illustrates the transmission of the byte L with space parity.

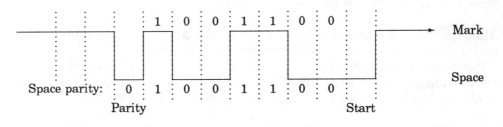

Figure 3.16   Space parity (parity bit is always space)

If the parity bit received is *not* a space, then a parity error is detected; otherwise, the byte is assumed to be error free.

3.2.2   Other Errors

There are two other common types of errors that can occur on an asynchronous channel:

- An *overrun error* occurs when the receiving DTE does not process the incoming data bytes quickly enough. A typical sequence is outlined in Figure 3.17. In Figure 3.17, three bytes have been sent by the transmitting DTE; however, before the receiving DTE has had time to receive and process the second byte (it is still processing the first byte), the third byte arrives, overwriting the second byte. Overruns can be avoided by reducing the processing load on the receiving DTE or by reducing the line speed.

Transmitting DTE		Receiving DTE
First byte sent	⟶	Receives first byte
Second byte sent	⟶	Processing first byte
Third byte sent	⟶	Receives third byte

Figure 3.17   Example of an overrun error

- A *framing error* occurs when the receiving DTE cannot detect the end of the frame (i.e., the stop bits cannot be detected). There are two reasons that the DTE can miss the stop bit(s):
  - noise may have caused the stop bits to be inverted, causing the receiving DTE to detect one or more spaces instead of marks.
  - noise may have caused the start bit to be inverted, causing the DTE to start assembling the byte with the wrong bit.

  Regardless of the cause of the framing error, there is no mechanism available to allow the receiving DTE to determine the correct value of the transmitted byte (other than the retransmission of the byte).

Further explanation of overrun and framing errors is given in Section 3.3.

3.2.3   The Break Condition

In addition to the characters found on a terminal's keyboard, many DTEs with keyboards have a key marked BREAK. The break key does not have an equivalent ASCII (or EBCDIC) character code; rather, it is intended to cause the user's DTE to generate a *break condition* on the channel. A break can be used for a number of reasons. In many applications, it is intended to signal the receiving DTE that attention is required.

A break condition is indicated by holding the channel in the space state for *at least* the amount of time required to send an entire frame (i.e., a start bit, the data bits, the parity bit, and the stop bits). See Figure 3.18.

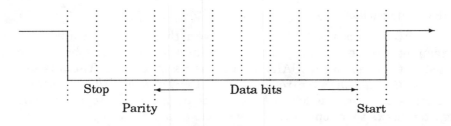

| Stop | Parity | ←――― Data bits ―――→ | Start |

Figure 3.18   Break condition (all of frame is held in space state)

How the receiving DTE handles the break condition is determined by a higher level of protocol. For example, software may be designed to treat the reception of a break as an indication that an executing process is to be aborted.

3.3   ASYNCHRONOUS COMMUNICATIONS HARDWARE

Data within a DTE is usually stored and moved in a parallel fashion (the start and stop framing bits do not exist); however, the data sent across the channel is usually sent serially. The DTE is therefore required to convert the internal data to a form that can be transmitted on the channel (in serial form with start, stop, and parity bits). Similarly, the serial data received from the channel must be changed into parallel for use within the DTE.

The conversion of the data for transmission and reception is done in hardware by a device known as a *Universal Asynchronous Receiver/Transmitter (UART)*. The UART can be represented diagramatically as shown in Figure 3.19.

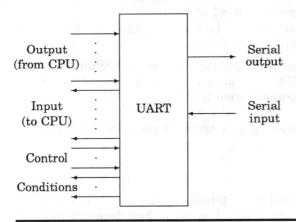

Figure 3.19   Basic UART connections

The UART is responsible for generating the start, stop, and parity bits, as well as for removing them. Channel conditions such as the break condition, framing, and overrun errors are signalled by the UART back to the processor. The processor can send control signals to the UART, including line speed, word size, parity, and the number of stop bits.

3.3.1   UART Transmission

When transmitting data, the UART must convert the internal parallel byte into a stream of serial bits using *parallel-to-serial conversion*. The byte to be transmitted is supplied to the UART by the DTE's processor. The bits are stored in a *Shift Register* (often referred to as the *Transmit Shift Register*). The start bit is sent first, followed by the bits in the Shift Register. The Shift Register *clocks* them onto the channel, one at a time, at the line speed (Figure 3.20).

How and when the parity bit is generated (and subsequently sent), depends upon the parity selected (Table 3.1).

Odd and even parity are calculated by exclusive or'ing the data bits as they are shifted onto the channel. The parity bit is initialized to 0 for even parity and 1 for odd parity. Figure 3.21 illustrates how a feedback loop can be used

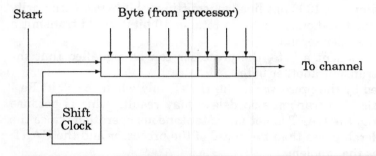

Figure 3.20 UART Shift Register

TABLE 3.1 UART Parity Generation

Parity	How generated
None	Parity bit is not sent
Odd	Generated by exclusive or'ing the outgoing data bits
Even	Generated by exclusive or'ing the outgoing data bits
Mark	Parity bit is set to 1
Space	Parity bit is set to 0

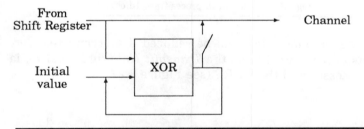

Figure 3.21 Use of feedback loop to calculate parity

to calculate the parity (the initial value of the parity bit depends upon the parity being calculated).

Each bit that is sent is included in the parity generation. Once the final data bit is included in the parity, the parity bit can be clocked onto the channel for transmission. If mark or space parity is selected, a 1 or 0, respectively, is put onto the channel after the final bit, regardless of the value in the parity-generation hardware.

The parity bit is followed by one or more stop bits. Stop bits are "generated" by the UART entering an idle state in which the channel idles with marks and blocks transmission for at least the time it would take to transmit the required number of stop bits.

It is important to note that the line speed indicates the *total* number of bits that the UART can transmit in one second. Therefore, when determining the number of bytes that can be transmitted in one second, it is necessary to include the number of data bits as well as the number of start, stop, and parity bits. For example, a 1200 bps line transmitting 7-bit bytes, with parity (odd or even), one start and one stop bit (a total of 10 bits), could transmit a maximum of 120 bytes per second.

Once the UART has sent a byte, the processor can be signalled that the UART is ready to transmit another byte.

If data is supplied by the processor to the UART only when the Shift Register is empty, noticeable transmission delays may result. This is because transferring a byte to the UART is not an instantaneous operation, since the line speed is considerably less than the speed of the processor and the UART. Table 3.2 illustrates the problem.

TABLE 3.2   Channel Throughput Reduced Due to Speed of UART

Time	Processor	UART	Channel
1	Supplies byte to UART		Idle
2		Shifts	*Active*
3		Data	*Active*
4		Bits	*Active*
5		Signals completion to processor	Idle
6	Supplies byte to UART		Idle
7		Shifts	*Active*
8		Data	*Active*
9		Bits	*Active*
10		Signals completion to processor	Idle

The periods when the channel is idle can be reduced if a second register, a *Holding Register* (usually referred to as the *Transmit Holding Register*), is placed between the processor and the UART (see Figure 3.22).

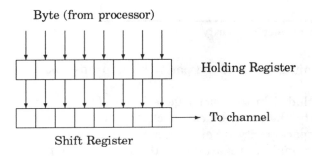

Figure 3.22   UART Transmit Holding Register

Delays are now reduced because the UART can be transmitting a byte from the Shift Register while the processor fills the Holding Register (see Table 3.3.)

This technique, whereby two registers are used in a transmission is known as *double buffering*. In addition to accepting bytes from the processor, most UARTs can signal the processor when the Transmit Holding Register is empty and when the Transmit Shift Register is empty.

TABLE 3.3 Channel Throughput Increased by Use of Holding Register

Time	Processor	Holding Register	Shift Register	Channel
1	Supplies byte to HR*	Empty	Empty	Idle
2		Supplies byte to SR*	Empty	Idle
3		Signals processor	Shifts	*Active*
4	Supplies byte to HR	Empty	Data	*Active*
5		Supplies byte to SR	Bits	*Active*
6		Signals processor	Shifts	*Active*
7	Supplies byte to HR	Empty	Data	*Active*
8		Supplies byte to SR	Bits	*Active*

* HR denotes Holding Register; SR denotes Shift Register

3.3.2 UART Reception

The UART receives nothing while the channel is in an idle (i.e., mark) state. Upon detection of a channel state change (that is, the channel changes from a mark to a space), the UART determines the center of the start bit and then reads bits from the channel at regular intervals using a *sampling clock*. The bits are assembled in a *Shift Register*; each time the sampling clock "ticks," the register is shifted to the right and the next bit from the channel is read. When all of the bits from the channel have been read (the number of bits read is determined by the word size), the resulting byte is supplied to the processor (Figure 3.23).

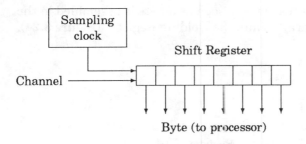

Figure 3.23   UART Reception Shift Register

The UART also scans for the start and stop bits, and if required, calculates and performs a parity check. How parity is handled depends upon the parity chosen:

No parity. The UART ignores parity checking altogether.

Mark or *space parity.* The channel can be sampled after the last data bit is read. The value of the bit can be compared to that expected by the receiving UART. If the received parity bit is the same as that expected, the data is assumed to be correct, otherwise a parity error is signalled.

Odd or *even parity.* Both the incoming data bits *and* the parity bit are used to determine whether a parity error has occurred. The UART initializes its parity check circuit to 0 (even parity) or 1 (odd parity) and proceeds to generate parity by exclusive or'ing the incoming data bits with the parity.

If no errors are detected, the value of the parity calculated by the UART should be the same as that received by the UART. At this point, the UART can explicity compare the parity bit received with that calculated and signal the DTE accordingly.

Alternatively, the UART can include the incoming parity bit in the parity calculation. If the parity in the frame received is the same as that calculated by the UART (i.e., both 0 or both 1), the result of this final exclusive or'ing is 0. However, if the values are different, the final exclusive or'ing will result in a value of 1. This result can be made available to the DTE; for example, a zero could indicate that no errors were detected, while a one would signal a parity error.

Once a complete byte has been assembled in the Shift Register, the UART can signal the processor that a byte is available. At this point, the processor can copy the byte from the Shift Register into a memory location.

If the assembled byte is kept in the Shift Register and the processor does not read the Shift Register before the first bit of the next byte arrives, an *overrun error* will occur. Since there is only one Shift Register, either the incoming byte must be discarded or the byte in the Shift Register must be overwritten. Ideally neither the incoming byte nor the byte in the Shift Register should be lost; meaning that the byte in the Shift Register should be read by the processor as quickly as possible. The reception technique is similar to that used in transmission: a second register is placed between the processor and the Shift Register (i.e., double buffering). As soon as a byte is assembled in the Shift Register, it is copied (in parallel) into the Holding Register (Figure 3.24).

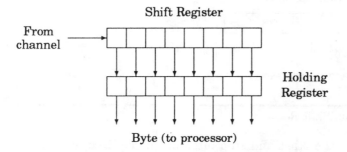

Figure 3.24   UART Reception Holding Register

The addition of the Holding Register does not eliminate the possibility of an overrun occurring, it merely reduces the probability. For example, a byte could be copied into the Holding Register and the processor signalled; if the processor did not remove the byte from the Holding Register before a second byte was copied into the Holding Register, an overrun error would still occur.

The other errors discussed in Section 3.2.1 are also handled by the UART's reception hardware. If the parity calculated as the byte is received does not agree with the parity supplied with the byte, the UART should signal the processor that a *parity error* has occurred. If a stop bit (i.e., a mark) is not detected after the last bit (data or parity, depending on whether parity is required), the UART should signal the processor that a *framing error* has occurred.

The UART should also be able to detect a *break condition*. Specifically, after the line has been in the space state for at least the start bit, data bits, parity bit, and stop bits. Often, a UART will signal a framing error when detecting a break because the framing error condition can be indistinguishable from the break condition. For example, an inverted (missing) stop bit on a null character sent with even parity is equivalent to a break condition.

The value of the byte assembled by the UART clearly depends upon the bits that are sampled from the channel. Although the signal diagrams have shown the rising and falling edges of a transmitted character to be sharp and square, in reality the edges may be much less distinct. In fact, over time, the signal may become *attenuated* or weakened, so that it is extremely difficult to determine the value of the bit, for example, see Figure 3.25.

Transmitted:

Received:

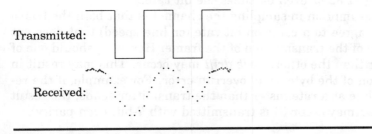

Figure 3.25   Signal attenuation

Since the value of a bit may become harder to determine at its edges, UARTs are normally designed to sample the line as close to the *center* of each bit as possible.

The center of each bit is found by first locating the center of the start bit. Once the center of the start bit has been found, the UART can sample the line once per *bit time* (i.e., the inverse of the line speed; for example, a 1200 bps line would have a bit time of 1/1200 of a second), to find the center of the remaining bits in the transmission.

The algorithm to find the center of the start bit is as follows:

1. Wait for a mark-to-space transition.

2. When a transition has been found, sample the line at 16 times the bit rate.

3. After 8 "ticks" (i.e., one-half a bit time), sample the line:
   - if a space (0) is found, a start bit is assumed and the line can be sampled once per bit time.
   - if a mark (1) is found, a false start bit was found, and the line sampling can be abandoned.

For example, if the letter S is sent, the sampling of the channel occurs as depicted in Figure 3.26.

Since the UART may not start its sampling clock at the exact edge of the start bit's mark-to-space transition, using a 16 times counter could prove to be

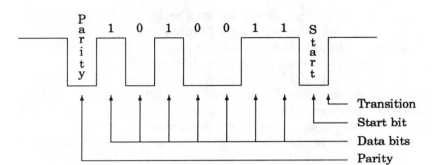

Figure 3.26 Channel is sampled at center of each bit

inaccurate in determining the center of the start bit. The error can be made smaller by sampling at 32 or even 64 times the bit rate.

The underlying assumption in sampling the channel is that both the transmitter and receiver agree to a common bit rate (or line speed) that does not vary over the period of the transmission of the frame. However, should one of the clocks be slower than the other, *clock drift* may occur. This may result in the misinterpretation of the byte or an overrun error. For example, if the receiver samples the line at a rate faster than the transmitter sends, the result shown in Figure 3.27 may occur (S is transmitted with 7-bit, even parity).

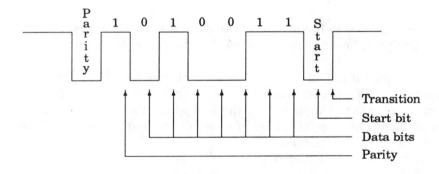

Figure 3.27 Clock drift: center of bit is not found

Because of the slower receiver clock speed, the value of the byte received by the DTE will not be the same as was transmitted. Depending upon the degree of signal attenuation, the DTE could receive one of a number of possible byte values, for example (the leftmost bit is the parity bit):

10100111   The third bit received (sampled at the space/mark transition between the second and third bits transmitted) is read as a 1. A parity error will occur.

10100011   The third bit is read as a 0, meaning that the parity bit and the data bits are assumed to be correct.

In each of these two cases, the parity bit may be misinterpreted as the start bit of the next byte. Regardless of the value of the byte received by the DTE, it is wrong, meaning that one or both UART clocks need to be reinitialized and the data retransmitted.

3.4 THE PC UART

A typical PC is supplied with at least one UART (also referred to as a *serial interface*, or *asynchronous communication adapter*, or *serial port*). Although there is no single supplier of UARTs, most PC UARTs are compatable with the Intel 8250 UART. Commkit supports the 8250 UART.

The 8250 UART is programmable and permits:

- Variable word size (5-, 6-, 7-, or 8-bit words)
- Variable number of stop bits (1, $1\frac{1}{2}$, or 2)
- Choice of parity (none, mark, space, odd, or even)
- Choice of line speeds (50 bps to 9600 bps, or higher)

The UART permits the transmission and reception of data, and can signal the processor with the following status indications:

- Data ready (i.e., data is available in the receive buffer)
- Reception errors (i.e., overrun, parity, and framing)
- Break condition detected
- Transmit Shift Register Empty
- Transmit Holding Register Empty

The UART also supports interrupts, three of which are of interest at this point:

- Receive Line Status (a change in the status of the line has occurred, typically an error or a break)
- Data Available (a byte has been received)
- Transmit Holding Register Empty (a byte has been copied into the Shift Register and the UART can accept another byte)

UART interrupts occur through device vectors 11 (serial port 2) and 12 (serial port 1). The type of interrupt (i.e., Data Available, Transmit Holding Register Empty, or Receive Line Status) can be determined by the processor reading the Interrupt Identification Register (see Section 3.4.1).

3.4.1 Programming the UART

As with the other PC devices that have been discussed, the UART can be accessed through a series of ports using the three instructions: `inportb()`, `outportb()`, and `outport()`.

Although there are a total of seven ports for the UART, only five will be discussed in this chapter (the remaining two are discussed in Chapter 8). The five ports, their addresses, offsets, and uses are listed in Table 3.4 (note that some ports have multiple uses).

TABLE 3.4   UART Port Addresses and Uses

Port 1	Port 2	Address offset	Uses
0x3F8	0x2F8	Base address* + 0	– Transmission Register Buffer – Receive Register Buffer – Line speed (least significant byte)
0x3F9	0x2F9	Base address + 1	– Interrupt Enable – Line speed (most significant byte)
0x3FA	0x2FA	Base address + 2	– Interrupt Identification Register
0x3FB	0x2FB	Base address + 3	– Line Control Register
0x3FD	0x2FD	Base address + 5	– Line Status Register

*The base address refers to 0x3F8 (Port 1) or 0x2F8 (Port 2).

For the sake of brevity, the remainder of this section will refer only to serial port 1. However, everything discussed for serial port 1 is applicable to serial port 2.

UART initialization   When a computer is first powered on, the hardware is often in an undetermined state; for example, when the contents of the computer's memory are unknown. Similarly, the internal settings of the UART are unknown and must be initialized. That is, the line speed, word size, parity, and number of stop bits must be written to the UART before it is used. Three registers serve to initialize the UART: the two line speed registers (0x3F8 and 0x3F9) and the Line Control Register (0x3FB).

The UART's line speed is generated by dividing its internal clock rate (1.8432 MHz) by a programmable 16-bit divisor, which is set up in the two line speed registers, 0x3F8 and 0x3F9. The value resulting from the division is *sixteen times* the actual line speed. Once a mark-to-space transition has been detected, the center of the start bit can be determined by examining the channel after eight "ticks" of the clock have occurred. As soon as the center of the start bit has been found, the center (and value) of each subsequent bit can be obtained after every sixteen "ticks" of the clock. The value selected for the line speed is used for both transmission and reception.

Although any 16-bit value between 1 and $(2^{16} - 1)$ can serve as the divisor, specific values must be used in order to obtain "well-known" line speeds. For example, Table 3.5 lists some of the divisors and their associated line speeds. As an example, consider the effect of setting the line speed to 9600 bps. First, the UART's internal clock rate of 1.8432 MHz is divided by 0x0C (decimal 12) to obtain the line speed: 0.1536 MHz or 153,600 "ticks" per second. Remember, this is still 16 times the actual line speed. Every 16 of these ticks is equivalent

TABLE 3.5   **Sample Divisors and Line Speeds**

Divisor (hexadecimal)	Line speed
0x0900	50
0x0180	300
0x0060	1200
0x0030	2400
0x000C	9600

to the time taken to send a single bit, resulting in an effective speed of 153,600 divided by 16, or 9600 bits per second. (To find the center of the start bit, the UART samples the channel eight "ticks" after the mark-to-space transition is found.)

The 16-bit value of the line speed divisor is written into the two line speed register ports. Since the two line speed registers (0x3F8 and 0x3F9) are used both in the transmission and reception of data as well as indicating which interrupt has occurred, the UART must be informed of the function of the two registers *before* they are used. If bit 7 of the Line Control Register (the Divisor Latch Access Bit, or DLAB) is set, ports 0x3F8 and 0x3F9 can be accessed as the line speed divisor registers (Figure 3.28).

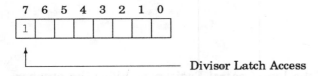

Figure 3.28   Line Control Register: Divisor Latch Access Bit

The line speed register ports can now have the value of the line speed written into them: the lower 8 bits into 0x3F8 and the upper 8 bits into 0x3F9. For example, to set the line speed to 9600 bps, register 0x3F8 would be set to 0x0C and register 0x3F9, to 0x00 (Figure 3.29).

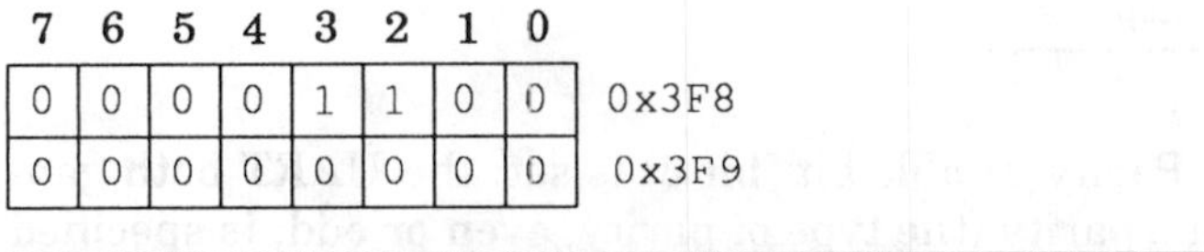

```
7   6   5   4   3   2   1   0
0   0   0   0   1   1   0   0    0x3F8
0   0   0   0   0   0   0   0    0x3F9
```

Figure 3.29   Line Speed Register: ports 0x3F8 and 0x3F9

The word size, parity, and stop bits are also initialized through the Line Control Register. The contents of the Line Control Register are shown in Figure 3.30 (note that the Divisor Latch Access Bit is cleared), and the terms used in the figure are defined in the following list and associated tables.

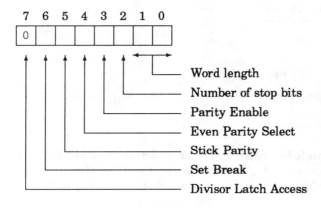

Figure 3.30 Line Control Register

Word length. The word length is specified in bits 0 and 1 of the Line Control Register, permitting 4 different word lengths (Table 3.6).

TABLE 3.6   Word Length Bit Combinations

Bit 1	Bit 0	Word length
0	0	5 bits
0	1	6 bits
1	0	7 bits
1	1	8 bits

Number of stop bits. Bit 2 of the Line Control Register signifies the number of stop bits in each transmitted or received frame. The number of stop bits generated depends upon whether this bit is set and the number of bits in each word (Table 3.7).

TABLE 3.7   Possible Stop Bit Values

Bit 2	Word length	Number of stop bits
0	Any length	1 stop bit
1	5-bit	1-1/2 stop bits
1	6-, 7-, 8-bit	2 stop bits

Parity Enable. When the Parity Enable bit (bit 3) is set, the UART both generates and checks frame parity (the type of parity, even or odd, is specified in bit 4).

Even Parity Select. Bit 4, Even Parity Select, is set to indicate even parity and cleared to indicate odd parity. This bit has meaning only if bit 3 (Parity Enable) is set.

Stick Parity. Stick Parity is a mechanism whereby the transmitted byte can be sent (and received) with either mark or space parity. When both the

Stick Parity bit and Parity Enable bits are set, parity generation is disabled and the value of the parity bit is set to the inverse of whatever parity (odd or even) has been selected in bit 4. Table 3.8 shows the required settings to generate mark or space parity and assumes that the stick parity bit is set.

TABLE 3.8 Bit Settings for Mark and Space Parity

Parity required	Parity Enable	Even Parity Select
Mark	1	0
Space	1	1

As always, both the transmitting and receiving DTEs must agree to the same parity (mark, space, odd, even, or none).

Set Break. The Set Break bit can be used to force the line into a break condition, that is, when this bit is set, the line is held in the space state until the bit is cleared. Transmitting a break requires the processor to determine the amount of time needed for a break, given the line speed, and then to set the Set Break bit. Once the time has expired, the processor can clear the Set Break bit.

Divisor Latch Access Bit. The Divisor Latch Access Bit (bit 7) when set, allows the processor to change the line speed (see previous discussion). When cleared, the speed cannot be altered.

The Line Control Register settings are applicable to both transmission and reception. For example, if the UART is initialized to 7-bit data and even parity, the UART will transmit *and* receive 7 bits of data per frame with even parity.

To initialize the UART to 7-bit data, 1 stop bit, and even parity, the Line Control Register will contain the information shown in Figure 3.31.

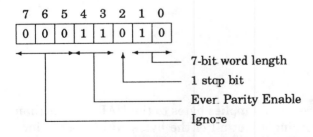

Figure 3.31 Line Control Register settings for 7-bit data, 1 stop bit, even parity

The C software used to set the primary port UART to 9600 bps, 7-bit bytes, 1 stop bit, and even parity could be written as follows:

```
#define DLABon      0x80
#define DLABoff     0x00
#define BPS96K      0x0c
#define SEVENBIT    0x02
#define STOPBITS    0x00
#define PRTYENA     0x08
#define EPS         0x10

#define DIVLTCHLSB 0x3F8
#define DIVLTCHMSB 0x3F9
#define LCR         0x3FB

initialize()
{
outportb(LCR, DLABon);
outport(DIVLTCHLSB, BPS96K);
outportb(LCR, DLABoff + SEVENBITS + STOPBITS + PRTYENA + EPS);
}
```

UART transmission   The UART has two registers associated with data transmission: the Transmit Holding Register and the Transmit Shift Register. Although the UART can signal when either of these registers are empty, the processor can write only to the Transmit Holding Register.

The Transmit Holding Register is an 8-bit register accessed through port 0x3F8. A byte written to this port (using outportb()) is normally copied by the UART to the Shift Register and transmitted serially. For example, to transmit the character A:

```
/* UART has been initialized */
outportb(0x3F8, 'A');
```

However, should the byte be written to the port before the previous byte has been copied into the Shift Register, data will be lost, causing a form of internal overrun to occur, for example:

```
main()
{
char ch;

/* Initialize UART */

for (ch = 'A'; ch <= 'Z'; ch++)
    outportb(0x3F8, ch);
}
```

In this code fragment, the processor supplies bytes to the UART faster than they can be transmitted. Accordingly, not all of the bytes will be sent since the UART is slower than the processor. This problem can be overcome by reducing the rate at which the processor supplies the data to the UART, either by polling the UART to determine when the next character can be supplied, or by allowing the UART to interrupt, signalling that the Transmit Holding Register is empty.

Polling the UART is done through the Line Status Register, port 0x3FD. The Line Status Register signals the condition of the UART's transmission and reception facilities as shown in Figure 3.32.

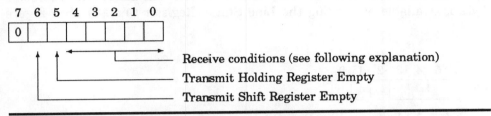

Figure 3.32   Line Status Register: Transmission Status bits

The status of the Transmit Holding Register Empty flag and the Transmit Shift Register Empty flag are indicated by their values: zero (the register is empty) or one (the register is busy). To maximize throughput, data should be written to the Transmit Holding Register as soon as the Transmit Holding Register Empty bit is set. A typical polling sequence could be written as follows:

```
#define TXR          0x3F8
#define LSR          0x3FD
#define THRE         0x20

main()
{
char ch;

/* Initialize UART */

for (ch = 'A'; ch <= 'Z'; ch++)
{
    while ((inportb(LSR) & THRE) == 0) ;
    outportb(TXR, ch);
}
}
```

UART transmission using interrupts is described in the following section.

UART reception   The UART makes data available to the processor through the Receive Buffer Register (port 0x3F8). The port is read and a copy of whatever is in the Receive Buffer is returned to the processor:

```
#define RCVR       0x3F8

main()
{
/* Initialize UART */

for(;;)
    printf(" %c\n", inportb(RCVR));
}
```

As when supplying data to the Transmit Holding Register, the UART assembles characters at a much slower rate than the processor can read them, meaning that the Receive Holding Register should only be accessed after a byte has been read from the line. The processor can determine whether a byte is available by reading the Line Status Register (0x3FD). (See Figure 3.33.)

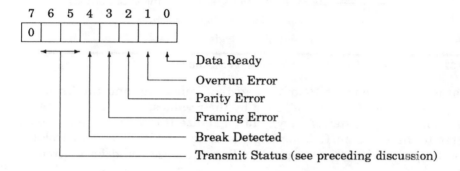

Figure 3.33   Line Status Register: Receive Status bits

The Data Ready bit is used to signal that a byte has been assembled and placed in the Receive Buffer Register (0x3F8). A value of 0 means that no new data has been placed in the buffer since the last time it was read, while a value of 1 indicates that new data is now available.

Data can be read from the UART and displayed using the following polling routine:

```
#define RCVR      0x3F8
#define LSR       0x3FD
#define DA        0x01

main()
{
/* Initialize UART */

for (;;)
{
     while ((inportb(LSR) & DA) == 0) ;
     printf("%c \n", inportb(RCVR));
}
}
```

Port 0x3F8 supports both transmission and reception because the processor can never perform both operations simultaneously and the UART can determine action being performed upon the port (i.e., read or write). If port 0x3F8 is being written to, it means that a byte is to be transmitted, while if the port is being read from, it means that the byte in the receive register is to be supplied to the processor.

Finally, before the UART is used, as part of the initialization procedure, both the Line Status Register and the Receive Buffer Register should be read, thereby ensuring that meaningless data or old line status values are ignored:

```
void clear_regs()
{
    /* Clear registers */
    (void) inportb(LSR);
    (void) inportb(RCVR);
}
```

How UART reception can be handled through interrupts is described in the following section.

UART errors Reading the Line Status Register indicates more than whether a byte can be transmitted or whether a byte is available; four other conditions are detectable as well:

Overrun Error. The UART reads and places a byte into the Receive Buffer Register before the processor has read the original byte in the Receive Buffer, thereby overrunning the original byte. The Overrun Error bit is set if an overrun error has occurred; it is cleared by the processor reading the Line Status Register. The original byte is lost.

Parity Error. An incoming byte is received with a parity error. The Parity Error bit is set if a parity error has occurred; it is cleared by the processor reading the Line Status Register. The processor can read the byte from the Receive Buffer Register.

Framing Error. A stop bit is not found when one is expected, causing a framing error and resulting in the UART setting the Framing Error bit. The Framing Error bit is cleared by the processor reading the Line Status Register.

Break Detected. The UART has detected a condition whereby the line has been in the space condition for at least the time it takes to send a single byte in a complete frame (i.e., start bit, data bits, parity bit, and stop bits). This condition is signalled by the UART setting the Break Detected bit, and is cleared by the processor reading the Line Status Register. As mentioned earlier, when a break is detected, many 8250s will set the Framing Error bit as well.

Whenever the Line Status Register is read, the processor obtains the value of the register; however, the original contents of the register are lost. This means that if two or more bits are set (for example, Data Ready and Parity Error), the register must be read and its value saved so that *all* the status bits can be checked. As an example, the following code fragment checks for any occurrence of the four conditions described in the previous list:

```
#define LSR      0x3FD
#define DA       0x01      /* Data Available */
#define OE       0x02      /* Overrun Error */
#define PE       0x04      /* Parity Error */
#define FE       0x08      /* Framing Error */
#define BRKFND   0x10      /* Break Found */

void check_lsr()
{
char lsr_value;

lsr_value = inportb(LSR);

if (lsr_value & DA) data_avail();
if (lsr_value & OE) overrun_error();
if (lsr_value & PE) parity_error();
if (lsr_value & FE) framing_error();
if (lsr_value & BRKFND) break_found();
}
```

Line status changes can also be signalled using interrupts.

UART interrupts Thus far, all UART access has been done using polling. From the material covered in Chapter 2, it should be clear that polling wastes processing power since the processor could be performing other tasks. To overcome this problem, the UART has been designed to generate four different types of interrupts, three of which are now considered: line status change, data available, and transmit ready. The fourth type of interrupt is discussed in Chapter 8.

Before the UART can signal an interrupt, both the UART and the 8259 Interrupt Controller must be initialized. In the case of the UART, the Interrupt Enable Register (port 0x3F9), should indicate which interrupts the processor will service (note that bits 4 through 7 are ignored) (Figure 3.34).

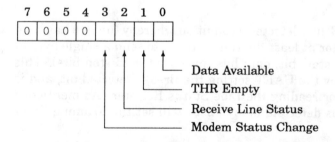

Figure 3.34 Interrupt Enable Register

To enable an interrupt, the corresponding bit in the Interrupt Enable Register must be set. For example, to enable the Data Available and Receive Line Status interrupts, the Interrupt Enable Register would have to be set to 0x05 using outportb():

```
#define IER      0x3F9    /* Interrupt Enable Register */
#define DATA_AV  0x01     /* Data available */
#define TX_HR_MT 0x02     /* Transmit Holding Register empty */
#define RVC_LS   0x04     /* Receive Line Status */
#define MDM_CHG  0x08     /* Modem status change */

uart_init()
{
/* Other initialization statements */
outportb(IER, DATA_AV+RCV_LS);
}
```

In addition to setting the Interrupt Enable Register, the 8259 must also be initialized so that interrupts from the UART will be made available to the PC. The UART differs from the other devices studied so far in that the PC can support *multiple* UARTs. Accordingly, for each UART on the PC, there must be a device bit mask available in the 8259 Interrupt Controller. In a typical one UART PC configuration, bit 4 of the Interrupt Controller is assigned to the UART; while in a two UART PC, bits 3 and 4 are assigned to the second UART and the first UART respectively (Figure 3.35).

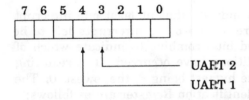

Figure 3.35 8259 interrupt mask: UART bit positions

To enable either of these interrupts, the corresponding bit in the Interrupt Controller mask should be cleared. For example, to allow interrupts from both UARTs, the keyboard, and the clock, one could write:

```
#define INT_MASK 0x21    /* 8259 Interrupt Control Mask Register */
#define CLKENA   0xFE     /* Clock enable:            11111110 */
#define KEYENA   0xFD     /* Keyboard enable:         11111101 */
#define SP1ENA   0xEF     /* UART 1 enable:           11101111 */
#define SP2ENA   0xF7     /* UART 2 enable:           11110111 */
#define PPENA    0x7F     /* Parallel port enable: 01111111 */

initialize()
{
/* Other initialization statements */
outportb(INT_MASK, CLKENA & KEYENA & SP1ENA & SP2ENA & PPENA);
}
```

If UART interrupts are *not* required, either the Interrupt Enable Register should be cleared or the UART's bit in the Interrupt Controller mask should be assigned 0xFF.

The interrupt vectors associated with the two UARTs are 12 (UART 1, addresses 0x30 through 0x33) and 11 (UART 2, addresses 0x2C through 0x2F). Setvect() can be used to establish the entry points to the UART interrupt handlers.

Once enabled, the UART can cause interrupts to occur. A UART interrupt only signals the processor that a change has occurred to the UART, it does not indicate the cause of the change. To determine the cause of the interrupt, the processor must read the Interrupt Identification Register, port 0x3FA, using inportb() (Figure 3.36).

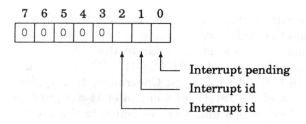

Figure 3.36   Interrupt Identification Register

Bit 0 (interrupt pending), is cleared to indicate that at least one interrupt is pending and if set, signals that there are no other interrupts left to be serviced. Bits 1 and 2 (the interrupt id bits) combine to indicate which of the four possible UART interrupt conditions have occurred. The resulting combinations are assigned priorities, the highest being 6, the lowest, 0. The priorities and values of the Interrupt Identification Register are as follows:

Highest (iir = 6). A change in the line status (i.e., an overrun, parity, or framing error, or a break interrupt) will cause a Receive Line Status interrupt. The interrupt is cleared by the processor reading the Line Status Register (port 0x3FD); the value read indicates the cause(s) of the interrupt.

Second (iir = 4). If the UART receives data, the Received Data Available interrupt is signalled. The interrupt is cleared by reading the Receive Buffer Register (port 0x3F8).

Third (iir = 2). The Transmit Holding Register Empty interrupt indicates that the UART is able to transmit another byte. The interrupt can be cleared by either the processor reading the Interrupt Identification Register (0x3FA) or by the processor writing to the Transmission Register (port 0x3F8).

Lowest (iir = 0). The status of the modem has changed. Modem status change interrupts are discussed in Chapter 8.

Clearing an interrupt condition does *not* necessarily mean that all UART conditions have been serviced: other interrupts may still be pending. For example, it is possible to clear the line status change interrupt (iir = 6), only to be confronted with a received data available (iir = 4). Unless *both* of these conditions are cleared during the same interrupt cycle, some UARTs will "lock-up" and stop receiving altogether. Therefore, whenever an interrupt is detected and the condition is cleared, the interrupt-pending flag of the Interrupt Identification Register must be checked. If it is still zero, other UART conditions are waiting to be serviced.

The 8250 UART is no different from any of the other devices that have been discussed. First, access to the UART takes place through a series of ports; and second the 8259 must be signalled the interrupt is over.

3.5   POINT-TO-POINT COMMUNICATION USING COMMKIT

The Commkit module commkit.c contains software to control two UARTs: serial port 1 (base port address 0x3F8) and serial port 2 (base address 0x2F8). The UART base addresses are defined in devices.h; and stored in the array serial_addr (found in commkit.c):

```
#define SP1        0x3F8
#define SP2        0x2F8

int serial_addr[2] = {SP1, SP2};
```

The Commkit software distinguishes between the two UARTs by assigning each a unique queue identifier (SP1IH for serial port 1, and SP2IH for serial port 2). Whenever a UART interrupt occurs, the identifier is used to differentiate between the two serial ports. Since there is no guarantee that the identifiers SP1IH and SP2IH will equal 0 and 1, it is necessary to subtract SP1IH from the supplied serial port number to obtain the correct subscript:

```
int base_addr;
int port_num;   /* Set to either SP1IH or SP2IH */
...
base_addr = serial_addr[port_num - SP1IH];
```

Once the base address is obtained, all other port register addresses associated with the serial port can be determined.

3.5.1   Initialization

Both UARTs are initialized by the procedure port_init() (found in commkit.c), which takes the identifier (SP1IH or SP2IH) and the line speed of the UART. Port_init() then determines the base address and initializes:

- Speed of the serial port
  Devices.h contains constants for a number of commonly used line speeds and the Divisor Latch Access Bit DLABon:

```
#define DLABon       0x80
#define BAUD96K      0x00c
    ...
#define BAUD50       0x900
```

First, the Line Control Register (base_addr + 3) is set to DLABon. Then the line speed (baudrate) is written, as a word, to port base_addr.

The line speed is passed to Commkit from the mainline of the program as an integer value. The value of the line speed can be hard-coded into the program, or the user can be allowed to enter a value from the command line when the program is run. The utility get_line_speed() takes a string value and converts it to the equivalent integer line speed value; the integer value is then returned to the calling procedure. The version of get_line_speed() supplied with Commkit accepts one of six possible values (50, 300, 1200, 2400, 4800, or 9600).

- Word length, the number of stop bits, and parity.

    Constants for setting the Line Control Register are defined in devices.h:

```
#define DLABoff      0x00
#define SEVENBIT     0x02
#define EIGHTBIT     0x03
#define WORDLEN      EIGHTBIT
#define ONE_STOP     0x00         /* 1 stop bit (5, 6, 7, 8 bits/word) */
#define TWO_STOP     0x04         /* 2 stop bits (6, 7, 8 bits/word) */
                                  /* 1.5 stop bits (5 bits/word) */
#define PEN          0x08         /* Parity enable */
#define EPS          0x10         /* Even parity select */
#define STICK        0x20
#define PARITY       (ONE_STOP+PEN)
#define LCR_DEFN     (DLABoff+WORDLEN+PARITY)
```

The value of LCR_DEFN is written to the Line Control Register (base_addr + 3).

- The enabling of interrupts.

    The Modem Control Register is initialized using the devices.h constants:

```
#define DTR         0x01        /* Data terminal ready */
#define RTS         0x02        /* Request to send */
#define OUT2        0x08        /* Enable serial port interrupts */
#define LOOPBK      0x10
#define MCR_DEFN    (DTR+RTS+OUT2)
```

The constant MCR_DEFN is written to base_addr + 4. Note that for the UART to generate interrupts, OUT2 must be written to the Modem Control Register as well.

- All interrupts are enabled (data available, Transmit Holding Register, line status, and modem status).

    The constants for each are also defined in devices.h:

```
#define DATA_AV     0x01        /* Data avaiable interrupt */
#define TX_HR_MT    0x02        /* Transmit Holding Register empty */
#define RCV_LS      0x04        /* Receive Line Status */
#define MDM_CHG     0x08        /* Modem status change */
```

The Interrupt Enable Register (base_addr + 1) is initialized to the preceding constants.

As with all other devices that Commkit accesses, the original interrupt vectors are saved and the new values are written using `setvect()` in the procedure `initialize()`:

```
initialize()
{
    ...
    old_sp2 = getvect(11);
    old_sp1 = getvect(12);
    ...
    setvect(11, sp2_ih);
    setvect(12, sp1_ih);
    ...
}
```

`Sp1_ih()` and `sp2_ih()` are the entry points for the interrupt handlers associated with each serial port (see the following section).

The UART interrupt handler   Initially, interrupts from either UART cause control to be passed to `sp1_ih()` (serial port 1 interrupt handler) *or* `sp2_ih()` (serial port 2 interrupt handler). Both `sp1_ih()` and `sp2_ih()` call a separate procedure, `port_handler()`, which is responsible for processing UART interrupts. The `port_handler()` software distinguishes between the calling procedures by accepting the interrupt handler's identifier (either `SP1IH` or `SP2IH`) as its argument. This eliminates the need for two sets of identical software, one for each interrupt handler. See Figure 3.37.

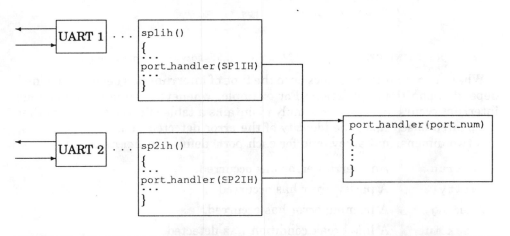

Figure 3.37   How Commkit supports multiple UARTS

`Port_handler()` obtains the base address of the UART in question from the `serial_addr` array, indexed by `port_num`. With the base address (address either `0x3F8` or `0x2F8`), the Interrupt Identification Register (`address + 2`) can be read to determine the type of interrupt that has occurred. By reading the Interrupt Identification Register in a loop, all pending interrupts can be serviced until no further pending interrupts are detected (that is, when `iir` = 1):

```
while ((iir = inportb(address + 2)) != 1)
{
switch (iir)
{
case 6: /* Receiver Line Status Interrupt */
        ch = inportb(address + 5) & 0x1E;
        /* Update error statistics */
        break;

case 4: /* Data Available Interrupt */
        ch = inportb(address);
        low_level(port_num, RECVDONE, ch);
        break;

case 2: /* Transmit Holding Register Empty Interrupt */
        low_level(port_num, XMITDONE, 0);
        break;

case 0: /* Modem Status Change Interrupt */
        /* See chapter on telephones */
        ch = inportb(address + 6);
        low_level(port_num, MODEMSTATUS, ch);
        break;

default: /* Unknown IIR value */
         /* Update error statistics */
   }
}
outportb(INT_CTL, 0x20);   /* Reset 8259 for more interrupts */
```

What `port_handler()` does once the type of interrupt has been determined depends upon the application. For example, whenever a line status change interrupt occurs, `commkit.c` simply maintains a table of error conditions that is updated based upon the identity of the error detected. The table, `errors`, is a two-dimensional array (one for each port) defined in `commkit.c`:

`overrun`	An overrun error has occurred.
`parity`	A parity error has occurred.
`framing`	A framing error has occurred.
`break_int`	A line break condition was detected.
`modem`	A modem status change has occurred.
`unknown`	An unknown `iir` value was detected.

The contents of `errors` can be displayed using `serial_port_stats()`; specifying the starting line number as the argument.

To accept calls from the serial port software, the procedure `low_level()` must be extended to recognize the following:

`device`	The serial port identifier (one of `SP1IH` or `SP2IH`).
`code`	The event associated with the device; one of:

`RECVDONE`	A data available interrupt has occurred.
`XMITDONE`	The Transmit Holding Register is empty.
`MODEMSTATUS`	A modem status change interrupt has occurred.
`MSG_AVAIL`	A message is available for either of the serial ports (call from `send()`).

`data`	The value of the register read after the interrupt has occurred. For `RECVDONE`, `data` is the incoming character; while for `MODEMSTATUS`, `data` is the value of the Modem Status Register. The value is zero for `XMITDONE` and `MSG_AVAIL`.

3.6 EXAMPLE

In the following section, a PC telephone utility will be designed and implemented using Commkit.

3.6.1 The Problem

Many multi-user computer systems support "phone" utilities that allow any number of users to carry on a conversation via asynchronous terminals. The problem addressed here is how to support a similar feature that permits electronic communications between two people sitting at a pair of interconnected PCs.

The requirements are:

- Anything that is typed on one terminal should also appear on the other (i.e., remote) terminal.

- Each screen should be divided in half, with the upper half (ten lines long) reserved for the local user's input and the lower half for the remote user's output.

- The two PCs are connected via their serial ports. The configuration should look like that shown in Figure 3.38.

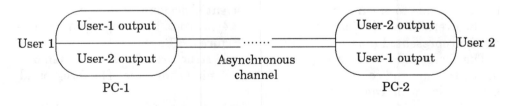

Figure 3.38   PC Telephone utility configuration

- A character, when entered, should be displayed on the local user's screen as well as being transmitted. Characters received from the asynchronous channel should be displayed in the remote user's half of the screen.

■ The end of session is indicated by either user typing CTRL-C. This should cause the program to terminate, returning to MS-DOS. If the remote user signals end of session, the local user should receive the message `Remote user signed off`, at which point the session ends and control should return to MS-DOS.

■ Once the local user's half of the screen is filled, either with characters or one too many carriage returns, the local user's half screen should be cleared. Similarly, when the remote user's half of the screen is filled, either with characters or one too many carriage returns, the remote user's half of the screen should be cleared.

Note that there is no end-to-end signalling (i.e., the DTEs do not explicitly signal one another to clear the screen). It is assumed that both stations are in "lock-step," so that when one station's software clears its local user's half of the screen, it is assumed that the same action is taking place on the other station with the remote user's half of the screen.

3.6.2   The Design

This problem can be broken down into two distinct parts: (1) handling characters from the keyboard, and (2) handling characters from the communications channel. To simplify the design, the foreground process will handle the routing (i.e., from keyboard to channel and vice versa) as well as the display of characters.

Input (from keyboard)   Characters entered by a user from the local keyboard are displayed on the local screen and forwarded to the remote station. Part of the problem has already been solved since keyboard input is handled by the keyboard interrupt handler (`keyboard_handler()`) calling `low_level()` with the character. `Low_level()` can then forward the character to the process associated with the APPLICATION queue.

Upon receipt of a character from the keyboard interrupt handler, the foreground process must examine the character. If the character is an *ETX*, it should be forwarded to the remote DTE; once forwarded, execution should stop. All other characters must be displayed locally and then forwarded to the remote DTE. However, before the character can be displayed, a check must be made to ensure that there is sufficient space on the screen.

The overall flow of information from the keyboard to the foreground process can be represented diagramatically as in Figure 3.39.

The foreground process requires two data structures for screen management: the line and column position of the incoming character. The foreground process algorithm can be written as follows:

1. Accept a character from the `keyboard_handler()`.

2. Check the character:
   if *ETX*:
   a) Forward *ETX*.
   b) Stop the process and return to MS-DOS.

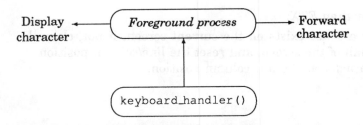

Figure 3.39 Keyboard information flow

anything other than *ETX*:

a) Clear the local user's half of the screen if no positions are available and reset the line/column position.

b) Display the character in the next line/column position available on the screen.

c) Forward the character.

Input (from remote station) Characters from the remote station are received by the serial port interrupt handler to which the cable is connected. The interrupt handler forwards each character to the foreground process for display, as illustrated in Figure 3.40.

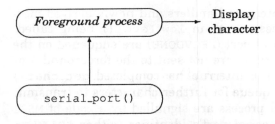

Figure 3.40 Serial port information flow

Since the remote DTE does not send any indication of when its half of the local screen should be cleared, it is the responsibility of the foreground process to maintain data structures for the line and column position of the incoming remote characters. Initially, the first available character position is in the first column of the lower half of the screen. This position is updated each time a character is displayed. Using this information, foreground process can then either display the character or erase the screen.

The algorithm for handling characters from the serial port can be written as follows:

1. Accept character from `serial_port()`.

2. Check the character:

    if *ETX*:

    a) Stop the process and return to MS-DOS.

any character other than *ETX*:

a) Check whether a space exists on the current screen, if not, clear the remote user's half of the screen, and reset the line/column position.

b) Display the character at the line/column position.

3.6.3 Implementation

An implementation of the point-to-point telephone utility can be found in the file pt2pt.c on the Commkit diskette. The software is divided into two distinct parts: (1) the low-level routines for keyboard and serial port handling, and (2) the foreground process for character routing and displaying.

Low-level   Three procedures support the low-level software:

system_initialize(). This clears the screen and proceeds to divide the screen into an upper and lower half to separate the local input and remote output. The variable handler_id is initialized to either SP1IH or SP2IH, depending upon the serial port through which the communications are to take place.

All software that is called by commkit must include a routine called system_initialize(). System_initialize() is called from initialize() in commkit.

low_level(). All data from the interrupt handlers and newly arrived messages from the foreground process result in low_level() being called. Data from the keyboard and serial port (RECVDONE) are enqueued on the APPLICATION queue; clock interrupts are not sent to the foreground process. When a serial port transmission interrupt has completed, get_char() is called to check the serial port queue for further characters to transmit.

Messages from the foreground process are signalled by a code of MSG_AVAIL being received with the serial port's identifier (either SP1IH or SP2IH). If the serial port is idle (indicated by the variable transmitting having a zero value), get_char() is called; get_char() is not called. In either case, transmitting is incremented. Transmitting ensures that messages from the foreground process are not tranmsitted while the serial port is in the process of sending a previously transmitted character.

get_char(). This is called when the serial port is no longer transmitting. This is indicated by either an XMITDONE being signalled by the serial port or a message arriving from the foreground process when the serial port is idle. If a character is on the serial port's queue, it is removed (using recv()) and transmitted. The variable transmitting is decremented.

To ensure that the telephone utility has time to transmit an *ETX* to the remote, the global variable running is assigned FALSE after an *ETX* has been transmitted by get_char().

Foreground process   Three procedures are used to support the foreground process:

do_pt2pt(). Waits for characters from either the keyboard or the serial port using the recv() primitive. Characters from the keyboard are passed to do_lcl_scr(), while characters from the serial port are passed to do_rmt_scr().

Control remains in do_pt2pt() until the global variable running is set FALSE by either do_rmt_scr() receiving an *ETX* from the remote PC or by get_char() detecting an *ETX* in the output data stream.

do_lcl_scr(). Is responsible for displaying and forwarding locally entered data supplied from do_pt2pt(). It maintains line and column information for displaying each character. Once a character is displayed, the send() primitive is envoked to forward the character to the output serial port.

do_rmt_scr(). Displays characters on the lower half of the screen sent from the remote PC. The screen clearing algorithm in do_rmt_scr() is identical to that found in do_lcl_scr().

Message flow   The overall message flow in the point-to-point telephone utility is outlined in Figure 3.41.

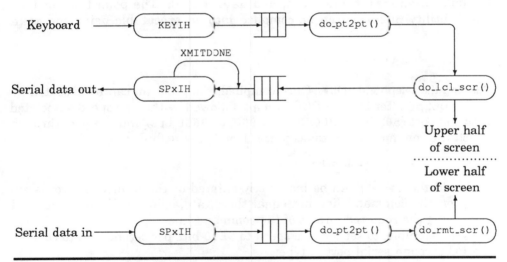

Figure 3.41   Message flow in PC telephone utility

The foreground process is shown in two parts simply to distinguish between keyboard input and serial port input. The foreground process waits for messages sent to queue APPLICATION; the keyboard and serial port both forward their messages to queue APPLICATION.

3.6.4 Using the Telephone Utility

The Commkit diskette contains both source and executable versions of the point-to-point telephone utility. The telephone utility can be run at one of a number of speeds using either serial port.

Hardware requirements Two PCs are required, each with at least one serial port. The physical configuration is shown in Figure 3.42.

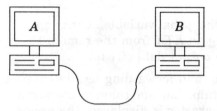

Figure 3.42   Physical configuration of PC telephone utility

The cable should be connected to the chosen serial port when starting the program. The local and remote serial ports need not be the same (that is, serial port 1 can connect to serial port 2 or serial port 1, and vice versa).

Creating the telephone utility The telephone utility is created from pt2pt.c, commkit.obj, intrpt.obj, primitiv.obj, and the header files required by Commkit (general.h, ascii.h, and devices.h). The point-to-point telephone utility pt2pt.c can be compiled into an executable using the make utility:

```
C:\> make pt2pt.exe
```

Running the telephone utility Once compiled, the program can be executed by typing pt2pt after the MS-DOS prompt, followed by the line speed associated with the port (50, 300, 1200, 2400, 4800, or 9600 bps) and the port through which the communication takes place (1 or 2, the default is 1):

```
C:\> pt2pt LineSpeed Port
```

Should the LineSpeed be incorrectly entered or the number of words entered on the command line not equal three, a diagnostic will be generated explaining the required format of the command line.

As an example, to set the line speed to 9600 bits per second and to connect the PC through serial port 2, type:

```
C:\> pt2pt 9600 2
```

The screen will clear, and appear divided, with the upper half for the display of local input and the lower half for remote output. Whatever is typed should appear on both the local and the remote PC.

The software forwards characters received from either serial port to queue APPLICATION. This can mean that if the cable is connected to a port other than the one selected when running pt2pt, characters will still be received and displayed, but characters entered at the local station will not be transmitted. The solution is to connect the cable to the port selected in the command line.

Finally, should the connection be broken for any reason and either of the users continue to enter characters, the local and remote stations will be out of step, since the number of characters sent by the PC do not equal the number entered by the user.

3.7 SUMMARY

This chapter has examined asynchronous point-to-point communications and how it can be achieved using a device known as a UART or Universal Asynchronous Receiver/Transmitter.

An asynchronous communications is one in which data, in the form of bytes, is sent from one DTE to another at random, unpredictable intervals. All bytes are sent serially (i.e., one bit at a time) between DTEs communicating asynchronously. To distinguish between the communication channel idling and a byte, the bits making up a byte are enclosed in a frame consisting of a start bit and one or more stop bits. Asynchronous communications also offer a limited form of error detection known as parity checking. There are five types of parity: none, mark, space, odd, and even.

The UART handles the conversion of parallel bytes (within the DTE) to serial for transmission on the communication channel. As well as handling serial-to-parallel conversion for reception. The UART is also responsible for framing and error detection. To a programmer, a typical UART consists of at least the following:

Transmission Register through which the program supplies bytes for transmission to the UART.

Receive Register from which the program copies the bytes received by the UART.

Status Register indicating the UART's status, and includes information such as whether

- the transmitter is ready.
- a byte has been received.
- an error has been detected (parity, overrun, or framing).
- a break condition has been detected.

Control Register that allows the programmer to specify the number of stop bits, whether parity is required (and the type of parity), the number of bits per character, and the line speed.

For communications to take place between two UARTs, both must agree upon the number of bits in a character, the speed of the transmission, the number of stop bits, and the parity. Most UARTs allow these options to be programmed.

3.8 EXERCISES

1. What is the value of the missing bit required in order to get the specified parity (the missing bit is indicated by a ?):

1	0	?	0	1	1	0	0	Even
0	0	0	1	0	?	0	1	Mark
1	0	0	1	1	1	1	?	Odd
0	0	0	0	?	0	0	0	Space
1	?	1	1	1	1	1	0	None

2. Does the width of each bit get larger or smaller as transmission speeds increase? Does the time between the transmission of asynchronous characters increase or decrease as transmission speeds decrease? Explain your answer.

3. Describe the two types of overrun that a UART can experience.

4. Calculate the number of bits sent in one minute if a UART is to send at 9600 bps with odd parity and two stop bits. Does the number change if even parity is used? Does the number change if one stop bit is sent?

5. All characters except CTRL-C (*ETX*) can be transmitted using the telephone utility; explain why this is so. Propose, implement, and test a method to allow *ETX* to be sent.

6. Extend the sample telephone utility to permit entire lines to be transmitted rather than one byte at a time. Suggest a method to ensure that the line transmitted is received correctly by the remote PC.

7. Modify the telephone utility to emulate a VT-100 type terminal. Use this program to connect to a remote host. You will need to have access to a description of the control characters used by the terminal in order to do this exercise.

8. Determine how sensitive a UART is to minor changes in line speeds. Have one UART transmit a string of characters and a second UART receive them. Now, modify the line speed slightly on the receiving UART. At what point does the data become garbled?

9. Show that the recommended divisors for 300 and 1200 bps actually produce the required line speeds.

10. Write a small program to demonstrate that the contents of the UART's receive buffer remain unchanged, regardless of the number of times the buffer is read.

11. Show, by means of a series of examples, that parity checking (even or odd) will detect only an *odd* number of errors.

12. Explain the conditions whereby mark parity will be equivalent to even (or odd) parity and space parity will be equivalent to even (or odd) parity.

13. In Section 3.3.2, the number of samples on the line performed by the UART each second was calculated for a 9600-bps channel. Try calculating line speeds for 2400, 2000, and 1200-bps channels. Do they all work out exactly using the 1.8432 MHz clock?

14. Parity calculations were performed in this chapter by exclusive or'ing the outgoing data bits. Show that the same result can be achieving using exclusive nor'ing.

15. Modify the PC telephone utility to support the following:
    1. CTRL-B (*STX*) indicates that a session is about to begin. As soon as the telephone utility is "activated," it should start transmitting a series of *STX* characters (about once a second). Upon receipt of an *STX*, the software should respond with another *STX*; inform the user that a connection has been made and then start the session.
    2. CTRL-H (*BS*) signals that a character is to be deleted. When a user types *BS*, the character to the left of the cursor should be deleted. Any character, including carriage returns can be deleted; this means that a user can delete all of the characters on the local part of the screen. *BS* should be ignored if there are no characters left on the screen.

       If a character can be deleted, the *BS* should be transmitted to the remote PC. The remote PC should delete the character to the left of the last character displayed.
    3. CTRL-L (*FF*) signifies that the user explicitly wishes to clear the local part of the screen. Upon detection of a *FF*, the upper-half of the local user's screen should be cleared, regardless of the amount of text on the screen.

       FF should also be sent to the remote PC; when the *FF* is received, the remote user's half of the screen should be cleared.

    The screens should remain "in-step" after the transmission/reception of either the *FF* or *BS*.

16. Modify the `commkit.c` routine `get_line_speed()` so that it will take *any* number as a line speed and convert it into the equivalent 16-bit line speed value. Devise a method to test your implementation.

17. Write code fragments to show how the 8250 UART would be initialized for each different type of parity (i.e., none, even, odd, mark, and space).

18. If an `XMITDONE` interrupt is lost, all further communications will cease, since `get_char()` is only called after an `XMITDONE` interrupt. As messages arrive from the foreground process (signalled by `MSG_AVAIL`), `get_char()` will not be called as long as there are messages on the queue (indicated by `transmitting` being greater than zero). Add software to `pt2pt.c` to handle the situation when an `XMITDONE` interrupt is lost.

    The placing of an upper bound on a piece of software is sometimes called a *sanity check*, and it is used to handle those situations when a signal, such as `XMITDONE`, goes missing. This problem will be discussed in more detail in Chapter 5.

Physical Connections

4.1 INTRODUCTION

Up to now, any device that can communicate with another has been called a
DTE. Internally, all DTEs are assumed to represent information in the same
way: as series of bits with individual values of either 0 or 1. Similarly, the
transmission of information between DTEs is assumed to take place through
a UART, across a serial communication channel of an unspecified length, to
the other DTE (Figure 4.1).

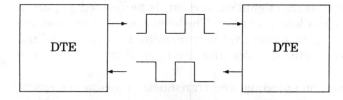

Figure 4.1   Transmission of information between DTEs

Although this is a perfectly reasonable view of how communications take place,
little or no consideration has been given to the following issues:

■ The technology chosen by the manufacturer of DTE for the storage and
movement of information may not be compatible with the technology chosen
by another manufacturer.

For example, one manufacturer may chose bipolar circuitry (such as TTL, or transistor-transistor logic), while another may chose a metal-oxide semiconductor (such as CMOS, complementary metal-oxide semiconductor). Connecting a TTL circuit to a CMOS circuit is not impossible; however, there are a number of technical differences that must be overcome, including speed and power (TTL is much faster and consumes more power than CMOS), as well as differences in the voltages used to represent the 0s and 1s.

- Even if two DTEs are electrically compatible, the electrical signals used within the DTE may only have sufficient power to propagate a limited distance. For example, TTL signals cannot be sent more than about one meter, meaning that the maximum separation between the two DTEs could be no more than one meter.

This chapter presents a brief introduction to the electrical characteristics and the representation of information in some of the technologies presently available to support the transfer of information between physically connected DTEs.

4.2   INTERCONNECTING DTES

From the discussion in the previous section and from our everyday experiences with DTEs, one can conclude that there are three issues that should be addressed to insure that information can be transmitted between the interconnected DTEs:

- The information within the transmitting DTE must be converted to a signal that can reach the receiving DTE.
- The signal must be carried across a channel (a medium such as a wire, optical fiber, or air) to the receiving DTE.
- The signal, before supplied to the DTE must be converted to the internal format used by the receiving DTE.

The first and last of these issues (signal conversion) is performed as part of the DTE in a device known as a *level converter*. The level converter *encodes* the information into an agreed upon signal that is transmitted across a medium that the receiving level converter *decodes* into the equivalent value on the receiving DTE.

Level converters, information encoding, and transmission media are examined in this section.

4.2.1   Level Converters

At events involving large numbers of people, if an official wants to convey information to the crowd, the official doesn't bother yelling (since the yell might not be heard by everyone), instead a device such as a megaphone is used, amplifying the official's voice to a level that can be heard by the people in the crowd.

Similarly, since the binary information within a DTE typically cannot propagate over distances of more than about a meter, a device that changes the information into a set of signals that can reach and be recognized by the receiving DTE is necessary. To avoid having unique conversion devices for all possible DTEs, the information is converted into signals agreed to by the various manufacturers. Once the signal reaches the remote DTE, the signal can be converted to the internal binary representation used by the receiving DTE.

The conversion of the information to the signal required on the channel takes place between the UART and the physical connection with the remote DTE using a level converter (Figure 4.2).

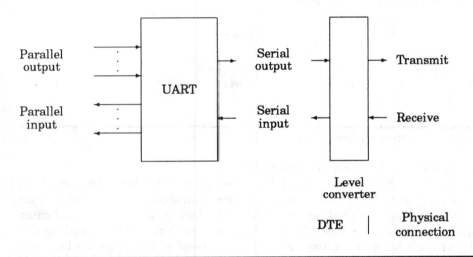

Figure 4.2 The level converter

The level converter is responsible for changing the DTE's internal binary information to that agreed to by the various DTE manufacturers for use on the channel. For example, a mark (1) may be converted to −10 volts, while a space (0) may be converted to +10 V.

Upon reception of a signal from the physical connection, the level converter must change the signal into an internal value acceptable to the DTE. Continuing with the example, a physical signal of −10 volts would be changed into a binary 1 and a signal of +10 V would be changed into a binary 0.

4.2.2 Information Encoding

When converting the information within the DTE into a signal that can be transmitted to another DTE, several factors must be considered. First, by increasing the line speed, more information can be transmitted. Second, an increase in the line speed increases the probability that a bit will be received in error. Fortunately, there are a number of techniques that can allow the line speed to be increased while reducing the chances of receiving the signal in error.

Nonreturn to zero The simplest type of encoding is known as **nonreturn to zero–Level** (or NRZ-L) in which each bit value is associated with a *constant* signal level, either positive or negative (hence the name NRZ-L, since during the transmission of a bit, the signal level remains constant and does not return to zero). For example, a mark may be associated with a negative voltage; while a space may be associated with a positive voltage. The only transition that occurs is when the signal changes from a mark to a space (or vice versa). NRZ-L can be implemented with little difficulty.

For example, the character S transmitted using NRZ-L would appear as shown in Figure 4.3. Remember, the right-most bit is being transmitted first in this and subsequent examples.

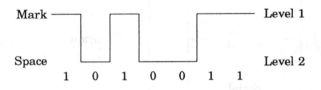

Figure 4.3   Nonreturn to zero–Level

All of the examples in Chapter 3 used NRZ-L.

Variations on NRZ include NRZ-I (or **nonreturn to zero–Inverted**) in which a *transition* from one level to another indicates a mark, rather than an absolute value of signal, as in NRZ-L. The lack of a transition indicates a space; the presence or lack of a transition can be detected by sampling the middle of each bit and comparing it with the level of the previous bit. For example, in NRZ-I, a transition occurs each time a mark is transmitted. This means that the letter S would be sent as shown in Figure 4.4.

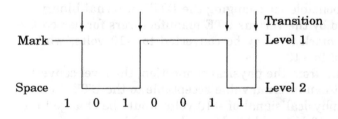

Figure 4.4   Nonreturn to zero–Inverted

As the line is sampled at the receiving DTE, a transition is taken to indicate a mark, while the absence of a transition indicates a space.

NRZ-I is also known as NRZ-M or **nonreturn to zero–Mark**. In NRZ-S (or **nonreturn to zero–Space**), a transition indicates a space and the lack of a transition, a mark.

Since NRZ-I and NRZ-S do not refer to an absolute signal value, but rather the presence or lack of a transition, they can offer better reliability over noisy channels than NRZ-L.

Return to zero (RZ) A major limitation in the NRZ signal encoding technique is that if there is a long sequence of 0s or 1s (in NRZ-L), 1s (in NRZ-S), or 0s (in NRZ-I), a constant signal level is produced. A constant signal level can result in the transmitting and receiving clocks losing synchronization.

This problem can be minimized by putting the transition in the *middle* of the bit and requiring the UART to maintain its bit synchronization from the value of the transition (i.e., from high-to-low or from low-to-high). A simple example of this encoding technique is **return to zero** or RZ.

RZ uses two signal levels: zero and nonzero. A space can be represented by a zero value (i.e., no transition) while a mark requires *two* transitions in the time it takes to send one bit. The first transition (from the zero signal level to the nonzero signal level) occurs at the *start* of the mark bit, while the second transition (from the nonzero signal level to the zero signal level) occurs in the *middle* of the mark bit. The last half of the mark bit is the zero signal level. Return to zero insures that the receiving DTE receives a transition (at least for marks), thereby allowing a degree of clock synchronization.

For example, the character S could be sent as illustrated in Figure 4.5 using RZ.

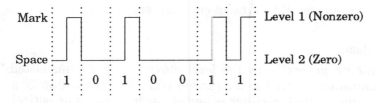

Figure 4.5 Return to zero

Although each mark causes a transition, potentially allowing the receiving clock to synchronize with the transmitting clock, a sequence of spaces could still result in the clocks drifting. Note also that in the NRZ-L encoding scheme, there is a one-to-one relationship between the bit and the transition; however, in RZ, one bit is represented by *two* transitions.

Biphase Return to zero attempts, but does not succeed, in reducing the problem of the two stations losing bit synchronization. By extending the RZ encoding technique to include a transition on *every* bit, it is possible to embed the transmitter's clock directly in the data stream. For example, a mark could be represented as a high-to-low signal transition, while a space could be a low-to-high signal transition. This technique, known as *biphase* encoding, allows the receiving DTE to extract both clocking information (thereby staying in synchronization with the transmitter) and data from the received signal.

As an example, to transmit the character S using a biphase encoding technique in which the first half of the signal is equal to the bit and the second half is equal to the inverse of the bit, the situation shown in Figure 4.6 would occur.

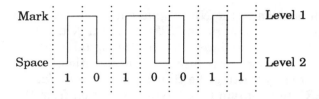

Figure 4.6   Biphase

Now every bit causes a transition: a transition from Level 1 to Level 2 indicates a 1, while a transition from Level 2 to Level 1 indicates a 0.

Clock resynchronization can be achieved by the receiving DTE sampling the
channel when the center of a bit (i.e., a transition) is expected. If a transition
is detected, the clocks are in synchronization. Should the transition occur
after it was expected, the receiver's clock is running slower than that of the
transmitter and must be adjusted. However, if the transition is detected
before the receiving DTE expected it, the receiver's clock is running faster
and must be adjusted.

Probably the best known example of biphase encoding is *Manchester encoding* and is widely used in high-speed communications. Manchester encoding
will be discussed in greater detail in subsequent chapters.

4.2.3   Transmission Media

Once the signal has been generated by the level converter, it is transmitted
through the communication channel to the remote DTE. The communication
channel consists of a media that is either *bounded* (such as wires or optical
fibers) or *unbounded* (the air or the vacuum of space). Some of the more
common media are now considered.

Two-wire open lines   A two-wire open line consists of two wires, insulated from
each other, one wire carrying the signal (typically a voltage or a current), the
other wire carrying the ground reference. The receiving DTE determines the
value of the signal by comparing the signal with the ground reference.

Two-wire open line systems are best used in applications requiring low bit
rates (less than 19.2 kilobits per second) and limited distances (less than
50 meters). Two-wire systems are susceptible to electromagentic interference:
should the noise affect only one of the two wires, the receiving DTE can mis-
interpret the signal. For example, consider the situation in which the ground
reference is taken as 0 volts with mark being represented by a voltage greater
than the ground reference, and space being represented by a voltage less than
the ground reference. If a mark is transmitted and noise causes the ground
reference to be greater than the voltage used for mark, the receiver, taking
the difference, could interpret the mark as a space (Figure 4.7).

Twisted pair   Considerable improvements can be made upon two-wire systems
by taking the pair of insulated wires and *twisting* them together. Any electromagnetic interference should affect *both* wires (not just one). If the receiving

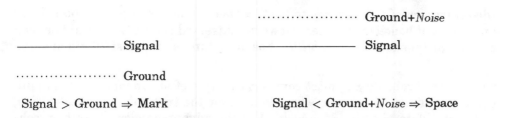

Figure 4.7   The effect of noise on a two-wire open line

DTE determines the value of the signal from the difference between the signal and the ground reference, and if both wires have been affected by noise, then ideally, the difference will be the same.

Other benefits of twisted pair over two-wire includes potentially higher line speeds and longer distances (for example, line speeds in the range of one million bps at distances of up to one kilometer can be achieved). In addition, the effects of crosstalk can be minimized by enclosing a number of twisted pairs within the same cable. Twisted pair is another example a bounded medium.

Coaxial cable   Although twisted pair offers numerous advantages over two-wire open line systems, it still has a limited bandwidth and at higher frequencies twisted pair suffers from signal attenuation. Both of these limitations can be overcome using *coaxial cable*, another bounded medium.

Coaxial cable consists of a signal conductor and a ground reference conductor separated by a *dielectric* material (that is, a material that does *not* conduct electricity) and encased in an insulating material. One of the conductors is a wire that passes through the center of the dielectric while the other conductor is wrapped around the dielectric (typically as a wire braid). Signals transmitted by coaxial cable are less prone to the effects of electromagnetic radiation and signal attenuation. Consequently, much higher line speeds are possible, up to 800 million bits per second (Mbps) over distances of about 1.5 kilometers.

Optical fiber   All of the bounded media examined thus far are constructed from metallic material, and as such are subject to the effects of electromagnetic interference, crosstalk, and limited bandwidths. The development of *optical fibers* that carry signals in the form of light rather than currents or voltages can overcome many of the limitations associated with metallic media at extremely high bandwidths.

Optical fibers are known as dielectrics and are made from plastic or glass. The optical fiber (the core) is enclosed in a cladding and a sheath. The signals sent through an optical fiber are sent as light, generated by light-emitting diodes (LEDs) or injection laser diodes (ILDs). Although ILDs consume less power than LEDs and produce better signals, the cost and lower reliability of ILDs make LEDs more attractive. Signals are detected by the use of a photo-detector.

Finally, it is worth noting that signals in an optical fiber are subject to various forms of attenuation: scattering, the radiation of the signal; absorption, the conversion of light energy to heat; connection losses at joints and splices; and losses at bends in the fiber. However, if treated carefully, optical fiber can operate at speeds of up to 8 *billion* bps at distances of almost 70 kilometers.

Microwave Probably the most common example of an unbounded communications media is microwave, which is used for the transmission of television, voice, and data signals. Microwave has the advantage over the other techniques previously described because there is no physical connection between the transmitting and receiving DTEs. The limiting factor of microwave is that it cannot pass through objects. This means that microwave transmitters and receivers must have *line-of-sight* transmission. It is not uncommon to find microwave in use between buildings.

Communication satellites can also be used for microwave transmission. Ground stations communicate with a geostationary satellite, a satellite that remains in a fixed position above the Earth. As with microwave transmissions, the ground stations must be able to "see" the satellite. Transmissions to the satellite are sent on one frequency (the *uplink*) and returned on a second frequency (the *downlink*). Different groundstations are assigned different uplink and downlink frequencies. The signals received and transmitted by the satellite are *repeated* using a device known as a *transponder*.

4.3 STANDARDS

Before a communication can take place, both DTEs must agree to a common protocol, which covers things such as line speed, word size, parity, and error-recovery methods. Similarly, there must be agreement as to the physical connection of the DTEs covering aspects such as: the voltages used to represent mark and space, the type of information encoding on the channel, and the physical properties of the channel itself. Protocols used to describe the physical connections between the DTEs are often referred to as *standards*.

Standards are rules created by groups or organizations in an effort to ensure that equipment from different manufacturers can exchange information. The standards describing the physical connection cover a wide range of issues, including how signals (i.e., marks and spaces) are to be encoded, and the maximum allowable distance between DTEs.

There are many organizations involved in the defining of communication standards; however, some of the more widely known that are responsible for defining the physical connections between interconnected DTEs are:

- Electrical Industry Association (EIA), a U.S. based organization to which many North American manufacturers of electrical equipment belong. EIA standards are often prefixed by the letters RS, which mean recommended standard.

- Comité Consultatif International Téléphonique et Télégraphique (CCITT), is an organization sponsored by the United Nations, and is responsible for producing international communication standards. CCITT membership is made up of representatives from national PTTs (Post, Telephone and Telegraph) and governmental organizations. All countries and many companies belong to the CCITT.

CCITT defines a number of standards for communication systems, including: analog (designated by the prefix **V.**), digital (designated by the prefix **X.**), and ISDN (designated by the prefix **I.**).

- Other standards organizations that will be discussed in subsequent chapters include the International Organization for Standardization (ISO) and the Institute of Electrical and Electronic Engineers (IEEE).

There are a number of DTE interconnection standards available defined by both EIA and CCITT. The remainder of this chapter considers one of the most widespread interconnection standards, RS-232-C (and its CCITT equivalent, V.24), as well as briefly considering some other interconnection standards.

4.4   RS-232-C

RS-232-C (CCITT V.24) defines the electrical, physical, and mechanical properties of a widely used (and often abused) EIA standard. Almost all existing DTEs support RS-232-C; for example, the serial communication ports supplied with most PCs usually support RS-232-C.

4.4.1   Physical Characteristics

An RS-232-C connector (Figure 4 8) has 25 *pins* and is known as a *D-connector* because of its shape (one side is slightly longer than the other, making it look like a D).

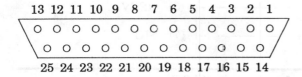

Figure 4.8   The 25-pin D-connector

Since not all 25 pins are necessary for a DTE-DTE connection, 9 pin D-connectors are also available (see Chapter 8). Of the 25 pins, only three are of interest at the moment (the remaining pins are discussed in detail in Chapter 8):

Pin 2. Serial data is transmitted on this pin. (On a 9-pin connector, the transmit pin is pin 2.)

Pin 3. Serial data is received on this pin. (On a 9-pin connector, the receive pin is pin 3.)

Pin 7. Used to establish signal ground. (On a 9-pin connector, signal ground is pin 5.)

There are two "genders" of RS-232-C connector: male (the connector with little pins), and female (the connector with little holes). The displayed illustration of a D-connector has female numbering (the male is reversed, so that when the connectors are coupled, the numbering corresponds correctly). The RS-232-C standard expects all DTEs to have male connectors, meaning that the cable connecting two DTEs should have female connectors. However, since RS-232-C is a (very) loose standard, it is possible to find DTEs with female connectors. When the cable's connector is the same gender as that of the DTE, a device known as a *gender mender* is required; the gender mender is, simply, a very short RS-232-C cable with the same gender of connector at either end.

The maximum recommended separation between two DTEs connected by an RS-232-C cable is 50 feet (15 meters); while the maximum recommended bit rate is 9600 bps. As with most aspects of RS-232-C, these maximums are often exceeded; for example, it is possible to run 9600 bps at distances up to 250 feet (75 meters). An RS-232-C cable connects each pin at one end of the cable to the same pin at the other end of the cable (i.e., pin P connects to pin P).

4.4.2 Interconnecting DTEs

Before a pair of DTEs can communicate, they must be connected. In the case of RS-232-C, the standard RS-232-C cable previously described will *not* work. The reason for this is fairly straightforward: if a DTE is connected to another DTE, both transmit pins will connect through to one another and both receive pins will do the same (assume a 25-pin connector). See Figure 4.9.

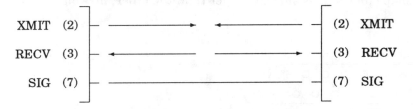

Figure 4.9   The result of directly connecting a pair of DTEs

To allow one DTE to connect to another (without modifying the pin connections on the RS-232-C port), something must be done to the cable to ensure that the communications can take place. The solution is to *swap* the transmit and receive lines, so that whatever is sent on a DTE's pin 2 appears on the other DTE's pin 3. A cable wired in this fashion is known as a *null-modem* cable. The minimum null modem wiring is as depicted in Figure 4.10.

4.4.3 Signal Levels

The typical voltage range for RS-232-C is ±15 volts, with a positive voltage (in the range +3 V to +15 V), which indicates that the line is in a space condition and with a negative voltage (in the range −3 to −15 V) indicating the mark condition (Figure 4.11).

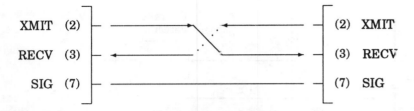

Figure 4.10 Minimum wiring for a null modem

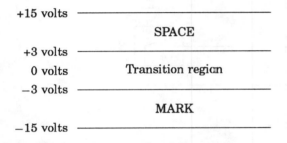

Figure 4.11 RS-232-C signal levels

RS-232-C uses NRZ-L for its signal encoding.

4.5 OTHER INTERCONNECTION STANDARDS

RS-232-C is by no means the only nor the best interconnection method available. This section examines two other interconnection methods. The first, the 20-milliampere (mA) current loop, is quite old and is not associated with a particular standard; while the second, RS-449, is the proposed successor to RS-232-C.

4.5.1 20-mA Current Loop

The 20-mA current loop predates the computer since the current loop was (and still is) used in teletype communications. The basic operation consists of sending a 20-mA current pulse from the local DTE to the remote DTE. The presence of the current indicates a mark, while the absence indicates a space. The presence and absence of a current to represent mark and space is known as *neutral working* (a variation, in which the current flows in one direction for mark and the other direction for space is known as *polar working*).

The fundamental components of a 20-mA current loop are a current source, a current switch, and a current detector. Each DTE interface consists of two parts: (1) the transmitter, containing the current switch; (2) and the receiver, containing the current detector. For a full-duplex communication, two current loops are required (a total of four wires), one for each direction of the data (Figure 4.12).

The interface which supports the current source is said to be the *active* interface while the interface without the current source is the *passive* inter-

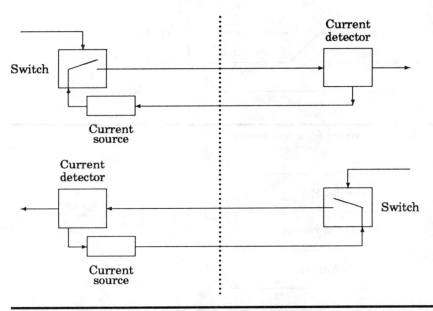

Figure 4.12   A full-duplex 20-mA current loop implementation

face. Typically, one DTE is active and the other is passive (as in the previous diagram). Regardless of the configuration, an active transmitter must send to a passive receiver or a passive transmitter to an active receiver. In those situations where both the transmitter and the receiver are "the same," an intermediate device is required either to supply a current source (if both are passive), or to act as a passive receiver and passive transmitter (if both are active).

The 20-mA loop is suitable for distances up to about 1500 feet (roughly 450 meters). Crosstalk is one of the disadvantages of using the 20-mA loop over long distances.

The main problem with the 20-mA loop is that there is no standard defined. A good example of this is to apply Ohm's law (current is voltage divided by resistance) to the circuit: if one DTE uses a 400-V source and a 20,000 ohm resistor and the other DTE uses a 4-V source and a 200 ohm resistor, both produce 20-mA currents; however, interconnecting the two will result in the 200 ohm resistor being destroyed by the 400-V source.

Fiber optics can be used to isolate the two DTEs, thereby avoiding the voltage problem (Figure 4.13).

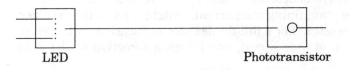

Figure 4.13   Isolating DTEs by fiber optics

Some PCs support a current loop interface. For example, some asynchronous adapters for the IBM PC have an internal switch that can select either RS-232-C or 20-mA current loop (pins 9 and 11 for the transmit current loop, and pins 18 and 25 for the receive current loop).

4.5.2 Other EIA Standards

RS-232-C, for all its seeming popularity, has a number of serious limitations that restrict the distances over which it can be used. For example, due to line capacitance, it is possible for signals to become distorted to the point where the data is received incorrectly. Similarly, should the ground reference (pin 7) be different for the two DTEs, undesirable electrical characteristics can be applied to the transmitted signal.

In recognition of these and other limitations of RS-232-C, the EIA proposed three new standards: *RS-449*, *RS-422-A*, and *RS-423-A*. RS-422-A and RS-423-A define the electrical circuits that use the physical interface defined in RS-449.

The RS-449 standard defines the physical connections required to support either RS-422-A or RS-423-A. RS-449 is procedurally similar to RS-232-C and is intended to offer an orderly means of migrating from the old standard to the new standard. Some of the differences between RS-449 and RS-232-C are listed:

- The RS-449 standard calls for *two* sets of connectors: a 37-pin connector for data, control, timing, and diagnostics; and a 9-pin connector for a secondary channel circuits. RS-232-C has a single 25-pin connector carrying all signals.

- RS-449 supports both *balanced* and *unbalanced* circuits; whereas RS-232-C only supports unbalanced circuits.

  A balanced circuit is one in which the signals are carried between the DTEs on a *pair* of wires. Signals are sent as a current down one wire and return on the other; the two wires create a complete circuit. An unbalanced circuit is one in which the signal is sent over a single wire, with the DTEs sharing a common ground. Electrical problems can arise if the ground potential differs between the two DTEs.

  A balanced circuit is less affected by noise and produces less noise than does an unbalanced circuit. In a balanced circuit, the receiving DTE determines the value of the signal (i.e., mark or space) by comparing the difference between the transmitted signal and the ground. Should the line be affected by noise, the difference between the transmitted signal and ground should be the same as if the noise is not present (Figure 4.14).

The equivalent CCITT standard for RS-449 is V.35.

The standards RS-422-A (CCITT V.11) and RS-423-A are intended for balanced and unbalanced circuits, respectively:

RS-422-A. Since RS-422-A supports balanced circuits, two separate wires are used for each signal (i.e., transmit and receive); doubling the number of circuits, but permitting higher data rates (see Table 4.1).

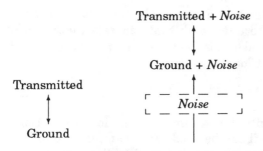

Figure 4.14   The effect of noise on a twisted-pair (RS-449) cable

In RS-422-A the differences between the voltages on the two wires determines whether a mark or a space is sent. If the signal difference between the two wires is positive and more than +0.2 V, a mark is received, whereas a negative difference of more than −0.2 V indicates a space. The smaller transition region (0.4 V in RS-422-A compared to 6 V in RS-232-C) is due to the use of the balanced circuit.

RS-423-A. RS-423-A supports unbalanced transmission and is designed, in part, as a method whereby RS-232-C users can migrate to RS-449, since RS-423-A can support *both* RS-422-A and RS-232-C.

In RS-423-A, a mark is indicated by a −4-V difference between the signal and the *common* ground wires, while a space is indicated by a +4-V difference. These voltages are compatible with the existing RS-232-C standard, thereby permitting RS-423-A interconnection with RS-232-C. (Since RS-423-A receivers also handle the RS-422-A 0.4-V transition region, RS-422-A transmitters can be used with RS-423-A receivers.)

The differences between balanced and unbalanced circuits are also illustrated when comparing the speeds and distances attainable with RS-422-A and RS-423-A. See Table 4.1.

TABLE 4.1   Effect of Distance on Line Speed

Standard	At 1000 meters	At 10 meters
RS-422-A	100,000 bps	10,000,000 bps
RS-423-A	3,000 bps	300,000 bps

4.6 SUMMARY

This chapter has introduced some of the concepts surrounding the generation of signals and the technology available for the transmission of data between DTEs.

The chapter examined three aspects of the physical connection:

Encoding of signals. Data within a DTE cannot simply be transmitted to a remote DTE for a number of reasons: the signals might not be strong enough to reach the destination, or the electrical representation of the signals may differ from DTE to DTE. To overcome these problems, devices known as level convertors are used to "boost" the signal strength as well as convert the signal to an encoding agreed upon by both DTEs.

Connecting DTEs. For information to reach one DTE from another, some form of connection is required. In all of the applications considered thus far in the text, the connection has been physical (typically copper wires); however, there are alternatives to wire, including optical fibers and microwave.

Standards. Standards are need to ensure that DTEs from different manufacturers can be connected. These standards define how signals are encoded, the physical wiring of the devices, and even the shape of the connectors. Without these agreements, data communications would be extremely difficult.

In subsequent chapters, RS-232-C will be examined in more detail and additional standards will also be discussed.

4.7 EXERCISES

1. Draw the bit pattern for the transmission of the letter S using NRZ-S (space) encoding. Compare this to NRZ-I (inverted) encoding.

2. Show, by means of a diagram, that a sequence of marks in NRZ-S will produce a constant signal level. What is generated if a sequence string of spaces is encoded using NRZ-S?

3. Show, by means of a diagram, that a sequence of spaces in NRZ-I will produce a constant signal level. What is generated if a sequence of marks is encoded using NRZ-I?

4. The illustration of the RS-232 D-connector was said have female numbering. Find a male RS-232 connector and show how the numbering differs.

5. Read through your PC's technical reference manual to determine the electrical signals used within the PC. What is the maximum distance these signals can be propagated? (You might want to visit a library and reference an electronics handbook to answer this question.)

6. If you have access to an ohm-meter, take an RS-232-C cable and determine if the cable is a null-modem cable or a "standard" RS-232-C cable. This can be done by holding one of the meter's probes onto pin 2 at one end of the cable and the other probe onto pin 2 on the other end of the cable. If the meter does not register any current flow, you can assume that pin 2 does not connect through to pin 2. This implies that you have a null-modem cable. Verify this by checking pin 2 with pin 3: the meter should register something this time otherwise you have a very strange cable.

   Be careful how you test male connectors, since pins 2 and 3 are adjacent you might find yourself applying a probe to both pins 2 and 3, giving a false reading on the ohm-meter. If you cannot get the probe to make contact with a pin in female connector, you can always use a paper clip to complete the circuit (unbend the paper clip and place it about 5 mm into the pin-hole).

7. Determine experimentally what distance an RS-232-C signal can be successfully propagated by connecting a number of RS-232-C cables together. Use the point-to-point telephone utility developed in Chapter 3 to transmit the data from one DTE to the other. Remember to check for the type of cable (null-modem or standard); if the cables are null-modem, you'll have to use an odd number of cables. Why?

Tools for Testing Communication Systems

5.1 INTRODUCTION

In Chapter 3, you were expected to work with software that supports point-to-point asynchronous communications between pairs of DTEs. In your work, you may have encountered problems in determining:

- which DTE was actually transmitting (or receiving)

- which DTE was correctly following the protocol

As you no doubt discovered, either or both of these problems can result in untold hours of wasted time while trying to determine "which end is doing what." Not surprisingly, people implementing or maintaining communication systems in the "real" world also run into these problems, especially when interconnecting DTEs from different manufacturers, even though the manufacturers claim to have implemented the same protocol.

Ideally, tools are needed that allow the person attempting to solve the problem to monitor the activities on the communication channel and to determine exactly which end is transmitting or where the protocol is not being observed. Fortunately, a number of tools are available that satisfy the the listed requirements.

5.2 BUILT-IN TOOLS

Many UARTs support "built-in" hardware facilities that permit the programmer to perform numerous software tests. Broadly speaking, these tests fall into two categories: *loopback testing* and *interrupt generation*.

5.2.1 Loopback Testing

A loopback test causes all data normally supplied to the UART for transmission to be returned to the processor as if the data had just been received. This permits the testing of the local software by removing any chance of errors being introduced by the remote DTE or the communications channel, since the UART is separated from the communication channel. For example, a loopback test makes it possible to test both transmission and reception software locally.

When a loopback test is being performed, the serial transmission hardware continues to transmit marks, and the serial-receive hardware is disconnected (Figure 5.1).

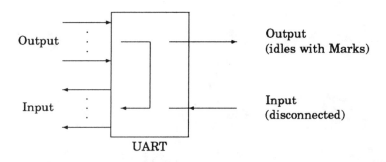

Figure 5.1   UART loopback test

In the 8250 UART, loopback is set by writing `0x10` to the Modem Control Register (address `0x3FC` for serial port 1, and address `0x2FC` for serial port 2) (Figure 5.2).

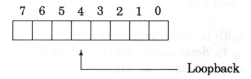

Figure 5.2   Modem Control Register: loopback bit

Commkit can be used to demonstrate the UART's loopback feature by changing the Modem Control Register (MCR_DEFN, defined in file `devices.h`) to include the constant LOOPBK:

```
#define MCR_DEFN    (DTR+RTS+OUT2+LOOPBK)
```

If the preceding change is made to `devices.h` and the telephone utility described in Chapter 3 (using `make`, `commkit.c` will also be recompiled), the UART will be placed in loopback mode next time `pt2pt.exe` is run. Running the newly compiled version of the telephone utility should cause everything that is typed locally (and appearing in the upper half of the screen) to appear on the lower half of the screen as it would had a remote user sent the information. If the modified software does nothing (i.e., the lower half of the screen doesn't echo what you type on the upper half), don't despair—not all 8250 UARTs support loopback. Try running the software on another PC.

The UART is switched out of loopback mode by writing (DTR+RTS+OUT2) to the Modem Control Register.

5.2.2 Generating Interrupts

All software, whether it's a simple first-year assignment or a commercial database package must be tested before being released. The same holds true for data communications software. However, testing communications software has the added problem that certain errors are caused by random or spurious events that are hard to duplicate. For example, events such as overrun errors and framing errors are unpredictable, and may take many hundreds of hours of testing before the event occurs (and when the event does occur, it is difficult to duplicate).

Fortunately, the 8250 UART has been designed so that hardware interrupts (such as overrun and framing errors) can be generated through software; meaning that error-handling software can be thoroughly tested before being released.

There are six hardware interrupts that can be software generated by the 8250 from the Line Status Register (Data Available, Overrun Error, Framing Error, Parity Error, Break Interrupt, and Transmit Holding Register Empty), as well as four hardware interrupts from the Modem Status Register (the use and testing of the Modem Status Register will be discussed in more detail in Chapter 8). These interrupts are caused by writing to any of the corresponding status bits in the Line Status Register and having the UART in loopback mode. The specific bits in the Line Status Register are given in Figure 5.3.

For example, the steps required to test the overrun error-handling software on the second serial port (`SP2`, base address `0x2F8`), are as follows:

1. Turn loopback on (port `0x2FC`).

2. Write `0x02` to the Line Status Register (port `0x2FD`).

3. A line status interrupt is then generated by the UART, causing control to be passed to the interrupt handler responsible for serial port 2 (`sp2_ih()`).

4. The Interrupt Identification Register will have a value of `0x06` (Receiver Line Status Change) and the Line Status Register will have a value of `0x02`.

5. The interrupt is serviced and cleared as if it were any other interrupt.

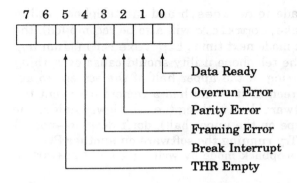

Figure 5.3   Line Status Register bits affected in loopback mode

Software-generated interrupts can continue as long as the UART remains in loopback mode.

5.3 CHANNEL MONITORING TOOLS

Built-in testing can force the hardware to emulate certain conditions for software verification; however, these tests still offer no suggestion as to the state of the channel itself. For example, if data transmitted from one DTE fails to arrive at the other, and both DTEs are "working perfectly," then something is happening to prevent the data from arriving at the receiving DTE. There are three possibilities:

- The data *isn't* being sent by the transmitting DTE.
- The data is being sent, but the communication channel is failing to pass the data to the receiving DTE.
- The data is being sent from the transmitting DTE across the channel correctly, but isn't being *received* by the receiving DTE.

The first two of these possibilities (and perhaps the third) can be overcome by having the capability of observing the activities on the communication channel.

Broadly speaking, there are two types of tools available that permit the observation of the activity between two DTEs on a communication channel: *break-out boxes* and *line analysers*.

5.3.1 The Break-out Box

In the previous chapter, it was shown that a single communication channel interconnecting two DTEs consists of a number of different connections, each responsible for a specific signal. Since these signals are typically electrical impulses, the signals can be detected and displayed to the person monitoring the channel.

The break-out box is a tool designed to indicate which signals on each of the different connections between the two DTEs are active. In a break-out box, the state of a signal (i.e., active or inactive) is indicated by a light-emitting diode associated with the connection in question. A break-out box monitoring the signals on an RS-232 communication channel would typically signal the conditions on any or all 25 pins. For example, as data is transmitted between the two devices, the light-emitting diodes displaying pins 2 and 3 would become active and inactive, depending upon the value of the transmitted byte (marks turn the LED on, while spaces turn it off).

In addition to monitoring the various signals on the channel, break-out boxes can allow the person testing the channel to activate a nonexisting signal. For example, if pin 2 (transmit) is idling (with marks), the breakout box allows the person testing the channel to force the pin into the space state. Similarly, a signal can be deactivated by breaking the connection. Break-out boxes generally cost between $50.00 and $200.00.

5.3.2 Line Analysers

Although break-out boxes are useful in determining the state of various signals between the DTEs, they give no indication as to the data that is actually being sent. For example, when a byte is transmitted, the break-out box's transmission LED simply flashes on and off.

Line analysers (or *data analysers*), like break-out boxes, monitor the various signals that occur between the two DTEs. However, line analysers are designed to *show* the data that is being transmitted on the communication channel rather than only indicating that a signal is present. For example, if the byte A is transmitted between a pair of DTEs, a break-out box simply flashes on and off; whereas, the line analyser displays the byte A.

At a minimum, a line analyser permits the user to monitor the data on a communication channel by displaying the transmissions from both DTEs, with the data from each DTE appearing on alternate lines of the display. To allow as much flexibility as possible, line analysers often have keyboards that permit the user to specify the configuration of the channel (including line speed, parity, and word size); while more sophisticated and expensive line analysers will do this automatically. In addition, some analysers can be programmed to recognize specific protocols and will search for control sequences associated with the protocol before displaying the captured data. Line analysers are considerably more expensive than break-out boxes, usually costing anywhere from $3,000 to over $20,000.

5.4 THE COMMKIT LINE ANALYSER

Commkit is supplied with a software line analyser for monitoring the communication channel between pairs of DTEs. The Commkit line analyser can be found in the file analyser.c on the Commkit diskette.

5.4.1 Hardware Requirements

The Commkit line-analyser software requires a PC with two serial ports (SP1, serial port 1; and SP2, serial port 2). For example, to monitor the traffic between two PCs, a third PC is required to act as the line analyser. A possible configuration of the three PCs is shown in Figure 5.4 (the analyser is the PC with the A on the screen).

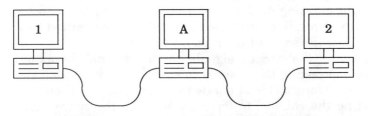

Figure 5.4   The Commkit line analyser interconnecting two PCs

As in all other cases, the PCs must be connected by null modem cables.

5.4.2   Design

The basic algorithm associated with the Commkit line analyser is as follows:

1. Read a byte (from either port).
2. Display the byte.
3. Send (forward) the byte on the "other" port.

The algorithm, as written, simply displays each received byte on the screen. In order to make the line-analyser output less confusing, each serial port can be associated with a specific set of lines on the analyser's screen. For example, data received on serial port 1 could be displayed in inverse video on odd-numbered lines (1, 3, 5, etc), while the data received on serial port 2 could be displayed in normal video on even-numbered lines (2, 4, 6, etc).

Another useful technique often used by line analysers is to interleave the display of the incoming bytes. That is, when a sequence of one or more bytes from one DTE stops, the next sequence of bytes (from either DTE) starts up where the last DTE stopped. This permits the line analyser to display the events as they occur. For example, in a half-duplex connection, all line-analyser output would be associated with one set of lines (odd or even) until the communication channel was turned around, at which point the second DTE would be transmitting, and the line analyser's output would be on the other set of lines (even or odd). However, in a full-duplex connection, output on the line analyser could appear from either DTE, thereby resulting in the interleaving of output (i.e., a combination of normal and inverse video on alternate lines).

5.4.3   Implementation

The line analyser is implemented using the message-passing facilities of Commkit. As bytes are received from either of the serial ports on the line-analyser

PC, they are sent in messages to the (foreground) line-analyser process which writes the byte to the screen and then forwards the byte to the other port.

The line-analyser software is divided into three distinct parts: the interrupt handlers, the display/control process, and the character-forwarding software.

The interrupt handlers Four Commkit interrupt handlers (sp1_ih(), sp2_ih(), clk_ih(), and kb_ih()) are used by the line-analyser software:

sp1_ih() and sp2_ih(). The two serial ports communicate with the analyser process by making calls to low_level() after the reception of a character (RECVDONE) or after a character has been transmitted (XMITDONE).

Each received character is forwarded to the analyser process via queue APPLICATION. The transmit done interrupt causes the queue associated with the serial port to be checked for further characters.

When the analyser process sends a message to either serial port for transmission (code MSG_AVAIL), the state of the port is checked. If the port is transmitting, the message is left on the port's queue; otherwise the queue is read and the byte is transmitted.

clk_ih(). The clock interrupt handler calls low_level() about 18 times a second, which keeps track of the number of "ticks." As soon as one second has elapsed, a one-byte message is sent to the analyser process via queue APPLICATION.

kb_ih(). The keyboard interrupt handler calls low_level() whenever a character is read from the keyboard. Each character is forwarded to the analyser process via queue APPLICATION.

The display/control process All bytes received from the serial ports, all keyboard input, and all timing signals are sent to the foreground display/control process, do_analyser(), via queue APPLICATION. Do_analyser() waits for messages and receives them using the recv() primitive.

Messages, containing a byte, from either of the serial ports are displayed on the PC's screen and then forwarded to the "other" serial port queue. The line analyser process can determine which port to forward the byte to since the source identifier associated with the byte's message indicates the port that the byte was received from (either SP1IH or SP2IH).

The variable base_line indicates the pair of lines (i.e., base_line and base_line + 1) upon which the output should be displayed. Characters (and their associated attributes, normal or inverse) are written to a specific column within a line (indicated by the variable column). Once a character is displayed, column is incremented. Should column exceed the screen width, base_line is incremented by 2 and column is cleared. When base_line exceeds the length of the screen (indicated by the constant END_OF_SCREEN), base_line is set to START_OF_SCREEN.

In addition to the displaying and forwarding of bytes, the line analyser supports a number of extensions to the original algorithm:

- Once a second, a timing signal is displayed on the screen, thereby allowing the person using the line analyser to get an indication of the amount of time taken for each transmission. The timing signal is generated by the clock interrupt handler (`clock_handler()`), and forwarded to the line-analyser process.

  The timing signal is displayed on the normal video line (the even numbered lines) as an inverse video blank character and on the inverse video line (the odd numbered lines) as a normal video blank character. The timing signal can be toggled (displayed or not displayed) by pressing CTRL-T (*DC4*), causing the variable `time_display` to be assigned TRUE or FALSE. By default, the timing signal is displayed when the analyser is first turned on (i.e., `time_display` is TRUE).

- Since output from the analyser can disappear rather rapidly if there is a large volume of traffic flowing between the DTEs, output to the screen can be toggled using CTRL-S (*DC3*) to turn the line analyser's output off (FALSE is assigned to the variable `display_all`), and CTRL-Q (*DC1*) to turn the line analyser's output on (TRUE is assigned to `display_all`).

  Although transmitted data is not displayed when the line-analyser display is toggled off, the line analyser still receives and forwards all data.

  If the line analyser's output has been toggled off, the timing signal is not displayed.

- At any time, the line analyser can be switched off (thereby returning to MS-DOS) by using CTRL-C (this changes the variable `running` to FALSE). At this point, all communications cease since the analyser is no longer forwarding the characters.

- When the line analyser is started, all received data is displayed (i.e., `display_all` and `time_display` are assigned TRUE).

Character forwarding software Once the character display sequence has finished, `do_analyser()` sends the character to the "other" serial port for transmission. However, before the character can be transmitted, the state of the serial port must be determined:

Port is busy. If the port is busy, the character cannot be sent and is left on the queue associated with the serial port. The character, or any intervening characters are removed one at a time from the queue when each XMITDONE interrupt is signalled.

Port is idle. If the port is idle, the character can be removed from the serial port's queue and transmitted immediately using `outportb()`.

The state of the serial port is maintained in the semaphore `transmitting` (an array of two elements, one for each serial port). Each element in `transmitting` is initially zero, indicating that no transmission is taking place; it is incremented whenever a message from the line analyser process arrives for a specific serial port.

Messages from the line-analyser process cause `low_level()` to be called with the code `MSG_AVAIL`. If the port's `transmitting` semaphore is zero, the queue is read and the character sent (`transmitting` is incremented in `low_level()` and decremented in `get_char()`). However, if `transmitting` is non-zero, `transmitting` is incremented and the character remains queued.

Whenever `XMITDONE` is signalled, the function `get_char()` is called and the queue associated with the interrupting serial port is read and the character transmitted. In addition, the serial port's semaphore `transmitting` is decremented.

It was found during some of the tests of the line-analyser software that once a week (usually on weekends) a serial port would fail to issue an `XMITDONE` signal. The loss of the `XMITDONE` signal stopped all data flow out the serial port because the queue is read and the data transmitted only when `XMITDONE` is detected.

The loss of the `XMITDONE` signal also meant that the serial port failed to read its serial port queue. By failing to read the queue, the pool of message buffers eventually reached zero (as more messages were forwarded to the unread queue), resulting in the line analyser crashing and returning control to MS-DOS.

The solution to this problem is to monitor each serial port using a *sanity check*. The sanity check works on the assumption that as long as `XMITDONE` signals are being generated, `transmitting` should have a value in the range of 0 (not transmitting) or 1 (transmitting). Any value much higher than say, 10 or 15, indicates that something is wrong with the serial port and an `XMITDONE` signal has been lost. When this point is reached, the sanity check takes over and forces the first character on the queue to be sent by calling `get_char()`. This character then results in the serial port generating an `XMITDONE` signal, meaning that transmissions can resume and the queue will eventually be emptied.

The sanity check occurs whenever a `MSG_AVAIL` is signalled. Should `transmitting` exceed `LIMIT` (defined in `analyser.c`), it is assumed that an `XMITDONE` is missing and a transmission is forced.

Message flow   The overall flow of messages within `analyser.c` is illustrated in Figure 5.5.

All devices send their messages to queue `APPLICATION` which is read by `do_analyser()`. Messages from the keyboard and the clock are processed by the analyser software; messages from either of the serial ports are displayed (if the display is enabled) and put onto the "outgoing" queue for transmission. All messages are a maximum of one byte in length.

5.5   USING THE COMMKIT LINE ANALYSER

The Commkit diskette is supplied with both the source code and executable code for the line analyser. The line analyser requires a PC with two serial ports.

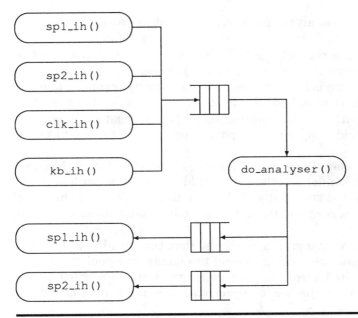

Figure 5.5   Message flow within the Commkit line analyser

5.5.1   Creating a Commkit Line Analyser

An executable line analyser is comprised of the line-analyser source code, `analyser.c`, `commkit.obj`, `intrpt.obj`, and the standard header files (`general.h`, `ascii.h`, and `devices.h`):

```
C:\> make analyser.exe
```

5.5.2   Running the Commkit Line Analyser

Once compiled, the line analyser can be executed by typing `analyser` and the required line speed (one of 50, 300, 1200, 2400, 4800, or 9600) after the MS-DOS prompt. For example, to run the line analyser at 2400 bps, one would type:

```
C:\> analyser 2400
```

When using the line analyser, remember to start the line-analyser software on the analyser PC *before* starting any of the other PCs. This ensures that all data transmitted between the two PCs will be forwarded rather than being blocked by the inactive line-analyser PC. Should the line analyser be shut down before a transmission has completed, the remaining bytes will not be forwarded.

The control characters recognized by the line analyser are as follows:

CTRL-C   Terminates the line analyser, control is returned to MS-DOS.

CTRL-T   Turns the one-second timing pulse on or off.

CTRL-S   Stops display of all output (data and timing signals).

CTRL-Q   Resumes display of all output (data and, if enabled, timing signals).

5.6 SUMMARY

This chapter has examined some of the tools that are available to assist in the testing and development of communications software. Some rudimentary tools are available within the UART itself, allowing conditions such as overrun and the break indication to be tested directly by the processor. For as useful as these tools are, they do not offer the user any indication as to what is happening on the communication channel itself.

Two different types of tools are available for examining the traffic on a channel: the break-out box and the line analyser. Break-out boxes permit the monitoring of various signals on the channel, such as whether a byte has been sent or received; however, no indication is given as to the value of the data. Line analysers, on the other hand, allow the user to actually see what is happening on the channel, thereby aiding in the development and implementation of communications software.

Commkit is supplied with a line analyser which can monitor the traffic flow between two DTEs. The analyser offers some of the features found on commercial analysers, at a somewhat reduced cost.

Finally, it is important to remember that there are three possible places to consider when testing communication software: the transmitter, the channel, and the receiver. Tools such as the line analyser allow a software developer to monitor the traffic on a channel and help in tracking down software errors.

5.7 EXERCISES

1. Run a loopback test on the telephone utility described in Chapter 3.

2. Run the PC-phone utility (developed in Chapter 3) with the line analyser connecting the two PCs. Try typing a message from one PC; what appears on the analyser? Use the timing signal to determine how long it takes to type an entire line of characters. Type messages from both PCs, what appears on the line analyser? Toggle the line analyser so that output does not appear on the line analyser's screen, now type messages on both PCs, does the information still get through?

3. Modify the line analyser to allow the user to see the data displayed in either hexadecimal, octal, or ASCII. Let the user enter the selection from the keyboard while the program is running (thereby permitting the user to change the output dynamically).

    Test your program by modifying the PC-phone utility so that it sends 7 bits of data and parity (i.e., one of mark, space, odd, or even). The line analyser should read 8-data bits and *no* parity. The value displayed by the line analyser will be the data and the parity bits.

    (*Note*: that for hexadecimal and octal output, a single character will map into two or three display characters.)

4. As mentioned in Section 5.4, some of the more sophisticated line analysers can dynamically configure themselves by monitoring the traffic on the line (i.e., without operator intervention). Modify the Commkit line analyser so that it will configure itself to the speed of the line and the word size.

   In order to answer this question you will need to consider the different line status signals generated by the serial ports. Instead of recording the error statistics in port_handler(), low_level() will have to be called with the value of the Line Status Register.

5. Add a clock facility to the line analyser by displaying a clock in the upper righthand corner of the screen. The clock can be useful in a number of situations; for example, the user can time the length of a transmission. Use CTRL-R (*DC2*) to reset to clock to zero.

6. Add a scanning feature to the line analyser. That is, allow the line analyser to search for specific sequences of bytes. Prior to finding the search string, no data should be displayed; however, once the search sequence is found, all subsequent data received should be displayed. Allow the user to change the sequence of characters that is being scanned while the analyser is running.

   By default, the analyser should not search for any strings. Use CTRL-F (*ACK*) to signal that the user wants to enter a search string (the number of characters in the string should not exceed 32). Once a string has been entered, the string should not be searched for until the user types CTRL-U (*NAK*), at which point a message should appear on the top line of the analyser's screen indicating that a search in underway. By typing CTRL-U again, the search is to be stopped.

   In many situations it is useful to search for both the starting and ending strings in a sequence of characters. Extend the analyser so that the user can specify an "end-string": the end-string should be accepted after the user types CTRL-E (*ENQ*). (The end-string should not be searched for until the starting string has been found.) As soon as the end-string has been found, the starting string should be scanned for once again and no data displayed until the starting string has been found.

   All data should be forwarded while the search is taking place.

7. Use the line analyser to determine the terminal control characters sent between your school's host and a terminal connected to the host. Once you have these characters, modify the point-to-point software to emulate the control characters sent from the host. Use the line analyser to help debug the terminal emulation program.

   Although the easier way of solving this problem is to get the manual associated with the terminal in question. If the manual is not readily available, this technique can be used to determine the terminal's control characters.

Longer Distance Communications

Consider the following situations:

- A file consisting of thousands of binary records (perhaps millions of bytes) must be transferred from one computer to another without the loss or corruption of any information. How long will the transfer take; and can the transfer take place using only asynchronous point-to-point communications?

- Imagine working in the branch of an office that is several hundred miles from the head office in which the central computer facility happens to be located. How will the branch office access the information stored at the head office?

Transferring large volumes of binary information using the point-to-point techniques discussed in Chapter 3 is both potentially error-prone and time consuming. Consider, for example, how the transmitting computer could determine whether the destination computer had received a byte correctly. In a terminal-host asynchronous configuration, the error check can be achieved using remote echoing, in which the character typed by the user is echoed by the remote host. If the character echoed is not the same as the character entered, the user can delete the erroneous character and type the character again. The same approach does not lend itself well to the transfer of large volumes of data for a number of reasons:

- Checking by echoing each character is a costly, time-consuming operation, since the throughput is essentially halved with all the characters being echoed.

- Just because a character is echoed, does not mean that it was received correctly. In the worst case, the character may be corrupted before being received (for example, from A to C), and then corrupted again as it is echoed (for example, from C back to A). In this situation, neither the transmitter nor the receiver has any way of telling that the character was received incorrectly.

- If the echoed character does not match the character that was originally sent, the transmitter can detect the error, but how can it be corrected? Retransmitting the character is of no use since the receiver has had no indication that there was an error with the initial character.

- If binary data is being sent, a delete character must not be interpreted as a delete operation, but rather as part of the data being sent.

There is a second problem that must be considered when dealing with the transfer of large volumes of data using asynchronous communications: the overhead associated with the transmission. When using an asynchronous frame format to transmit a byte of information, the number of control bits range from a minimum of two (if only one start and one stop bit are used) to a maximum of four (if the start, parity, and two stop bits are used); in the worst case, when sending a 7-bit byte (with the four control bits) a 36 percent overhead can be expected. For example, if the file in question contains one million bits, a total of more than 1.36 million bits must be sent in the transmission, a potentially costly overhead if the user is expected to pay connection charges.

Problems also arise when attempting to use RS-232-C (or any of the other standards that were discussed in Part 2) over long distances. For example, RS-232-C signals are attenuated once the distance between the DTEs exceeds roughly 100 meters; meaning that using RS-232-C to transmit over any reasonable distance (between buildings or between continents) is impossible without some form of assistance.

Part 3 presents a step-by-step examination of the techniques used to overcome the limitations of distance, volume, and error handling in data communications. Methods of increasing the amount of *useful* information transmitted (by decreasing the amount of framing information associated with each byte) using *synchronous* communications are discussed in Chapter 6. Chapter 6 also presents a number of different error-detection techniques which far surpass the simple parity check.

Chapter 7, introduces some of the concepts associated with transferring files between DTEs. The chapter examines problems such as reliable file transfer and file system interaction with the communication system.

The remaining three chapters look at methods of overcoming the distance limitations imposed by standards such as RS-232-C. Chapter 8 shows how the most ubiquitous communication system of all, the telephone, can be used to support data communications. Using the telephone system for data communications can prove to be an expensive solution, especially when the communicating DTEs are separated by distances that require charges applied to the call. In Chapter 9, a number of *multiplexing techniques* that can be used to share a single communication channel amongst a number of DTEs are presented, hence reducing the separate physical communication channels required.

Chapter 9 concludes with a discussion as to why using the existing telephone system for data communications is not necessarily a good thing and considers alternatives to the telephone system. Chapter 10 demonstrates how ideas associated with synchronous communications, the telephone system, and multiplexing all came together in the early 1970's to allow the development of long-distance communication facilities entirely devoted to data communications known as *wide area networks*.

Synchronous Communications

6.1 INTRODUCTION

Asynchronous communications are intended for *low-volume* data transfers, consisting of several bytes per second, typically between a user typing at a DTE connected to a remote DTE. However, if the transfer between the two DTEs is a *large-volume* transfer, consisting of thousands or even millions of bytes (as could easily happen if a file is being transferred), asynchronous communications may prove to be a less desirable method of data transfer. Consider the following:

Transmission overheads. Each byte that is sent requires at least two, and possibly as many as four, extra control bits. These control bits are necessary since they insure that the byte is properly framed (the start and stop bits), and offer a degree of error detection (the parity bit). With the inclusion of these control bits, each asynchronous frame transmitted has an overhead of between 20 percent (a 10-bit frame consisting of an 8-bit byte, the start bit, and one stop bit) to over 36 percent (an 11-bit frame consisting of a 7-bit byte, the start bit, parity bit, and two stop bits). Therefore, for every million bits that are sent, between 200,000 and 360,000 bits are transmitted as control information.

Error detection and correction. The only means available to the receiving DTE to determine whether the byte has been received correctly is the parity bit. Although the parity bit can help in detecting errors, it can only detect an odd number of bit changes. The parity bit is adequate for low-volume transfers in which each byte is echoed by the remote DTE, since the user can immediately tell whether what has just been typed is echoed correctly. However, echoing each byte in a high-volume transfer halves the throughput.

One way in which DTEs can transfer less control information and more data is to use *synchronous communications*. Synchronous communications are intended to:

- Minimize transmission overhead by reducing the amount of control information sent with each *message* (i.e., sequence of data bytes)

- Support better error handling, thereby making error detection and correction more efficient

The remainder of this chapter examines how the these two points can be achieved using synchronous communications.

6.2   REDUCING TRANSMISSION OVERHEADS

Ideally, when sending a message between a pair of DTEs, nothing other than data should be transmitted (Figure 6.1).

Data   Data   Data

Figure 6.1   Transmitting "pure" data

However, in Chapter 3, it was shown that two problems must be overcome if data is to be sent between DTEs:

Frame delimiting. The channel idles in the mark state, and any byte sent with one or more leading marks (1s) will not be detected correctly by the receiving DTE.

Timing. The transmitting and receiving DTEs must remain "in step" to insure that each bit is received as transmitted.

In an asynchronous communication, these problems are overcome through the use of additional control bits (i.e., the start and stop bits) and by restricting the number of bits that can be transmitted (i.e., the byte size plus the control bits).

Since synchronous communications permit the transmission of data without embedded control characters, techniques must exist to overcome the problems of frame delimiting and timing.

6.2.1 Frame Delimiting

In an asynchronous communication, all frames are prefaced with a start bit to distinguish the data from the channel's idle state. A similar solution can be applied to sending a message using synchronous communications. Before the first data byte is sent, the transmitting DTE forwards an indication (such as a special byte) that a message is about to follow. For example, see Figure 6.2. (Note, in this and subsequent examples, all transmissions occur from *left* to *right*.)

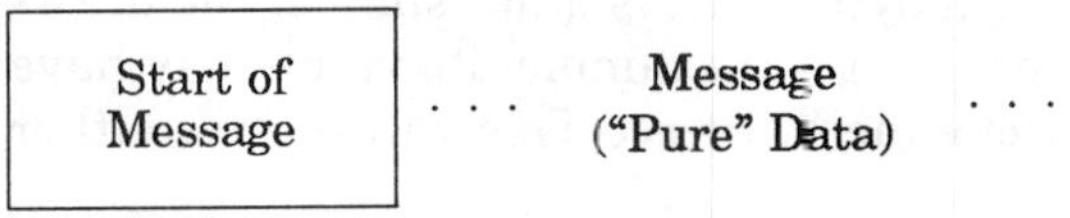

Start of Message	. . .	Message ("Pure" Data)	. . .

Figure 6.2   Prefacing a message with a start-of-message indicator

Upon receipt of the *start-of-message* indicator, the receiving DTE can then begin removing the message from the channel. If the start-of-message indicator is a byte, there is no need to support special hardware for the transmission and reception of the start-of-message indicator.

A similar argument can be applied to ending the message. The receiving DTE must be able to detect the *end-of-message*, otherwise the DTE will continue receiving indefinitely. Three ways in which a transmitter can indicate to the receiver where the end-of-message occurs include:

1. The simplest message delimiting technique is to have all messages consist of the same number of bytes. By using a *fixed-message size*, the receiving DTE always expects a message to consist of say, N data bytes. Once the start-of-message indication is detected, the receiving DTE samples the channel for N bytes of data. The transmitting DTE always sends N bytes of data after the start-of-message indication is sent.

   The problem with using a fixed-message size is that the message to be sent may consist of *less* than N bytes, requiring the message to be padded with extra bytes that are not part of the message itself. A mechanism must be available whereby the transmitting DTE can inform the receiving DTE of the number of data bytes actually sent.

2. Another message delimiting technique involves the transmitter sending the receiver a byte containing a count of the number of bytes in the message. The *byte count* is usually sent immediately after the start-of-message indication, for example, as in Figure 6.3.

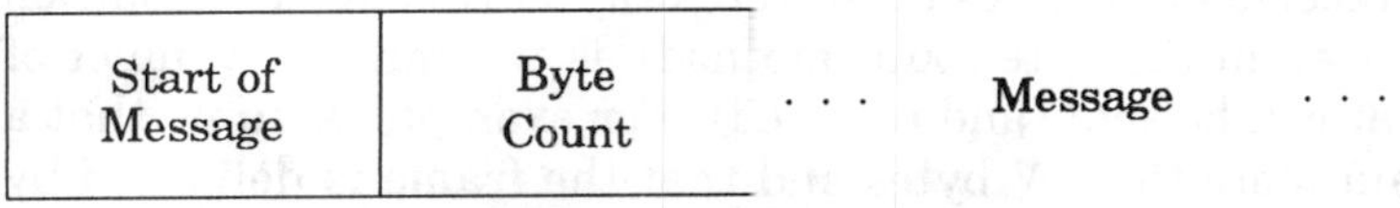

Start of Message	Byte Count	. . .	Message	. . .

Figure 6.3   Prefacing a message with a byte count

The byte count can be used by the receiving DTE to count the number of incoming bytes; when the count reaches zero, the receiving DTE can stop receiving data:

```
receive(Start_Byte);
receive(Count_Byte);

for (i = 0; i != Count_Byte; i++)
    receive(Message[i]);
```

Although the algorithm for using a byte count is quite simple, the drawback is that if the byte count is incorrect (for example, its value may have been changed because of a noisy channel), the receiver will receive either too many or too few bytes.

3. The final approach is to transmit a special end-of-message indicator after the last byte of the message. The incoming byte stream is always scanned for the end-of-message indicator; once this has been detected, the receiving DTE has received the entire message. For example:

```
receive(Start_Byte);
receive(Data_Byte);
i = 0;
while (Data_Byte != END_OF_DATA)
{
    Message[i++] = Data_Byte;
    receive(Data_Byte);
}
```

Messages sent with byte counts often have an end-of-message indicator appended to the last byte of the message.

The start-of-message, message, end-of-message sequence is known as a frame (Figure 6.4).

Figure 6.4   A frame

Should the end-of-message indicator be lost (for example, due to noise), the receiving DTE will receive more bytes than were originally sent. The solution (which can also be used in the byte-count method), is to limit the number of bytes in a frame that can be sent (and received). For example, assume that a frame cannot contain more than N bytes and that the frame is delimited by the bytes START and END, then the receive data algorithm could be written as follows:

1. Wait for START byte.

2. Set byte_count to zero.

3. Check each data byte as it arrives:

END byte   Message with valid number of bytes received. Terminate loop.

default   Check byte_count:

     0 .. N-1:   Store byte in buffer, increase byte_count by 1, repeat from Step 3.

     N: Error, missing END byte. Terminate reception process.

This algorithm insures that a receiving DTE does not continue receiving indefinitely, possibly causing it to run out of buffer space.

In an asynchronous communication, a frame consists of a single byte; the number of bytes in a synchronous frame depends upon several factors, including:

- The number of bytes needed to represent the control sequences and other framing information. Ideally, this should be very small in relation to the total frame size.

- The amount of storage available at the receiving DTE. The data bytes within the frame must not exceed the receiving DTE's storage capacity.

- The amount of information that must be retransmitted should an error be detected in a frame. For example, if a file of one million bytes is transmitted as a single frame, and if one byte is found to be in error, the entire one million bytes must be retransmitted. However, transmitting the file as a series of one thousand-byte frames means that the amount of information to be retransmitted is considerably less.

- The time required to transmit a frame must not exceed the length of time the hardware can remain in synchronization. If synchronization is lost, the contents of the frame will be lost, potentially requiring another transmission. This can be rectified by using a smaller frame size.

6.2.2 Timing

Information that is transmitted serially between DTEs is transmitted a bit at a time. To insure that there is a high probability that each transmitted bit is received correctly, both the transmitting DTE and receiving DTE must be synchronized.

In Chapter 3, it was shown that a UART's clock is designed to remain in step with the remote UART only for the time it takes to send a single byte. The transmitter's and receiver's clocks are synchronized by the start bit: once the center of the start bit is found, the channel can be read once every bit time. As soon as the receiving DTE has assembled the byte, the two DTEs are no longer synchronized, meaning that the next byte sent requires that a start bit be prefixed.

If "pure" data is sent between the communicating DTEs, the DTEs must still remain in step to insure that each byte sent is the same as the byte that is received. However, a synchronous communication, unlike an asynchronous communication, requires that the DTEs remain in step for tens, hundreds, or possibly even thousands of bytes. Keeping the DTEs synchronized is not a trivial matter, since clocks can drift and result in the loss of synchronization.

As with so many other aspects of data communications, there are a number of techniques available which permit the DTEs to transmit a frame of "pure" data at the same time staying "in step."

Special synchronization sequences   Special synchronization byte sequences can be scattered throughout the frame. These characters are detected by the hardware of the receiving DTE which can realign its clock to correct for any clock drift that may have occurred. Frames are often prefixed by the synchronization sequences to insure that the clocks are properly aligned before the transmission begins (Figure 6.5).

Synchronization Sequence	Start of Message	. . "Pure" Data . .	Synchronization Sequence	. . "Pure" Data . .	End of Message

Figure 6.5   Achieving synchronization using synchronization sequences

Since the synchronization sequence is being embedded within the frame of "pure" data, it is necessary to distinguish between synchronization sequences that are used to realign the clocks and data bytes that happen to have the same value as the synchronization sequence (an event that could occur if a binary file is transmitted). Protocols have been designed to overcome this problem and are discussed in subsequent sections.

Separate timing channel   Another solution to the problems associated with the synchronization of DTEs is to transmit on two channels: one reserved for the data bits, the other for a clocking signal. With this method, the receiving DTE knows exactly when to sample the channel since the transmitting DTE indicates the center of the data bit with a timing pulse (Figure 6.6).

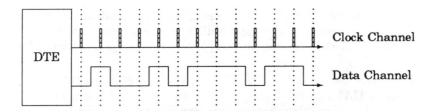

Figure 6.6   Data transmission using a separate clock channel

There is another reason for having one of the DTEs supply the clocking signal: the "other" DTE may not support a clock:

- If the transmitting DTE is supplied with the clock, it sends each data bit on one channel and a timing pulse on the other. The receiving DTE detects the timing pulse and reads the data channel to determine the value of the bit.

- If, however, the transmitting DTE is not supplied with a clock, the receiving DTE must supply the timing signal. In this situation, the transmitting DTE waits for a timing pulse and then sends a bit: the receiving DTE can sample the channel after the timing pulse has been sent (Figure 6.7).

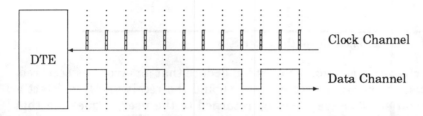

Figure 6.7   Data transmission using an external clock channel

Encoding the timing into the data   A third approach to keeping the communicating DTEs synchronized is to encode the clocking information directly into each bit as it is transmitted. In this way, as the signal arrives, the receiving DTE extracts both the value of the bit and the clock signal.

One of the best known examples of encoding the clock into the data stream is *Manchester encoding*, in which the middle of each bit contains the clock signal as well as an indication as to the value of the bit (Figure 6.8).

Figure 6.8   Manchester encoding

In Manchester encoding, a low-to-high transition in the middle of the bit interval means space (or 0), while a high-to-low transition indicates a mark (or 1). For example, the transmission of the byte S using Manchester encoding would appear as in Figure 6.9.

The extracted data is half a signal behind the transmitted data because the value of each bit is determined at the point where the clock signal is extracted (i.e., the center of the bit).

6.3 IMPROVING ERROR DETECTION

In a full-duplex asynchronous communication, error detection is typically the responsibility of the user. In remote echoing, if the character typed is not the

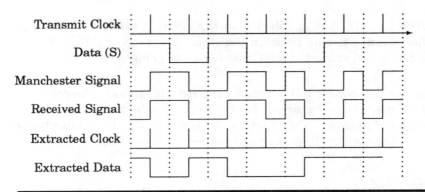

Figure 6.9   Manchester encoding of the letter S

same as the character echoed, the user can deduce that an error has occurred, forcing the user to retype the character. Should the receiving DTE detect a parity error, an error message can be returned to the user, requesting that the character be re-entered.

However, as Figure 6.10 illustrates, even if each byte is echoed when received, there is no guarantee that the transmitting DTE can determine, simply by checking the echoed byte and its parity, that an error has occurred.

Transmitting DTE		Receiving DTE
Send A	$\longrightarrow$ Corrupted to C $\longrightarrow$	Receive C
		$\Downarrow$
Receive A	$\longleftarrow$ Corrupted to A $\longleftarrow$	Echoed as C

Figure 6.10   A limitation of echo checking

Should the transmitting DTE determine that an error has occurred, it must inform the receiving DTE that the last byte sent was in error and the correct byte follows. For example, the character % could be sent by the transmitter when the echoed character is not the same as was originally sent (Figure 6.11).

Transmitting DTE		Receiving DTE
Send A	$\longrightarrow$ Corrupted to C $\longrightarrow$	Receive C
		$\Downarrow$
Receive C	$\longleftarrow$ C $\longleftarrow$	Echoed as C
Error: A $\neq$ C		
Send %	$\longrightarrow$ % $\longrightarrow$	Discard C
Send A (again)	$\longrightarrow$ A $\longrightarrow$	Receive A
		$\Downarrow$
Receive A	$\longleftarrow$ A $\longleftarrow$	Echoed as A

Figure 6.11   Error correction

This solution simply leads to further difficulties:

■ a mechanism must be devised whereby it is possible to send a % as data (that is, the receiving DTE must be able to distinguish a data % from a retransmission request %),

- a protocol must be devised which allows the transmitter to inform the receiver to discard the corrupted %, if an error occurs during a retransmission (especially if the % is corrupted)

- the receiver will accept the retransmitted byte, but not discard the original corrupted byte, if, for some reason, the % is lost.

Admittedly, it is possible to write software to handle the these and other issues, but in the end, the overhead (such as echoing each byte), will make the solution unnecessarily clumsy and expensive. In addition, the parity check is costly in terms of the amount of information that must be sent and the level of detection that is achieved. For example, if a message of 200 bytes is sent, 200 parity bits are also sent.

Fortunately, a number of techniques exist that are more accurate in their ability to detect errors and are less costly in terms of the amount of information transmitted when applied to large volumes of data.

6.3.1 Longitudinal Redundancy Check (LRC)

The parity check is used to check an individual byte by summing the bits *across* the byte. A second type of parity check, known as a *longitudinal redundancy check* (LRC), can be applied to a "column" of bits within a message. That is, whereas parity is applied to a single byte, the LRC is applied to *all* of the bytes.

The LRC is a byte, initially set to 0xFF. Prior to transmission, each data byte is exclusive-or'ed (XOR) with the LRC. (The output from an exclusive-or is 0 if the bits are the same and 1 if the bits are different.)

Once all of the data bytes have been transmitted, the LRC is sent. For example, consider the transmission of a message (msg) of length N:

```
LRC = 0xFF;
for (i = 0; i < N; i++)
{
    LRC ^= msg[i];  /* Same as: LRC = LRC ^ msg[i];  ^ denotes XOR */
    xmit(msg[i]);
}
xmit(LRC);
```

In Figure 6.12, five 8-bit bytes are sent followed by the LRC.

0	1	1	0	1	1	0	0	Byte 1
1	0	1	0	1	1	1	1	Byte 2
0	1	1	1	0	1	0	1	Byte 3
1	1	1	0	0	0	1	0	Byte 4
0	0	0	1	0	1	1	1	Byte 5
1	0	1	1	1	1	0	0	Check character (LRC)

Figure 6.12 The LRC after exclusive or'ing 5 data bytes

The receiver follows a similar algorithm, initially setting the LRC to 0xFF. As each byte is received, it is exclusive-or'ed into the receiver's LRC:

```
LRC = 0xFF;
for(i = 0; i < N; i++)
{
    recv(msg[i]);
    LRC ^= msg[i];
}
recv(last);
LRC ^= last;
```

Assuming that no errors have occurred during the communication, the transmitter's LRC will be the same as the receiver's: meaning that when the receiver exclusive-or's the transmitter's LRC, the result should be zero. For example, Figure 6.13 depicts the results of sending the previous 5-byte sequence.

Transmitter			Receiver
LRC = 11111111			LRC = 11111111
	send(01101100)	$\longrightarrow$ recv(01101100)	
LRC = 10010011			LRC = 10010011
	send(10101111)	$\longrightarrow$ recv(10101111)	
LRC = 00111100			LRC = 00111100
	send(01110101)	$\longrightarrow$ recv(01110101)	
LRC = 01001001			LRC = 01001001
	send(11100010)	$\longrightarrow$ recv(11100010)	
LRC = 10101011			LRC = 10101011
	send(00010111)	$\longrightarrow$ recv(00010111)	
LRC = 10111100			LRC = 10111100
	send(LRC)	$\longrightarrow$ recv(10111100)	
			LRC = 00000000

Figure 6.13 The transmission of a message and its LRC

When the last byte is received and the LRC is zero, it means that no errors were detected. Since the LRC algorithm, like that of the parity check, uses exclusive-or'ing to calculate the check information, it should not be surprising that the LRC is no more accurate than the parity check. For example, if an odd number of bits within a column are inverted due to noise, then the error can be detected; however, an even number of bit changes cannot be detected (Figure 6.14).

In some manuals you may find the term *vertical redundancy check* (VRC), in addition to LRC. VRC is simply another term for parity check. The terms VRC and LRC refer to the error checking used with magnetic computer tapes. In tape lexicon, vertical refers to information stored across the width of the tape (i.e., data bytes stored in parallel with a parity bit), while longitudinal refers to information stored along the length of the tape. A vertical redundancy check is applied across the tape and the longitudinal redundancy check is applied along the length of the tape (Figure 6.15).

Error detection can increase by two to four orders of magnitude over either VRC *or* LRC if the two techniques are used together (that is, each byte is sent with a VRC and is included in an LRC). In Figure 6.16, five 8-bit bytes are sent (with hardware-generated *odd* parity), followed by the LRC.

Transmitter   Receiver

LRC = 11111111   LRC = 11111111
                 send(01101100)   ⟶   recv(01101100)
LRC = 10010011   LRC = 10010011
                 send(10101111) *NOISE* recv(101011⬚0⬚1)
LRC = 00111100   LRC = 001111⬚1⬚0
                 send(01110101)   ⟶   recv(01110101)
LRC = 01001001   LRC = 010010⬚1⬚1
                 send(11100010)   ⟶   recv(11100010)
LRC = 10101011   LRC = 101010⬚0⬚1
                 send(00010111) *NOISE* recv(000101⬚0⬚1)
LRC = 10111100   LRC = 101111⬚0⬚0
                 send(LRC)   ⟶   recv(10111100)
                                                               LRC = 00000000

Figure 6.14 An error undetectable by LRC

0	1	1	1	1	0	1	1	1	0	1	1	1	1	1	1	Bit 7
1	0	0	0	0	1	0	0	0	1	0	0	0	0	0	0	Bit 6
0	1	0	1	0	0	1	0	0	0	1	0	0	0	0	1	Bit 5
0	0	0	0	0	0	0	1	0	0	0	1	0	1	0	0	Bit 4
0	0	0	1	1	0	1	0	1	0	1	0	0	1	1	0	Bit 3
1	1	0	1	0	0	0	0	0	0	1	0	0	0	0	1	Bit 2
1	1	1	0	1	0	0	0	1	0	1	0	1	0	1	1	Bit 1
0	1	1	1	0	0	0	1	0	0	0	1	1	0	0	1	VRC (Odd)

⇑
LRC

Figure 6.15 VRC and LRC encoding

1	0	1	1	0	1	1	0	0	Byte 1
1	1	0	1	0	1	1	1	1	Byte 2
0	0	1	1	1	0	1	0	1	Byte 3
1	1	1	1	0	0	0	1	0	Byte 4
1	0	0	0	1	0	1	1	1	Byte 5
0	1	0	1	1	1	1	0	0	Check character (LRC)

⇑
Parity check (hardware generated)

Figure 6.16 The inclusion of a parity check with an LRC

Although the LRC includes all the data bits, it does *not* include the hardware-generated parity check bit. In the preceding example, the LRC's parity check is 0 (because the LRC is sent as odd parity and it has an odd number of bits set in the LRC byte) rather than 1 (as it would be if the parity bits were included in the LRC).

However, even when used together, combinations of errors can still cause the error detection to fail. For example, consider the effects of an even number of bit changes in the same columns of an even number of bytes (Figure 6.17). In this example, neither parity nor LRC errors are detected, even though the message was received in error.

```
Transmitter                                                    Receiver

LRC = 11111111                                                 LRC = 11111111
send(01101100)   (Parity = 1)    ⟶     recv(01101100)         (Parity = 1)
LRC = 10010011                                                 LRC = 10010011
send(10101111)   (Parity = 1)   NOISE  recv(10|0|011|0|1)     (Parity = 1)
LRC = 00111100                                                 LRC = 00|0|111|1|0
send(01110101)   (Parity = 0)    ⟶     recv(01110101)         (Parity = 0)
LRC = 01001001                                                 LRC = 01|1|010|1|1
send(11100010)   (Parity = 1)    ⟶     recv(11100010)         (Parity = 1)
LRC = 10101011                                                 LRC = 10|0|010|0|1
send(00010111)   (Parity = 1)   NOISE  recv(00|1|101|0|1)     (Parity = 1)
LRC = 10111100                                                 LRC = 10|1|111|0|0
send(LRC)        (Parity = 0)    ⟶     recv(10111100)         (Parity = 0)
                                                               LRC = 00000000
```

Figure 6.17   An error undetectable by both LRC and VRC

6.3.2   Cyclic Redundancy Check (CRC)

In certain applications, sending blocks of information with an LRC, VRC, or both, may provide sufficient error detection, especially if the channel is known to be reliable and reasonably error free. However, there are situations which call for as near-to-perfect error detection as can possibly be applied. Consider the electronic transfer of funds between bank branches. If, during the transfer of funds, the channel is subject to noise, undetected errors could be disasterous for the bank and its customers, since the amounts received might not correspond to the amounts sent. Although LRC and VRC can detect odd numbers of errors, it is possible for errors to go undetected: what is needed is an error detection technique that is several orders of magnitude more effective than LRC and VRC.

The technique used in many applications requiring better error detection is a *cyclic redundancy check* (CRC).

CRC fundamentals   The principles associated with the other error detection techniques discussed earlier in the book are also applicable to the cyclic redundancy check algorithm. That is, the transmitting entity calculates the error check using the data from the message, appends a check sequence to the end of the message, and then transmits the message and the check sequence to the receiving entity in a frame. The receiving entity performs the same calculation on the incoming message and determines whether the message is valid by examining the result of the calculation. The cyclic redundancy check is particularly attractive since it offers greater error detection accuracy through the use of polynomial division.

Basically, the cyclic redundancy check algorithm treats the message as a single-bit stream in which each bit is taken as a coefficient of a polynomial. In general, a message k bits long, has k terms, and is a polynomial of order $k - 1$. A message with terms $m^{k-1} + m^{k-2} + \cdots + m^2 + m^1 + m^0$ can be written as the polynomial:

$$M(x) = m_{k-1}x^{k-1} + m_{k-2}x^{k-2} + \cdots + m_2x^2 + m_1x^1 + m_0$$

For example, the message 101101001 can be written as the polynomial:

$$1x^8 + 0x^7 + 1x^6 + 1x^5 + 0x^4 + 1x^3 + 0x^2 + 0x^1 + 1x^0$$

and simplified to $x^8 + x^6 + x^5 + x^3 + x^0$.

As with LRC and VRC, the message is transmitted with the check bits (commonly referred to as the CRC). Together, the message and the check bits make a unique cyclic code word. The objective of the CRC algorithm is to insure that the vast majority of possible errors are detected by the receiving entity. By dividing the message polynomial by a *generator polynomial*, a set of check bits unique to the message can be obtained.

The generator polynomial, $G(x)$, is a polynomial of degree g, which must be less than the degree of the message polynomial, $M(x)$. $G(x)$ is always odd (i.e., the lowest order term has a value of 1) and must have a value greater than 1. Unless otherwise indicated, all calculations are performed on binary digits using modulo 2 addition without carries ($\oplus$ denotes modulo-2 addition).

The transmission algorithm is as follows:

1. The message $M(x)$ is multipled by x^g, (i.e., the message is shifted left by g bit positions; these bit positions are cleared).

2. The result of the multiplication is divided by the generator polynomial, $G(x)$, giving a quotient, $Q(x)$, and a remainder, $R(x)$:

$$\frac{x^g \times M(x)}{G(x)} = Q(x) \oplus \frac{R(x)}{G(x)}$$

   The remainder, $R(x)$, is always less than the divisor $G(x)$ since the maximum number of bits in the remainder is g.

3. The remainder, $R(x)$, is added to the shifted message (i.e., the lower g bits), producing the frame to be transmitted, $T(x)$:

$$T(x) = x^g \times M(x) \oplus R(x)$$

The receiving entity receives the frame $T(x)$, and proceeds to divide the message by the generator polynomial, $G(x)$. Since the transmitted message includes the remainder from the original division, the frame $T(x)$ should be exactly divisible by the generator polynomial $G(x)$:

$$\frac{T(x)}{G(x)} = \frac{x^g \times M(x) \oplus R(x)}{G(x)}$$

substituting $Q(x) \oplus R(x) \div G(x)$ for $x^g \times M(x) \div G(x)$, one finds:

$$\frac{T(x)}{G(x)} = Q(x) \oplus \frac{R(x)}{G(x)} \oplus \frac{R(x)}{G(x)}$$

Since any number exclusive-or'ed with itself is zero (such as $R(x) \div G(x)$), a successful transmission will result in a remainder of zero.

Example 6.1 Consider the transmission of the message 101101001 using the generator polynomial 101001 ($x^5 + x^3 + 1$). Following the algorithm described previously, one finds:

1. The generator polynomial $G(x)$ has $g = 5$, meaning that the message $M(x)$ must be shifted left by five:

$$2^5 \times 101101001 = 10110100100000$$

2. The shifted message is then divided by the generator polynomial:

```
                              1 0 0 1 0 1 0 1 0   (Quotient)
1 0 1 0 0 1 | 1 0 1 1 1 0 1 0 0 1 0 0 0 0 0
            ⊕ 1 0 1 0 0 1
                1 0 0 0 0 1
              ⊕ 1 0 1 0 0 1
                  1 0 0 0 0 0 0
                ⊕ 1 0 1 0 0 1
                      1 0 0 1 0 0
                    ⊕ 1 0 1 0 0 1
                        1 1 0 1 0   (Remainder)
```

The quotient, $Q(x)$ is discarded.

3. The remainder $R(x)$, 11010, is added to the shifted message, producing $T(x)$, which consists of $M(x)$ and $R(x)$. $T(x)$ is therefore 10110100111010.

The receiving entity accepts the transmitted frame and performs the division using the same generator polynomial:

```
                              1 0 0 1 0 1 0 1 0   (Quotient)
1 0 1 0 0 1 | 1 0 1 1 1 0 1 0 0 1 1 1 0 1 0
            ⊕ 1 0 1 0 0 1
                1 0 0 0 0 1
              ⊕ 1 0 1 0 0 1
                  1 0 0 0 1 1
                ⊕ 1 0 1 0 0 1
                      1 0 1 0 0 1
                    ⊕ 1 0 1 0 0 1
                            0   (Remainder)
```

The result of the division is zero, indicating that no errors were detected in frame.

However, should one or more bits become inverted (i.e., 0 to 1 or vice versa), the division should result in a nonzero remainder. For example, if the frame received was 101 01 100111010 (rather than 101 10 100111010), the division would proceed as follows:

```
                              1 0 0 1 0 1 0 1 0   (Quotient)
 1 0 1 0 0 1 │ 1 0 1 0 1 1 0 0 1 0 0 0 0 0
           ⊕ 1 0 1 0 0 1
               1 0 0 0 1 1
             ⊕ 1 0 1 0 0 1
                 1 0 1 0 1 0
               ⊕ 1 0 1 0 0 1
                   1 1 1 0   (Remainder)
```

The receiving entity can reject the frame since the remainder after the division is nonzero.

CRC Generators All communication channels can be subject to some form of fault which leads to one or more bits in the transmitted frame becoming inverted. The CRC generator polynomial must be designed to detect invalid frames.

It is possible to represent the error itself as a polynomial that is exclusive-or'ed to the frame; if the bits in error are represented as coefficients, the corresponding bits in the frame will be inverted. Using the preceding example in which the transmitted frame, 10110100111010, is corrupted to 10101100111010, the bits in error are as follows:

Transmitted frame	10110100111010
Error bits	00011000000000
Received frame	10101100111010

In this example, the error polynomial $E(x)$ is $x^{10}+x^9$. Error bits corresponding to polynomials containing $G(x)$ as a factor will be undetected. The question is how to develop a generator polynomial that will detect errors within the transmitted frame.

The CRC generating polynomial is chosen to detect four types of error:

Single-bit errors. If the transmitted frame has a single bit in error, the error polynomial $E(x)$ contains a single term, x^e, where e has a value less than the total number of bits in the frame $T(x)$. By having more than one term in the generator polynomial $G(x)$, x^e cannot be divided evenly, meaning that all single-bit errors will be detected.

Double-bit errors. A double-bit error, like the single-bit error, can be represented by the error polynomial. In this case, the polynomial consists of two terms, $E(x) = x^i + x^j$; as before, i and j are both less than the number of bits in the frame, $T(x)$. $E(x)$ can be expressed as $E(x) = x^i(x^{j-i} + 1)$ if $i < j$. By insuring that the generator polynomial has a factor with three terms, neither x^i nor $(x^{j-i} + 1)$ are divisible by the generator, meaning that all double-bit errors will be detected.

Odd number of errors. If the frame is received with an odd number of errors, $E(x)$ will have an odd number of terms. Since no polynomial with an odd number of terms has $x + 1$ as a factor, if $G(x)$ has $x + 1$ as a factor, all frames with an odd number of errors will be detected.

Error bursts. An error burst is a sequence of at least two incorrect bits separated by a series of other bits that may be in error. Error bursts less than or equal to g bits in length (i.e., the degree of the generator polynomial) will be detected as errors. If the burst is exactly $g+1$ bits long (i.e., equal to the number of bits in the generator polynomial), the error will be detected if $E(x)$ does not equal $G(x)$. The probability of the error going undetected is $(1/2)^{(r-1)}$, since the first and last bits of $E(x)$ are the same as $G(x)$, This means that the remaining $r - 1$ bits must be equal. Finally, if the burst exceeds g, the probability of the error going undetected can be shown to be $(1/2)^r$.

The number of bits in the CRC is typically a function of the character (i.e., byte) size used by the communicating entities since the supporting hardware handles quantities of this size. For example, in 8-bit communications, the size of the remainder is typically 16 or even 32 bits in length, meaning that the generator polynomial can be 17 or 33 bits long.

There are a number of CRC generators available for use with synchronous communication protocols, some of the better known include (note, the X in CRC-X refers to the number of bits transmitted in the remainder):

CRC-12. A 12-bit CRC intended for use with synchronous protocols supporting 6-bit bytes. The generator polynomial is $x^{12} + x^{11} + x^3 + x^2 + x + 1$. The initial value of the CRC is zero. If, after the end-of-message is detected, the receiver's CRC result is zero, it is assumed that message was received correctly.

CRC-16. This is a 16-bit CRC used by IBM for the transmission of 8-bit character codes. The generator polynomial is $x^{16} + x^{15} + x^2 + 1$. The initial value of the CRC is zero. The message is assumed to be correctly received if the receiver's CRC result is zero.

CRC-CCITT. This is a 16-bit CRC developed by IBM for their SDLC protocol and also used by the ISO HDLC protocol (both protocols are discussed later); it employs the following generator polynomial: $x^{16} + x^{12} + x^5 + 1$. The CRC is initialized to 0xFFFF and the CRC bits are inverted upon transmission. The received message is deemed correct if, after the end of the message, the receiver's CRC has a value of 0xF0B8.

CRC-32. A 32-bit CRC intended for use primarily in local area networks and some military applications. The generator polynomial is:

$$x^{32} + x^{26} + x^{23} + x^{22} + x^{16} + x^{12} + x^{12} + x^{11} + x^{10} + x^8 + x^7 + x^5 + x^4 + x^2 + x + 1$$

The initial value of the CRC is 0xFFFFFFFF. As with the CRC-CCITT, the transmitter inverts the CRC bits prior to transmission. The receiving entity's CRC should equal 0xDEBB20E3 if the message is received correctly.

Although the generator polynomials are different, the basic algorithm is the same for each.

CRC implementations The first observation that one must make when considering the implementation of a CRC generation routine (in either hardware or software) is *how* is it possible to perform division on a message that could be thousands of bits long, when most machines can only perform 32-bit arithmetic (or less in many cases).

Interestingly enough, the entire division process can take place in a shift register and performed on each bit as it is being transmitted serially. For example, Figure 6.18 shows a possible Shift Register design for CRC-16 calculations (polynomial generator: $x^{16} + x^{15} + x^2 + 1$).

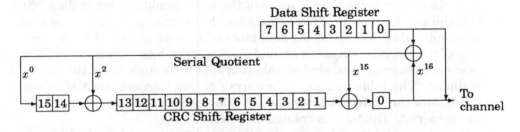

Figure 6.18 A Shift Register implementation of CRC-16

Prior to the first byte being transmitted, the CRC Shift Register is initialized to `0x0000`; the CRC Shift Register contains the intermediate remainder. The Shift Register emulates polynomial division by performing modulo-2 subtraction on the terms x^0, x^2, and x^{15}. The result of the exclusive-or between the low-order data bit and the high-order bit of the remainder (x^{16}) is either a 0 or a 1: a 0 value causes the remainder to rotate unchanged, whereas a 1 inverts the value of each divisor polynomial term; equivalent to obtaining a new intermediate remainder value by including bits from the dividend. Each bit from the Data Shift Register is put onto the channel for transmission as well as being fed into the CRC circuit. When the last data bit has been included in the intermediate remainder, the bits in the Shift Register are clocked onto the channel.

The Commkit CRC utilities Commkit is supplied with two CRC utilities that generate CRC-16 remainders. The first is a software emulation of the CRC shift register circuit previously described, while the second performs a table lookup:

Emulation. The Shift Register shown in Figure 6.18 can be emulated in software by looping through each bit in the data byte prior to the transmission of the data.

> `Crc_calc()` (found in the file `crcsr.c`) contains an implementation of the Shift Register written in C. The software is optimized, upon entry

to `crc_calc()`, an intermediate value of the remainder is produced by exclusive-or'ing the data `byte` with the `crc`. The low-order bit in the new intermediate remainder is right-shifted. Whenever a carry is detected, the polynomial `POLY` is exclusive-or'ed into the remainder (note that `POLY` is simply the octal representation of $x^{15} + x^2 + x^0$).

The intermediate remainder is returned by `crc_calc()`.

Table lookup. By studying the emulation software, a number of patterns emerge that can be used to reduce the time associated with division by repeated shifting. These patterns allow the creation of a table that can produce the next intermediate remainder from the current remainder and the data byte. A second, faster version of `crc_calc()`, which uses table lookup can be found in `crctbl.c`.

The table is based upon the observation that each bit in the new intermediate remainder is always made of the same combinations of data bits and the previous value of the remainder. For example, bit 15 of the new remainder always contains the data bits exclusive-or'ed with the low-order bits of the old intermediate remainder. Similarly, bits 1 through 5 of the new remainder are the shifted values of bits 9 through 13 of the old remainder. The table `crc_tbl` is an array of 256 integers, each of which represents the different intermediate remainder results associated with the subscript. The table is created in `gen_tbl()`.

Prior to the first call to `crc_calc()`, `gen_tbl()` must be called to generate the array `crc_tbl`. Upon entry into `crc_calc()`, the byte to be included in the CRC is exclusive-or'ed with the lower eight bits of the CRC, producing an index into the table. The `crc` is then shifted right and exclusive-or'ed with the bit pattern from `crc_tbl`; this is the new intermediate CRC.

Not surprisingly, both methods produce the same results for the same messages; however, table lookup is the faster of the two methods.

6.4   ERROR RECOVERY

The previous section has shown a number of techniques that allow a receiving DTE to determine if a frame has been received in error. The question now is: once the error has been detected, what steps should be taken to correct it?

Since there is only one transmitter and one receiver, the possible places where the error can be corrected are somewhat limited:

- The receiving DTE can attempt to correct the error itself. This is known as *forward-error recovery*.

- The transmitting DTE can retransmit the frame in error. This is known as *backward-error recovery*.

6.4.1   Forward-Error Recovery

If sufficient redundancy information is supplied with the frame, it may be possible for the receiving DTE to correct (and keep) the frame. For example, deep space probes with limited storage capacity cannot be expected to keep retransmitting frames that are received in error on the Earth; instead, additional information is sent with each frame to allow the recovery of corrupted information.

Forward error recovery techniques require the transmitted data to contain sufficient additional information so as to allow the receiver to correct the errors. The more redundant information that is sent, the more errors that can be corrected.

6.4.2 Backward-Error Recovery

Because of the distances and speeds involved, most terrestrial communications do not expect the receiving DTE to correct errors detected within the frame. Instead, most protocols are written so that the receiving DTE *discards* the frame(s) in error and requests a retransmission of the frame(s) using a technique known as *automatic-repeat request* (or ARQ). There are a number of different ARQ algorithms used in backward-error recovery as illustrated by the following protocols.

Stop-and-wait A *stop-and-wait protocol* requires the transmitting entity to send one frame at a time and await a reply from the receiving entity. The reply is an *acknowledgement* indicating whether the frame has been correctly received.

If the frame is correctly received, the receiving entity responds with a *positive acknowledgement* (or *ACK*). The following *time sequence diagram* (Figure 6.19) illustrates the basic cycle of a stop-and-wait protocol (unless otherwise indicated, it is assumed that the frame the DTE is about to transmit contains a message).

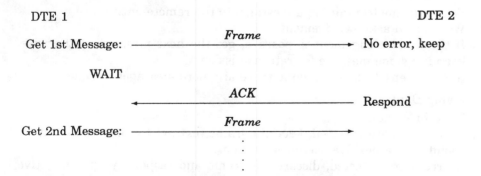

Figure 6.19   The basic cycle of a stop-and-wait protocol

In Figure 6.19, DTE 1 gets a message, transmits the message in a frame, and then waits for a reply from DTE 2. When DTE 2 receives the error-free message, an acknowledgement is returned. Upon receipt of the *ACK*, the transmitting entity (DTE 1) can discard the message just sent and get the next message for transmission.

However, if a frame is received incorrectly, the receiving entity (DTE 2) responds with a *negative acknowledgement* (or *NAK*), requiring the transmitting entity to *retransmit* the *original* frame. Once the frame is received correctly, transmission can continue with the subsequent frames (Figure 6.20).

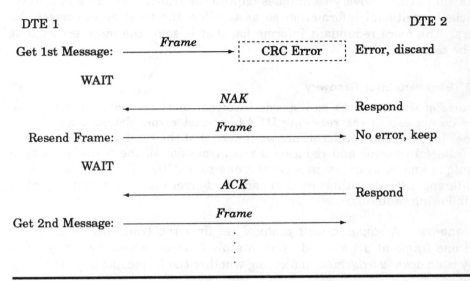

Figure 6.20   Error detection and correction in a stop-and-wait protocol

The transmit-frame and receive-acknowledgement (positive or negative) cycle continues until all messages have been sent (in frames) and acknowledged.

The algorithms for the stop-and-wait protocol can be written as follows:

- Transmitting data:
    1. Send a frame (containing a message) to the remote entity.
    2. Wait for an acknowledgement.
    3. If the acknowledgement is positive, get the next message. Otherwise, keep the same message for retransmission.
    4. Repeat steps 1, 2, and 3 while there are more messages to send.

- Receiving Data:
    1. Wait for a frame.
    2. If no errors are detected, keep the frame (extract the message) and respond with a positive acknowledgement.
    3. If errors are detected, discard the frame and respond with a negative acknowledgement.
    4. Repeat steps 1, 2, and 3 while there is more to be received.

The stop-and-wait protocol as described assumes that *all* frames and acknowledgements reach their intended destination. This could be a poor assumption since the flow of data may cease if a frame or an acknowledgement is lost (due to noise or a momentary loss of connection), leaving the transmitting entity waiting *indefinitely* for an acknowledgement. For example, if the acknowledgement (positive or negative) is lost, the transmitter of the original frame might wait forever, ceasing the flow of information (Figure 6.21).

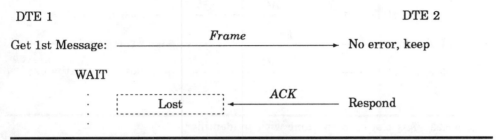

Figure 6.21   Information flow ceases if the ACK is lost

There are a number of ways in which the absence of an acknowledgement can be overcome to insure the continuing flow of frames. The most common means is to limit the amount of *time* the transmitting entity can wait for a response. That is, if a response isn't received within a specified time period, the transmitting entity simply retransmits the frame (Figure 6.22).

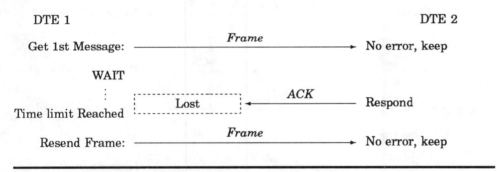

Figure 6.22   Using a time limit to detect the missing message

This solution, however, can lead to another problem: DTE 2 has now received a *second* copy of DTE 1's original frame (meaning that the same message has been received twice). The question arises: How can DTE 2 distinguish between frames that are retransmissions of previous ones and frames that are entirely new?

One possible solution is to have DTE 2 compare the contents of the previous frame (i.e., the message) with the one just received, if they are the same, the one just received can be discarded. This is not necessarily a good idea, since this ignores the possibility that two or more different messages may have the same value: such as a pair of blank lines in a file. An alternative is to have each frame associated with an identifier that allows the receiving DTE to distinguish between incoming frames. For example, the identifier could be an integer that is sent with the message as part of the frame and is unique to each frame (Figure 6.23).

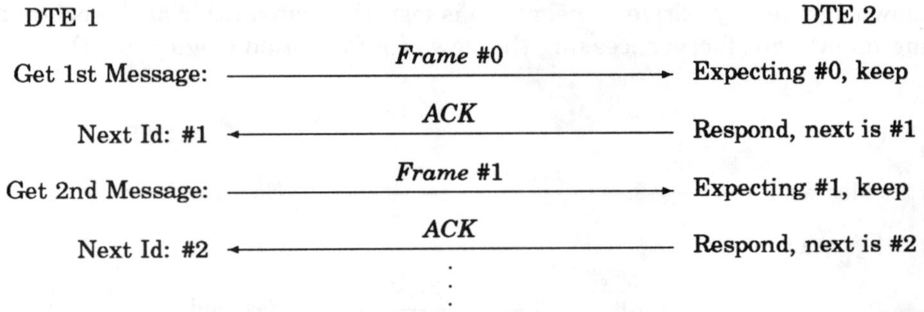

DTE 1   DTE 2

Get 1st Message: ——————— *Frame #0* ———————→ Expecting #0, keep

Next Id: #1 ←——————— *ACK* ——————— Respond, next is #1

Get 2nd Message: ——————— *Frame #1* ———————→ Expecting #1, keep

Next Id: #2 ←——————— *ACK* ——————— Respond, next is #2

Figure 6.23   Associating each frame with an identifier

The identifier is more commonly referred to as a *sequence number*.

Duplicate frames can be identified and rejected by having the receiving DTE examine the sequence number associated with each frame, for example, as in Figure 6.24.

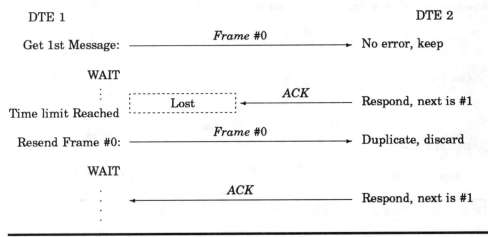

Figure 6.24   Recognizing a duplicate frame

In this example, DTE 1 sends frame #0 and waits for a reply. Since no reply is received before the time limit is reached, frame #0 is retransmitted. DTE 2 initially receives frame #0 and responds with an *ACK* since 0 is the expected sequence number; the expected sequence number is then increased to 1. When the next frame arrives with sequence number less than the expected sequence number, DTE 2 correctly assumes that the frame is a duplicate and discards it. The frame is a duplicate because the previous *ACK* was lost, meaning that DTE 2 must retransmit the acknowledgement.

Now, when a duplicate frame is received, the receiving DTE need only inspect the sequence number to determine whether the frame is new or a retransmission of the previous one. As before, when the transmitting DTE finally receives a positive acknowledgement, the next frame can be transmitted.

It may appear that each frame that is sent must have its own unique sequence number (for example, starting at 0 and proceeding to infinity). However, careful examination of the transmission-acknowledgement cycle reveals that at any particular moment, only a single frame requires an acknowledgement. This means that the stop-and-wait protocol needs, at most, *two* distinct sequence numbers: one for the frame about to be sent, and the other for the previous frame. By alternating between two sequence numbers (say, 0 and 1), the two DTEs can remain in-step and determine which frames are lost or are received in error. For an example see Figure 6.25.

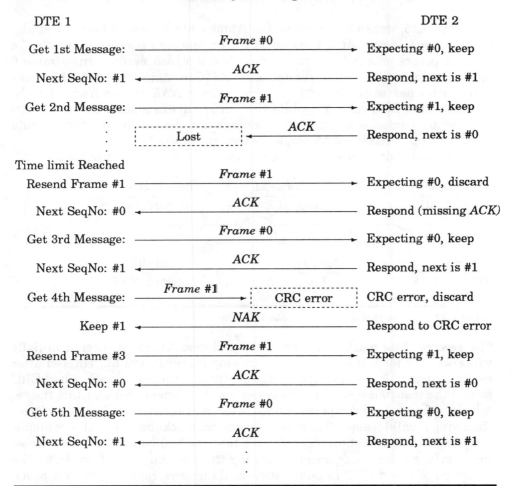

DTE 1		DTE 2
Get 1st Message:	——— *Frame #0* ———→	Expecting #0, keep
Next SeqNo: #1	←——— *ACK* ———	Respond, next is #1
Get 2nd Message:	——— *Frame #1* ———→	Expecting #1, keep
	Lost ←——— *ACK* ———	Respond, next is #0
Time limit Reached		
Resend Frame #1	——— *Frame #1* ———→	Expecting #0, discard
Next SeqNo: #0	←——— *ACK* ———	Respond (missing *ACK*)
Get 3rd Message:	——— *Frame #0* ———→	Expecting #0, keep
Next SeqNo: #1	←——— *ACK* ———	Respond, next is #1
Get 4th Message:	——— *Frame #1* ——→ CRC error	CRC error, discard
Keep #1	←——— *NAK* ———	Respond to CRC error
Resend Frame #3	——— *Frame #1* ———→	Expecting #1, keep
Next SeqNo: #0	←——— *ACK* ———	Respond, next is #0
Get 5th Message:	——— *Frame #0* ———→	Expecting #0, keep
Next SeqNo: #1	←——— *ACK* ———	Respond, next is #1

Figure 6.25   An example of the stop-and-wait protocol

The receiving DTE must maintain state information regarding the frame it is *about* to receive (i.e., the expected sequence number). Furthermore, both DTEs must agree to a common starting sequence number (typically 0).

A complete stop-and-wait transmission state machine can be represented as in Figure 6.26 (the first frame is sent with sequence number 0 and enters state **T2**):

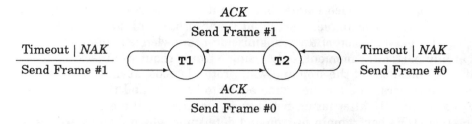

Figure 6.26   Stop-and-wait transmission state machine

In Figure 6.26, state **T2** is entered after frame 0 has been sent (either initially or after receiving an *ACK* in state **T1**). The machine stays in state **T2** if a timeout occurs or a *NAK* is received; either of which events cause frame 0 to be retransmitted. Upon receipt of an *ACK* in state **T2**, frame 1 is sent and control passes to state **T1**. A Timeout or a *NAK* causes frame 1 to be retransmitted from state **T1**, while an *ACK* results in a state change (to **T2**) and the transmission of frame 0. Although not shown, the machine should terminate upon receipt of an acknowledgement of the last frame.

A stop-and-wait receive state machine can be represented as in Figure 6.27.

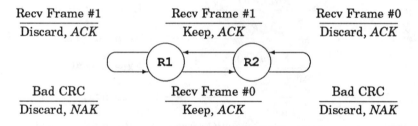

Figure 6.27   Stop-and-wait receive state machine

The receive state machine consists of two states: **R1**, to be entered initially while waiting for frame 0, or after receiving frame 1; and **R2**, entered after receiving frame 0. In both states, the reception of a frame with a bad CRC causes the transmission of a negative acknowledgement (*NAK*), while the receipt of a frame causes a positive acknowledgement (*ACK*) to be transmitted. Receiving a valid frame after it has already been acknowledged (for example, receiving frame 1 in state $R1$) indicates that the transmitter did not receive the previous acknowledgement, requiring the transmission of an *ACK*. The reception of a bad CRC in either state could be a retransmission of a previous frame (if the last *ACK* was not received), or it could be the transmission of a new frame. For example, in state **R2**, if frame 0 is received with an invalid CRC, the last *ACK* was not received and the retransmission was in error. If frame 1 is received with a bad CRC in state **R2** it means that the last frame was correctly acknowledged, but frame 1 was damaged during its transmission. In either event, the reponse is a *NAK*.

Interestingly enough, the stop-and-wait protocol does not require the negative acknowledgement: if the DTE receives a frame with a CRC error, there is no need to respond since the transmitter will eventually timeout and retransmit the same frame again. The advantage of using the negative acknowledgement is that throughput can be increased because a frame with a bad CRC is retransmitted as soon as the transmitting DTE receives the *NAK*.

Go-back-N   A closer examination of the stop-and-wait protocol reveals that it is essentially a half-duplex protocol. For example, after the transmitting entity sends a frame, the channel is turned around to allow the receiving entity the opportunity to respond with an acknowledgement. If the connection between the two entities is full-duplex, then using the channel in a half-duplex fashion is both a waste of time and bandwidth. The question now is: How can a full-duplex communication channel be used to increase throughput?

One potential way of increasing throughput is to allow the transmitting DTE to send a number of frames while simultaneously receiving responses. Figure 6.28 is an example of a possible scenario (the channel is assumed to be full-duplex since frames and acknowledgements are transmitted simultaneously; the X indicates simultaneous transmission and reception of frames and acknowledgements).

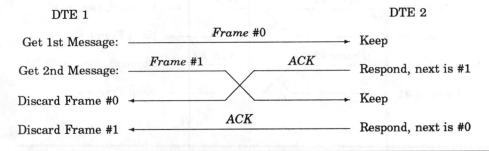

Figure 6.28   Simultaneous transmission of frames and *ACK*s

In this example, DTE 1 discards frame #0 upon receipt of the first acknowledgement and frame #1 upon receipt of the second acknowledgement. This approach will work correctly as long as no frames are lost, as Figure 6.29 illustrates.

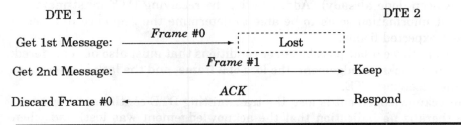

Figure 6.29   The *ACK* signals DTE 1 to discard the lost frame

In Figure 6.29, DTE 1 receives an acknowledgement and proceeds to discard frame 0: something that shouldn't happen because frame 0 is lost and never reaches DTE 2; and the acknowledgement that DTE 1 receives is for frame 1. What is needed is a mechanism whereby the acknowledgement can indicate the specific frame being acknowledged, rather than using a single acknowledgement for all frames.

A commonly adopted solution is to append an identifier to the acknowledgement (in much the same way the identifier is appended to the frame). The identifier indicates the sequence number of the *next* frame that the receiving DTE expects to receive. This is analogous to sending letters to someone, then telephoning and asking which letters they have received: the person might reply that they had received the first and second letters but are still awaiting the third; or if no letters had been received, the response might be that they were still waiting for the first letter. In the case of the transmitting DTEs, a typical transmission scenario could be as shown in Figure 6.30 (note that the acknowledgements indicate the sequence number of the *next* expected frame).

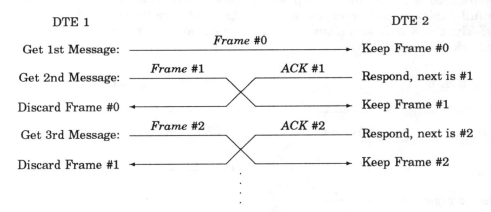

Figure 6.30   Adding a sequence number to the *ACK*

Upon receipt of an acknowledgement, the transmitting DTE can discard those frames with sequence numbers up to, but not including, the sequence number sent with the acknowledgement, since the acknowledgement is indicating the *next* frame expected by the receiver. For example, if an acknowledgement with sequence number 3 is received, frames 0, 1, and 2 can be discarded (if this has not been done already). Additionally, the receiving DTE must maintain sufficient information so as to be able to determine the sequence number of the next expected frame.

There are three other possible error conditions that must also be considered: the loss of an acknowledgement, the loss of a frame, and the lack of a response from the receiving DTE.

If an acknowledgement is lost, the transmitting DTE continues to transmit (since there is no indication that the acknowledgement was lost) and when the next acknowledgement is received, the transmitting DTE can determine which frames are to be discarded. (See Figure 6.31.)

In Figure 6.31, the acknowledgement for frame #0 (*ACK* #1) is lost but DTE 1 continues to transmit frames. Upon receiving *ACK* #2, DTE 1 can dispose

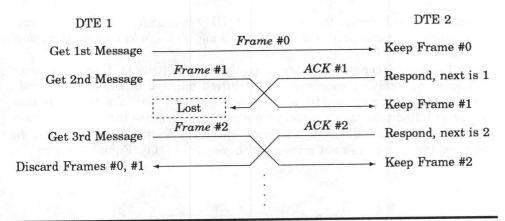

Figure 6.31   An acknowledgement sequence number includes all previous sequence numbers

of both frame 0 and 1 because the acknowledgement indicates that *all* frames with sequence numbers less than 2 have been accepted.

The second error condition that must be considered is how to handle the loss of a frame. If a DTE receives a frame with an invalid or out-of-sequence sequence number, the receiving DTE should respond with an indication that the sequence number is invalid, thereby permitting the transmitting DTE to restart its transmission with the correct frame. The transmitting DTE should resume with the frame that the receiving DTE expects next.

By replying with a negative acknowledgement (and the sequence number of the next expected frame), the transmitting DTE can distinguish between a normal acknowledgement and an error condition, as well as having the sequence number of the frame where retransmission is to resume. In Figure 6.32, frame 0 is lost, causing the receiving DTE to respond with a request for frame 0.

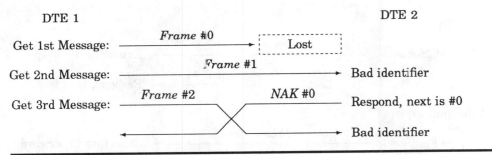

Figure 6.32   The retransmission of a lost frame

The negative acknowledgement received by the transmitting DTE indicates that the receiving DTE is still expecting frame 0, even though frames 0, 1, and 2 have been sent. Since the transmitting DTE has no indication as to which frames have been received correctly and which are in error, the worst is assumed and transmission resumes from the specified frame (in this case, frame 0).

Protocols which expect the transmitting DTE to retransmit all frames from the sequence number indicated by the receiving DTE are known as *go-back-N* protocols.

The third error condition occurs when the transmitting DTE sends a frame and does not receive a response. The solution adopted in the stop-and-wait protocol can also be applied to the go-back-N protocol: each frame that is sent must be replied to within a certain time period, otherwise the frame is again sent. There are two different scenarios where the frame loss may occur. In the first, the frame does not arrive at the receiving DTE (Figure 6.33).

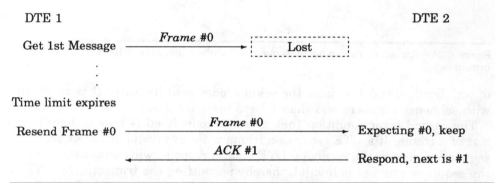

Figure 6.33   Using a timeout to retransmit a lost frame

The second scenario occurs when the frame has arrived and is acknowledged by the receiving DTE, but the acknowledgement is not received. In this situation, when the time limit expires, the frame is retransmitted but discarded by the receiving DTE. The receiving DTE responds with an acknowledgement indicating the next expected sequence number (Figure 6.34).

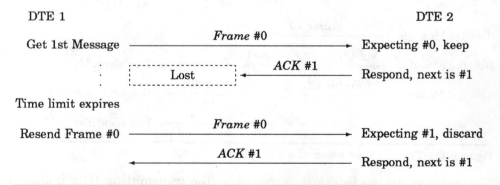

Figure 6.34   Acknowledging (and discarding) a duplicate frame

To avoid unnecessary retransmissions, the timer associated with the acknowledged frame is turned off as soon as the correct acknowledgement is received. Should several frames be waiting for acknowledgements and the incoming acknowledgement indicates that all of the frames have been accepted, each timer must be turned off and each frame discarded.

One of the arguments for the go-back-N protocol is that it can be implemented on a full-duplex channel, thereby increasing channel throughput. However, there are two competing objectives which must be considered when increasing channel throughput:

1. The transmitting DTE should be operated in such a way so it keeps the channel "full."

2. The acknowledgements must be returned at regular intervals in order to minimize the amount of retransmitting required should one of the previous frames be received in error.

In the stop-and-wait protocol, two sequence numbers are needed (one for the previous frame and one for the current frame). The quantity of sequence numbers required in a go-back-N protocol is not so readily apparent. If only two sequence numbers are used (as in stop-and-wait), then the number of frames that the transmitting DTE can send without receiving an acknowledgement is one, Figure 6.35 illustrates.

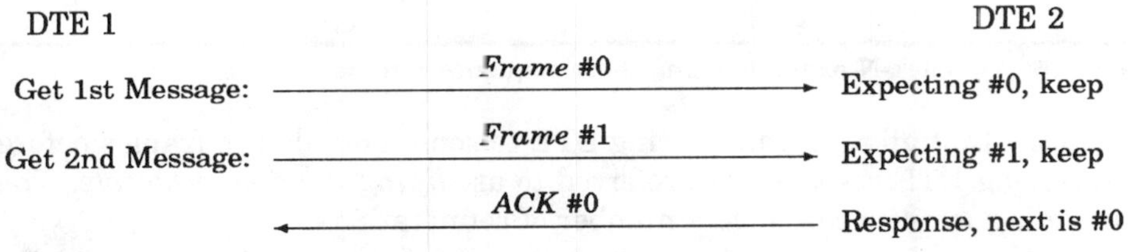

DTE 1   DTE 2

Get 1st Message: ──────────── *Frame* #0 ────────────▶ Expecting #0, keep

Get 2nd Message: ──────────── *Frame* #1 ────────────▶ Expecting #1, keep

◀──────────── ACK #0 ──────────── Response, next is #0

Figure 6.35   A problem with sequence numbers

The receipt of *ACK* #0 (by DTE 1) can mean *either*:

1. Two frames were received (0 and 1), and DTE 2 is expecting a third frame (sent with sequence number 0), *or*

2. DTE 2 is still expecting the first frame (that is, frame 0 was lost), meaning that both frames must be retransmitted.

Since it is necessary for protocols to be well defined and unambiguous, then the number of unacknowledged frames must be less than the total number of possible sequence numbers (otherwise problems such as those just described can occur). In short, if there are N sequence numbers available, then at most $N - 1$ frames can be unacknowledged.

Consider, for example, a protocol that supports 3 sequence numbers (0, 1, and 2). The transmitting DTE must wait for an acknowledgement after sending two frames (each with a unique sequence number). Upon receipt of the acknowledgement, further frames may be transmitted (or retransmitted if a negative acknowledgement is received). Figure 6.36 illustrates a typical frame/acknowledgement cycle ("Next pair" denotes the next pair of sequence numbers that DTE 2 is expecting).

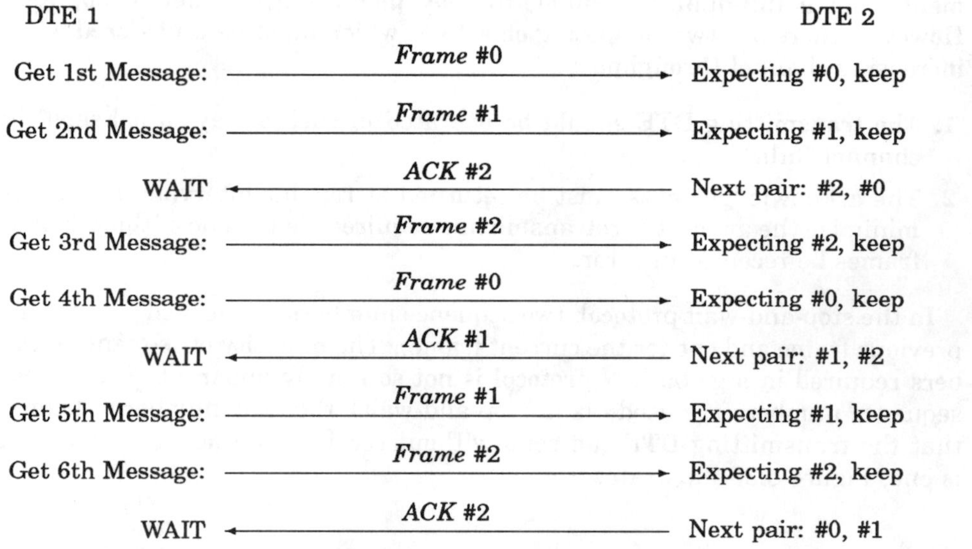

DTE 1   DTE 2

Get 1st Message: ──────── *Frame #0* ────────▶ Expecting #0, keep

Get 2nd Message: ──────── *Frame #1* ────────▶ Expecting #1, keep

WAIT ◀──────── *ACK #2* ──────── Next pair: #2, #0

Get 3rd Message: ──────── *Frame #2* ────────▶ Expecting #2, keep

Get 4th Message: ──────── *Frame #0* ────────▶ Expecting #0, keep

WAIT ◀──────── *ACK #1* ──────── Next pair: #1, #2

Get 5th Message: ──────── *Frame #1* ────────▶ Expecting #1, keep

Get 6th Message: ──────── *Frame #2* ────────▶ Expecting #2, keep

WAIT ◀──────── *ACK #2* ──────── Next pair: #0, #1

Figure 6.36   Go-back-N example using three sequence numbers

Protocols that allow a transmitting DTE to send a number of frames before the receiving DTE responds are referred to as *sliding window protocols*. The term sliding window can have a number of connotations:

- as each message is sent, the *transmission window* is decreased in size by one; transmissions continue until the window has a size of zero, at which point transmissions cease. Whenever an acknowledgement is received, the transmission window is opened (the exact amount depends upon the value returned by the receiver); transmissions can resume, decreasing the window size.

  In Figure 6.36, DTE 1 can send two frames before waiting for a reply, it therefore has a transmission window of size 2. Each acknowledgement received indicates that the two messages sent were received correctly, therefore fully opening the transmission window.

- the window "slides" forward, indicating the sequence numbers to be used for the next set of message(s) to be sent. In the preceding example, three sequence numbers exist (0, 1, and 2); since they are always being re-used, the list of available sequence numbers can be considered as a long repeating sequence of the same three values:

$$0\ 1\ 2\ 0\ 1\ 2\ 0\ 1\ 2\ \dots$$

At any moment, two of the sequence numbers can be in use; as acknowledgements are received, the window slides over the next set of possible sequence numbers. For example, after the initial transmission, the window sits over 0 and 1:

$$\boxed{0 \quad 1} \quad 2 \quad 0 \quad 1 \quad 2 \quad 0 \quad 1 \quad 2 \quad \dots$$

After the first acknowledgment, the window slides over the next two sequence numbers:

$$0 \quad 1 \quad \boxed{2 \quad 0} \quad 1 \quad 2 \quad 0 \quad 1 \quad 2 \quad \dots$$

The number of frames that can be sent without being acknowledged is known as the *window size*. Initially, the transmission window is set to the value of the window size. As each frame is sent, the transmission window is decreased until it reaches zero (i.e., the window is closed), at which point no further frames can be sent. In the last example shown, the window size is two.

To maximize throughput, the transmission window should never be allowed to close, which means that the receiving DTE must respond with sufficient acknowledgements to insure an uninterrupted flow of frames. This can be achieved in a couple of ways: every frame can be acknowledged, or the window size can be made large enough to require fewer acknowledgements. For example, with four possible sequence numbers, the receiving DTE could respond after every third frame (Figure 6.37).

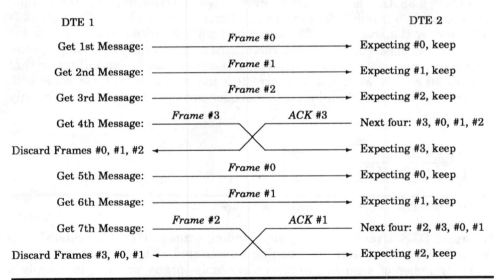

Figure 6.37   Four sequence numbers; DTE 2 responds every three frames

Similarly, the receiving DTE can impose *flow control* onto the transmitting DTE by restricting the rate at which frames are acknowledged (in the most extreme case, if the receiving DTE does not respond at all, the transmitting DTE is forced to retransmit all pending frames as their timers expire). For example, given a window size of two, the receiving DTE could turn the go-back-N protocol into a stop-and-wait protocol (assume three sequence numbers). (See Figure 6.38).

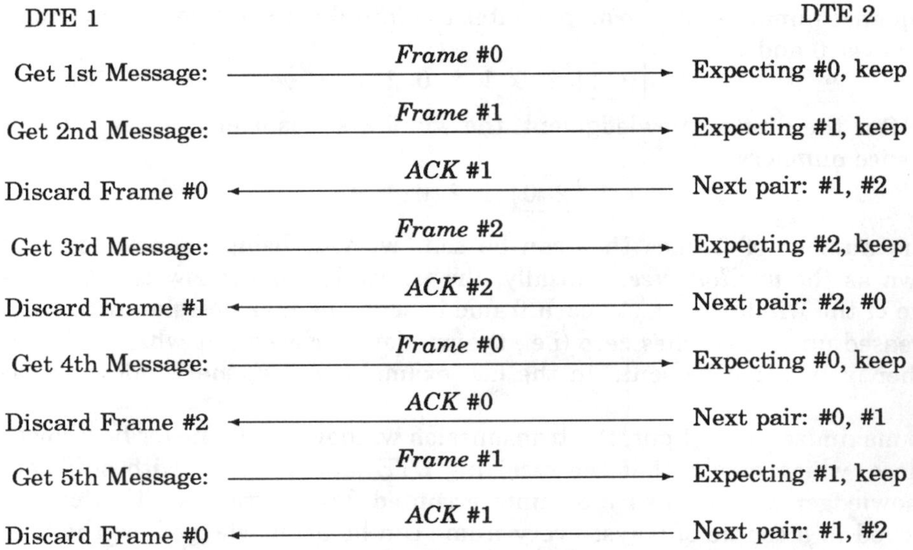

DTE 1   DTE 2

Get 1st Message: ————————— *Frame #0* —————————→ Expecting #0, keep

Get 2nd Message: ————————— *Frame #1* —————————→ Expecting #1, keep

Discard Frame #0 ←———————— *ACK #1* ————————— Next pair: #1, #2

Get 3rd Message: ————————— *Frame #2* —————————→ Expecting #2, keep

Discard Frame #1 ←———————— *ACK #2* ————————— Next pair: #2, #0

Get 4th Message: ————————— *Frame #0* —————————→ Expecting #0, keep

Discard Frame #2 ←———————— *ACK #0* ————————— Next pair: #0, #1

Get 5th Message: ————————— *Frame #1* —————————→ Expecting #1, keep

Discard Frame #0 ←———————— *ACK #1* ————————— Next pair: #1, #2

Figure 6.38 Go-back-N implementation of stop-and-wait

In Figure 6.38, the receiving DTE never allows the transmitting DTE to send more than one frame before the transmission window closes. This effect is achieved by the receiving DTE responding with an acknowledgement to the previous (as opposed to the most recent) frame received. For example, after receiving frames #0 and #1, instead of responding with #2 (an indication that frames #0 and #1 were received correctly), the receiving DTE responds with #1, thereby allowing the window to move forward one sequence number only (Figure 6.39).

0 1	2	Initial window setup	
0	1 2	After *ACK* #1	

Figure 6.39 The transmission window of Figure 6.38

To avoid DTE 1 retransmitting any pending frames, DTE 2's acknowledgements must arrive before the time limits associated with each message expire.

The number of sequence numbers available in any protocol is usually a power of two (if the sequence number is sent as a binary number) and depends upon the protocol. Most protocols vary the number of possible sequence numbers from 2 (a 1-bit sequence number, 2^1) to 8 (a 3-bit sequence number 2^3). In situations where there may be long transmission delays, up to 128 sequence numbers can be specified (a 7-bit sequence number, 2^7).

Until now, data transfer has been half-duplex; that is, one DTE has been transmitting frames and the other has been receiving them. Should both DTEs have information to exchange, the data transfer methods examined thus far force one station to wait until the other has completed its transfer.

Since the communication channel is full-duplex, it would appear that at the channel level, at least. There is no reason why information could not be sent in both directions simultaneously using a *bidirectional data transfer*.

To accomplish this transfer, the change required to the go-back-N protocol is actually quite simple: acknowledgements must be sent with the frames using a technique known as *piggybacking*. When piggybacking acknowledgements, each frame is sent with its own sequence number *and* the sequence number of the next expected frame to be sent by the destination DTE. The frame's sequence number is referred to as *Ns* (the *send count*), while the next expected sequence number is referred to as *Nr* (the *receive count*). The frame still carries a message.

When a DTE receives a frame, it must check the values of Ns and Nr:

Ns. The DTE maintains an incoming frame counter that contains the value of the next expected frame sequence number. If the incoming frame counter is equal to the value of Ns, the frame is accepted and the frame counter is incremented. However, if the values of the incoming frame counter and Ns are not equal, the frame is discarded.

Nr. The value of Nr is an acknowledgement, informing the local DTE of the frames that have been accepted by the remote DTE. A value of *N* acknowledges all frames up to frame *N − 1*; the acknowledged frames can be discarded by the local DTE.

A possible exchange between two DTEs performing a bidirectional transfer could appear as in Figure 6.40. (Note, the format of a frame is *Frame(Ns,Nr)*, "Dis" means discard the specified frame numbers, and "Keep" means the frame is to be kept.)

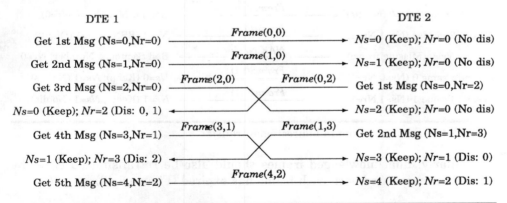

Figure 6.40 Go-back-N bidirectional transfer

If a station does not have information to send but has a frame to acknowledge, the station responds with an acknowledgement rather than a frame. The acknowledgement contains the value of the station's next expected sequence number (i.e., Nr). For example, if DTE 2 in Figure 6.40 only had one frame to transmit, the following sequence of frames might have transpired (Figure 6.41).

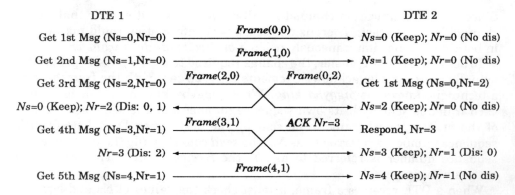

DTE 1   DTE 2

Get 1st Msg (Ns=0,Nr=0) ——————*Frame(0,0)*——————▶ Ns=0 (Keep); Nr=0 (No dis)

Get 2nd Msg (Ns=1,Nr=0) ——————*Frame(1,0)*——————▶ Ns=1 (Keep); Nr=0 (No dis)

Get 3rd Msg (Ns=2,Nr=0) ——*Frame(2,0)*——×——*Frame(0,2)*—— Get 1st Msg (Ns=0,Nr=2)

Ns=0 (Keep); Nr=2 (Dis: 0, 1) ◀   ▶ Ns=2 (Keep); Nr=0 (No dis)

Get 4th Msg (Ns=3,Nr=1) ——*Frame(3,1)*——×——*ACK Nr=3*—— Respond, Nr=3

Nr=3 (Dis: 2) ◀   ▶ Ns=3 (Keep); Nr=1 (Dis: 0)

Get 5th Msg (Ns=4,Nr=1) ——————*Frame(4,1)*——————▶ Ns=4 (Keep); Nr=1 (No dis)

Figure 6.41   Bidirectional transfer with acknowledgements

Note that in the go-back-N protocol, only frames are acknowledged, acknowledgements are not.

If a frame is lost or received in error, the same rules apply in a bidirectional transfer as in a unidirectional half-duplex transfer: the receiving DTE must inform the transmitting DTE of the error with a *NAK*; or if frames were not received, the transmitting DTE should timeout and retransmit the frames not yet acknowledged. For example, a frame received out of sequence, due to the loss of a previous one, should result in a negative acknowledgement (Figure 6.42). (Note, BSN indicates that a bad sequence number was detected.)

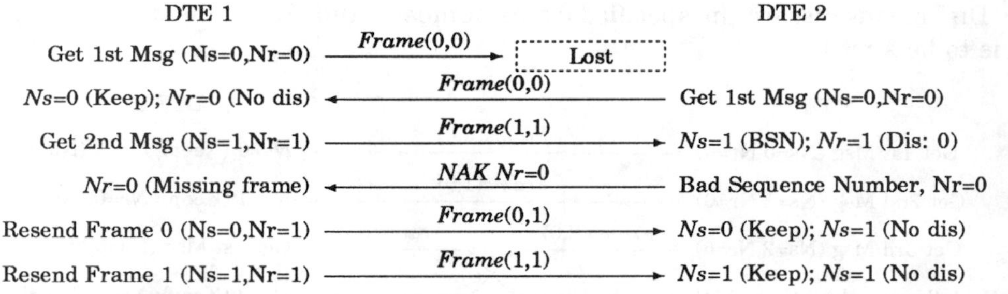

DTE 1   DTE 2

Get 1st Msg (Ns=0,Nr=0) ——*Frame(0,0)*——▶ ⌐ ‾ ‾ ‾ ‾ ⌐ Lost ⌐

Ns=0 (Keep); Nr=0 (No dis) ◀——*Frame(0,0)*—— Get 1st Msg (Ns=0,Nr=0)

Get 2nd Msg (Ns=1,Nr=1) ——*Frame(1,1)*——▶ Ns=1 (BSN); Nr=1 (Dis: 0)

Nr=0 (Missing frame) ◀——*NAK Nr=0*—— Bad Sequence Number, Nr=0

Resend Frame 0 (Ns=0,Nr=1) ——*Frame(0,1)*——▶ Ns=0 (Keep); Ns=1 (No dis)

Resend Frame 1 (Ns=1,Nr=1) ——*Frame(1,1)*——▶ Ns=1 (Keep); Ns=1 (No dis)

Figure 6.42   Error handling in bidirectional transfer

Similarly, unacknowledged frames should also be retransmitted once the time limit associated with each frame has expired (Figure 6.43).

Selective retransmission   The go-back-N protocol offers considerably more flexibility and throughput than the stop-and-wait protocol. However, go-back-N has a problem in that when a frame is received out of sequence or in error, all frames subsequently received are discarded until the frame with the correct sequence number is retransmitted. Consider the situation given in Figure 6.44, where frames 2 and 3 are retransmitted, even though only frame 1 was in error. Ideally, only those frames received in error should be retransmitted, thereby avoiding unnecessary retransmissions.

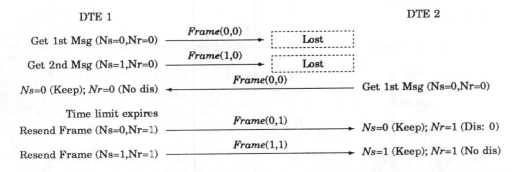

Figure 6.43 Frame timeout in a bidirectional transfer

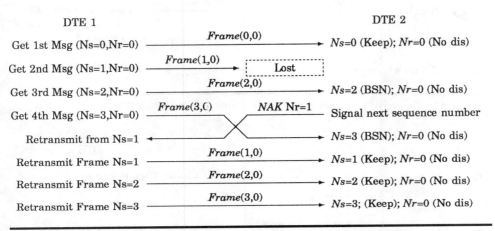

Figure 6.44 A go-back-N limitation: the retransmission of valid frames

Selective retransmission is a technique whereby only those frames that are not received correctly (or have apparently not been received) are retransmitted. Selective retransmission is achieved by the receiving DTE explicitly acknowledging each frame as it is received. A missing frame will not be acknowledged, causing the transmitting DTE to eventually retransmit the unacknowledged frame (either by detecting the missing acknowledgement or by the time limit associated with the frame expiring). (See Figure 6.45.)

The time it takes to recover from the loss of a frame depends upon the time limit associated with each frame. This delay can be reduced by having the receiving DTE transmit a *NAK* that explicitly identifies the missing frame. In Figure 6.45, DTE 2 can transmit a *NAK* #1 as soon as frame #1 is determined to be missing (i.e., after frame 2 is received). Upon receipt of the *NAK*, DTE 1 can retransmit frame #1.

The loss of an acknowledgement can lead to some interesting problems if there are a limited number of sequence numbers. For example, consider the situation in which two sequence numbers are used to represent the frames that are sent (Figure 6.46). When DTE 2 receives the retransmitted frames 0 and 1, there is no indication that these are retransmissions, with the re-

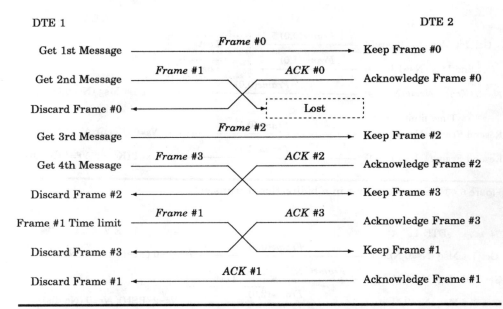

Figure 6.45 Selective retransmission: only frame 1 is retransmitted

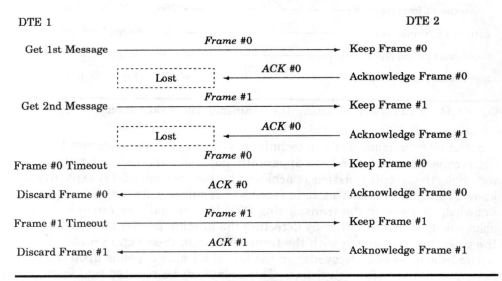

Figure 6.46 Sequence numbering problems with go-back-N

sult that DTE 2 will keep *two* copies of frames 0 and 1. The concept of a transmission window that slides as each acknowledgement is received will not work for selective retransmission. For example, by using three sequence numbers (0, 1, and 2), and requiring the transmitting DTE to have at most two frames waiting for acknowledgement and sliding the window forward as acknowledgements are received, fails if frames 0 and 1 are transmitted and an acknowledgement is received for frame 1 only. If the transmitting DTE sends frame 2 and retransmits frame 0, the receiving DTE once again has no indication that frame 0 is a retransmission.

A number of different solutions to this problem exist. For example, using a form of sliding window that moves the window forward only when the "oldest" frame has been acknowledged will overcome the problem.

Although selective retransmission may appear to offer numerous advantages, it is not widely used. The main problem with selective retransmission is the storage overhead required by the receiving DTE for holding frames while waiting for any intermediate missing frames.

6.5 SYNCHRONOUS PROTOCOLS

Broadly speaking, synchronous protocols are divided into two categories: *byte-oriented* and *bit-oriented* protocols.

6.5.1 Byte-oriented Synchronous Protocols

Byte-oriented synchronous protocols are those that use the control characters found in character codes (such as ASCII or EBCDIC) to delimit frames and support other aspects of the protocol. Although there are numerous byte-oriented protocols in existence, the following is a brief introduction to the grandparent of them all: IBM's early (and highly successful) Binary Synchronous Communications Protocol, also known as Bisync or BSC, (so named because it allows the synchronous transmission of binary data). Bisync was designed around the EBCDIC character set although ASCII implementations do exist.

The Bisync protocol is intended for batch processing in which users submit their "jobs" to a *remote job entry* (RJE) station, typically a punch-card reader and a line printer. The job, consisting of a deck of punch cards is read and transmitted to the central host for processing. Once the processing has finished, the output is *spooled* to disk and when the opportunity arises, sent to the user's RJE for printing.

Bisync is a stop-and-wait protocol that allows data transfer between pairs of *stations*. Bisync has a window size of one (i.e., there can be at most one pending data frame) and two sequence numbers (0 and 1). Each data frame is associated with a sequence number: the frames transmitted first, third, fifth, and so on, with sequence number 1; and frames transmitted second, fourth, sixth, and so on, with sequence number 0. Data frames do not carry the sequence numbers; instead, sequence numbers are returned with acknowledgement frames. Acknowledgement frames are transmitted as two characters (note that the sequences are different for ASCII and EBCDIC.) (See Table 6.1).

Whenever a data frame is received correctly, the receiving station changes the acknowledgement (from 0 to 1 or vice versa) and responds with the acknowledgement. Once a data frame has been properly acknowledged, the transmitting station changes the expected acknowledgement (from 0 to 1 or vice versa).

A typical transmission is given in Figure 6.47.

TABLE 6.1   Bisync Acknowledgement Sequences

Acknowledgement	EBCDIC	ASCII
ACK 0	DLE 0x70	DLE 0
ACK 1	DLE /	DLE 1

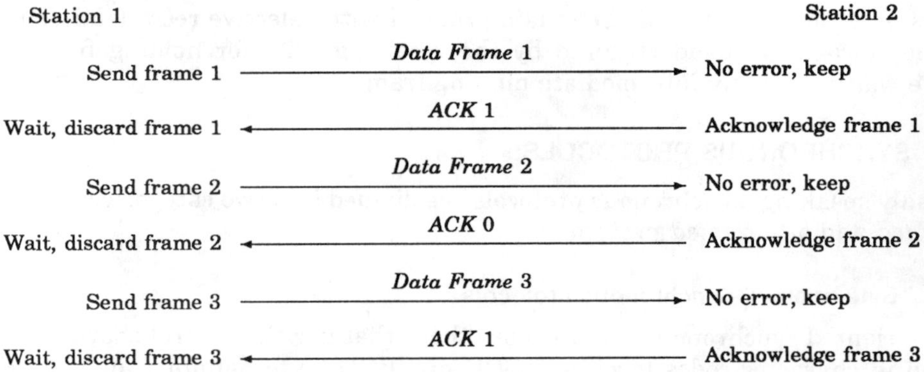

Station 1   Station 2

Send frame 1 ——————— *Data Frame 1* ———————→ No error, keep

Wait, discard frame 1 ←——————— ACK 1 ——————— Acknowledge frame 1

Send frame 2 ——————— *Data Frame 2* ———————→ No error, keep

Wait, discard frame 2 ←——————— ACK 0 ——————— Acknowledge frame 2

Send frame 3 ——————— *Data Frame 3* ———————→ No error, keep

Wait, discard frame 3 ←——————— ACK 1 ——————— Acknowledge frame 3

Figure 6.47   A typical, error-free Bisync sequence

Data frames received in error are negatively acknowledged (using a *NAK*). The transmitting station is expected to retransmit the frame, while the receiving station is to reply with the correct acknowledgement. In Figure 6.48, assume that the acknowledgement for frame N is *ACK* 1.

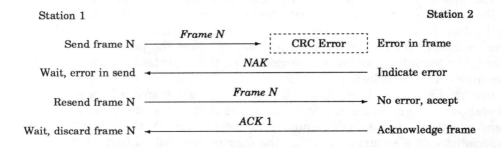

Station 1   Station 2

Send frame N ——— *Frame N* ——→ CRC Error   Error in frame

Wait, error in send ←——————— *NAK* ——————— Indicate error

Resend frame N ——————— *Frame N* ———————→ No error, accept

Wait, discard frame N ←——————— ACK 1 ——————— Acknowledge frame

Figure 6.48   Frame retransmission due to CRC error detection

If a frame is not acknowledged (i.e., the receiving station never receives the frame or the acknowledgement is lost) within 2 seconds, the transmitting station must poll the receiving station to determine the value of the last acknowledgement sent. Polling takes place using the *ENQ* (enquire) control character. There are four possible outcomes of the poll:

The correct acknowledgement is received. The frame was received correctly by the receiving station, but the acknowledgement was lost. The next frame can be transmitted at this point (assume that frame N is to be acknowledged with *ACK* 0). (See Figure 6.49.)

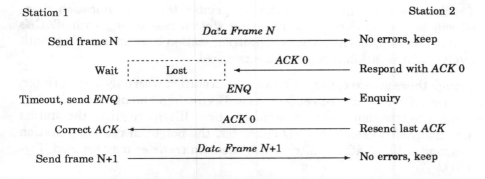

Figure 6.49   Correct acknowledgement signals transmission of next frame

The wrong acknowledgement is received. The receiving station never received the data frame and is still responding with the acknowledgement of the *last* correctly received frame. The transmitting station must retransmit the last data frame (Figure 6.50).

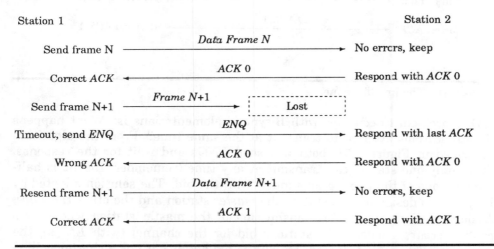

Figure 6.50   Last acknowledgement signals retransmission of current frame

The receiving station never responds. It is possible that the receiving station could be momentarily off-line or simply too busy to respond to the poll. To accommodate situations such as these, the transmitting station will wait for 3 seconds and poll again. If, after three such cycles, no response is obtained, the transmitting station aborts the transmission. There are a number of variations and exceptions to the time and the number of repeats the transmitting station performs. For example, in some installations the number of polls can be greater to accomodate transmission delays; or the time between polls can be increased.

Other responses. There are other responses allowed by Bisync. For example, should the receiving station be unable to accept more data frames because of such problems as no paper in the line printer, the communication channel can be kept active by the receiving station responding with *WACK*s (wait acknowledgement). The transmitting station continues polling (with *ENQ*s) until an acknowledgement is received.

Although there are exceptions (for example, a station with only a line printer, or a station with only a card reader), most Bisync implementations allow either station to transmit and receive information. Bisync requires the station about to transmit to send an *ENQ* character, the potential receiving station is to respond with an *ACK* 0, after which the data transfer may proceed (Figure 6.51).

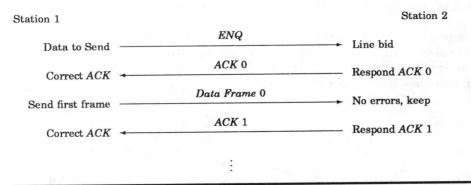

Station 1   Station 2

		ENQ		
Data to Send		———————————————→		Line bid
		ACK 0		
Correct *ACK*		←———————————————		Respond *ACK* 0
		Data Frame 0		
Send first frame		———————————————→		No errors, keep
		ACK 1		
Correct *ACK*		←———————————————		Respond *ACK* 1

$\vdots$

Figure 6.51   The line-bit sequence

One problem to consider with Bisync implementations is: What happens if both stations attempt to transmit at the same time? From the algorithm described in Figure 6.51, both will send *ENQ*s and wait for the response. Since only one station can transmit at any time (remember, Bisync is half-duplex), one of the two stations must "win" the bid. The solution adopted by Bisync is to designate one station the *master* station and the other the *slave*. A slave station must defer transmission to the master station whenever a conflict occurs. When both stations bid for the channel (with *ENQ*s), the master station is "guaranteed" to win the bid because it has a shorter polling wait period: 1 second for the master, as opposed to 3 seconds for the slave.

Once a station has finished transmitting, the receiving station is signaled with an end-of-transmission character or *EOT*. At this point, both stations return to the state where either can bid for the channel. *EOT* can also be used to abort a transmission. If the transmitting station sends an *EOT*, the receiving station the returns to the line-bidding state.

Although Bisync is half-duplex, there is a provision for forcing the transmitting station to give up the line, thereby allowing the receiving station to send a message. Either station, when receiving, can respond with an *RVI* or reverse interrupt, which is equivalent to an acknowledgement. Upon receipt of the *RVI*, the transmitting station sends one more block, waits for the acknowledgement and then sends an *EOT*. The receiving station can then bid for the line.

The Bisync frame Bisync, like any synchronous protocol, requires the use of framing information to allow a receiving DTE to distinguish between data and the idle channel. Bisync uses special control characters.

Start-of-frame is indicated by either of the following control characters:

SOH Start of Header, or

STX Start of TeXt.

End-of-frame is also a control character, represented by one of:

ITB Intermediate Transmission Block,

ETB End of Transmission Block, or

ETX End of TeXt.

ETB and *ETX* signal the receiving station that the line is to be turned-around for an acknowledgement. *ITB* on the other hand can be used to denote the end of a record; the *ITB* is followed by another record (typically, although not necessarily, starting with an *STX*). The number of *ITB* blocks allowed is implementation dependent; however, after a maximum of about four unacknowledged records, the fifth must be terminated by an *ETB* or an *ETX*. The *ETX* is a special case of *ETB*, indicating that no further frames will arrive (*ETX* is often used to signal that the end-of-file has been reached).

Frames consisting of *printable* bytes only (i.e., alphanumerics, carriage return, line feed, tab, and form feed) are known as *nontransparent* frames. (Note, unless otherwise indicated, all frames are sent from left-to-right; see Figure 6.52.)

$$\begin{bmatrix} SOH \\ STX \end{bmatrix} \cdots\cdots\cdots \text{Data} \cdots\cdots\cdot \begin{bmatrix} ITB \\ ETB \\ ETX \end{bmatrix}$$

Figure 6.52 The nontransparent frame format

A 16-bit cyclic redundancy check (CRC-16) is calculated on all the data bytes and is transmitted after the end-of-frame character. The CRC covers only the *data* from the start-of-frame character (*STX* or *SOH*) to the end-of-frame character (*ITB*, *ETB*, or *ETX*). A separate CRC is calculated for each frame, including *ITB* frames. The CRC associated with an *ETB* or *ETX* following a series of *ITB* blocks is generated only on the last block.

The Bisync protocol allows a limited number of control characters to be sent in nontransparent frames. This leads to another problem: how can messages, such as executable images or binary files, consisting of nonprintable control characters, be transmitted? For example (Figure 6.53), if part of a data stream consists of the control character *ETB*, the receiver cannot distinguish between the *ETB* indicating the end-of-message *ETB* and the data *ETB*; this means that the receiver will stop receiving after the first *ETB* (the *data ETB*!):

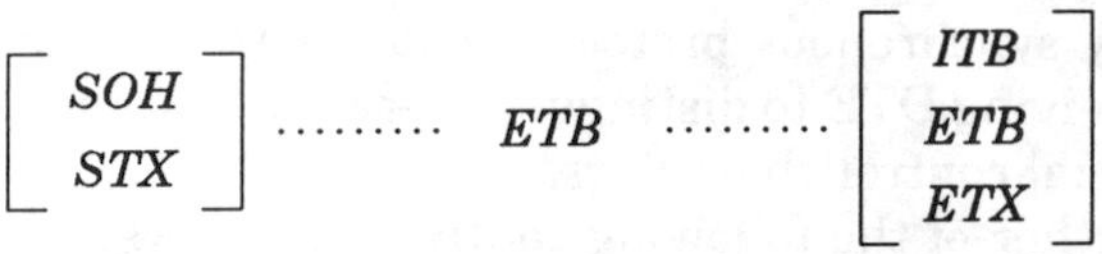

$$\begin{bmatrix} SOH \\ STX \end{bmatrix} \cdots\cdots\cdots \quad ETB \quad \cdots\cdots\cdots \begin{bmatrix} ITB \\ ETB \\ ETX \end{bmatrix}$$

Figure 6.53   Nontransparent data cannot include certain control characters

The solution to this problem is to have the transmitting DTE inform the receiving DTE that nonprintable characters are included in the transmission. A communication which permits the inclusion of control characters as data within the frame is known as a *transparent transmission*. A transparent transmission allows *any* byte to be transmitted as data. Control characters in a transparent frame are prefixed with the *DLE* character (Figure 6.54).

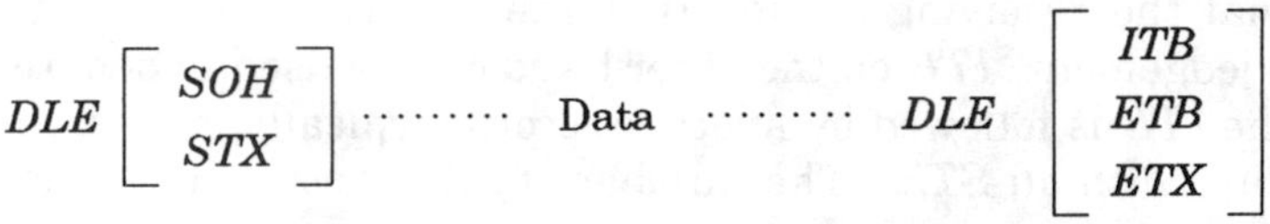

$$DLE \begin{bmatrix} SOH \\ STX \end{bmatrix} \cdots\cdots\cdots \quad Data \quad \cdots\cdots\cdots \quad DLE \begin{bmatrix} ITB \\ ETB \\ ETX \end{bmatrix}$$

Figure 6.54   The transparent frame format

Should an *ETB* or nearly any other control character be sent as data, it will accepted as data because it is *not* prefixed with a *DLE*.

Although prefixing framing control characters with *DLE* is intended to insure that *any* character can be sent as data, problems arise should a message contain a *DLE* followed by an end-of-frame character (i.e., one of *ITB*, *ETB*, or *ETX*). For example, the receiving DTE cannot distinguish between *DLE* followed by *ETX* sent as data or sent as an end-of-frame sequence (Figure 6.55).

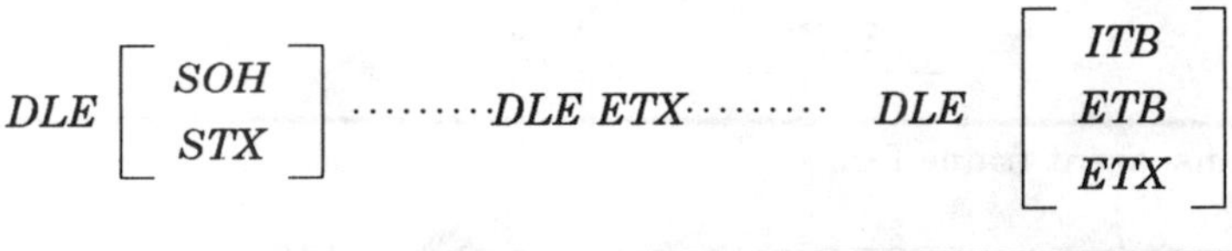

$$DLE \begin{bmatrix} SOH \\ STX \end{bmatrix} \cdots\cdots\cdots DLE\ ETX \cdots\cdots\cdots \quad DLE \begin{bmatrix} ITB \\ ETB \\ ETX \end{bmatrix}$$

Figure 6.55   A *DLE-ETX* data sequence cannot be sent in a frame

Since the *DLE* and the character that follows it are both data, neither can be left out of the transmission. The solution is to *prefix* any *DLE* found in a message with another *DLE*, then to transmit both *DLE*s (Figure 6.56).

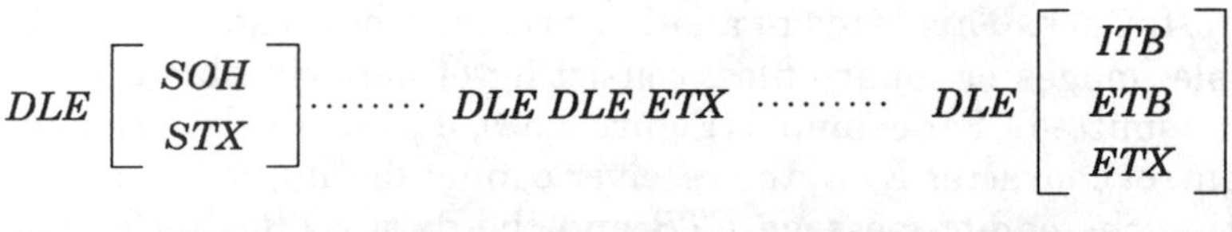

$$DLE \begin{bmatrix} SOH \\ STX \end{bmatrix} \cdots\cdots\cdots \quad DLE\ DLE\ ETX \quad \cdots\cdots\cdots \quad DLE \begin{bmatrix} ITB \\ ETB \\ ETX \end{bmatrix}$$

Figure 6.56   All data *DLE*s must be prefixed by *DLE*

When the receiving DTE receives a *DLE* in the data stream, the DTE enters a special state and waits for one of a *DLE* (taken as data) or a control character (typically signalling the end-of-frame).

Synchronization   Synchronization of Bisync DTEs is achieved through the use of a series of synchronization characters (*SYN*), prefixed to the start of every frame. The *SYN* characters synchronize the transmitting and receiving clocks, thereby allowing the transmission of "pure" data. *SYN* characters can be placed in a frame to insure that the receiver's clock maintains synchronization. There is yet another exception: If the frame is a transparent frame, the *SYN* character must be prefixed by a *DLE*.

6.5.2 Bit-oriented Synchronous Communications

Byte-oriented synchronous communications, such as those described for Bisync, although still in widespread use, suffer from a number of drawbacks, including:

- Two frame structures are required: one for transparent data and the other for nontransparent data. In fact, there are numerous exceptions when dealing with the two different frame structures, suggesting that Bisync is actually two protocols rather than one.

- There is an additional overhead in using a *DLE* to signal that the next byte should be treated as data, both in terms of processing (adding and removing the *DLE*) and throughput (the transmission of 16-bits of information to represent 8-bits).

Both of these problems can be overcome if *bit*-oriented rather than byte-oriented communications are used. A good example of a bit-oriented synchronous protocol is IBM's Synchronous Data Link Control (SDLC).

In SDLC, all frames containing information or acknowledgements have the same structure, notably:

Flag	Address	Control	Information	FCS	Flag

where:

Flag.   The **Flag** byte delimits the frame and is used to synchronize the two stations. Both the leading and trailing **Flag** bytes have the same pattern: 01111110. SDLC allows multiple frames to be sent with a single **Flag** byte separating each frame.

Address.   The **Address** field denotes the intended destination of the message (if the frame is sent by the *primary* station) or the address of the station sending the frame (if the frame is sent by the *secondary* station). The **Address** field is intended to allow several secondary stations to share a single communication channel, controlled by a single primary station through the use of polling.

Control. The Control field is 1-byte long and defines the function of the frame. A frame supports one of three formats, defining the frame's function, which are discussed in the following sections.

Information transfer format. The information transfer format Control field signals the receiving station that the frame is an *information frame*, and contains one or more bytes of data. The format of the information transfer Control field is as follows:

| 1 | Ns (3 bits) | P/F bit | Nr (3 bits) |

Ns is the send count, which is the sequence number of this information frame. Ns is applicable only to information frames. Nr is the receive count, indicating the sequence number of the next expected information frame from the station to which this frame is destined.

Supervisory format. The supervisory frame is intended to assist in the orderly flow of information frames between stations. The supervisory frame Control byte has the following format:

| 1 | 0 | Code (2 bits) | P/F bit | Nr (3 bits) |

Code is one of the following:

Ready-to-receive (00). Ready-to-receive or RR is an acknowledgement; it signals that the next expected frame is Nr.

Receive-not-ready (01). Receive-not-ready (RNR) is both an acknowledgement (the next expected frame is Nr) and an indication to the transmitting station that there is a temporary problem at the receiving station.

Reject (10). Reject (REJ) is a negative acknowledgement, requesting the transmitter to start transmission from frame Nr.

Nr is the receive count, indicating the sequence number of the next expected information frame.

Unnumbered format. Unnumbered frames are used to convey information specific to the function of the communication channel connecting the various stations. For example, the primary station can initialize secondary stations through the use of unnumbered frames and stations can report their status in an unnumbered frame. The format of an unnumbered Control frame field is as follows:

| 1 | 1 | Code (2 bits) | P/F bit | Code (3 bits) |

Code values include:

UI (unnumbered information). The frame contains data in the Information field.

DISC (disconnect). The primary station is disconnecting the secondary station specified in the Address field.

UA (unnumbered acknowledgement). An affirmative response to a command such as *DISC*.

The *P/F* (poll/final) bit is common to all `Control` field formats, its interpretation is given in Table 6.2.

TABLE 6.2

P/F bit	Transmitter	Interpretation
Set	Primary (to secondary)	Secondary is to start transmission.
Set	Secondary (to primary)	Secondary has finished transmission.
Clear	Either	A transmission is in progress.

`Information`.   The `Information` field contains data being sent from one station to another. If the frame is an unnumbered frame, the `Information` field may be present and carry information specific to the SDLC protocol, such as a test pattern or station identification data. Information frames carrying data for applications on the destination DTE use the `Information` field; there is no specified length of the `Information` field, but it must be a multiple of 8 bits. Supervisory frames do not have an `Information` field.

`FCS`.   The `FCS` is the Frame Check Sequence (another term for CRC). The `FCS` is calculated using CRC-CCITT and covers the entire frame, excluding the `Flag` bytes. The `FCS` is generated by the transmitting station and placed after the `Control` or `Information` field (the `Information` field is optional in some frames); the receiving station calculates its own version of the FCS until the trailing `Flag` pattern is detected. The result of the receiving station's calculation should be `0xF0B8`.

SDLC uses a sliding window protocol with a total of eight possible sequence numbers; the window size is application dependent, with the maximum size being seven. The section on the go-back-N protocol describes the basic functions of SDLC.

Transparency   To be truly useful, a protocol must be able to support transparent data, thereby allowing any bit pattern to be transmitted. In byte-oriented protocols such as Bisync, a special "escape" byte (*DLE*) allows the receiving DTE to distinguish between control bytes, sent as data, and control bytes, used for control sequences. As well, the "escape" byte requires a set of special rules to handle its own inclusion.

In bit-oriented protocols such as SDLC, the problem of transparency still remains, since the sequence `01111110` delimits the end-of-frame, meaning that a byte sent with the value `01111110` will cause the receiving DTE to stop receiving. The solution is to use a technique known as *bit stuffing* whereby the transmitting hardware inserts a `0` bit after any sequence of five `1`s (except when the end-of-frame sequence is sent).

The receiving hardware removes the extra bit using the following algorithm:

1. If a sequence of five `1`s has been received (i.e., `11111`), then wait for the next bit.

2. If the bit is a 0, discard it and continue assembling the stream of bits into bytes.

3. If the bit is a 1, keep it. This should be the end-of-frame sequence.

4. Reset the bit-stuffing sequence count and resume the count when the next 1 is received.

The following examples illustrate how bit stuffing works (0 bits that are inserted are enclosed as $\boxed{0}$ and the information received has the inserted bit removed):

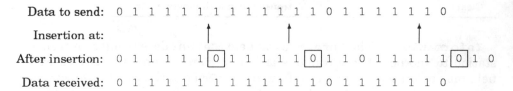

SYNCHRONOUS COMMUNICATIONS HARDWARE

6.6 SYNCHRONOUS COMMUNICATIONS HARDWARE

Synchronous communications, like asynchronous communications, require specialized hardware to support the transmission and reception of data. Not surprisingly, there are several different types of synchronous hardware available: at a minimum, the hardware is either byte-oriented or bit-oriented.

The exact functions of the hardware vary from manufacturer to manufacturer; however, it is not surprising to find features such as synchronization detection and CRC generation and checking on the hardware itself.

6.6.1 Byte-oriented Hardware

Many manufacturers of byte-oriented synchronous hardware make the hardware support asynchronous communications as well. Hardware that supports both synchronous and asynchronous communications is known as a *Universal Synchronous/Aynchronous Receiver/Transmitter (USART)*. The structure of the USART is similar to that of the UART (Figure 6.57).

The Intel 8251A is used on the IBM PC to support the Bisync protocol. Functionally, the 8251A USART is very similar to the 8250 UART in that the baud rate, character length, stop bits, and parity can be selected under program control. The program can also select asynchronous or synchronous operation. (The 8251A supplied with the PC operates in synchronous mode only.)

When transmitting a Bisync frame, the software is required to format the entire frame (including the *SYN* characters and the CRC). The frame is transmitted one byte at a time. The software is expected to supply data to the 8251A at such a rate that the transmit buffer is never empty. Should the transmit buffer become empty, the 8251A starts to idle with *SYN* characters. This can clearly lead to problems in transparent mode, since *SYN* characters sent as timing characters are to be prefixed with *DLE*.

If a Bisync station is to receive a frame, the 8251A must be put into *hunt* mode, scanning the channel for one or more *SYN* characters. The software

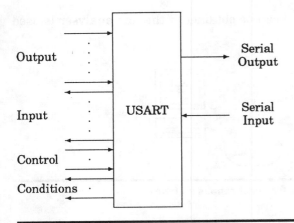

Figure 6.57   The USART

can also specify whether the search is for one or two *SYN* characters. The bytes are returned to the processor as they are received.

6.6.2 Bit-oriented Hardware

Intel also manufactures the Intel 8273, the PC's programmable SDLC communications adapter. The 8273 performs a number of tasks specific to SDLC, thereby reducing processor overhead. For example, if a frame is to be transmitted, the 8273 transmits the **Flag** byte followed by the **Address** and **Control** fields. If an **Information** field is to be transmitted, it is supplied to the 8273 using DMA (thereby reducing processor overhead). Lastly, the **FCS** and final **Flag** byte are sent by the 8273. Incoming frames are treated in a similar fashion, with the **Address** and **Control** fields being written to hardware registers and the **Information** field transferred to memory without processor intervention. The **FCS** is checked as well. The processor is interrupted upon reception of a frame.

6.7   COMMKIT SYNCHRONOUS SOFTWARE

Due to the costs involved, few PCs are supplied with synchronous communication hardware. As such, Commkit does not support software to control synchronous hardware.

However, Commkit can *emulate* byte-oriented synchronous protocols on asynchronous hardware by using the same frame delimiters, error-checking and recovery procedures, and other rules associated with the protocol. The remainder of this chapter examines Commkit's half-duplex stop-and-wait protocol, which functions as a synchronous protocol.

6.7.1 Hardware Requirements

The stop-and-wait implementation is point-to-point and requires, at a minimum, two PCs. Either of the serial ports (1 or 2) can be interconnected. A better appreciation of the protocol can be obtained if the line analyser is used (Figure 6.58).

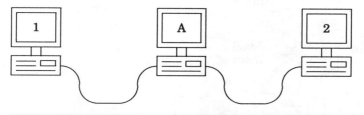

Figure 6.58   Hardware configuration for synchronous software

6.7.2   The Problem

The Commkit stop-and-wait protocol should be designed to allow a user on one PC to send a "block" of data to a remote PC. Transfer is to be uni-directional; that is, one PC transmits while the other receives. The problem can be divided into two distinct parts:

1. *Stop-and-wait protocol.* The stop-and-wait software should transfer frames of up to 80 bytes in length across the communication channel. Each frame will be sent with a sequence number and a 16-bit CRC. The receiving stop-and-wait software should acknowledge each frame as it is received.

2. *Block transfer.* The block transfer software should allow a user to type a message of up to ten lines of text on the transmitting PC. Each line of text is supplied to the stop-and-wait software for transmission after the tenth line is entered or when the user types CTRL-Z. The receiving block transfer software displays each line once it has been successfully received by the station's stop-and-wait software.

6.7.3   Design

A stop-and-wait protocol   The stop-and-wait protocol will allow a process on one PC to send frames of up to 80 printable (nontransparent) characters in length to a process on another PC. The protocol is to be a "typical" stop-and-wait protocol requiring the transmitting DTE to send a frame (with an embedded sequence number), to which the receiving DTE will reply with an acknowledgement: an *ACK*, if the frame is received correctly; or a *NAK*, if an error is detected. If the frame is positively acknowledged, the transmitting DTE will send another frame, while a negative acknowledgement causes the transmitting DTE to retransmit the old frame. A frame received with the wrong sequence number is discarded but positively acknowledged. If no response is received within 1 second of the transmission, the frame is sent again. A possible sequence is shown in Figure 6.59.

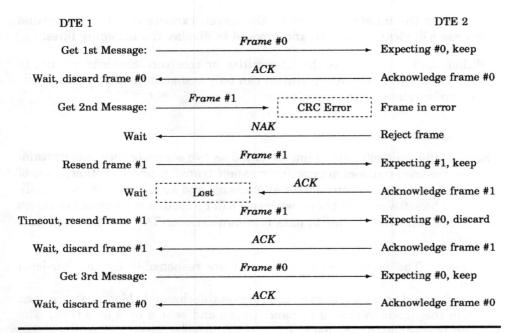

DTE 1   DTE 2

Get 1st Message: ———————— *Frame #0* ————————→ Expecting #0, keep

Wait, discard frame #0 ←———————— *ACK* ———————— Acknowledge frame #0

Get 2nd Message: ——— *Frame #1* ———→ [CRC Error] Frame in error

Wait ←———————— *NAK* ———————— Reject frame

Resend frame #1 ———————— *Frame #1* ————————→ Expecting #1, keep

Wait [Lost] ←———— *ACK* ———— Acknowledge frame #1

Timeout, resend frame #1 ——— *Frame #1* ———→ Expecting #0, discard

Wait, discard frame #1 ←———————— *ACK* ———————— Acknowledge frame #1

Get 3rd Message: ———————— *Frame #0* ————————→ Expecting #0, keep

Wait, discard frame #0 ←———————— *ACK* ———————— Acknowledge frame #0

Figure 6.59 The Commkit stop-and-wait protocol

The protocol uses Bisync control characters to delimit each data frame:

STX	seq	Data	*ETX*	CRC	CRC

The sequence number **seq** alternates between 0 and 1, while the **Data** consists of from 0 to 80 bytes. Any control character (other than *ETX*) can be sent as data. The 16-bit CRC, generated using Commkit's CRC-16 utility, and sent as two 8-bit bytes (**CRC**) includes *both* **Data** and the sequence number **seq**. The data to be transmitted is supplied by a process; once the transmission has completed, a completion code is to be returned to the process, indicating that the next line of data can be transmitted.

The acknowledgement characters (*ACK* and *NAK*) are the ASCII positive and negative acknowledgement characters respectively.

Block transfer There are *two* foreground processes:

- On the transmitting PC, the foreground process will accept up to ten lines of text from the user, and when signalled, send the text to the stop-and-wait software for transmission to the receiving DTE. When all the lines on the transmitting station have been sent, the screen is cleared and then ready for further input. Data is forwarded if one of two conditions are met: (1) whenever ten lines of text are entered, and (2) a CTRL-Z will cause all messages (at least one and less than ten) to be sent.

- On the receiving PC, when a line is received correctly by the stop-and-wait software, it will be forwarded to the local foreground process for displaying.

Whenever the number of lines on the screen exceeds ten, the foreground process will clear the screen and proceed to display the incoming lines.

Either station can act as the transmitter or receiver. Stations are not to change roles; the transmitting station can only transmit blocks of data, while the receiving station can only receive.

6.7.4   Implementation

The stop-and-wait software is implemented as two separate files, one containing the low-level routines supporting message transfer, and the other, a set of high-level routines, responsible for all message and keyboard display. The division of the software into these two levels will be used in subsequent chapters to demonstrate other issues in data communications. The two stop-and-wait files are:

`s&wlow.c`. The procedures in `s&wlow.c` are responsible for the low-level trans-

mission and reception of messages across the channel. Messages are read from the queue indicated in `handler_id` and sent a byte at a time. The port is specified by the user.

A station receiving a frame responds with an acknowledgement (*ACK* or *NAK*), extracts the message from the frame and sends the message to the process associated with queue `APPLICATION`.

`s&wex.c`. `S&wex.c` contains the high-level software responsible for displaying messages received from queue `APPLICATION`. All keyboard input is also sent to `APPLICATION` for display and formatting into messages. Once ten messages or **CTRL-Z** is typed, the messages are sent to queue `handler_id` for transmission.

This problem can be divided into four parts: high-level transmission, high-level reception, low-level transmission, and low-level reception.

High-level transmission   The high-level transmission software, `do_lcl_msg()`, is in one of two states:

`READING`. In state `READING`, characters are accepted from the keyboard and stored in the structure `msg_to_go` until a **CTRL-Z** or end-of-buffer is detected. Structure `msg_to_go` is an array of ten elements (one for each line):

```
struct
{
int size;
char data[81];
} msg_to_go[10];
```

As each character is accepted, it is displayed on the screen at location `line`, `column`. The character is stored in `msg_to_go.data` and `column` is assigned to `msg_to_go.size`.

When msg_to_go is filled or the user signals CTRL-Z, do_lcl_msg() begins its writing sequence by calling write_message_number(), which sends the first line stored in msg_to_go.data to the low-level transmission routine. All messages are sent to one of the serial ports (SP1IH or SP2IH) indicated by handler_id. The state then changes to WRITING. The variable current_msg contains the number of the next line to be transmitted.

A CTRL-C from the keyboard will abort the process, returning control to MS-DOS.

WRITING. The WRITING state is entered whenever the low-level transmission routine has completed sending a message to the remote PC. If there is another line of data to be sent (indicated by current_msg being less than line), write_message_number() is called with current_msg.

Control remains in the WRITING state until all the lines of data are transmitted, at which point the state changes to READING.

High-level reception   Frames received by the low-level reception software are forwarded for display to do_rmt_msg(), the foreground process, through queue APPLICATION. The lines are displayed as received starting at the top of the screen; after the tenth line, the screen is cleared and display starts again from the top line.

In both the high-level reception and transmission software, there are two common routines: (1) diagnostic(), which writes a diagnostic message on the last line of the screen; and (2) check_clock(), which erases the last line of the screen after about five seconds of display have elapsed.

Low-level transmission   All entry to the transmission software takes place through low_level(). Interrupts from either serial port or the clock handler are eventually routed to xmit_protocol() which is responsible for the transmission of the frame. Xmit_protocol() is implemented as a state machine consisting of the following states, the value of the current state is stored in s_and_w.state (all data structures are defined in s&w.h):

AWAIT_MSG. State AWAIT_MSG is entered initially and after a message has been successfully transmitted. If a message is available for transmission, start_transmission() is called and an *STX* is sent. The state changes to SEND_SEQNO.

SEND_SEQNO. As soon as the serial port signals that the *STX* has been sent, control passes to state SEND_SEQNO. The sequence number, s_and_w.seq_no, is transmitted and included in the CRC. The state changes to SEND_MSG.

SEND_MSG. The message bytes, stored in s_and_w.msg, are transmitted as each XMITDONE indication is received. Each byte is included in the CRC. When end-of-message is detected and the last byte has been sent, the state changes to SEND_ETX.

SEND_ETX. State SEND_ETX is entered after the last byte of the message has been sent. An *ETX* is transmitted and the state changes to SEND_CRC1.

SEND_CRC1. The first half of the CRC is sent; the state changes to SEND_CRC2.

SEND_CRC2. The second half of the CRC is sent; the state changes to AWAIT_ACK. The timer, s_and_w.ticks, is cleared.

AWAIT_ACK. The AWAIT_ACK state is entered after a message has been sent; the transmission state machine is awaiting an acknowledgement from the remote station. There are three possible outcomes:

No response. If no response is received after one second, the frame is re-transmitted by calling start_transmission(). The state changes to SEND_SEQNO.

Response is NAK. A negative acknowledgement results in the frame being retransmitted by a call to start_transmission(). The state changes to SEND_SEQNO.

Response is ACK. A positive acknowledgement means that the remote station received and accepted the frame just sent. At this point, the sequence number is updated and the high-level software informed of the successful transmission. The state changes to AWAIT_MSG.

Any other responses are ignored.

Low-level reception Entry to the low-level reception software takes place through low_level() whenever an interrupt is received from either the serial port or the clock handler. Recv_protocol() handles the reception and acknowledgement of any incoming frames through the use of a state machine, the state of which is indicated in s_and_w.state. The action of the state machine depends upon the current state and the condition for changing state:

WAIT_STX. This state is entered initially and after a message has been received. When an *STX* is received, control passes to state WAIT_SEQNO.

WAIT_SEQNO. The byte following the *STX* is taken to be the sequence number of the frame and is stored in s_and_w.recv_no. The sequence number is included in the CRC. The state then changes to WAIT_MSG.

WAIT_MSG. The bytes following the sequence number are stored in the array s_and_w.msg and included in the CRC. When an *ETX* is detected, control passes to state WAIT_CRC1.

WAIT_CRC1. The byte following the *ETX* is taken as the first half of the CRC. This byte is included in the CRC being calculated for the frame. The state then changes to WAIT_CRC2.

WAIT_CRC2. This byte is taken to be the second half of the CRC and is included in the CRC. Process_message() is then called, which examines s_and_w.crc. If the value of the CRC is zero, the frame is acknowledged; if the sequence number is the one expected (indicated by comparing s_and_w.recv_no with s_and_w.seq_no), the message is forwarded to queue APPLICATION and the sequence number is incremented.

In each state (except WAIT_STX), there is a timed sanity check. Should the transmitting station fail to send a byte within one second, a diagnostic message is displayed on line 0 and control passes back to state WAIT_STX.

The state of the low-level software (i.e., either transmitting or receiving) is indicated in `s_and_w.protocol`: `XMIT` or `RECV`. All keyboard messages are sent to the foreground process.

6.7.5 Compiling and Running the Stop-and-Wait Software

The stop-and-wait software is also supplied on the Commkit diskette as the executable file `s&wex.exe`. A new executable can be created using the `make` utility:

```
C:\> make s&wex.exe
```

The `s&wex.exe` is created from `s&wex.c`, `s&wlow.c`, `commkit.obj`, `crc.obj`, and `intrpt.obj`.

Once created, `s&wex.exe` can be executed by typing the file name followed by the desired line speed, the port in question (i.e., 1 or 2), and an indication of the function of the PC, either transmitting (`X`) or receiving (`R`, the default). For example, to run a PC as a transmitter at 300 bps through port 2, type:

```
C:\> s&wex 300 2 X
```

Both stations (transmitter and receiver) cause the screen to be cleared upon initialization. If the preceding format is not followed or the line speed is not recognized, control returns to MS-DOS and a diagnostic is issued. Data is entered at the PC designated as the transmitter. Either station can be terminated by typing CTRL-C.

As data is entered on the transmitting station, it is echoed on the screen. A new line is obtained after each carriage return or after the user attempts to enter a character onto a full line. The contents of the screen are forwarded, a line at a time, once ten lines have been entered and the user attempts to move to the eleventh, or the user types CTRL-Z.

Each line, as it is received, is displayed on the receiving PC, starting on the second line down from the top of the screen. Any errors (such as bad sequence number, or invalid CRC) detected by the receiving PC are displayed on the top line.

Once the transmission has completed, the transmitting PC's screen is cleared and the user can enter more data. The receiving PC's screen is cleared before the first line of any incoming data is displayed.

6.8 SUMMARY

This chapter has examined synchronous communications and their uses, notably the transfer of large volumes of data with the minimum of overhead. Many of the issues involved in synchronous communications have been discussed:

- Synchronous communications involve the transmission of "pure" data (i.e., no start and stop bits); to achieve this, special frames are needed with some form of delimiter.

- The receiving DTE can verify that the transmitted frame was received correctly through the use of a series of one or more check bytes that are generated by the transmitter. Techniques such as the longitudinal redundancy check (LRC) can be used, but they offer limited checking capabilities on the data within the frame. However, more accurate frame checking is possible using cyclic redundancy checks or CRCs. A CRC treats the entire message as a long dividend, and divides the message by a CRC generator; the remainder is transmitted as part of the frame. A number of different CRC standards exist; CRCs can be generated in hardware and software.

- Once the frame has been received, the receiving station needs a mechanism whereby the transmitting station can be informed of the status of the message (i.e., was it received correctly, or was the CRC in error). Such a mechanism is the acknowledgement, in which the station receiving the frame replies to the transmission with either a positive or negative acknowledgement.

- Two common classifications of protocol have been developed for use with synchronous communications: stop-and-wait and go-back-N. Stop-and-wait protocols involve a transmitting station sending a frame and then waiting for an acknowledgement, at which point the next frame can be sent. go-back-N protocols permit potentially higher throughput by the use of sliding windows, which allow the transmitter to send a number of frames before an acknowledgement is required. Go-back-N protocols also allow for the bi-directional transfer of information by piggybacking acknowledgements on data frames.

The chapter has also shown that synchronous communications can be emulated, in part, using asynchronous communications. The Commkit stop-and-wait protocol is such an example.

6.9 EXERCISES

1. Show that synchronous communications offer better throughput than asynchronous.

2. If synchronous communications are so much more efficient that asynchronous, would it make sense to replace all asynchronous terminals with synchronous terminals? Consider the types of overhead.

3. Compare the types of overhead involved in the calculation of a message's CRC using the software shift-register implementation against the table lookup method.

4. Show, by means of illustrations or examples, why throughput can be improved in the stop-and-wait protocol by using a *NAK* rather than a time-out.

5. Show, by means of illustrations or examples, how *NAK*s can improve throughput for selective retransmission.

6. Show, by means of illustrations or examples, how a sliding window protocol can be used to support selective retransmission.

7. In Bisync, why does a timing *SYN* require a *DLE* prefix when transmitting transparently? What happens if the *DLE* is omitted?

8. How does SDLC distinguish between its three different frame formats?

9. Using the state machine descriptions for the stop-and-wait protocol, show how the protocol recovers from the loss of a frame (Figure 6.60).

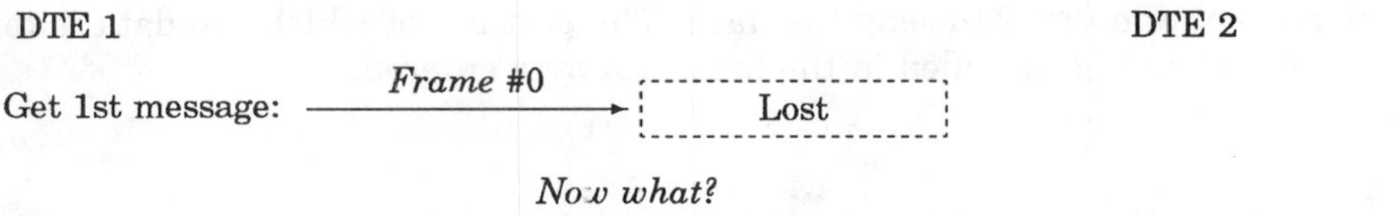

Figure 6.60

10. Run s&wex.exe between two PCs connected by the line analyser. Identify the different fields in the frame. What are the values of the sequence numbers?

11. Run s&wex.exe from one PC connected through the line analyser. What happens when several lines of message are sent? How many messages are sent? Why?

    On the line analyser, the frame delimiters appear as ☺ (*STX*) and ♡ (*ETX*). Note that the CRC bytes follow the *ETX*.

12. Modify the s&wex.exe software so that CTRL-C does not terminate the transmitting PC. Next, run s&wex.exe between two PCs connected by the line analyser. Insert several *ETX* characters as data into the messages (type CTRL-C, it echos as a heart). What happens when the message is transmitted?

    What modifications are necessary to the stop-and-wait software to allow the transmission of an *ETX* as data? Make the modifications and retest the software.

13. The stop-and-wait protocol supplied with Commkit has a problem: If the receiving DTE misses the *ETX* and the transmitting DTE retransmits the frame before the receiving DTE can abort the first reception, a very long message will be received. This can cause various areas of memory to be overwritten. Modify the existing state machine and the software to handle errors such as the one described here.

14. The example stop-and-wait protocol has another problem: If a frame is continuously *NAK*ed, the transmitter will never stop transmitting and the receiver will never stop receiving. A constant SEND_ABORT has been defined in s&w.h, but isn't used. Modify the stop-and-wait software so that after five retransmissions of the same packet, the transmission will be aborted.

Develop a means whereby this could be tested. What changes are needed in s&wlow.c?

15. Many test situations may require an error to be introduced into the transmitted data. For example, in order to check an implementation's error-handling routines, it would be necessary to send messages with invalid CRC values. (It may be easier to have the line analyser cause the errors, than it is to rewrite the transmission software to generate errors!)

Modify the line analyser software so that the user may enter data that is subsequently sent out a specified port. Use CTRL-J to enter the data to be sent and CTRL-V to send the data. The port out of which the data is to be sent can be specified in the first data byte entered.

File Transfer

7.1 INTRODUCTION

The examples illustrating both asynchronous and synchronous point-to-point communications have thus far been confined to short messages entered by the user at a PC. Not surprisingly, this is only one of the many different types of application that can use a communication facility. There are others, such as *file transfer*, involving the transfer of a file from one DTE to another. Protocols designed for large-volume transfer, such as those discussed in the previous chapter, are ideal for file transfer, since large numbers of bytes can be reliably transferred with the minimum of acknowledgement overhead.

Although the concept of file transfer is straightforward (a copy of a file is sent from one DTE to another), there are, as usual, a number of important issues that must be considered to ensure that the file arrives at the intended destination complete and in the same form that it left the source. For example:

- Are the file attributes transferred? The file attributes are information about the file, such as its name and extension, ownership, time and date of creation, size, and the type of file (i.e., sequential, direct, or indexed).

  At a minimum, the file name and extension should be transferred. However, there are situations in which it is necessary to transfer all of the attributes associated with the file. This may not be as simple as it seems. If an indexed file is to be transferred and the index refers to absolute disk block locations on the original disk, transferring the index may be a meaningless operation. Similarly, one type of file may not be supported on the destination DTE, requiring the file to be converted to a common file type.

A case in point would be transferring an indexed file with its indexes to a DTE that only supports sequential access.

- What is to happen to the file on the destination DTE if the file transfer fails? File transfer can fail should one (or both) DTEs or the communications channel cease to function. If part of the file has already been written to the disk, should it be left on the disk or deleted?

- Should an acknowledgement indicating that a message is properly received by the remote DTE also be taken to mean that the message has been successfully written to the disk?

  In some situations, a message may be received correctly by the communications software, but may not be written correctly to the disk. For example, the disk may fail. *Additional* protocols may be needed to indicate that the message has been received *and* successfully written to the file on the disk.

This chapter presents a overview of how file systems function and how files can be transferred. The basic concepts associated with file transfer are examined in detail. A general-purpose file transfer application using Commkit's stop-and-wait software developed in the previous chapter is discussed and implemented.

7.2 FILE SYSTEMS

Central to any file transfer is the operating system's *file system*. The file system is responsible for the organization and access of files stored on some external medium, typically a disk. There are many different approaches to the development and implementation of a file system; fortunately, there are a number of operations common to most file systems, some of which are discussed in this section.

7.2.1 Disks

Disks are a magnetic (or electronic) medium that can store information. Information on a disk is divided into collections of bytes referred to as *sectors*. Sectors are organized into rings on the disk; a single ring is known as a *track*. Information on the disk is read and written by a *read-write head* moving from track-to-track as the disk rotates. If a disk consists of multiple surfaces, each surface has its own read-write head that moves across all tracks. A *cylinder* is defined as the tracks of a multiple-surface disk that can be accessed without moving the read-write heads.

In many file system implementations, sectors are grouped into *blocks* and disk-access requests are expressed in terms of blocks rather than individual sectors.

7.2.2 Files

Files consist of a series of bytes often grouped into structures known as *records* and stored in one or more blocks on the disk. The blocks associated with a file are maintained in a structure (usually a list structure, linked or sequential). The file system maintains a *directory* (also made up of a number of blocks), which contains the names of the files on the disk. The attributes associated with each file are kept on the disk, as well, often as part of the directory or in a separate data structure. One of the attributes is a pointer to the file's first block.

7.2.3 File Access

At a minimum, a file system allows a process to access files for both reading and writing. Typical file system operations include:

Creation Initially, before any files are put onto the disk, the disk contains an empty directory and a list of available blocks. Processes that require the storage of information can request the creation of a file. The file system adds the name of the file to the file directory along with any other necessary attributes. Once the file is created, the process may proceed with writing information to the file.

Opening An existing file (i.e., one with a name in the directory) is accessed by the application requesting that the file be opened, usually for reading or writing. Many file systems will check the attributes associated with the file before performing the open request; for example, only processes with certain privileges may be allowed to open a file.

There are numerous special cases of file opening. For example, a file can be opened in "append" mode, allowing the application to write to the end of the file, thereby preserving the original contents of the file. Other file systems can open files for both reading and writing, permitting the updating of specific records in the file. Finally, it is worth noting that file creation is simply a special case of opening a file for writing from the beginning of the file.

Closing When a process has finished accessing a file, the file system usually expects the application to close the file. By closing the file, other processes can be granted access to the file (assuming that there is a limit of one process per open file).

Reading Files are opened for reading to allow processes access to the information within the file. Exactly *how* the file is read depends upon the type of file and the file system. For example, sequential access returns the next available record to the process, whereas direct access can return any record in the file. When reading a sequential access file, mechanisms exist to signal the process that the end-of-file is reached.

Writing Files can also be opened for writing, thereby allowing the process to update existing information or add entirely new information to the file. As the process adds information, the file system places it into blocks and when the block is filled, writes the block to the disk.

Since the file system may allow many files to be opened simultaneously, each opened file is associated with a handle or *file descriptor*. The file descriptor is used by the file system to distinguish the various file requests from the different processes, and it is used by the process to distinguish among the different files it may have open.

Other commands that are associated with file manipulation can be made out of the previous operations. For example, a file copy involves creating a new file and opening an old one. The old file is read and each record is written to the newly created file. Once the copying has completed, both files are closed.

7.3   FILE TRANSFER PROTOCOLS

A file transfer protocol is a set of rules that describe the steps required for a file transfer to take place. There is no single set of rules for file transfer protocols; for example, some are full-duplex, permitting simultaneous bi-directional file transfer; while others are half-duplex, allowing one file to be sent at a time. Similarly, some file transfer protocols operate using a stop-and-wait protocol while others are implemented using go-back-N protocols.

In its simplest form, a file transfer protocol can be thought of as a file copy command operating between a pair of DTEs. Ideally, the protocol should be written so that it is independent of the underlying communication software, for example:

File transfer protocol software
_____
Communication software (DTE-to-DTE)
_____
Physical interconnection

By separating the file transfer software from the communication software, a number of benefits can be obtained, including:

Portability. If the file transfer protocol makes no references to the communication protocol, then changing the communication protocol should be transparent to the file-transfer protocol. For example, if one pair of DTEs use a stop-and-wait communication protocol and another pair use a go-back-N protocol, a truly portable file transfer protocol would operate atop either protocol (this assumes that both communication systems offer the same set of communication primitives to the file transfer software).

Testing and verification. Software testing and subsequent verification is simplified if the different layers are written independent of each other. Quite simply, the number of places for which an error must be searched is greatly reduced if each part of the system is tested independently.

Having said this, the underlying communications software and its implementation can affect the types of files that can be transferred. For example, if the communication software only supports 7-bit ASCII and the file contains 8-bit binary data, file transfer may not be be possible.

Regardless of the implementation, a file-transfer protocol describes three basic operations for the transfer of a file. These are described in the following sections.

File identification The existing file must be opened for reading on one DTE and the new file created on the other DTE. In both cases, a file name (and possibly a path indicating the storage unit and the directory) must be specified on both machines. Additionally, file attributes must be associated with the new file; these attributes can either be those of the original file or they can be the default attributes assigned by the file system on which the file is created.

The file transfer can be aborted at this point for any number of reasons (note that most of these points are implementation dependent):

- The file to be copied does not exist. If the file does not exist, the transfer cannot take place. (Some implementations will ask the user for the name of another file.)

- The file name is already in use on the receiving DTE. A common solution is to rename the newly created file to something other than the existing file name, rather than to abort the transfer.

- The user requesting the transfer does not have the necessary access rights to the file. Some files will be associated with certain privileges which dictate who can access the file.

Where the file transfer is initiated is, once again, implementation dependent. The simplest approach is to have the transfer initiated on the DTE where the file exists and to have a user on the remote DTE specify the file name and path of the file to be created. Ideally, a user on either DTE could request a transfer to (or from) the other DTE. If the transfer can be initiated from either DTE, regardless of the file's location, the file name must be passed between the DTEs with an indication as to whether the file is to be created or opened for transfer.

Record transfer Once the file has been opened for reading on one DTE (the source) and created for writing on the other DTE (the destination), the contents of the file must be transferred. In their simplest forms, the algorithms for transferring the contents of a file can be summarized as follows:

- The source algorithm:
  1. Open the file for reading.
  2. Read a record from the file.
  3. Pass the record to the communication software for transmission.
  4. Repeat steps 2 and 3 until end-of-file is detected.

- The destination algorithm:
  1. Create the file.
  2. Wait for a record from the communication software.
  3. Write the record to the newly created file.
  4. Repeat steps 2 and 3 until end-of-file is indicated.

Although these are the basic steps in transferring the contents of the file, the algorithms are very often extended in light of the following:

- It is not always advisable to allow the unchecked transfer of records as is suggested in the source algorithm. If the communication software runs slower than the file transfer software, records can be lost should the communication software's queue overflow. One solution is to use a so-called *hand-shake* between the file transfer software and the communication software; the file transfer software proceeds to supply another message only when permitted to do so by the communication software.

- If the communication software is prone to losing messages, many file transfer protocols will implement end-to-end acknowledgements between the two halves of the file transfer protocol. These acknowledgements are handled by the file transfer protocol independently of the communication software, meaning that there are potentially two sets of acknowledgements taking place: those in the communication software and those in the file transfer software.

Finally, it is not a good idea to assume that the receipt of an acknowledgement indicates that the message just sent was actually written to the remote file. It is possible that the record was received correctly but not written to the file; for example, the disk might fail during a write operation.

End-of-file indication   As already suggested in the previous section on transferring the contents of the file, an end-of-file indication must be sent to the destination. The end-of-file signal is typically *not* written to the file, it is simply an indication to the file transfer software to close the file. The file system takes care of updating the end-of-file information.

7.4   COMMKIT FILE TRANSFER EXAMPLE

Commkit is supplied with s&wdisk.c, a file transfer utility that can transfer files between PCs using the low-level stop-and-wait software: s&wlow.c. S&wdisk.c is a simple file transfer utility that operates in one of two modes:

Source. In source mode, s&wdisk reads the contents of a given file and supplies each record, one at a time, to s&wlow for transmission.

Destination. In destination mode, s&wdisk waits for records received by s&wlow and writes them to the newly created file.

7.4.1   Design

The file transfer utility, s&wdisk, is to be written independently of the s&wlow software, but designed so that s&wlow can support the transfer without any modification. Accordingly, there are a number of restrictions placed upon the design of s&wdisk because of decisions taken in the original design of s&wlow:

1. A maximum of 80 bytes can be transferred.
2. Communications are half-duplex; the PC initiating the transmission is the only one that can send messages, the receiving PC can only send acknowledgements.

In light of these restrictions, the file transfer can only be initiated from the PC which has the file to transfer. Additionally, end-to-end acknowledgements between the file transfer software is impossible because of the half-duplex restriction. Finally, recall that s&wlow signals the transmitting process that the last message sent has been acknowledged.

The following algorithm supports file transfer from the source PC using s&wlow:

1. Open the file for reading.

2. Read a record from the file.

3. If end-of-file is not detected:
   a) Pass the record to s&wlcw for transmission.
   b) Wait for s&wlow to indicate that the acknowledgement was received.

4. Repeat steps 2 and 3 until end-of-file is detected.

5. Pass an end-of-file indication to s&wlow for transmission.

The following algorithm uses s&wlow for reception on the destination PC:

1. Create the file.

2. Wait for a record from s&wlow.

3. If the record does not indicate end-of-file:
   a) Write the record to the newly created file.

4. Repeat steps 2 and 3 until end-of-file is indicated.

5. Close the file.

In addition to the above algorithms, a message structure is required to permit the transfer of the individual records. This data structure requires two fields, one specifying an option and the other, the data associated with the option (Table 7.1).

TABLE 7.1 The Option and Associated Data

Option Field	Data Field
DATA	File record
END_OF_FILE	Empty

7.4.2 Implementation

The two algorithms described in the design section can be implemented directly in Turbo C using the UNIX file access functions open(), close(), read(), and write() (these functions and their associated options are defined in the include files fcntl.h and sys\stat.h). Communications between the foreground process and s&wlow are supported by send() and recv().

To simplify the design, the file name must be specified on both the source and destination PCs. The file name is not transferred (implementation of this is left as an exercise).

Two mutually exclusive foreground processes implement the source and destination algorithms (which one is called depends upon whether the PC is the source or the destination of the file):

read_and_send()   The read_and_send() procedure opens the file specified by the user. Each record is read, REC_LEN bytes at a time, into the structure message.data. If end-of-file is detected, message.option is set to EOF, otherwise it is set to MORE_TO_COME.

Message is forwarded to the serial port specified in handler_id for transmission by s&wlow. Read_and_send() then waits for an indication that the transmission has been completed or that an CTRL-C from the keyboard is detected. Note that read_and_send() does *not* terminate as soon as the end-of-file is detected; this is to allow s&wlow the time needed to transfer the EOF message.

Once the transfer has completed, the file is closed.

receive_and_write()   The receive_and_write() procedure creates a file of the name specified by the user. The attributes associated with the file are S_IREAD and S_IWRITE (indicating that the file can be read and written).

Once the file is opened, receive_and_write() accepts each message (containing the option and data); if the option is MORE_TO_COME, the data is written to the newly created file. When message.option indicates EOF, the file is closed and receive_and_write() terminates.

The overall flow of messages between the source and destination PCs can be represented as shown in Figure 7.1. The associated list defines the events.

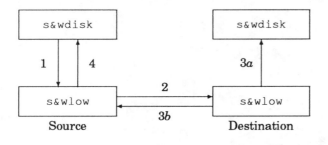

Figure 7.1   The file transfer protocol message flow

1. S&wdisk uses the send() primitive to pass message to s&wlow via queue SP1IH or SP2IH (depending upon the port specified by the user).

2. S&wlow transmits the message in a frame to the destination copy of s&wlow.

3a and 3b. S&wlow puts the message onto queue APPLICATION for processing by s&wdisk (step 3a); while simultaneously acknowledging the frame (step 3b).

4. S&wlow indicates to s&wdisk (via a completion code put onto queue APPLICATION) that the message has been received by the destination PC. At this point, s&wdisk can send another message.

7.4.3 Compiling the File Transfer Software

The file transfer example, s&wdisk.c, can be compiled and linked with s&wlow.obj, commkit.obj, intrpt.obj, and crc.obj along with the various support routines using the make utility:

```
C:\> make s&wdisk.exe
```

7.4.4 Running the File Transfer Software

Once created, s&wdisk.exe can transfer files between PCs connected by a null modem RS-232-C cable; either serial port can connect to the other (i.e., 1 to 2, 1 to 1, or 2 to 2).

Since the stop-and-wait software is half-duplex, one PC must be designated the source (of the file), and the other PC, the destination.

The source PC is invoked by typing s&wdisk followed by the line speed, the port (1 or 2), an X (signifying that this station is transmitting the file), and the name of the file to transfer, after the MS-DOS prompt. Error messages are issued if the line speed is incorrect, if the wrong number of arguments are placed on the line, or if the file does not exist.

For example, to transfer commkit.c to the destination PC on a 9600-bps line through port 2, type:

```
C:\> s&wdisk 9600 2 X commkit.c
```

The transfer will continue until an error occurs or the file is completely transferred to the destination. Upon completion of the transfer, control returns to MS-DOS.

The destination station is initialized in a similar fashion; however, an R is used rather than an X to indicate that the station is receiving, and the file created and written to by s&wdisk is given the file name. Error messages are issued if the line speed is incorrect, if the wrong number of arguments are placed on the line, or the file already exists.

For example, to create a file commkit2.c with the information received from a 9600-bps line on port 1, type:

```
C:\> s&wdisk 9600 1 R commkit2.c
```

Control is returned to MS-DOS when the receiving station receives the end-of-file signal from the transmitting station. If things go wrong, the receiving station can be aborted using CTRL-ALT-DEL.

7.5 SUMMARY

This chapter has examined file transfer and how it is achieved using a simple file transfer protocols running atop the Commkit stop-and-wait protocol. Other file-transfer protocols are possible and will be discussed further in subsequent chapters.

It is worth noting that protocols are used in almost all aspects of computing science. For example, consider the transfer of information between to two DTEs involved in the file transfer. Rules are applied to the transfer of the message: the message must conform to a certain format; files cannot be accessed unless they are opened; and files can only be accessed according to the way they are opened.

7.6 EXERCISES

1. Perform a file transfer with the line analyser between the sending and receiving PCs. Identify the various fields in the data packets.

2. Run s&wex as a receiver and s&wdisk in source mode—does the file transfer take place? Just because s&wdisk receives an acknowledgement for each record, does that mean that the file is being written to disk? Explain.

3. Start s&wdisk in source mode on one DTE before starting s&wdisk in destination mode on a connected DTE. Does the transfer still work? Explain.

4. Does the disk speed dictate when the destination s&wdisk software terminates?

5. Try transferring an executable file. Does the transfer work? Explain. The line analyser will help solve this exercise.

6. Modify s&wlow.c so that executable files can be transferred, then transfer an executable file between the two PCs. Does the transferred file function properly on the receiving PC? Since there is no end-to-end verification that the file transfer is successful, is this the only method of determining that the file was sent (and received) correctly?

7. Modify s&wdisk so that the file name is supplied to the destination DTE by the source DTE. The software should still accept files with duplicate file names. Hint: add an option to the list of available options.

Command	option	data
Open file	O	Name of file
File data	D	One record from the file
Close file	C	Empty

8. Is it possible to transfer file attributes so that the newly created file looks "the same" as the original? The UNIX file functions chmod() and stat() offer some interesting possibilities. Now the tricky bit, can the file's original time of creation be kept?

9. Modify `receive_and_write()` so that **CTRL-C** will abort the receive software.

10. One limitation of the existing file transfer utility is its inability to transfer more than one file without returning to MS-DOS. Rewrite the file transfer software so that a series of files can be transferred without requiring the software to be restarted. For example:

```
C:\> s&wdisk 9600 1 X

file1.c
TRANSFER STARTED
TRANSFER COMPLETED

commkit.obj
TRANSFER STARTED
TRANSFER COMPLETED

s&wdisk.exe
TRANSFER STARTED
TRANSFER COMPLETED

CTRL C

C:\>
```

The file name can be obtained in one of two ways:

- the keyboard software in `low_level()` can assemble the file name until a carriage return is detected; at which point the string can be forwarded to `APPLICATION`. This involves changing both `s&wlow.c` and `s&wdisk.c`.
- the file name can be assembled in `read_and_send()`, one byte at a time until a carriage return is detected. This involves only changing `s&wdisk.c`.

11. Many line analysers have the ability to record data displayed on the screen for subsequent play back. Since Commkit supports simultaneous file access and UART interrupts, implement a data capture routine on the line analyser.

The Telephone System

8.1 INTRODUCTION

Consider the situation in which a small local company grows in size and opens branch offices in a number of different cities. For the company to function successfully, the people in the branch offices will need to communicate with the head office: either by telephone, courier, or mail.

In addition, the people in the branch offices may need to access information maintained on the computer(s) at the head office. The problem is: How can this be done? Surface mail and courier may be too slow for most applications. Ideally, the information should be transferred electronically; however, given the distance limitations placed on RS-232-C (and most of the other standards discussed in Chapter 3), these standards cannot directly support the required transfer.

What is needed is a communication facility that will allow the interconnection of two DTEs, regardless of their location (either in the same building or on different sides of the world). The most obvious answer is, of course, the telephone system, simply because it is the most readily available.

This chapter examines the telephone system and its use as a medium for the transmission of data, and outlines the equipment needed to access the telephone system. The chapter includes a comparison of RS-232-C and RS-449. The Commkit software demonstrates how the telephone system can transmit and receive data using the PC.

8.2   THE TELEPHONE SYSTEM

The telephone system was originally designed to transmit voice information from one subscriber, through a *central* or *end* office, to another subscriber. The central office was (and still is) responsible for setting up, maintaining, and taking down the connection. The mechanisms for supporting these operations have changed substantially over the past century: from direct operator intervention, through a series of electromechanical devices (originally the Strowger step-by-step switch and eventually the cross-bar switch), to the digital switching of today. The future appears to be changing as rapidly as the past, with a move away from analog-voice technology to worldwide digital transmission known as *Integrated Services Digital Network* (ISDN).

The basic concepts associated with the telephone have not changed as drastically. Subscribers still take the telephone handset *off-hook* to establish a connection with the central office. The central office detects the off-hook condition (current is drawn) and responds with a *dial tone*. The number selected by the subscriber (either through dialing, which breaks the current at precise intervals, or by creating tones at precise frequencies) is recorded by the central office. Once the number is obtained, the central office attempts to make the connection with the other party. If the other party's line is not engaged (i.e., is busy), the central office generates a signal which causes the telephone to ring. When the call is answered, a *circuit* is then dedicated for the duration of the call. The circuit is freed by either party putting their handset *on-hook*.

The central office is designed to handle local calls for a limited number of subscribers (in North America, roughly 10,000 per central office). Since most telephone companies have more than 10,000 subscribers, the telephone system consists of thousands of central offices. Although every subscriber's telephone is connected to a central office through a *two-wire local loop*, the central office has only sufficient equipment to handle about 10 percent of attempted calls (up to 20 percent in some locations where there is a great deal of business traffic).

Not all calls are local to the subscriber's central office; some calls are intended for subscribers connected to other central offices. These are *long distance* calls and require special signalling to allow a central office to determine that the call is for a different central office. The call is routed from the subscriber's central office through one or more circuits to the central office of the specified party. In North America this is achieved by prefixing the dialed party's number with a 1 and possibly an *area code*.

The technology used to create and maintain the circuit is known as *circuit switching*. The paths taken through the telephone system can vary, depending upon a number of factors, such as the time of day and the day of the week. Once the circuit is established, it remains in place until the call is freed.

Figure 8.1 illustrates the basic structure of the present North American telephone system, consisting of some 150 million subscribers.

The circuit eventually established for the call is dictated primarily by the number of potential circuits between the two central offices and the volume of traffic on the telephone system at the time the call is placed. Ideally, the call should be routed across the shortest path connecting the two central

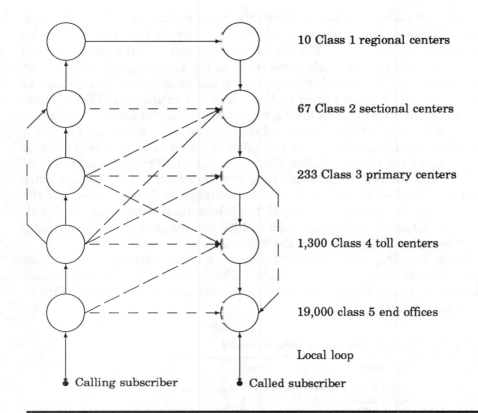

Figure 8.1   Basic structure of present North American telephone system

offices; however, in some cases the path may be fully utilized by other calls. Recognizing this, telephone engineers have developed a network of *trunks* that allow the calling subscriber to reach the called subscriber through one of a number of different paths. Some heavily used paths, represented by dashed lines in the previous diagram, are known as *high-usage trunks* and can be thought of as "shortcuts" across the network between end-offices or centers. If the path across a high usage trunk is unavailable, traffic overflows are placed onto the next available high-usage trunk, or as a last resort, onto a *final trunk* (represented by a solid line in the above diagram). (The present hierarchical structure is evolving to support a dynamic routing structure that is not restricted to preplanned high-usage trunks and final trunks.)

The equipment connecting the subscriber's telephone to the central office is typically analog and is designed for voice frequencies in the 300 to 3400 Hz range. As has been shown in previous chapters, signals sent across wires are subject to attenuation and can eventually die out entirely. To avoid the loss of signals, signals are "boosted" using some form of signal regeneration technique. Prior to the development of digital signalling, the signals on a telephone circuit were boosted using amplifiers. If the signal was subject to noise, both the voice and the noise were amplified; in the worst case, all that could be heard by either subscriber would be the noise!

Digital technology has helped eliminate many of these problems. In digital central offices, the analog-voice signals are converted to digital using an analog-to-digital converter. The digital-voice signals are converted back to analog (using a digital-to-analog converter) in the receiving subscriber's end office. Digital signals sent between centers are *multiplexed* into groups of signals using a technique known as *time-division multiplexing* (*TDM*). Time-division multiplexing involves taking a number of different telephone circuits, sampling them at precise intervals and sending the value of the sample over a communication channel to another end-office or center. The receiving office or center samples the communication channel at the same rate as the transmitter and routes the resulting sample to either the subscriber or another office or center. Sampling theory states that by sampling at *twice* the highest signal frequency, the sample contains all the information of the original signal. Since voice data falls in the range of 0 to 4000 Hz, sampling the channel 8000 times a second will capture all of the voice data.

In North America, a multiplexing hierarchy has been developed to support circuits between central offices. Table 8.1 illustrates the North American hierarchy, while similar ones exist for telephone transmission rates in Europe and Japan.

TABLE 8.1   The North American Multiplexing Hierarchy

Designation	Data Rate	Circuits
T1	1.544 Mb/s	Twenty-four 64-kb/s digital voice
T2	6.312 Mb/s	Four 1.544 Mb/s T1
T3	44.736 Mb/s	Seven 6.312 Mb/s T2
T4	274.176 Mb/s	Six 44.736 Mb/s T3

8.3   CONNECTING TO THE TELEPHONE SYSTEM

As has already been shown at the start of this chapter, the obvious solution to communicating over distances that cannot be supported by RS-232-C and other standards is to use the telephone system. However, there are several problems that must be addressed before the communication can take place, notably:

■ The telephone operates at frequencies in the range of 300 to 3400 Hz, while a DTE generates voltages of extremely low frequencies that a telephone will not detect.

■ How are the connectors found on the back of a DTE to connect to the telephone system?

In short, it is not possible to hold a telephone handset up to the back of a DTE in the hope that the DTE's signals will be detected and transmitted. A device needed that can *modulate* (convert) the DTE's electrical signals into a frequency that can be used by the telephone. This device must also be able to *demodulate* (convert) the telephone frequency signals into electrical impulses that can be understood by the DTE.

The device that converts the DTE's signals into telephone frequencies and vice versa is known as a *data communications equipment* (*DCE*). More commonly, the DCE is referred to as a *modem*, indicating the functions the DCE performs: *modem* is referred to as a *modem*, indicating the functions the DCE performs: *mo*dulating the voltage into a frequency and *dem*odulating the frequency into a voltage.

8.3.1 Modems

Whenever a telephone call is made, there are two stations involved: the one that originates the call and the one that answers the call. The same terminology is applied to pairs of modems involved in a communication. The modem where the call originates is the *originating modem,* and the modem where the call is answered is the *answering modem.*

Modems can be purchased as originate-only (that is, they can only be used to place calls), answer-only (the modem can only receive calls), or originate/answer (the modem can be selected to act as either an originate or an answer modem). An originating modem can only communicate with an answering modem; that is, originate-originate and answer-answer combinations are not possible.

8.3.2 Modem Signalling

The telephone works in the frequency range of roughly between 300 and 3400 Hz. The modem, using the telephone system, therefore has about 3000 Hz in which to modulate and demodulate the binary information. There are three basic techniques that can be used to encode binary information on the telephone system, all of which are now considered.

Amplitude modulation   In amplitude modulation (AM), a mark (1) is represented by one amplitude of a *carrier* frequency and a space (0) is represented by another; for example, as illustrated in Figure 8.2.

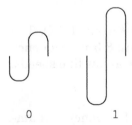

0   1

Figure 8.2   Amplitude modulation

The binary information to be transmitted is *keyed* (or switched) between these two frequencies by the modem. For example, the ASCII byte S (with bit pattern 1010011) could be transmitted as shown in Figure 8.3.

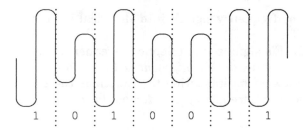

Figure 8.3 Amplitude modulation of the letter S

The above pattern represents the byte S being sent as "pure" data. Had the byte been sent asynchronously, the start, parity, and stop bits would also be included in the signal.

Since the amplitude modulation signal is prone to signal attenuation, modems using amplitude modulation are not in common usage other than at very low line speeds, such as 300 bps.

Frequency modulation Frequency modulation (FM) differs from amplitude modulation in that the amplitude of the carrier is fixed but the frequency of the carrier changes in accordance with the binary data being transmitted. In other words, a mark (1) is sent at one frequency and a space (0) at another, as shown in Figure 8.4.

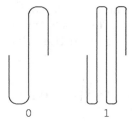

Figure 8.4 Frequency modulation

Frequency modulation is also known as *frequency-shift keying* (FSK). The transmission of the byte S could appear as shown in Figure 8.5 in frequency modulation. FSK modems are generally designed to operate at low line speeds, usually in the range of 300 to 1200 bps.

Phase modulation In phase modulation (PM), the carrier's frequency and amplitude are kept constant, but the *phase* of the carrier is shifted to represent a mark (1) or a space (0). For example, mark and space could be shifted 180° to one another (Figure 8.6). When binary signals are encoded this way, it is known as *phase-coherent phase shift keying* or phase-coherent PSK. If the byte S is transmitted using PSK, the pattern could appear as depicted in Figure 8.7.

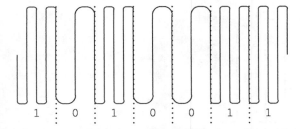

Figure 8.5   Frequency modulation of the letter S

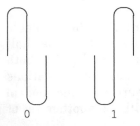

Figure 8.6   Phase modulation

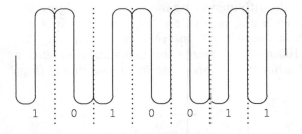

Figure 8.7   Phase modulation of the letter S

In phase-coherent PSK, the modem maintains internal reference signals that are compared against the incoming signal. Phase-coherent PSK modems suffer from several drawbacks, including the need for complex demodulation circuitry and their susceptibility to random phase changes in the signal.

A variation on phase-coherent PSK is *differential PSK*. A differential PSK signal differs from the phase-coherent PSK signal in that the signal used to represent a bit is *relative* to the last bit signal. For example, a phase shift of 90° could indicate a space, while a phase shift of 270° could indicate a mark. The byte S transmitted using differential PSK and using the above shifts would appear as shown in Figure 8.8. A differential PSK modem need only determine the magnitude of the phase shift to obtain the value of the bit.

Example 8.1   The modem offers a limited bandwidth of about 3000 Hz; if the entire frequency is devoted to one DTE or the other, the result is a simplex communication (or half-duplex, if a protocol is in place to allow the channel to be turned around).

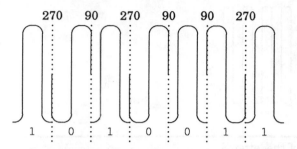

Figure 8.8   Differential PSK of the letter S

To achieve a full-duplex communication would require that the available frequency (3000 Hz) be divided in two: half for transmission, the other half for reception. This raises a problem: there are two modems, and if they both transmit at the same frequency, their signals will collide, and communications will cease. Some type of agreement is necessary to ensure that one modem will use one set of frequencies, and the other modem will use another set of frequencies.

Fortunately, it is possible to assign frequencies based upon whether the modem is originating or answering the call (hence the reason for allowing only originating modems to communicate with answering modems). An originating modem will transmit on frequency X and receive on frequency Y, while the answering modem will transmit on frequency Y and receive on frequency X.

For example, a 300-bps Bell-103 modem assigns the following frequencies to the modem, depending on whether it is in originate or answer mode (Figure 8.9).

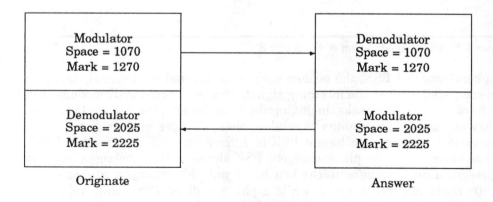

Figure 8.9   Frequency assignment of a 300-bps Bell-103 modem

The CCITT equivalent 200-bps modem (CCITT Recommendation V.21) uses the frequencies given in Figure 8.10.

Bits per second vs. baud   Up to this point in the text, all references to line speed has been in terms of *bits per second*. However, reading through the

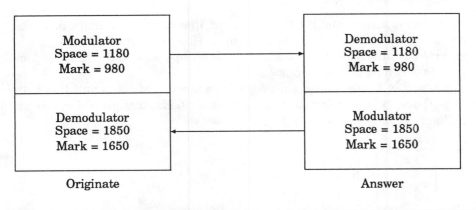

Figure 8.10 Frequency assignment for a CCITT 200-bps modem

literature, one finds that modems are often described in terms of *baud* rather than bits per second. Baud (named in honour of Emile Baudot, inventor of the Baudot code), is defined as follows:

A unit of signalling speed equal to the number of discrete conditions or signal events per second.[1]

Baud is equivalent to bits per second if each signal event is equal to exactly 1 bit. As an example, 300 bps is the same as 300 baud if there is 1 signal event every 1/300 of a second. If the channel uses 2400 Hz (cycles per second) to indicate a mark, then the number of cycles required to represent a mark is:

$$\frac{1}{300} \text{ sec} * 2400 \text{ Hertz} = 8 \text{ cycles}$$

Diagramatically, one bit would appear as shown in Figure 8.11.

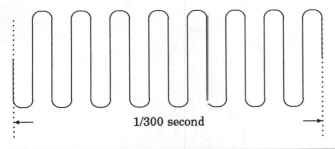

Figure 8.11 A 300-bps bit at 2400 Hz

Similarly, 600 bps is equivalent to 600 baud at 2400 Hz if 1 bit is sent every 4 cycles. If the modem can be designed to recognize 1 bit per cycle, then the modem can support 2400 bps. Since the maximum frequency the telephone

[1]J.E. McNamara, *Technical Aspects of Data Communications*, Second Edition, Digital Press, Bedford, Mass., 1982.

system allows is about 3400 Hz, the maximum line speed that can be achieved if 1 bit is equivalent to 1 baud, is 3400 bps. However, the U(S)ART can be programmed to much higher speeds than 3400 bps and still use a modem: The question is how is this accomplished?

One answer is to use phase shifting. For example, at 600 baud there are 600 "signal events" occurring each second. At 2400 Hz, this gives 4 cycles per baud (Figure 8.12).

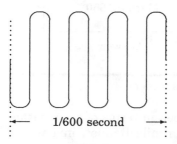

1/600 second

Figure 8.12   One signal event (baud) at 2400 Hz and 600 baud

By shifting the phase of the signal by 90°, four distinct patterns emerge, allowing the assignment of four different bit combinations (Figure 8.13).

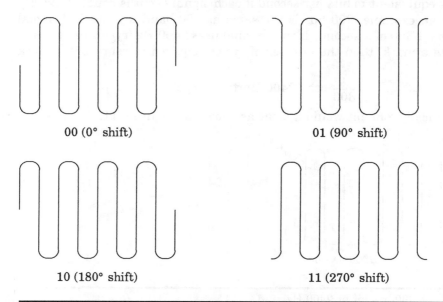

00 (0° shift)   01 (90° shift)

10 (180° shift)   11 (270° shift)

Figure 8.13   The 90° phase shift allows two bits per baud

Now each signal event contains *two* bits. Two bits per baud is known as a *dibit*. The phase shift allows the 600-baud channel to support 1200 bps. For example, to transmit the 7-bit ASCII character S on a 600-baud channel at 2400 Hz would produce the signal shown in Figure 8.14 (assuming phase-coherent PSK).

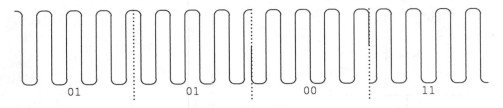

01　　　　01　　　　00　　　　11

Figure 8.14　The letter S at 2400 Hz and 600 baud phase-shifted

Note that an even number of bits are required and, in this case, the eighth bit is sent as a zero. In an asynchronous transmission, the entire frame is sent (i.e., start, stop, parity, and data bits). If the resulting number of bits is odd, the next start bit or an idle mark would be encoded into the last dibit. Similarly, in a synchronous communication, a dibit may contain the last bit of one data byte and the first bit of the next data byte.

The Bell 212 is a full-duplex modem that supports either low-speed (i.e., 300 bps) or high-speed (1200 bps) communications. In low-speed mode, the modem generates FSK signals and is compatible with the Bell 103 modem described previously. High-speed mode is achieved using PSK operating at 600 baud, there is a single transmission frequency and a single reception frequency (Figure 8.15).

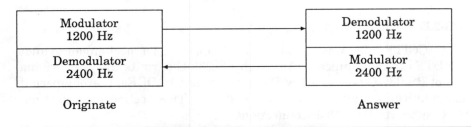

Originate   Answer

Figure 8.15　1200-bps Bell 212 frequency assignments

The Bell 212 achieves 1200 bps on a 600-baud channel by encoding the data into dibits using differential PSK (Table 8.2).

TABLE 8.2　Bell 212 Dibit Values

Dibits	Phase Differential
00	−135
01	−45
10	+45
11	+135

Higher channel speeds can be achieved by using combinations of phase shifting and amplitude modulation. For example, *tribits* (or three bits per baud), can be obtained by having two different amplitude levels and four different phase angles (Figure 8.16).

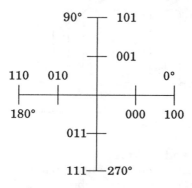

Figure 8.16   Tribits or three bits per baud

A phase shift of 90° to the first amplitude level would indicate a value of 001; while a phase shift of 270° to the second amplitude level would indicate 111. Using tribits it is possible to attain 1800 bps on a 600-baud channel.

Through other combinations of phase angles and amplitude shifts, even higher speeds can be attained; for example, at 4 bits per baud, 2400 baud can support 9600 bps. This is known as as *QAM (quadrature amplitude modulation)*.

8.4   RS-232-C (CCITT V.24)

RS-232-C (CCITT V.24) was introduced in Chapter 4 as a mechanism to allow pairs of DTEs to communicate. Although RS-232-C permits this, the original purpose of RS-232-C was to allow DTEs to connect to DCEs, thereby permitting communications across telephone systems. This section examines how RS-232-C supports DTE-DCE connections.

The signals between the DTE and the DCE are digital 0s and 1s, while the signals on the telephone network are analog. RS-232-C carries digital signals between the DTE and the DCE (Figure 8.17).

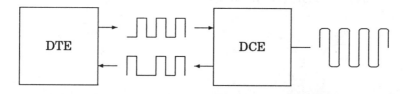

Figure 8.17   RS-232 carries digital signals between the DTE and DCE

RS-232-C requires a minimum of three connections between the DTE and the DCE: signal ground, transmission, and reception. To ensure that all manufacturer's equipment (DTE or DCE) can communicate, RS-232-C defines both its signal levels and the physical wiring between the DTE and the DCE. RS-232-C connectors support either 25 or 9 pins. Each RS-232-C pin performs a specific task and is given a unique label. All signals are defined in relation to the DTE; that is, signals are sent *to* the DCE or *from* the DCE.

8.4.1 Required Connections

Although RS-232-C supports a 25-pin connector, only three connections are required for the transmission and reception of data (two circuit labels are given, the first for RS-232-C, the second for CCITT V.24):

Pin 2. Transmitted data (to DCE). Circuit BA (CCITT: 103).

Data generated by the DTE is sent to the DCE on this circuit. The circuit is kept in the mark state at all times when there is no transmission in progress.

Pin 3. Received data (from DCE). Circuit BB (CCITT: 104).

Signals are generated on this circuit by the DCE based upon the signals received from the remote DCE. The circuit is kept in the mark state at all times when there is no transmission in progress.

Pin 7. Signal ground or common return (there is no direction on this circuit). Circuit AB (CCITT: 102).

This circuit establishes the common ground between the DTE and DCE. It is used as the reference for determining whether a signal is a mark or a space.

8.4.2 Minimum Line Control Requirements

Transmit data, receive data, and signal ground are the minimum number of connections required between the DTE and DCE to ensure data transfer. The following circuits are used to control access to the telephone channel:

Pin 22. Ring Indicator (from DCE). Circuit CE (CCITT: 125, "calling indicator").

Set by the DCE when an incoming ringing signal has been detected. The signal is *on* during a ring and *off* between rings and at all other times when ringing is not being received.

Pin 20. Data Terminal Ready, more commonly DTR (to DCE). Circuit CD (CCITT: 108/2).

Used by the DTE to control the DCE's access to the communication channel. The *on* condition causes the DCE to connect to the telephone channel (this can be set at any time, either before Ring Indicator is set or during the ringing sequence).

The *off* condition causes the DCE to disconnect from the communication channel. It is important to note that because most U(S)ARTs are double buffered, one or more bytes may still be in the UART when the *off* condition is to be raised. To avoid losing these bytes, the software should be written so that it waits for an indication that the last byte has been sent (on the PC's 8250 UART, the signal is Transmit Shift Register Empty) before setting DTR *off*.

Pin 8. Received Line Signal Detector, more commonly Carrier Detect (from DCE). Circuit CF (CCITT: 109, Data Channel Received Line Signal Detector).

This circuit indicates that the local DCE has detected a valid line signal from the remote DCE. The circuit is *on* when the signal meets the signal levels specified by the type of DCE; it is *off* when the signal no longer meets the required levels.

Pin 6. Data set ready, more commonly *DSR* (from DCE). Circuit CC (CCITT: 107).

An indication as to the status of the local DCE. *On* indicates the following conditions:

1. the local DCE is connected to a communication channel, and
2. the local DCE is not in test, talk, or dial mode, and
3. it has reached the stage where a call can be established (see Section 8.4.3).

An *off* indicates that the DTE is to ignore the signals from the DCE.

8.4.3 Full-Duplex Communications

In a typical full-duplex communication, each DTE is given half of the carrier, thereby allowing simultaneous transfer of information. Before a communication can take place across the telephone network, the call must be set up (or established) by the modems (one originating the call, the other answering it). Although the exact sequence can vary from manufacturer to manufacturer, the steps required to setup, maintain and eventually clear a full-duplex communication are essentially as follows.

Originating modem At the originating modem, the call is placed by a user following these or a variation of these steps:

1. The user dials the digits of the answering modem.
2. The telephone at the answering modem rings. The answering modem responds with a carrier once the telephone has been answered. (There can be a delay in this step if the answering modem requires operator intervention at the answering modem; see the discussion on answering the modem).
3. The user presses the Data/Talk button.
4. The telephone is hung up. (Note, this does not clear the call since the modem is in control of the telephone line).

Within the DTE itself, the following algorithm can be applied:

1. wait for carrier and Data Set Ready (DSR)
2. once detected, respond with Data Terminal Ready (DTR)
3. commence and maintain the data transfer

Note that most modems have been designed to allow steps one and two to be reversed.

Answering modem   At the answering modem, call setup can be achieved by the DCE and DTE or by operator intervention. If the call is answered by the operator, the steps are as follows:

1. The telephone rings and is answered by the operator.
2. The DCE is in answer mode (to allow the transfer of data).
3. The operator presses the Data/Talk button.
4. The carrier is generated.
5. The operator hangs up the handset.

Internally, the software must wait for Carrier Detect (CD) and DSR. The subsequent steps are the same as those of the originating modem.

It is also possible to have the DTE answer the call in conjunction with the DCE. In such situations, the following steps occur:

1. DCE detects a ring and signals the DTE with a Ring Indicator (RI).
2. DTE responds by asserting DTR.
3. DCE generates a carrier and signals CD and DSR to DTE.
4. Data transfer is performed as usual.

Call clearing   The call can be cleared by either end through one of a number of methods:

- The Data/Talk button on the modem can be pressed, resulting in the carrier being dropped. This causes CD and DSR to drop, allowing the software to determine that the call has been cleared.
- The software can stop asserting DTR. When the modem detects that DTE is no longer active, the carrier is dropped.
- The carrier (from the remote DCE) drops. When the modem detects that the carrier has been dropped (usually a signal that the remote has disconnected), CD and DSR are dropped, once again, allowing the software to clear the call.

In all of the above cases listed, the modem is usually designed to wait a period of time (on the order of 50 milliseconds) to ensure that the event has actually ocurred. For example, a modem detecting a loss of carrier waits 50 milliseconds before clearing the call; should the carrier return during this period, the call is not cleared.

8.4.4   Half-Duplex Communications

A half-duplex communication requires that a single modem generate a carrier at any one time and differs from a full-duplex communication in that once one

DTE has finished transmitting, the line can be "turned around" so that the other DTE can transmit (Figure 8.18).

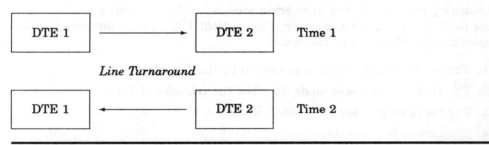

Figure 8.18   Half-duplex communications require line turnaround

This then raises the issue: How does a modem "know" when to turn the line around, start (or stop) transmitting and stop (or start) receiving? Since RS-232-C is not an end-to-end protocol (that is, no information, other than DTE data, is passed between the two modems), the signal to perform line turnaround must therefore come from another source.

The solution is to use a higher level of protocol to which both DTEs agree. For example, the half-duplex Bisync protocol defines which DTE can be transmitting at any moment in time. Certain agreed upon control sequences cause the DTEs to exchange control of the line (Figure 8.19).

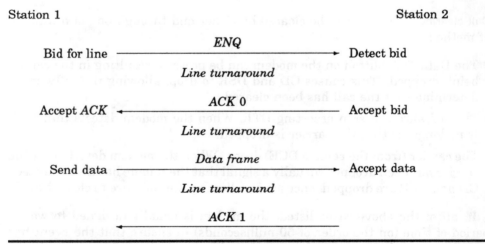

Figure 8.19   In Bisync, stations signal their modems to turnaround

Since the modem is responsible for generating the carrier, it must be signalled to start (and stop) carrier generation. RS-232-C defines two other signals to allow the DTE and modem to achieve line turnaround:

Pin 4. Request to Send, commonly known as RTS (to DCE). Circuit CA (CCITT: 105).

This signals the DCE that the DTE has data to send. However, the DTE cannot start transmitting at this point, it must wait for the DCE to indicate clear to send.

Pin 5. Clear to Send, commonly known as CTS or *"Ready for Sending"* (from DCE). Circuit CB (CCITT: 106). Indicates that the DCE is able to send data to the remote DCE. *On* indicates to the DTE that data can be sent, while *off* indicates that the DCE is not prepared to transmit. Once the DTE detects CTS, it can start to transmit.

In a full-duplex communication, CTS can be wired to the carrier detect signal, meaning that as long as there is a carrier, it is clear to send data (this is known as *CB-CF common*). See Figure 8.20.

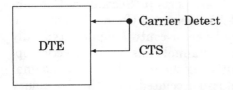

Figure 8.20   CB-CF common

In some full-duplex modems, the RTS signal is ignored since it is assumed that the DTE will always be in a state that allows transmission.

In a typical half-duplex RS-232-C application, the DTE sends a RTS to the DCE, to which the DCE responds with CTS. However, since RS-232-C is not an end-to-end protocol, the local DCE has no indication of whether the remote DCE-DTE is ready to accept data (remember, the CTS signal is simply between the local DTE and local DCE). To avoid having the local DTE transmit data before the remote DCE-DTE is ready to accept it, the RTS can invoke a timer which, upon expiring, causes CTS (this is known as *CB-CF separation*). See Figure 8.21.

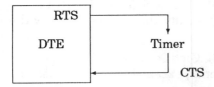

Figure 8.21   CB-CF separation

When the line is to be turned around, each DTE is responsible for certain actions to ensure that the communication can continue:

DTE about to receive. The DTE that is about to receive (i.e., the former transmitter) must signal its modem to stop generating the carrier signal; this is achieved by dropping RTS. The DTE waits for its modem to detect the carrier from the remote modem, at which point carrier detect is signalled. Data can then follow.

DTE about to transmit. The DTE about to transmit (i.e., the former receiver) signals its modem to start generating the carrier signal by raising RTS. After a given time period (see previous discussion), the modem signals CTS to the DTE. The DTE can then start to transmit.

8.4.5 Miscellaneous Connections

In addition to the nine circuits already described, there are a number of other RS-232-C circuits used to support a variety of communication situations. In general, these circuits are used in exceptional circumstances, which are now outlined.

Secondary communication channel   RS-232-C supports a "Secondary Communication Channel" or *reverse channel* (CCITT: Backward Channel) that is intended for the transmission of supervisory or error-control signals, typically in a half-duplex communication. The reverse channel runs in the direction opposite to the main transmission, thereby allowing the receiving DTE to signal without turning the line around. The circuits associated with the Secondary Communication Channel are:

Pin 14. Secondary Transmitted Data (to DCE). Circuit SBA (CCITT: 118).
  Equivalent to circuit BA, except that SBA is used by the secondary channel.

Pin 16. Secondary Received Data (from DCE). Circuit SBB (CCITT: 119).
  Equivalent to circuit BB, except that SBB is used by the secondary channel.

Pin 12. Secondary Received Line Signal Indicator (from DCE). Circuit SCF (CCITT: 122).
  Equivalent to circuit CF (carrier detect), except that SCF is used by the secondary channel.

Pin 13. Secondary Clear to Send (from DCE). Circuit SCB (CCITT: 121).
  Equivalent to circuit CB (Clear to Send), except that SCB is used by the secondary channel.

Pin 19. Secondary Request to Send (to DCE). Circuit SCA (CCITT: 120).
  Equivalent to circuit CA (Request to Send), except that SCA is used by the secondary channel.

Other Signals

Pin 1. Protective ground. Circuit AA (no equivalent CCITT circuit). This circuit is grounded to the DTE.

Pins 9, 10. Reserved for testing purposes.

Pin 23. Data signal rate selector.
  This signal permits the changing of the data signal rate: if *on*, the higher speed supported by the DCE is chosen; if *off*, the lower speed is chosen.

This signal can be set by either the DCE or the DTE. If the signal direction is to the DCE, pin 23 is circuit CH (CCITT: 111), otherwise pin 23 is circuit CI (CCITT: 112), from the DCE.

Pin 21. Signal quality detector (from DCE). Circuit CG (CCITT: 110).

If the telephone channel appears to be error free, this signal is set on. However, if the DCE detects an error on the telephone channel, the signal is turned off.

Pin 17. Receiver Signal Timing Element (from DCE). Circuit DD (CCITT: 115).

If the DTE does not support a receive clock that permits it to determine the center of each received bit, the clocking signal must be supplied by the DCE. This circuit allows the DCE to signal the center of each bit sent by the DCE.

Pin 24. Transmitter Signal Timing Element (to DCE). Circuit DA (CCITT: 113).

If the DCE does not supply its own clocking signal (to determine the center of each bit), the signal must be supplied on this circuit by the DTE. The *on/off* transition of the timing signal indicates the center of each bit.

Pin 15. Transmitter Signal Timing Element (from DCE). Circuit DB (CCITT: 114).

If the DTE does not supply it own clocking signal, the signal is supplied by the DCE on this circuit. The DTE supplies a bit between each timing signal.

Pins 11, 18, 25. Unassigned.

8.4.6 9-Pin Connectors

From the above discussion on RS-232-C it should be clear that the majority of the pins on the standard 25-pin connector (also known as a *DB-25 connector*) can usually be safely ignored. As such, many manufacturers now produce 9-pin (or *DB-9*) RS-232-C connectors. The assignment of pins on an RS-232-C 9-pin connector are given in Table 8.3 (there is *not* a one-to-one correspondence to the 25-pin connector).

TABLE 8.3   RS-232 9-Pin Signal Names

9-Pin Connector	25-Pin Equivalent	Signal Name
1	8	Carrier detect
2	2	Transmit data
3	3	Receive data
4	20	Data Terminal Ready (DTR)
5	7	Signal Ground
6	6	Data Set Ready (DSR)
7	4	Request to Send (RTS)
8	5	Clear to Send (CTS)
9	22	Ring Indicator

8.4.7 The Null Modem

In theory, two DTEs cannot communicate unless they are connected via a pair of DCEs because the transmit and receive pins connect directly. However, in Chapter 4, it was shown that if two DTEs are spaced less than 50 feet (15 meters) apart, a special null-modem cable will permit the DTEs to communicate. The null-modem cable crosses pins 2 (transmit) and 3 (receive), thereby ensuring whatever is sent by one DTE will be received by the other. The minimum null-modem wiring is as shown in Figure 8.22.

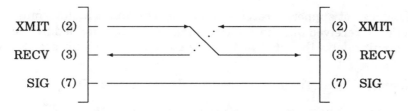

Figure 8.22   The minimum null-modem wiring

In many cases, application software is written to support more than simply the transmit and receive connections. For example, an application written for half-duplex communications will probably not work with the above null-modem cable because it expects signals such as CTS to be set. A complete null-modem cable (supporting both half- and full-duplex communications) could be wired as illustrated in Figure 8.23 (the diagram assumes an RS-232-C 25-pin connector).

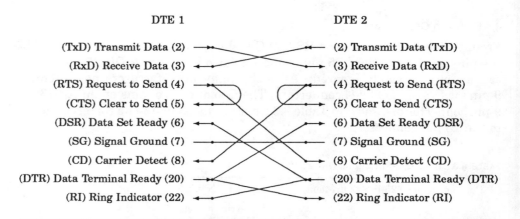

Figure 8.23   A complete null-modem wiring

The results of the above connections cause the following to occur:

- local DTR *on* turns remote RI *on* and remote DSR *on*.

- local RTS *on* turns local CTS *on* and remote CD *on*.

■ local TxD *on* turns remote RxD *on*.

8.4.8 Limited-Distance Modems

In certain situations, the distance between the two DTEs does not warrant the installation of a separate telephone circuit and modem, while at the same time, RS-232-C signals are not strong enough to reach the remote DTE. Instead, a *limited-distance modem* can be employed to interconnect the two DTEs.

Limited-distance modems draw power from the DTE's RS-232-C port to help boost the RS-232-C signal (for example, power can be taken from pins 4 (RTS) or 20 (DTR)). The maximum separation between the two DTEs depends upon the manufacturer of the limited-distance modem, but typically cannot exceed about 2.5 kilometres.

8.5 RS-422-A, RS-423-A, AND RS-449

In Chapter 4, several other connection standards were discussed, notably RS-422-A, RS-423-A, and RS-449. These three standards, like RS-232-C, define the physical and electrical standards of a DTE-DCE interconnection. Table 8.4 shows RS-449 with its corresponding RS-232-C and CCITT V.24 signals.

Although the Electrical Industries Association intends to replace RS-232-C with RS-422-A, RS-423-A, and RS-449, the popularity and widespread use of RS-232-C means that the replacement process will probably be a slow one. In addition, the trend for DTE-DCE interconnection is towards *less* wires, rather than more, meaning that these new standards may already be outdated.

8.6 PC MODEM CONTROL

The 8250 UART supplied with the PC supports a limited number of RS-232-C modem functions, specifically:

■ the ability to control a number of modem conditions (through the Modem Control Register)

■ the ability to determine the modem's status (from the Modem Status Register)

The UART can be programmed to interrupt the PC when modem status changes occur.

8.6.1 The Modem Control Register

Previous chapters have shown a number of uses of the Modem Control Register (port 0x3FC or 0x2FC), including loopback and enabling UART interrupts. The Modem Control Register can also be used by the PC to send DTR (Data Terminal Ready) and RTS (Request to Send) signals to the UART.

TABLE 8.4   RS-449 and Corresponding RS-232 and CCITT V.24 Signals

	RS-449		RS-232-C		CCITT V.24
SG	Signal Ground	AB	Signal Ground	102	Signal Ground
SC	Send Common			102a	DTE Common
RC	Receive Common			102b	DCE Common
IS	Terminal in Service				
IC	Incoming Call	CE	Ring Indicator	125	Calling Indicator
TR	Terminal Ready	DC	Data Terminal Ready	108/2	Data Terminal Ready
DM	Data Mode	CC	Data Set Ready	107	Data Set Ready
SD	Send Data	BA	Transmitted Data	103	Transmitted Data
RD	Receive Data	BB	Received Data	104	Received Data
TT	Terminal Timing	DA	Transmitter Signal Element Timing (DTE)	113	Transmitter Signal Element Timing (DTE)
ST	Send Timing	DB	Transmitter Signal Element Timing (DCE)	114	Transmitter Signal Element Timing (DCE)
RT	Receive Timing	DD	Receive Signal Element Timing	115	Receiver Signal Element Timing (DCE)
RS	Request to Send	CA	Request to Send	105	Request to Send
CS	Clear to Send	CB	Clear to Send	106	Ready for Sending
RR	Receiver Ready	CF	Received Line Signal Detector	109	Data Channel Received Line Signal Detector
SQ	Signal Quality	CG	Signal Quality Detector	110	Data Signal Quality Detector
NS	New Signal				
SF	Select Frequency			126	Select Transmit Frequency
SR	Signalling Rate	CH	Data Signal Rate Selector (DTE)	111	Data Signalling Rate Selector (DTE)
SI	Signalling Rate Indicator	CI	Data Signal Rate Selector (DCE)	112	Data Signalling Rate Selector (DCE)
SSD	Secondary Send Data	SBA	Secondary Transmitted Data	118	Transmitted Backward Channel Data
SRD	Secondary Receive Data	SBB	Secondary Received Data	119	Received Backward Channel Data
SRS	Secondary Request to Send	SCA	Secondary Request to Send	120	Transmit Backward Channel Line Signal
SCS	Secondary Clear to Send	SCB	Secondary Clear to Send	121	Backward Channel Ready
SRR	Secondary Receiver Ready	SCF	Secondary Received Line Signal Detector	122	Backward Channel Received Line Signal
LL	Local Loopback			141	Local Loopback
RL	Remote Loopback			140	Remote Loopback
TM	Test Mode			142	Test Indicator
SS	Select Standby			116	Select Standby
SB	Standby Indicator			117	Standby Indicator

The structure of the Modem Control Register is shown in Figure 8.24, and is defined as follows.

DTR. When set, the modem is signalled that the PC has connected to the modem and is able to send and receive data.

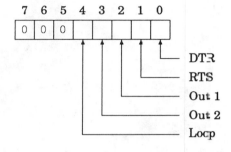

Figure 8.24 The 8250 Modem Control Register

RTS. The PC is requesting access to the channel. This is often ignored in full-duplex modems, but is necessary for half-duplex configurations.

Out 1. Not used.

Out 2. Must be set to enable VART interrupts.

Loop. Set to enter loopback mode (see Chapter 5).

Bits 5, 6, and 7. Permanently zero.

For example, to signal the modem that the PC is connected to the channel and has data to send, one could write:

```
#define MCR      0x3FC
#define DTR      0x01
#define RTS      0x02
#define OUT2     0x08

outportb(MCR, DTR+RTS+OUT2)
```

To clear the modem, one could use the following (note that OUT2 must be written to the Modem Control Register to ensure that all serial port interrupts will be allowed to continue):

```
outportb(MCR, OUT2);
```

8.6.2 The Modem Status Register

The Modem Status Register (port address 0x3FE or 0x2FE) can be used to determine a limited number of status indications of the modem. Specifically, the Modem Status Register indicates a change in state of any of four different RS-232-C connections as well as the current value of connection (Figure 8.25). The register bits are defined as follows:

△**CTS.** There has been a change in the CTS signal since the last time the modem status register was read. The new value of CTS can be obtained by examining bit 0x10 of the Modem Status Register.

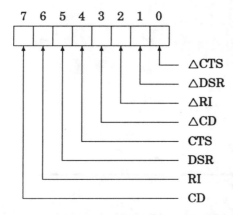

Figure 8.25   The 8250 Modem Status Register

△**DSR.** There has been a change in the DSR signal since the last time the Modem Status Register was read. The new value of DSR can be obtained by examining bit `0x20` of the Modem Status Register.

△**RI.** There has been a change in the Ring Indicator (RI) signal since the last time the Modem Status Register was read. The new value of RI can be obtained by examining bit `0x40` of the Modem Status Register. This bit is set everytime the telephone rings and stops ringing.

△**CD.** There has been a change in the Carrier Detect (CD) signal since the last time the Modem Status Register was read. The new value of CD can be obtained by examining bit `0x80` of the Modem Status Register.

CTS. This is the value of the CTS signal. In full duplex applications, CTS is usually permanently set; while in half-duplex applications the value of CTS depends upon whether the DTE is attempting to transmit.

DSR. This is the value of the DSR signal. If the modem is functioning properly, this signal will be *on*, otherwise it is cleared. For data transfer to proceed, DSR must be *on*.

RI. This is the value of the RI signal. If a ringing tone is detected, RI is set *on*, otherwise it is set *off*. Ring Indicator only has meaning to answer-mode modems. Once the call is established, RI should not be generated.

CD. This is the value of the CD (Received Line Signal Detector) signal. If a carrier is present, data transfer can take place, subject to the rules of the protocol.

Depending upon the signals available from the modem, a data transfer should wait for `CTS`, `DSR`, and `CD`. For example, to wait for modem signals from serial port 2, one could write:

```
status = inportb(SP2 + 4);

if ((status & (CTS+DSR+CD)) == (CTS+DSR+CD))
    /* Data transfer can now proceed */
```

8.6.3 Modem Interrupts

Modem status changes can be made to cause interrupts by setting the UART's Interrupt Enable Register to 0x08. Then, whenever a change in the modem status occurs, an interrupt will occur and the UART's Interrupt Identification Register will contain a value of 0x00 (indicating a modem status change). The status of the modem can be obtained by reading the Modem Status Register:

```
while ((iir = inportb(address + 2)) != 1)
{
    switch(iir)
    {
    case 6: /* Line status */
        ...
    case 4: /* Data available */
        ...
    case 2: /* Transmit done */
        ...
    case 0: /* Modem status change */
        status = inportb(address + 6);
        /* Process status */
    }
}
```

8.7 MODEM TESTING

Although the addition of modems and the telephone network extends the distance over which a DTE can communicate, it also means that there are more things that can go wrong. Fortunately, most modems support a number of tests that can assist in tracking down communication errors.

8.7.1 Self-Tests

Some modems can perform *self-tests* in which a specific binary test pattern is generated and then modulated. The modulated signal is looped back and demodulated. If the demodulated pattern is the same as the original test pattern, the self-test was successful. Ideally, both the originate and answer frequencies should be tested. If an error is detected, it is usually signalled through an error-indication light on the front panel of the modem.

During a self-test, the connections to the DTE and the telephone network are disconnected (Figure 8.26).

8.7.2 The Analog Loopback Test

An *analog loopback test* is designed to check the operation of the local DTE. Signals transmitted by the DTE enter the modem where they are modulated, demodulated, and then returned to the DTE. To allow modem software to be tested, CD is set high. The test is successful if the transmitted data is equal to the received data.

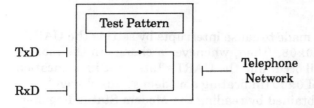

Figure 8.26   Modem self-test

In an analog loopback test, the DCE is isolated from the telephone network (Figure 8.27).

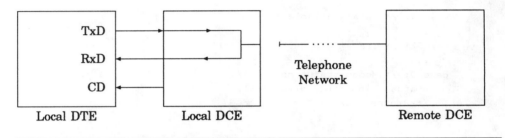

Figure 8.27   Analog loopback test

8.7.3   Digital Loopback Test

The *digital loopback test* is intended to test local demodulation and modulation of remote data; the local DTE does *not* partake in the test. The *remote DTE/DCE* transmits data across the telephone network while the local DCE demodulates the data and loops it back through the modulation circuitry (Figure 8.28).

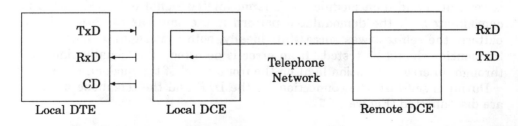

Figure 8.28   Digital loopback test

The test is successful if the data received by the remote DTE is the same as that sent by the remote DTE.

A variation on the digital loopback is the *modified digital loopback* in which the *local* transmitter is looped back at the modem (Figure 8.29).

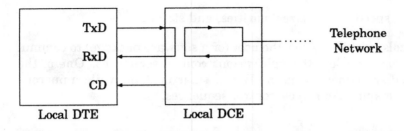

Figure 8.29 Modified digital loopback test

8.7.4 Remote Loopback Test

The *remote loopback test* permits testing of both modems and the telephone network (Figure 8.30).

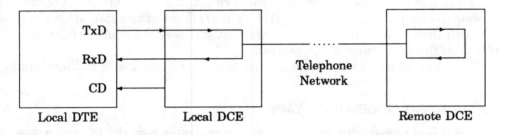

Figure 8.30 Remote loopback test

Signals are transmitted across the telephone network and looped back at the remote DCE. The remote DCE enters digital loopback test mode. The tests are successful if, at the local DTE, the data sent is the same as that received.

8.8 MODEM VARIATIONS

A number of interesting extensions to the modem are available commercially. The first are known as *smartmodems* and the other, a variation on smart-modems are *automatic calling units* (*ACU*s).

8.8.1 Smartmodems

Smartmodems are modems that contain a processor to help the user in placing and maintaining the call. In its simplest form, a smartmodem maintains a list of telephone numbers of different remote DTEs. When the user selects one of the numbers, the smartmodem places the call (by pulsing the digits or generating the tones associated with the digits).

Smarter smartmodems can have a variety of other options, including:

- The ability to perform self-tests
- The ability to associate a name along with the telephone number of the remote DTE; to permit a name rather than the number to be specified

■ a choice of line speeds, word sizes, parities, and stop bits.

Special protocols exist that allow the user (or a software package) to communicate with the smartmodem through various control sequences. One of the most widely used smartmodems is the Hayes' smartmodem; while numerous other smartmodems use the Hayes' control sequences.

8.8.2   Automatic-Calling Units

An automatic-calling unit is a hardware/software package that can place an outgoing call to a remote DTE.

One common application of the ACU is to place data transfer calls late at night to take advantage of low-cost telephone rates. Another application is to permit the verification of the source of the incoming call. In these situations, the DTE with the automatic-calling unit is called, the DTE obtains an identification associated with the calling DTE. The DTE with the automatic-calling unit can then contact the DTE to verify that this was the source of the call. If it was, the data transfer can proceed.

The EIA standard, RS-366 provides specifications for automatic-calling units.

8.9   COMMKIT MODEM SOFTWARE

Commkit is supplied with software that demonstrates how the PC and a modem can be made to interact. The software, modem.c, extends the point-to-point telephone utility developed in Chapter 3 to handle modems. Modem.c supports both originating and answering modems.

8.9.1   Hardware Requirements

Two different test configurations are possible. For example, if two PCs, two modems, and two telephones are available (Figure 8.31), all of the testing can take place using the modem software (*Org* is the originating station, while *Ans* is the answering).

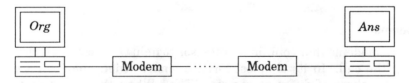

Figure 8.31   Hardware configuration if two modems are available

However, testing can still take place with a single modem if a remote host with dial-in facilities is available. In this case, an outgoing call is placed to the remote host; output from the remote host will appear on the lower half of the screen, while the local input will appear on the upper half of the screen (Figure 8.32).

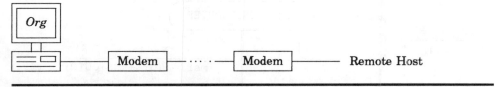

Figure 8.32   Hardware configuration if one modem is available

Finally, regardless of the configuration, the PC and the modem must be connected by a straight-through cable rather than a null-modem cable.

8.9.2   Design

The original point-to-point software will not support a modem. Any modem status changes detected by the `commkit` module and passed to `low_level()` with a `code` value of `MODEMSTATUS` are simply ignored. This must be modified if modem status changes are to be recognized and acted upon.

The number of modem status changes that are recognized by the 8250 UART is limited to:

Clear to Send (CTS). The modem is ready for transmission.

Data Set Ready (DSR). The modem is in data mode.

Ring Indicator (RI). The modem is receiving a ring from the telephone line.

Received Line Signal Detect (CD). The modem is receiving carrier (also referred to as Carrier Detect).

The major difference between the answering modem and the originating modem is whether Ring Indicator is detected. (Ring Indicator should only be detected by the answering modem.)

Once carrier is detected (by the answering modem asserting carrier or the user at the originating modem pressing the Data/Talk button), the modem should enter the DSR state and signal both `DSR` and `RLSD` to the UART. Upon detection of `DSR` and `RLSD`, the DTE can respond with D*T*R and RTS, since these are the only two signals supported by the UART. At this point the DTE is connected to the DCE and communications can commence.

Communications will continue until either end drops the carrier, or after the detection of an CTRL-C.

8.9.3   Implementation

Modifying the point-to-point software to support modems essentially entails adding modem control software to monitor the state of the modem before and during the exchange of information between the DTEs. A two-state finite-state machine can be defined as in Figure 8.33 to control both an originating as well as an answering modem (`mcr` is the value of the Modem Control Register and `msr` is the value of the Modem Status Register).

When a modem status change occurs, control is passed to `low_level()` with `device` indicating the serial port, a `code` value of `MODEMSTATUS`, and

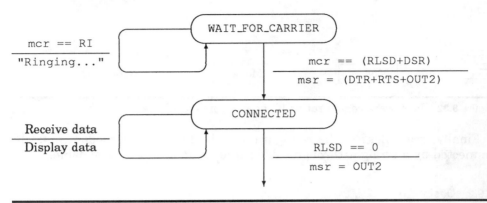

Figure 8.33   Modem control software state machine

the value of the modem status register in `data`. Although it would be a simple matter to forward the value of `data` to a process, and have the process check the modem status, the low-level Commkit modem software interprets the modem status and forwards a code to the foreground process. Similarly, the foreground process does not access the Modem Control Register, instead a message is sent to the low-level modem software indicating the required actions.

To support this design, the following changes are necessary:

1. A mechanism is needed whereby the foreground process can send messages to the serial port for transmission or for controlling the modem. A number of solutions are possible, such as sending a two-byte message to the modem serial port: one byte containing the data, the other containing a code indicating whether the byte is for transmission or to control the modem. The solution adopted involves creating two new process identifiers: `MODEM_DATA` and `MODEM_CHANGE`, defined as `SP1IH` and `SP2IH`, respectively.

   Now, all data to be transmitted is sent to `MODEM_DATA` and all modem control information is sent to `MODEM_CHANGE`.

2. `Low_level()` is modified to recognize the two different process identifiers. `Code` values associated with `MODEM_DATA` are taken to mean the standard actions associated with any serial port software; while the only acceptable `code` value associated with `MODEM_CHANGE` is `MSG_AVAIL`.

   A `MODEM_DATA` code value of `MODEMSTATUS` *or* a message for `MODEM_CHANGE` causes control to pass to `modem_change()`. `Modem_change()` is responsible for interpreting either the value of the modem status register or the message code from the foreground process:

   `MODEMSTATUS`. `Modem_change()` examines the value of the modem status register for one of the values given in Table 8.5 and, if found, sends the associated modem code to the foreground process.

   `MODEM_CHANGE`. The foreground process instructs `modem_change()` to change the Modem Control Register to a new value (Table 8.6).

TABLE 8.5 Modem Code (to Foreground Process)

Value of `msr`	Modem Code
RI	RINGING
RLSD + DSR	CARRIER_AVAIL
RLSD == 0	CARRIER_LOST

TABLE 8.6 New Modem Value (from Foreground Process)

Modem Code	New Value of `mcr`
ACCEPT_CALL	(DTR + RTS + OUT2)
CLEAR_CALL	OUT2

Note that when the modem software asserts DTR and RTS, OUT2 is also asserted to ensure that the 8250 still generates interrupts. Similarly, when the call is cleared, OUT2 must still be asserted.

3. The foreground process consists of two procedures: keyboard_data() and do_modem(). Keyboard_data() accepts characters from the keyboard (via do_modem()), displays them and forwards them to MODEM_DATA. CTRL-CS are forwarded by keyboard_data().

Do_modem() is an implementation of the finite-state machine presented at the start of this section with an additional state, DISCONNECTING. Control remains in state WAIT_FOR_CARRIER until a MODEM_CHANGE value of CARRIER_AVAIL is detected, at which point the modem control message ACCEPT_CALL is sent to MODEM_CHANGE. Note that messages of type RINGING cause the string "Ringing..." to be displayed.

Once the call is accepted, control passes to state CONNECTED, remaining here until either the carrier is lost (message CARRIER_LOST from MODEM_CHANGE) or the user enters CTRL-C. If an CTRL-C is detected, control passes to state DISCONNECTING, which waits two seconds before causing the carrier to be dropped, thereby permitting any pending characters to be sent to the remote DTE.

4. No changes are required for the background process BACKGROUND_1, do_rmt_scr(); it still receives bytes to be displayed on the screen from the serial port.

8.9.4 Compiling the Modem Software

An executable version of the modem software, modem.exe, can be created using the make utility:

```
C:\> make modem.exe
```

Modem.c includes the header files general.h, ascii.h, and devices.h. The object file modem.obj is linked with commkit.obj to produce modem.exe.

8.9.5 Running the Modem Software

Once an executable version of the modem software exists, it can be run by typing `modem` followed by the line speed (the modem software is written to communicate with an external modem attached to serial port 1):

```
C:\> modem 1200
```

Execution begins by the screen clearing. What happens next depends upon whether the DTE is the originating or the answering DTE:

Originating The number of the remote DTE/DCE must be dialed. When the carrier is heard, the Data/Talk button should be pressed and the telephone handset replaced in the cradle; the connection is now made (which lights appear on the modem depends upon the modem). As you type, the modem's Send light should flash on and off. If the parity, word size, and line speed are set correctly, a communication should be able to take place.

Answering The modem must be in answer mode (this might mean opening the modem and changing some settings; check the modem's instruction manual *before* embarking on this adventure).

Have someone at the remote modem dial the number of the local modem. When the telephone rings, the word `Ringing` should appear on the screen. What happens next depends upon the modem. If CD and DSR are set, the connection will be made. `Modem.c` may require changes to allow the communication to take place.

Once the connection is established, whatever is typed at the PC will be transmitted to the remote.

If the PC's modem is *internal* it is probably a so-called smart modem; meaning that `modem.c` may not function properly. It may be possible to configure the smart modem to act as an originating or answering modem and to issue commands to set, for example, DSR or to place the call; thereby creating an environment in which `modem.c` can work. Should the serial port used by the internal modem be something other than serial port 1, the constants `MODEM_DATA` and `MODEM_CHANGE` may have to be changed, along with serial port interrupt vector. Check the owner's manual for more details.

8.10 SUMMARY

This chapter has shown one way in which the distance limitations associated with standards such as RS-232-C can be overcome; notably, using the telephone network. Signals from a DTE cannot be placed directly onto the existing telephone system without the use of data communications equipment (DCE) or, more commonly, modems. Modems are responsible for modulating the signals from the DTE into a frequency that is acceptable to the telephone system and then demodulating the telephone frequencies back into a signal acceptable to the DTE. A variety of modulation technique exist including amplitude modulation, frequency modulation, and phase modulation. Phase modulation permits the transmission of much higher data rates using a variety of techniques such as phase and amplitute shifting, resulting in "more bits per baud."

The connection of the DTE to the DCE is also subject to standards, one of the most popular being RS-232-C. RS-232-C has a limited number of features, most of which are ignored by both manufacturers and users. RS-232-C modem control is limited as well because there is no mechanism to allow for end-to-end modem communications.

8.11 EXERCISES

1. Show that the complete null-modem cable (shown in Section 8.4.7) exhibits the same functions as a half-duplex modem.

2. What RS-232-C connections does your PC support? What RS-232-C connections does your modem support? Can the PC control all of the modem connections?

3. Obtain two PCs, two modems, and two telephones. Try running modem.c. The software was developed for a Bell 212 modem, therefore it might not work with your modem(s). If it doesn't, check the modem's instruction manual and modify modem.c so that software can control the modem properly.

4. As soon as do_modem() enters the DISCONNECTING state, all incoming characters are lost because only messages from CLKIH are processed. Extend do_modem() so that any keyboard characters that arrive while do_modem() is in the DISCONNECTING state are displayed. It may be necessary to lengthen the time taken between entering the DISCONNECTING state and the issuing of the CLEAR_CALL to allow testing of the software.

5. Rewrite modem.c so that when the call is cleared, instead of terminating the modem software, the software waits for another call.

6. Add modem software to the file transfer software; try transferring file to remote PCs.

7. Is it possible to write software which emulates a break-out box? That is, given the signals that the serial port supports, can we monitor and display the signals, while at the same time forwarding them (perhaps out the "other" port, somewhat like the line analyser)? The short answer to this problem is, yes it can be done, however the model fails in certain conditions. Write software to emulate the break-out box and identify the conditions in which the software cannot operate as a 'true' break-out box.

   This questions requires that you modify the serial port modem status change software in commkit.c. *Hint*: consider the issues surrounding the forwarding of modem status signals. Remember to take a copy of commkit.c before making any changes to it.

Multiplexing

9.1 INTRODUCTION

When people work at a terminal, they often pause, look around, think, scratch their heads, turn the page of the material they happen to be working on, the end result being that the channel connecting the terminal to the central computer is idle a considerable amount of the time. Even data-entry clerks who can type over a hundred words a minute and are working "flat-out" cannot keep the channel busy for any more than a fraction of its total capacity. As an example, the number of 10 character "words" that a typist would have to type each minute to keep a 9600-bps line full is:

$$\frac{9600 \text{ bits per second} \times 60 \text{ seconds per minute}}{10 \text{ bits per byte} \times 10 \text{ bytes per word}} = 5760 \text{ words per minute}$$

From this simple example, it is clear that a channel devoted to a single terminal is typically idle much more than it is active. If the channel could be *shared* amongst several terminals, the number of individual cables from user's DTEs to the central computer could be reduced dramatically, thereby cutting down on the expense of laying and maintaining the cables. The sharing of a single communication channel amongst several DTEs is known as *multiplexing*.

In addition to reducing cabling costs, multiplexing can also reduce the costs associated with telephone access of remote DTEs. For example, consider the costs to a company that has five telephone lines dedicated to data traffic. It may be possible to cut costs by up to 80 percent if the five telephone lines can be replaced by a single, multiplexed telephone line.

9.2   BACKGROUND

Multiprocessing DTEs such as timesharing computers are designed to support literally dozens of remote DTEs (PCs, terminals, and so on). Each remote DTE connection is made through a *port*, an interface to the central computer. Most operating systems allow the various ports to be configured (by either the system manager or the operating system) to specific terminal types such as: dial in, asynchronous, synchronous.

A typical set of DTE connections in a multiprocessing environment might consist of the configuration shown in Figure 9.1, in which three interactive terminals (DTE 1, DTE 2, and DTE 3) are connected by a series of individual asynchronous channels to ports E, L, and S, respectively, on a shared central processor (host DTE).

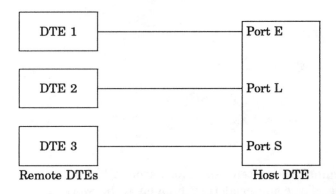

Figure 9.1   Remote DTEs connected to dedicated ports

If the individual channels connecting the interactive terminals to the ports on the host are only partially in use, it may be possible to have some or all of the terminals multiplex their communications onto a single channel; for example, see Figure 9.2.

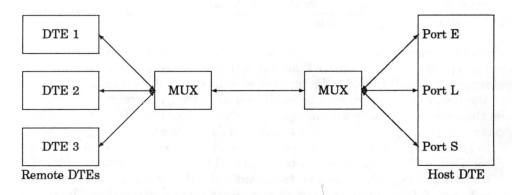

Figure 9.2   Remote DTEs sharing a channel by multiplexing

The equipment controlling the multiplexing is known as a *multiplexer* (or MUX) and performs two operations:

- the multiplexer takes information from the various DTEs and puts the information onto the multiplexed channel. This is known as *multiplexing*.

- the multiplexer takes information from the multiplexed channel and supplies it to the intended destination DTE. This is known as *demultiplexing*.

The operation of the multiplexer should be transparent to the DTEs that are being multiplexed. In this situation, transparency refers to the effect of the multiplexer on the communications. For example, there should be no detectable difference in communication speeds regardless of whether the multiplex is or is not present. Similarly, the data that is sent should not be altered in any way by the multiplexer.

The multiplexed channel is typically full-duplex, thereby allowing some DTEs to be transmitting information while others are receiving. Having said this, the connections between a multiplexer and its multiplexed DTEs can be any or all of full-duplex, half-duplex, or even simplex. It is also possible to have the multiplexer support a mixture of synchronous and asynchronous DTEs. In some cases, the connection between the DTEs and the multiplexer is asynchronous and the information sent between the multiplexers is synchronous. In short, the characteristics of the multiplexed channel should not have any bearing on the information that is being multiplexed. As with all other communicating devices, for the communications to succeed between a pair of multiplexers, both must agree to a common protocol.

9.2.1 Multiplexer Internals

A multiplexer is another example of the input-processing-output cycle. The multiplexing task consists of:

1. checking a connection for data
2. formatting the data according to the protocol used by the channel
3. transmitting the data on the channel

The demultiplexing algorithm is somewhat similar:

1. read the data from the channel
2. determine the destination of the data
3. forward the data to the specific connection

Physically, the multiplexer consists of two parts: connections to external devices and a connection to the remote multiplexer. The connections used depend upon the distance from the multiplexer to the external devices and the remote multiplexer; meaning that multiplexers usually support both direct connections and modems.

9.3 MULTIPLEXING TECHNIQUES

The multiplexer is responsible for ensuring that the information supplied by one DTE arrives at the correct destination DTE. There are three multiplexing techniques: *frequency-division multiplexing*, *time-division multiplexing*, and *statistical multiplexing*.

9.3.1 Frequency-Division Multiplexing

Frequency-division multiplexing (FDM), involves dividing the multiplexed channel into a number of unique frequencies, with each frequency assigned to a pair of communicating entities. FDM can be achieved only if the available bandwidth on the multiplexed channel exceeds the bandwidth needs of all the communicating entites.

Whenever a multiplexer receives data for transmission, the data is transmitted by the multiplexer on the frequency allocated to the transmitting entity. The receiving multiplexer forwards the information received on a specific frequency to the destination associated with that frequency.

The example given in Table 9.1 illustrates how a frequency-division multiplexer could connect DTEs 1, 2, and 3, with ports E, L, and S on a central host, respectively. The frequency allocation is as given in Table 9.1.

TABLE 9.1   Frequency Allocation for Figure 9.3

DTE-port pair	Frequency (Hz)
1 and E	10000–14000
2 and L	5000–9000
3 and S	0–4000

The 1000-Hz separation between the channels is known as the *guard band* and is used to ensure that one set of signals does not interfere with another.

Diagramatically, the connections are as shown in Figure 9.3.

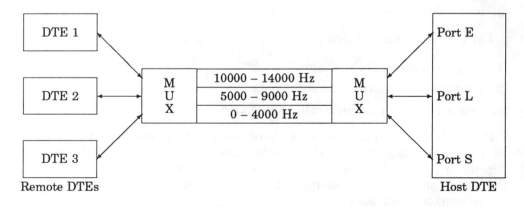

Figure 9.3   Frequency-division multiplexing

The advantage of FDM is that each DTE is assigned a unique frequency which can be treated as an unshared channel. However, FDM is not widely used in data communications because of the costs involved in having hardware that can transmit and receive signals on a variety of frequencies. An everyday example of FDM is cable television, in which many signals are "stacked up" and transmitted simultaneously over the cable. The user selects a viewing channel by tuning to that channel's frequency.

9.3.2 Time-Division Multiplexing

Time-division multiplexing (TDM) requires the multiplexer to timeshare the channel between the various DTEs involved in the communication. That is, at a specific moment, the remote multiplexer will send a byte from, say, DTE 1; at the next instance a byte from DTE 2 will be sent, and so on until all DTEs have been polled; the cycle is then repeated.

In Figure 9.4, DTEs 1, 2, and 3 are in communication with ports E, L, and S, respectively. The multiplexed channel is full-duplex and shared amongst all the communicating DTEs (the identifier in each box in the multiplexed channel between the two multiplexers should be read as "data from" the specific port or DTE; that is, it contains data rather than the identifier).

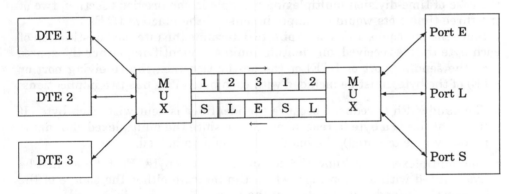

Figure 9.4   Time-division multiplexing

In Figure 9.4, the topmost channel contains data from DTEs 1, 2, and 3. The rightmost multiplexer is about to receive a byte from DTE 2, this is followed by a byte from DTE 1. On the lower channel, data is sent from ports E, L, and S; the leftmost multiplexer is about to receive a byte from port S.

To avoid the situation in which information arrives at the wrong DTE, both multiplexers must be synchronized. That is, the bytes must be sent in an agreed upon order and each byte that is received must be for the specific DTE (or port) to which it was intended. Synchronization can be achieved in a number of ways. A common approach is to use a special bit pattern that is used to indicate the start of a new cycle; for example, if N DTEs are being multiplexed, the $N+1$th byte to be transmitted would be the special, synchronizing bit pattern.

A time-division multiplexer polls each DTE to determine if there is information to be sent. However, a problem arises if one of the DTEs has nothing to send: What does the multiplexer transmit? Something *must* be sent because not sending a byte will mean that the time allotted to one DTE may be used by another, potentially resulting in the information arriving at the wrong destination. For example, if DTE 2 had nothing to send to port L, data from DTE 1 might be sent to port L instead.

This problem can be overcome in several ways, including:

- having a reserved-bit pattern (for example, the null character) that is sent whenever a DTE (or port) has nothing available for transmission

- transmitting *nine* bits between the multiplexers, eight bits for data, and the ninth to signal whether the byte contains data or is empty

9.3.3 Statistical Multiplexing

Statistical multiplexing attempts to overcome the problem of idling DTEs by only sending information from a DTE when information is available. For example, if three DTEs are sharing a channel and only one DTE is active, then as much of the channel as possible should be given over to the active DTE. (In the case of time-division multiplexing example in the previous section, two of the three time slots would be empty because of the inactive DTEs.)

Since the multiplexers must be able to determine the intended destination of each byte that is received, an identifier uniquely identifying either the source (i.e., the sending port or DTE) or the destination (i.e., the receiving port or DTE) of the byte, must be included with each byte. This has two implications:

- The bandwidth is reduced because the identifier is sent with each byte. If the identifier is a byte (a reasonable choice since the multiplexed channel is probably byte-oriented), the bandwidth would be halved.

- The multiplexer must know the destination of the byte. Each byte must be transmitted with an identifier, which can indicate either the source of the byte or the intended destination of the byte.

  If the identifier is the source's address, the remote multiplexer must map the source address into a destination connection. Similarly, if the identifier is a destination address, the local multiplexer must map the local device's identifier into the destination address. Either of these approaches can be achieved through the use of mapping tables.

In addition to the reasons already noted, statistical multiplexing differs from time-division multiplexing in that if none of the DTEs are active, the multiplexed channel will be idle.

The example given in Figure 9.5 shows how a pair of statistical multiplexers can function. As bytes are sent, they are prefixed with an identifier that allows the receiving multiplexer to determine the destination of the byte. In this example, each data byte is sent as two bytes: the address of the destination (displayed in **bold**) and the data.

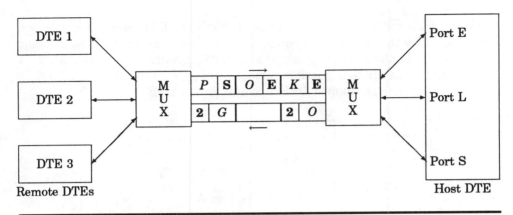

Figure 9.5   Statistical multiplexing

In Figure 9.5, the topmost channel (flowing from left to right) contains two bytes destined for port E (*K* followed by *O*) and one byte (*P*) for port S. The lower channel has two bytes for DTE 2 (*G* followed by *O*); additionally, there is a period during which nothing is being transmitted on the channel.

If all devices connected to a multiplexer transmit simultaneously for a sustained period, there may not be sufficient bandwidth to handle all of the traffic. To handle these situations, the multiplexers may simply discard the additional input, or buffers may be used to hold the data until transmission can take place.

9.4   PORT SELECTORS

In most multiprocessing systems, there are more users than there are possible connections to the central computer; and in some cases, there may be more remote DTEs than there are ports to the computer. From the system manager's point of view this is quite reasonable, since few users want to be on the computer 24-hours a day (there are exceptions), and the manufacturer of the computer may place a limit on the maximum number of ports that the computer can support.

In those situations where there are more remote DTEs than there are ports on the central host, a device known as a *port selector*, (or *front end, switch,* or *terminal concentrator*), is employed to manage the connections from the remote DTEs to the host's ports. The port selector supports two sets of connections: those to the remote DTEs and those to the host's ports. The port selector is typically connected to *all* possible remote DTEs and to all ports on the central host.

When a user on a remote DTE wants to initiate a communication with the central host, some form of signal is sent by the user to the port selector. For example, a series of characters (typically one or more carriage returns), or a break indication, or the detection of a carrier signal generated when the DTE is powered on. If a free port on the central host is available, the port selector makes a *logical* connection between the remote DTE and the free port.

Thereafter, all communications between the remote DTE and the host's port are handled by the port selector mapping the data from the DTE to the port or vice versa. In the example given in Figure 9.6, a central host has 2 ports (A and B), and there are four possible remote terminals (DTE 1 through DTE 4). The port selector has mapped DTE 1 to port A and DTE 3 to port B:

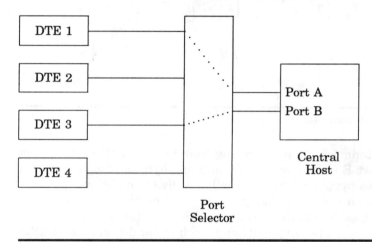

Figure 9.6   A port selector

When the communication finishes, the logical connection is broken and another DTE can use the port. Over a period of time, a DTE might be involved in any number of communications with the central host; however, each communication may be using a different port. If all ports are in use, the port selector ignores the incoming requests (possibly issuing a diagnostic message to the user at the remote DTE).

Port selectors can offer multiplexing capabilities as well. That is, one or more remote DTEs might share a single channel from a remote site; the port selector would demultiplex the channel and make logical connections to free ports using the same techniques as for the directly connected remote DTEs.

9.4.1   Other Multiplexer Applications

Until now the examples of multiplexing showed a multiplexer connected to a group of remote DTEs, while the second multiplexer is connected to a central host. In some situations it may be necessary to have the several (rather than one) central host. For example, a system may support two central hosts and several remote DTEs (Figure 9.7).

The connections between the various DTEs can be:

Static. If the connections are static, the multiplexers "know" the destination of each byte that is sent. This can be implemented using statically allocated mapping tables, meaning that, for example, each byte from DTE 2 is always sent to DTE S (and vice versa).

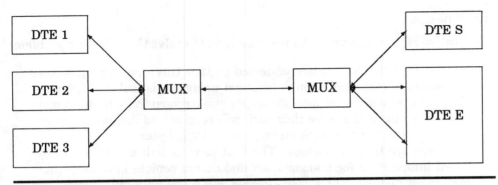

Figure 9.7   Multiplexing with multiple central hosts

Dynamic. Static connections force users to "seek-out" terminals that connect to specific DTEs. By making the connections dynamic by using some form of a port selector, users can choose their intended destination DTE. When the remote user is allowed to select one of several possible central DTEs, it is necessary for the user to indicate the required destination to one of the multiplexers. Once the destination is known, the information can be used by the multiplexers to establish a path from the user's DTE to the central DTE. If dynamic connections are allowed, the multiplexers may be required to support a protocol whereby the connection information (i.e., the source and destination addresses of the devices) is exchanged.

9.5   MULTIPLEXING WITH COMMKIT

Commkit can be used to illustrate multiplexing across a single channel between two PCs. The Commkit diskette is supplied with an example of statistical multiplexing between three separate processes. Time-division multiplexing and frequency-division multiplexing can also be implemented using Commkit: they are left to the reader as exercises.

9.5.1   Hardware Requirements

The multiplexing software is intended to be run on two PCs interconnected by a serial port. The traffic associated with the statistical multiplexers can be monitored if a line analyser is included (Figure 9.8).

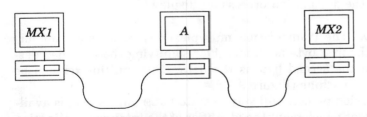

Figure 9.8   MUX hardware-configuration (*MX*-MUX, *A*-analyser)

9.5.2   Design

The statistical multiplexer software is designed to solve the following problem:

> Two PCs should be interconnected so that three pairs of processes can communicate over a single channel using statistical multiplexing. Each process will accept local messages and forward them to the remote process, while at the same time each will receive and display messages from the remote process. A message is a single byte.
>
> There are three processes. The first process will accept local keyboard information for transmission and accept remote keyboard information for display. The second process will transmit a byte every 18th of a second while displaying bytes from the remote process. The final process will transmit a byte once a second and display the byte sent by its remote process.

Process design   From the description of the problem, one can design a generic process that accepts local data and forwards it for transmission, while accepting remote data for display (Figure 9.9).

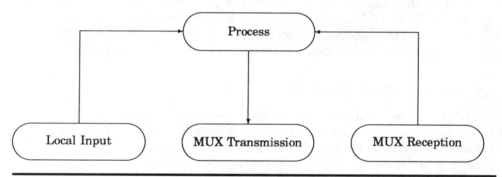

Figure 9.9   Overall structure of statistical multiplexer

Local input comes from two devices: the keyboard interrupt handler, KEYIH, and the clock interrupt handler, CLKIH. The clock interrupt handler generates two messages: one every 18th of a second; the other, once a second. Each of the three processes sends a message to the local MUX for transmission to the remote MUX. At the same time, messages that are received by the local MUX will be forwarded to the destination process for display.

The transmission MUX   The transmission multiplexer is responsible for forwarding two bytes: the first byte is an identifier signifying the intended destination process, and the second byte is the data. The multiplexer can be represented as a state machine (Figure 9.10).

The MUX Transmission process will stay in state IDLE until a byte is available for transmission, at which point the identifier of the intended destination (*DST*) is transmitted and the state changes to DST_ID. As soon as the transmission of the identifier has completed, control is passed to state CHAR and

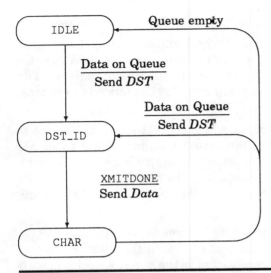

Figure 9.10 The transmission MUX state machine

the data is sent. When this transmission has completed, the queue is checked again. If there is data in the queue, the destination identifier is sent and control is passed to state DST_ID. If there is no data in the queue, the state returns to IDLE.

The reception MUX The reception multiplexer must wait for two bytes: the first byte contains the destination process identifier, and the second byte carries the data to be displayed by the specified process. A state machine consisting of two states can be created to represent the reception multiplexer (Figure 9.11).

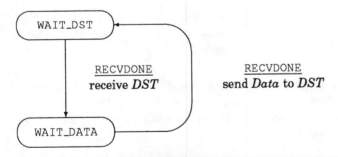

Figure 9.11 The reception MUX state machine

The reception MUX enters the WAIT_DST state and waits for input. The first byte received is assumed to identify the destination process (*DST*) and the state changes to WAIT_DATA. The second byte received is the data (*Data*). When the data is received, it is forwarded to the process indicated by the first byte received. Control returns to the WAIT_DST state.

9.5.3 Implementation

The implementation of the Commkit statistical multiplexer is based upon the design described in previous section. Implementation requires the use of three processes, as well as all of the low-level interrupt handlers. The processes and their associated queues are explained in the following sections.

do_mux()   This is the foreground process, which accepts single bytes sent to the APPLICATION queue from the KEYIH interrupt handler. These bytes are sent to the serial port responsible for emulating the multiplexer (indicated by handler_id). Bytes received from the channel by the multiplexer process for do_mux() are put on queue APPLICATION until they are received for display.

do_18_clk()   This process receives messages 18-times-a-second from CLKIH. After receiving a message from CLKIH, do_18clk() sends the "next" character from the string abcdefghijklmnopqrstuvwxyz to the queue associated with the multiplexer serial port (handler_id). A single character is sent each time a message from CLKIH is received—starting at a and proceeding one character at a time to z. When the end of the string is reached, the cycle is repeated. The do_18_clk() process is associated with queue BACKGROUND_1. This process displays all bytes that are received from the channel and forwarded by the local multiplexer to BACKGROUND_1. Do_18_clk() displays the bytes received from this queue.

do_1_clk()   This is associated with queue BACKGROUND_2, which receives messages once a second from the clock interrupt handler, CLKIH. Upon receipt of the message, do_1_clk() sends the "next" byte from the string 1234567890; when the end of string is reached, the cycle is repeated. Messages sent to the BACKGROUND_2 queue by the multiplexer are displayed by do_1_clk() after they are received.

Data is sent to and received from the remote multiplexer through one of the serial ports (specified by the user). Low_level() is called whenever a message is to be sent or when a byte is received:

Transmission MUX   The transmission MUX is an implementation of the transmission multiplexer described in the design section. The multiplexer is implemented in low_level() and mux_send(); there are two conditions under which a transmission can occur:

1. If the multiplexer is idle (indicated by mux_send_state having a value of IDLE), and if low_level() is called with a code of MSG_AVAIL. Mux_send() is called at this point and the transmission commences. If the multiplexer is not idle, the message remains queued.

2. If the multiplexer has completed a transmission of a data byte (indicated by a code of XMITDONE), the multiplexer state is CHAR and data is on the multiplexer's queue, a transmission will occur.

Reception MUX The reception multiplexer, mux_recv(), is an implementation of the reception multiplexer state machine described in the design section. Once the destination identifier and the byte have been received, the byte is forwarded to the destination process (Figure 9.12).

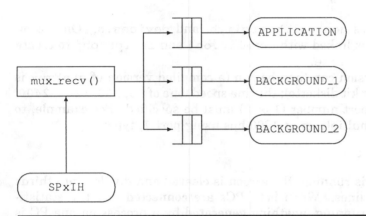

Figure 9.12 Information flow: MUX reception

To allow the user the opportunity to distinguish between the different messages that are sent by the various processes, the PC's screen is divided into thirds. The top third (lines 0 through 6) displays the data received from the remote keyboard process. The middle third (lines 8 through 14) shows the data received from the remote 18-times-a-second process. The lower third of the screen (lines 16 through 22) displays the data received from the remote once-a-second clock process. Once a process's screen is filled with information, the screen is cleared and output resumes in the top left-hand corner of the process's screen.

The identifier associated with the intended destination is simply the identifier of the transmitting process. For example, keyboard characters sent from BACKGROUND_1 on one PC are received by the BACKGROUND_1 process on the remote PC.

Finally, there is a problem in the implementation as it now stands: quite simply, when both multiplexers are started, one may start transmitting before the other. There may well be the loss of data; but more importantly, neither MUX can tell whether the byte received is a data byte or a destination identifier. This means that the two multiplexers could be out of synchronization, with one (or possibly both) treating the data as the destination identifier and the destination identifier as the data.

The solution adopted in the multiplexer software is to set the eighth bit when transmitting the identifier and to clear the bit when sending data. Then, when a byte arrives at a MUX, it is immediately possible to determine whether the byte is a destination identifier or a data byte simply by checking the eighth bit.

9.5.4   Compiling and Using the Statistical Multiplexer

The statistical multiplexer is written in Turbo C and can be found in `statmux.c` on the Commkit diskette; an executable version is also on the diskette. An executable version can be created using the `make` utility:

```
C:\> make statmux.exe
```

`Statmux.c` includes `general.h`, `ascii.h`, and `devices.h`. Once compiled, `statmux.obj` is linked with `commkit.obj` and `intrpt.obj` to create the executable `statmux.exe`.

The executable version can then be run (a compiled version of `statmux` is supplied on the Commkit diskette); the line speed (one of 50, 300, 1200, 2400, 4800, or 9600) and port number (1 or 2) must be specified. For example, to start the statistical multiplexer at 1200 bps using port 1, type:

```
C:\> statmux 1200 1
```

Once the program is running, the screen is cleared and divided into thirds by a pair of dashed lines. When both PCs are connected and the statistical multiplexers are running, anything generated by a process on one PC is displayed on the other in its corresponding part of the screen.

If the line analyser is used, pairs of bytes will appear on the analyser screen. The first byte is the destination process and the second byte is the data. The destination bytes are listed in Table 9.2.

TABLE 9.2   Line Analyser Output from Statistical Multiplexers

Destination	Byte Value	Displayed as
APPLICATION	0x84	ä
BACKGROUND_1	0x85	à
BACKGROUND_2	0x86	å

If the chosen line speed is too slow, the message queues may be dumped, since data is being supplied to the serial port faster than it can be sent. Communication will continue but in a very degraded fashion. The problem can be remedied by selecting a higher line speed; which line speed is left as an exercise.

9.6   SUMMARY

This chapter has examined another method of reducing line charges, notably the sharing of a channel amongst several DTEs or processes through the use of a multiplexer. The basic function of a multiplexer is to accept data from a number of devices and transmit it on a single, shared channel; while simultaneously receiving data from the channel and routing the information to the correct destination device. Three different multiplexing techniques were examined:

Frequency-division multiplexing   Frequency-division multiplexing requires each pair of communicating devices to be given their own frequency on the multiplexed channel. The multiplexers put data onto the channel using the frequency associated with the devices. The frequency at which data is removed indicates the destination of the data.

Time-division multiplexing   Time-division multiplexing requires that data from each device is sent at a precise time interval on the multiplexed channel. If the device has nothing to send, a signal is sent indicating that at this moment, the device associated with this slot has nothing to send. The receiving multiplexer is synchronized with the transmitter to ensure that the received data is supplied to the correct destination device.

Statistical multiplexing   Statistical multiplexing attempts to reduce the amount of wasted bandwidth associated with time-division multiplexing by transmitting information only when a device has information to send. To allow the receiving multiplexer determine the intended destination of the data, an identifier is sent with every data byte.

9.7   EXERCISES

1. Describe how device polling works. Compare device polling with multiplexing.

2. Two approaches to handling idle connections were described for time-division multiplexing. Describe the advantages and disadvantages of each.

3. Determine, both analytically and experimentally, the minimum line speed needed to allow the data to pass without loss (or crashing Commkit due to lack of queue space). The important numbers to consider are:

Process Name	Bytes/Second
APPLICATION	18
BACKGROUND_1	18
BACKGROUND_2	1

   If the channel is set to 9600 bps, approximately what percent of the channel is being used? Assume 10 bits per byte (8 bits data, 1 start, and 1 stop).

4. The statistical multiplexing example has "well-known" destinations already assigned in the software. Devise and implement an algorithm that allows the destination process to be assigned dynamically.

5. Develop and implement an algorithm to support frequency-division multiplexing using Commkit.

   One possible solution is to treat each 8-bit byte that the multiplexer transmits as a collection of eight different frequencies, each one assigned to a separate process. If there is nothing to be sent, the multiplexer sends 0xFF (each bit position having a value of 1). If a process supplies a byte to be transmitted, the multiplexer should change the bit position associated with the process to 0 (to indicate the start of data). Then, for the remaining eight data bits, the bit associated with the transmitting process contains the "next" data bit in the data to be sent. Once the data has been sent, the bit position should return to sending 1s. The reception multiplexer must scan each received byte for a nonzero bit value (the start-of-data signal). The data should be assembled from the next eight incoming bytes.

This solution requires a considerable degree of coding, analagous perhaps to the extra work required to support multiple frequencies.

6. Design and implement a time-division multiplexing program using Commkit to support the transmission of 7-bit data. The eighth bit can indicate whether the transmitted byte is data or is empty.

7. In light of the last question, consider how to transmit 8-bit data using time-division multiplexing and Commkit. It *might* be possible to use mark and space parity.

10

Wide Area Networks

10.1 INTRODUCTION

The material covered thus far in Part 3 has illustrated techniques for minimizing transmission overhead, overcoming distance limitations, and maximizing channel utilization. However, even these techniques cannot resolve problems such as the following:

- A branch office uses a multiplexer and modem to connect to their head office located several hundred kilometers away. In order to allow "instant access" to the head office, a telephone connection is maintained throughout the working day (including during coffee breaks, lunch time, and meetings).

  Although the occasional file transfer and some busy periods during the day may, from time to time, keep the channel at near capacity, there is insufficient network demand to warrant the telephone charges paid by the company.

- A telephone company analyzes its network traffic and discovers that the average duration of a voice call is about 5 minutes, while data calls can last for hours. Meanwhile, the annual growth in data traffic exceeds that of voice by roughly a 4 to 1 margin.

These two examples highlight an interesting contradiction: although more data traffic may suggest additional revenue to the telephone company, it can also result in more customer dissatisfaction because of failed call attempts (by both data and voice customers) due to congestion in the telephone network caused by the data traffic.

There are a number of possible solutions to this problem, including:

- installing more telephone circuits, thereby reducing the probability of failed calls,
- offering inducements to existing and potential data customers to get them off the voice network.

The first solution, increasing the number of circuits, will alleviate the situation only for the short term, since data traffic continues to grow. This leaves the second solution, getting data customers off the voice network, as the only real alternative. The problem is: where do those data customers go?

10.2   ALTERNATIVES TO THE PUBLIC TELEPHONE NETWORK

10.2.1   Private Lines

A common approach to getting data customers off the voice network is for the telephone company to lease them a *private line*, also referred to as a *leased* or *dedicated* line. The private line connects the data customer's DTE directly to the remote DTE. There are a number of advantages in having a private line, including minimal line noise (private lines are usually *conditioned* to reduce noise and static); guaranteed access to the telephone network; and the reacquisition of a voice circuit.

This solution has been taken even further: some larger companies rent entire private telephone networks from telephone companies or other organizations, thereby ensuring that all their calls (both data and voice) can be placed. It is becoming increasingly commonplace to find private companies (other than the telephone companies) with their own private T1 networks (see Chapter 8).

10.2.2   Public Data Networks

In some countries, *public data networks* (PDNs) have been installed, and are designed specifically for the transmission of data rather than voice. Circuit-switched data networks provide digital transmission facilities (i.e., the modulation and demodulation of signals is not required) for high-speed, high-volume communications. A typical digital data network may allow full-duplex communications for both asynchronous and synchronous DTEs at speeds of up to 56 kilobits per second. Many telephone companies support data networks designed specifically for digital (as opposed to voice) communications. For example, in the United States, AT&T offers *Data-Phone Digital Services* (DDS), while in Canada, Telecom Canada offers a service known as *Dataroute*.

Access to the voice network can be avoided by attaching DTEs directly to the digital network, using a DCE (*data circuit-terminating equipment*) designed specifically for digital technology.

Accessing public data networks In Chapters 4 and 8, RS-232-C and its proposed successors: RS-422-A, RS-423-A, and RS-449 were discussed. To overcome the well-known limitations of RS-232-C, the new standards increase the number of connectors from a single 25-pin D-connector to a pair of D-connectors for RS-449: a 37-pin primary channel connector and an optional 9-pin secondary channel connector. For all of the benefits associated with these new standards, the number of level converters (see Chapter 3) and connector pins increase the cost. Ideally, a mechanism that supports *fewer* connections but offers at least the same number of functions is needed.

CCITT Recommendations *X.20* (asynchronous) and *X.21* (synchronous) are examples of standards defining digital access to public data networks. In these standards, functions are coded as digital messages and passed between the DTE and DCE as streams of character strings using 15-pin connectors rather than devoting a single pin to a specific function. X.20 and X.21 provide services other than data transfer; for example, automatic-calling features are also supported, as well as signals that allow the DTE to determine the state of a call.

The X.21 circuits are defined as depicted in Figure 10.1.

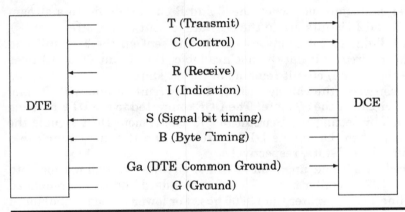

Figure 10.1 X.21 circuits defined

In X.21, both the DTE and DCE are defined as state machines, with the various states assigned to one of four phases: quiescent, call control, data transfer, and clearing (call) circuits. State transition is caused by changing the value of the signals on the T (transmit), C (control), R (receive), and I (indicate) circuits. T and C are associated with the DTE, while R and I are associated with the DCE.

For example, if both the DTE and DCE are in the quiescent phase (i.e., a call can be signalled by either the DTE, as an outgoing call, or the DCE, as an incoming call), the T and R circuits idle with a continuous stream of 1s, while the C and I circuits are in an *off* state (signalled by a continuous stream of 1s). The DTE can signal a call request by changing the value of the T and C circuits to a stream of 0s and entering the *on* state (a stream of 0s), respectively. The DCE responds with either a stream of +s indicating that the DTE can proceed to place the call or a stream of *BEL* characters, signalling that the outgoing call has collided with an incoming call. Either response (i.e., the + or the *BEL*) is prefixed by a pair of *SYN* bytes and is sent on the R circuit; the I circuit remains in the *off* state.

In the case where the call can be placed, the DTE supplies the DCE with the number of the party called as a stream of ASCII (IA5) digits on the T circuit. The DTE can request specific facilities (such as making the call a "collect call") as part of the data stream; these facilities are defined in CCITT X.2. The final digit is followed by a continuous stream of 1s on the T circuit, after which the DTE waits for the DCE to signal the progress of the call. While the DCE is attempting to place the call, the R circuit continues to idle with a stream of + characters. The DCE can inform the DTE of the progress of the call (for example, Number Busy or Invalid-Facility Request) by sending Call-progress signals on the R circuit in place of the + characters. Call-progress signals are defined in CCITT X.96.

A DTE is informed of an incoming call by receiving a *BEL* on the R circuit (prefixed by a pair of *SYN* characters) while in the quiescent phase. The DTE accepts the call by changing the C circuit from a stream of 0s to a stream of 1s.

Data transfer can commence when the T and R circuits indicate a stream of 1s and the C and I circuits are in the *on* state (a continuous stream of 0s). X.21 supports full-duplex communications; data is sent on the T circuit and received on the R circuit. If data is not available, the circuit (T or R) idles with 1s, while the C (or I) circuit remains in the *on* state.

Either DTE can clear the call by setting the T circuit to idle with 0s and returning the C circuit to the *off* state. The DCE connected to the DTE clearing the call responds by setting the I circuit to *off*. The remote DCE signals the call-clearing request to the remote DTE by setting the R and I circuits to a stream of 0s and the *off* state, respectively.

Both balanced (X.27) and unbalanced (X.26) circuits are defined for both X.20 and X.21. X.27 is similar to the RS-422-A standard and is recommended for DTE-DCE line speeds greater than 9600 bps. For lower speeds, unbalanced circuits may be specified using X.26, which is similar to RS-423-A.

Two CCITT standards, X.20*bis* and X.21*bis*, are available for DTEs that are configured to support either RS-232-C or V.24. X.21*bis* and X.20*bis* are designed to convert X.21 and X.20 signals into an equivalent RS-232-C or V.24 value; thereby allowing a DTE with analog equipment access to a digital public data network.

10.2.3 Sharing Channels

The impact of data traffic on the voice network is clearly minimized through the use of private lines or public data networks. However, the problem of channel utilization still exists: There will be periods throughout the day for which the channel is being paid but when it is not in use.

Ideally, what is needed is a communication channel that is always available to the customer, but for which the customer is only charged when transmitting or receiving information. If this channel could be shared among a number of different customers, costs (based, perhaps, on the volume of data transmitted each month) could be shared, as well. For example, a number of different customers in city A could share a channel to city B. Multiplexing could be used to ensure that the information sent by a customer in city B arrives at the correct DTE in city A and vice versa. By using statistical multiplexing, the channel would be used by only those customers who actually required the channel at any particular moment (Figure 10.2).

Figure 10.2   A shared channel between cities A and B

In Chapter 9, all communications were assumed to take place between one or more central hosts and a group of remote DTEs multiplexing the same channel that is owned by a single organization. However, in this situation, there can be a number of DTEs at either end of the multiplexed channel belonging to different customers, as depicted in Figure 10.3.

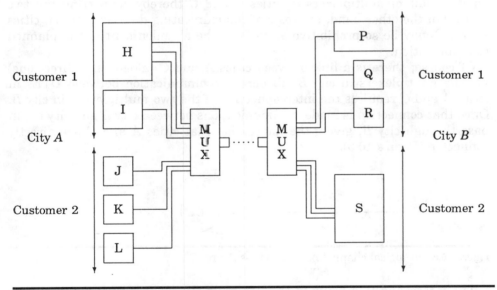

Figure 10.3   A MUX shared by different customers

There are essentially two approaches that can be used to support the transfer of information between the DTEs:

- First, all DTEs can be statically paired using a predefined connection (for example, DTE L in city A is always connected to DTE S in city B). The static connection is simple to implement and requires very little processing on the part of the multiplexers; however, users are given little flexibility.

- The second approach is to allow the various DTEs to dynamically select their intended destination (for example, the user of DTE I in city A may want to connect to any of DTEs P, Q, or R). The dynamic connection is more difficult to implement for a variety of reasons: mechanisms are needed to detect whether the remote DTE is available, as well as to determine if both DTEs are owned by the same customer. However, the advantage of this approach is the flexibility it offers the user.

It may turn out that organizations in a third city (city C) also need to communicate with facilities in city B: resulting in another multiplexed channel, this time between cities B and C (Figure 10.4).

Figure 10.4   Two multiplexed channels connecting three cities

Now, what happens if a customer in city A wants to communicate with the group's office in city C? There may not be sufficient traffic to warrant putting another pair of multiplexers in cities A and C thereby connecting the two cities. On the other hand, the costs of communicating directly between cities A and C may be so prohibitive as to force the abandonment of the planned communication.

Of course, there *is* a link between cities A and C (albeit an indirect one) via the multiplexers in city B. To permit communication between DTEs in cities A and C requires the interconnection of the two multiplexers in city B. Once that connection is made, communications between city A and city C can pass through city B, giving the impression that cities A and C are directly connected (Figure 10.5).

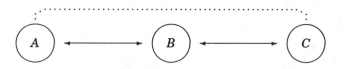

Figure 10.5   A logical channel between cities A and C

The interconnection between the two multiplexers in city B can be either *direct* or *indirect*.

Direct   The two multiplexers can be directly connected by having each multiplexer treat the other multiplexer as one of its DTEs (Figure 10.6).

The functions performed by the multiplexers depend upon a number of issues. For example, if the connection(s) are dedicated to specific DTEs in cities A and C, the multiplexers simply pass the data through the related connection. The connection between the two multiplexers is configured to give the illusion to MUX1 that MUX2 is the DTE in city C; while the illusion given to MUX2 is that MUX1 is the DTE in city A.

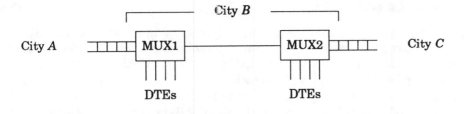

Figure 10.6 Direct MUX interconnection

However, if the connections between the two multiplexers are accessible by any DTE, then additional information must be passed between the DTEs prior to beginning any information transfer. For example, if a DTE in city A is to send information to a DTE in city C, then the following steps will probably be required:

1. obtain a free channel connecting MUX1 to MUX2
2. inform MUX2 of the intended destination DTE in city C
3. allow the communication to proceed

Indirect The two MUXs can be indirectly connected by passing information between a DTE that is connected to both MUXs (Figure 10.7).

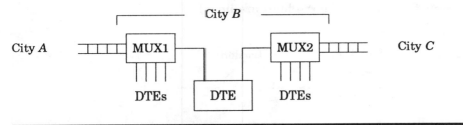

Figure 10.7 Indirect MUX interconnection

When data is sent to a DTE in a remote city (say, from city A to city C), it is first passed to a port on the DTE that is connected to both multiplexers. The DTE can then forward the data out the port associated with the destination DTE in city C. The shared DTE can be made to support both communication methods described for directly connected multiplexers.

This approach offers considerably more flexibility than directly connecting multiplexers, since the tasks are *well defined*. That is, the multiplexers are responsible for handling multiplexed data and forwarding the data to a specific port; while the shared DTE is responsible for establishing the connections and taking the data from an incoming port and supplying it to an outgoing port.

In addition to the above, a subtle change has occurred in the way the communication takes place. Until now, all communications have been point-to-point with no intermediate devices other than those directly involved in the communication. Now however, communications can take place between a *number* of intermediaries.

10.3 WIDE AREA NETWORKS

The previous section proposed designing a system of interconnected multi-plexers to support data traffic, rather than a combination of voice and data as in the existing telephone network. In addition, if statistical multiplexing is utilized, the bandwidth is employed only when necessary, potentially reducing the costs associated with using the telephone system.

In the mid-1960's, people working in the field of data communications rec-ognized the potential of developing computer *networks* that would allow the transmission of data between geographically dispersed DTEs. Since these networks were envisaged to span whole continents (or even the entire world), they were called *wide area networks* (WANs).

A wide area network is an interconnection of a number of multiplexing devices known as *nodes*. Each node in the network is directly connected to at least one other node through a communication channel known as a *link*. If a node is directly connected to N other nodes, it is associated with N links. Links are typically high-speed communication channels such as optical fiber, coaxial cable, microwave, or even satellite.

Additionally, each node supports a number of DTEs. A DTE can be directly connected to a node, or the node may support "dial-in" facilities whereby re-mote users can access the wide area network. Once connected to the network, a DTE potentially has access to any other DTE on the network.

A hypothetical wide area network could be as illustrated in Figure 10.8 (each circle is a node, while the lines are links).

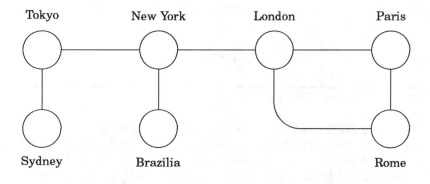

Figure 10.8 A hypothetical wide area network

The internal structure of a node closely resembles the multiplexer-DTE-multiplexer combination discussed in the previous section. A node performs a variety of functions, including:

- Allowing DTEs to send and receive information on the network
- Routing information to DTEs via other nodes. For example, in the wide area network shown in Figure 10.8, a DTE in Sydney could send information to a DTE in Paris via the Tokyo, New York, London (and possibly Rome) nodes

■ Multiplexing information on the links, thereby sharing the links amongst a number of DTEs. For example, all the DTEs attached to the Sydney node would share the link to Tokyo in order to reach DTEs on nodes other than Sydney.

How these functions are realized in a wide area network depends upon a number of issues, some of which are now considered.

10.3.1 Network Structures

There is no prescribed "shape" to a wide area network, since the geographic area covered may vary from country to country or continent to continent. However, if the geographic factors are ignored, there are a limited number of topologies.

Fully connected network A fully connected network is one in which every node on the network connects to every other node. If the network consists of N nodes, each node will require $N - 1$ links (Figure 10.9).

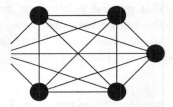

Figure 10.9   A fully connected network

Fully connected networks are usually very costly because of the number of links required. However, they are usually very fast (since there are no intermediate nodes to handle a message), and they offer a high degree of reliability (if a link fails, there should be an alternate path to the intended destination).

Star network A star network is one in which all nodes connect to a single, central node (often referred to as the *hub*). All communications between nodes pass through the hub node (Figure 10.10).

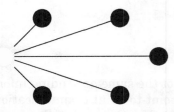

Figure 10.10   A star network

Although the star reduces the number of links to a minimum (i.e., N nodes require $N-1$ total links), the failure of the hub node will result in the complete cessation of all communications.

Mesh network   Another network, probably the most common of all wide area networks, is known as a mesh or partially connected network. In a mesh network, usually distance or known traffic volumes determine which of the nodes are connected (Figure 10.11).

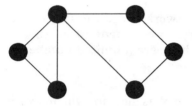

Figure 10.11   A mesh network

Mesh networks can also evolve as communication patterns change over time. For example, a city might not have a node, but if it gained political or economic stature, a node might be added. Similarly, the traffic volumes between two cities might be low, justifying the use of an intermediate node; however, over time the volumes might grow to the point where a separate link directly connecting the two cities might be needed.

Other network structures   There are a number of other topologies possible. Two specialized topologies that will be discussed later in the book are the *ring* and *bus networks* (Figure 10.12).

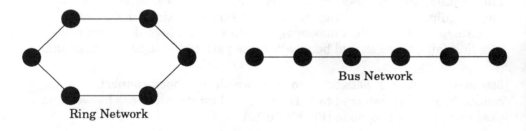

Bus Network

Ring Network

Figure 10.12   The ring and bus network structures

10.3.2 Addressing DTEs

Sending information on a wide area network is not the same as sending information in a point-to-point communication. In a point-to-point communication there is only one possible destination (the DTE at the other end of the channel), whereas in a wide area network there can be any number of possible destinations. Therefore, at a minimum, whenever a DTE supplies information to a node for transmission, the node must know the intended destination.

The intended destination is simply another DTE attached to a node somewhere on the network. How much information does the node require in order to get the information to the destination? Consider how a letter addressed to someone in another country is processed by the post office. The one thing the post office doesn't have is a list of all the people in the world; however, it does have a list of countries and regions within countries. The letter is first sent to the country in question; then to a region within the country; then to the city; and so on down to the person's house. In other words, there is a *hierarchy* used to route the letter.

The same approach can be applied to sending information in a wide area network: the information is not sent directly to a DTE or a port on a DTE. Instead, the information is sent to the node to which the destination DTE is attached. The node can then supply the information to the DTE or perhaps a port on the DTE (assuming the DTE supports several connections to the node).

All networks require some form of *address* to ensure that the information arrives at the intended destination. Broadly speaking, there are two types of addresses:

Hierarchical. A hierarchical address is a single address consisting of a series of fields, each of which is used to identify part of the destination. For example, a hierarchical address could consist of the node, the DTE, and the port on the DTE.

Global. A global address is a single address that uniquely identifies a single entity on the network (typically a DTE attached to a network node).

All DTEs attached to the network are associated with an address, potentially meaning that any pair of DTEs can communicate; assuming they agree to the same protocol.

In addition to the destination address, most, if not all, wide area networks require the address of the transmitting DTE (the *source address*) to also be sent. The source address can be used for a number of different purposes: the most obvious is that it allows the receiving entity a means whereby a reply or an acknowledgement can be returned.

10.3.3 Information Representation

To be effective and to attract as large a market as possible, wide area networks often support a variety of protocols, thereby allowing different DTEs access to the network. For example, the network should permit asynchronous DTEs to coexist with synchronous DTEs. In addition, the wide area network should be transparent: DTEs accessing the network should not be required to change their protocol. For instance, if a telephone circuit between a pair of asynchronous DTEs is replaced by a wide area network, the asynchronous communications should continue as before.

These two seemingly contradictory objectives (coexistence of protocols and transparency) require the wide area network to support a universal data structure that is internal to the network and recognized by the nodes, regardless of the DTE information carried. The structure, commonly known as a *packet*, should be able to carry the information specific to the protocol as well as control information specific to the wide area network. Typical control information can include the source and destination addresses as well as some form of error checking. A generalized packet structure can be visualized as in Figure 10.13.

Packet Specific Information	DTE Specific Information	Packet Checksum

Figure 10.13   A generalized packet structure

10.3.4 Packet Routing

The various nodes that make up the network are responsible for the *routing* of packets through the network; from the source node, to the destination node, and eventually to the destination DTE. There are a number of similarities between a circuit-switched telephone call and packet routing; accordingly, wide area networks are often labeled *packet switching networks* (PSNs). The terms *packet switching exchange* (PSE) and *packet switch node* (PSN) are synonymous with node.

The algorithms chosen to support packet routing in a network depend upon factors such as:

- The cost of sending a packet across a specific link. Some links may be more costly than others. For example, terrestrial links are typically cheaper than satellite links.

- The length of time it will take the packet to reach the intended destination. Time-critical information may be required to move through the network with a higher priority than other information.

- The volume of traffic on the network. As the number of packets on the network increases, *congestion* can occur, leading to delays and other problems (see later discussion).

- The order the packets will arrive at the intended destination. If multiple paths exist in the network and packets are permitted to take any path; then packets taking a longer path may arrive at the intended destination later than other packets, even though the packet that arrived late was sent earlier.

- The way that lost or duplicate packets are handled. In any communication, information can be lost through some form of error. In a wide area network, mechanisms may be required to ensure that information always reaches the intended destination. Similarly, if multiple paths exist and a packet somehow is sent on two or more links, mechanisms may also be required to recognize the duplication.

When a packet is transmitted through a wide area network, the packet will be handled in three different ways:

1. The node attached to the source DTE will accept the DTE's information, store it in a packet, and transmit the packet onto the network.

2. The node attached to the destination DTE will remove the packet from the network. The information in the packet will be transmitted to the destination DTE using the DTE's protocol.

3. Any intermediate nodes will route the packet to the final destination node using some type of *routing strategy* or *routing algorithm*.

Routing algorithms   There are many different algorithms that can be used to support packet routing through a network. At one extreme, the node can simply forward the packet out of all its links in the hope that eventually a copy of the packet will reach the intended destination node. This is known as *flooding*, and although there is a very good chance that a copy of the packet will reach the destination, there is also a very good chance that many other copies of the packet will also reach the destination. In addition, copies of the packet could be travelling through the network for indefinite periods of time before reaching the destination (this is especially true if there are loops or cycles in the network). Two ways of improving this algorithm are:

■ Supply each packet with a *hop count*; that is, a counter that is given an initial value by the source node and decremented by each node that receives the packet. When the hop count reaches zero, the receiving node discards the packet. The hop count must be large enough to ensure that nodes at opposite ends of the network can communicate.

■ Transmitting the packet out all links *except* the one on which it was received. This helps to reduce the number of unnecessary transmissions between pairs of nodes. The assumption behind this algorithm is that if a node forwards a packet, it was not the intended destination, therefore there is no need to retransmit the packet back to the original node.

There are a number of limitations to the these approaches, the chief among them being the unnecessary routing of packets to nodes that aren't on the path to the intended destination.

An alternative to flooding and its variations is to supply each node with a data structure known as a *routing table*. In its simplest form, the routing table contains a list of all possible destination nodes and the link to the next node on the path to the specified destination. For example, using the network illustrated in Figure 10.14, station *A*'s routing table could be as shown: where the *Destination* is the intended destination of the packet supplied to the node and *Next node* indicates the link to be taken to reach the destination (a '–' signals that there is no next node). For example, to reach nodes *B*, *D*, *E*, and *F* from node *A*, all packets would take the link to node *B*; however, to reach *C*, packets would be sent directly on the link to node *C*.

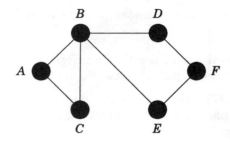

Destination	A	B	C	D	E	F
Next node	–	B	C	B	B	B

Figure 10.14   Station A's routing table

The choice of routes becomes somewhat more complex when considering node F. The routes from F to nodes D and E are readily apparent; however, there are two choices from F to B (either via node D or node E).

There are many ways in which the routing table can be constructed, organized, and used; some of which include:

Static allocation.   If the traffic patterns on the network are well known and the topology is stable (i.e., the addition or removal of a node or link is a rare event), it may be possible to decide upon the routes when the network is initially implemented. These routes can be placed in the routing tables of the different nodes and the network left to function. This is often referred to as *static allocation*. For example, it may be decided that the route from node F to node B is to go via node E, producing Table 10.1, routing table for node F.

TABLE 10.1   Node F's Routing Table

Destination	A	B	C	D	E	F
Next node	E	E	E	D	E	–

The choice of routes can be based upon any number of factors. Typical reasons include the cost of transmitting packets across a link, traffic patterns (some nodes may be subject to delays), and distance.

If multiple paths exist between nodes, the routing table could contain information about the different possible routes; this is known as *multipath routing*. For example, node F's routing table could be expanded to show that a route to node B also exists via node D (in addition to the route through node E). Multipath routing has a number of uses: (1) traffic can be shared between the different routes, and (2) should a route become inactive due to a link or node failure, an alternate route may be available.

Dynamic or adaptive routing.   In many situations, the topology and traffic patterns of the network can change, for example, due to node or link failures and variable traffic patterns during certain times of day. For example, if node

E fails, traffic from node F may have to be rerouted through D to reach B. Algorithms that allow the modification of routing tables are known as *dynamic* or *adaptive routing strategies*.

A variation on the use of static allocation is to have a network control center that periodically sends new routing tables to the nodes. These tables are based upon information that the network control center receives from all of the nodes; each node sends packets containing network status information. For example, the network control center could be informed of node E's failure; it could then produce new routing tables that would have node F's traffic flowing via node D.

Backward learning. The use of a centralized network control center performing routing table updates can be costly to the network because a percentage of the network bandwidth is lost to the exchange of status information. Ideally, the amount of bandwidth lost should be minimal. One such technique is known as *backward learning*.

In backward learning, every packet contains a count that is increased as the packet is transmitted by each node (the further away a packet is from its source, the greater the value of the count). Each routing table entry has a distance count associated with every destination in the table (the count indicates the number of nodes the destination is away from this node). Initially, all routing table distance counts are set to infinity.

The backward learning algorithm works as follows. Whenever a packet is received by a node, the destination entry in the routing table that corresponds with the *source* address in the packet is found. The routing table count is compared with the packet's count; if the packet count is less, the routing table entry is changed to the packet count, otherwise nothing is done.

For example, if the link between B and D is not functioning, the routing table for D might look like that in Table 10.2.

TABLE 10.2   Node D Routing Table (Link B–D Not Functioning)

Destination	A	B	C	D	E	F
Next node	F	F	F	–	F	F
Count	4	3	4	–	2	1

Should the B–D link become active, a packet from B might arrive across the link at D with a count of 1. Since this count is lower than the existing routing table count of 3 for destination B, the *Next node* for *Destination B* changes to B and the *Count* changes to 1 (Table 10.3).

TABLE 10.3   Node D Routing Table (Link B–D Now Functioning)

Destination	A	B	C	D	E	F
Next node	F	B	F	–	F	F
Count	4	1	4	–	2	1

As soon as a packet from D arrives at B, B's routing table count for D will change, meaning that messages from A and C can take the shorter route.

10.3.5   Methods of Packet Transmission

Packets are transmitted across a network one node at a time. Ideally, the packet will reach the intended destination with the minimum of difficulty. However, over a period of time, nodes may fail (i.e., crash due to a software or hardware fault) and links may fail (e.g., being cut by someone digging a trench). Should either of these types of fault occur, the transmitted packet might not reach its destination. The remedial action depends upon the type of service being offered by the network. Three common methods of service are now considered.

Datagram   A *datagram service* is a *best-effort* communication service that does not guarantee anything about the transmission of the packet. For example, a packet may be sent and then lost because of a network fault or the packet might simply be discarded due to heavy network traffic flow. On the other hand, duplicate copies of the packet might arrive at the destination because of routing problems in the network or simply as result of the routing algorithm (consider the possible effects of flooding).

In a datagram service, it is assumed that the DTEs are responsible for handling any errors associated with datagram transmission. For example, the DTEs could construct their own go-back-N protocol atop the datagram service.

Messaging   A *messaging system* is one in which a message is sent as a series of packets that are reassembled into the complete message at each node before being forwarding onto the next link.

In a typical messaging application, a DTE divides a large set of data, the *message* (such as a file), into a series of packets. Packets are transmitted between nodes; the receiving node reassembles the message from the incoming packets. Once the message is assembled, the node performs its routing algorithm and determines the next link. The message might not be transmitted immediately, the node may perform some type of scheduling. Typical scheduling criteria include the amount of buffer space available on the next node and the amount of traffic on a particular link. Networks that support messaging are also referred to as *store-and-forward* networks.

Messaging systems normally offer "guaranteed" service, in which a message sent from one DTE will eventually arrive at the intended destination DTE. To achieve this level of service, the communications *between* each node must ensure that each packet has been successfully transmitted. Protocols similar to Bisync or SDLC are often used by the individual nodes when communicating across the link.

Messaging is often used in situations where interactive computing is not required and the arrival of the data at the destination is not time critical.

Virtual circuits   There are applications that cannot function using datagrams or messaging. Consider, for example, an interactive terminal connected via a wide area network to a remote host. The user of the terminal wants to make sure that the data entered arrives at the remote host when, and in the order, it is entered. Imagine the fun of trying to edit a file in which each line is sent as a datagram: some lines might never arrive, others could arrive several times.

Network designers have recognized these limitations and have set about developing a system analogous to the public telephone network's "switched circuit" known as a *virtual circuit*. A virtual circuit is a path through a wide area network that is maintained for the duration of the communication (as is a switched circuit in the telephone network). The data entered by the user follows the same path through the circuit until the communication is ended. If another communication to the same destination is started at a later time, the path taken can differ from the previous one because of traffic conditions and changing topology. Virtual circuits are reliable: The data supplied by a transmitting DTE arrives in the order sent, without loss, duplication, or error at the receiving DTE. Over a period of time, there can be hundreds of simultaneous virtual circuits established across the network. A virtual circuit consists of three distinct phases.

Call establishment.   The calling party (a DTE) must indicate to its node that a virtual circuit is requested: a request that includes the address of the called party (normally a DTE attached to another node). This information is put into a *Call-Request* packet that is routed through the network by the various nodes on the path between the two DTEs. The network's routing algorithm dictates the path taken by the Call-Request packet.

As the Call-Request packet progresses through the network, a logical path for this one specific call is established between the nodes on the network. Each node is responsible for maintaining its part of the virtual circuit for the duration of the call in its *virtual-circuit table*. When the Call-Request packet finally arrives at the destination node, the destination DTE is "called," and if the call can be accepted, a *Call-Connected* packet is returned to the calling DTE. However, if the call cannot be accepted (for example, if the DTE is inactive) the call will be cleared by the called node returning a *Call-Clearing* packet to the calling DTE.

Although a virtual circuit itself is full duplex, the path created by the Call-Request packet need not be full duplex. For example, the Call-Request packet could set up a simplex channel; in these situations, the Call-Connected packet establishes a return-simplex channel. It is possible that the two halves of the virtual-circuit take completely different paths through the network.

Data transfer.   Once the call has been established, data transfer can take place. Data sent by either DTE passes through the network in a *Data packet* using the virtual circuit created in the call-establishment phase. Since there can be any number of virtual circuits in use, each packet is sent with an indication of its virtual circuit, the *virtual-circuit number*. As the Data packet arrives at each node, the virtual-circuit number, used in conjunction with the virtual-circuit table indicates the next leg of the packet's journey.

To ensure the reliability of the data transfer, Data packets are acknowledged, typically as they move between nodes. In some cases, there can be *end-to-end acknowledgements*, confirming the arrival of the packet at the destination node.

Call clearing.   As in any communication, there comes a time for the connection between the two DTEs to be terminated. Since there are a finite number of possible virtual circuits in the network (there is a limit to the size of the virtual-circuit tables), both the DTEs *and* the nodes involved in a virtual circuit must be informed that the call is being terminated.

A call is terminated by either DTE sending a *Call-Clearing* packet. The packet passes through the original path created during the call-establishment phase; each node is responsible for freeing its part of the virtual circuit. The normal response to a Call-Clearing packet is a Confirmation packet.

Although it may appear that a single virtual-circuit number is used to identify a virtual circuit through the network, this is seldom the case since the overhead associated with maintaining globally unique virtual circuit numbers outweigh their benefits. Instead, what appears to be a single virtual circuit is usually made up of a number of separate virtual circuits, allocated on a node-by-node basis. For example, consider the virtual circuits that exist on the links connecting nodes **X**, **Y**, and **Z** (Figure 10.15), in which virtual circuits exist for DTEs *A* and *D*, as well as DTEs for *B* and *C*.

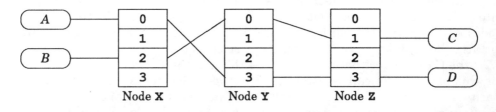

Figure 10.15   Virtual circuits connecting DTEs *A* and *B* to DTEs *D* and *C*, respectively

In the above example, process *B* communicates with process *C* through node **X**'s virtual circuit number **2**, whereas *C* uses virtual circuit number **1** on node **Z**. Since the virtual circuit numbers change from link-to-link, the node is for responsible changing the packet's virtual-circuit number prior to being transmitted out the next link. Consider a packet sent from *B* to *C*: the initial virtual-circuit number is **2**, which is changed to **0** when the packet is sent to node **Y**; at node **Y** the number is changed to **1**, and then sent to node **Z**, which forwards the packet to process *C*.

To distinguish between datagrams and virtual circuits, datagram services are often called *connectionless* while virtual circuits are called *connection-oriented*.

Many wide area networks offer combinations of the above services. For example, virtual circuits for interactive users may be needed during working hours, but during the quiescent periods at night, large volume transfers can be sent using a messaging service.

10.3.6   Node Design

The exact functions of a node depend upon a number of factors such as the protocol used by the wide area network and the protocols supported by the

DTEs. However, there are a number of generic features that a node should support:

- transmitting and receiving packets from other nodes
- routing packets from one node to the other nodes
- controlling the DTEs' network access

Although it is possible to design a node so that all of these functions are performed in one large maze of software, network designers have, over the years, come to recognize that dividing node software into *layers* or distinct parts offers a number of benefits, including:

- faults are easier to isolate and fix
- modification to one layer can be accomplished while it is isolated from the other layers
- software testing is simplified

The most natural (and perhaps obvious) division of the node is between that part of the node which controls the network and the part that allows the DTEs access to the network. The network part is responsible for forwarding packets and maintaining the virtual circuits; while the DTE part allows DTEs to send and receive information across the wide area network (Figure 10.16).

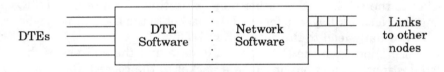

Figure 10.16 Functional division of a node

Within each of these two broad divisions, further layering is possible.

Network software layering Consider the functions associated with the transmission and reception of packets in a network supporting virtual circuits or messaging:

- Nodes are connected to other nodes by links. A single node may be associated with a number of links, not all of which will support the same medium. For example, some may be high-speed synchronous lines, while others might be asynchronous, and still others could be satellite.

  In many wide area networks, the lowest layer is known as the *Physical Layer* and defines the electrical and mechanical properties of the link. The nodes at the end of each link must agree to the same Physical Layer protocol.

- Both virtual circuits and messaging require that packets sent across a link arrive undamaged and in the correct sequence at the receiving node. Since the underlying Physical Layer only offers a transmission medium, another layer that supports the following features is required:

- Device driver specific to the underlying medium. The device driver is responsible for the transmission and reception of packets.
- Reliable, node-to-node protocol, such as stop-and-wait or go-back-N. This feature ensures that any packet sent across the link will either arrive correctly or will be received in error and a retransmission requested. (In a datagram network, the node-to-node protocol need not be reliable.)

This layer, often referred to as the *Data Link Layer*, is intended to ensure that packets sent across the underlying link arrive at the next node in the correct order and error-free. Although the device driver will be unique to each different type of link, the reliable protocol software need not be unique to the link. That is, packets are formatted with the correct sequence number and control fields by the protocol software, while the underlying device driver and the Physical Layer simply transmit the information supplied. Once again, the argument for using a single set of software deals primarily with maintenance: by using one set of software, "fixes" are universal.

- Finally, calls must be established and packets routed through the network. Since these functions cannot be justifiably performed by either the Physical Layer or the Data Link Layer, a third layer, the *Network Layer* is introduced. The Network Layer is responsible for a number of functions, including:

  - Inspecting packets received by a Data Link Layer to determine the destination of the packet. The packet may be intended for a DTE attached to this node, in which case the Network Layer supplies the information in the packet to the DTE. Or the packet may be destined for a remote DTE, requiring the Network Layer to forward the packet to the Data Link Layer that will eventually lead to the destination DTE.
  - Taking information from the DTE (typically data and the address of the intended destination) and passing it in a packet to the correct Data Link Layer for eventual transmission. Additionally, Call-Request and Call-Clearing packets are also handled by the Network Layer, and forwarded to a Data Link Layer for transmission.

    Should the destination DTE be attached to the same node as the transmitting DTE, the Network Layer need not attempt to transmit the information; instead, the information can be supplied directly to the specified DTE.

- The Network Layer acts as a multiplexer both to the DTEs that are attached to node and to the links. Diagramatically, a node can be represented as in Figure 10.17.

The concept of layering involves more than simply dividing tasks into logical functions: it encompasses data structures and in some respects, programming style. Many layered communication systems define a single-layer structure and apply this structure to all layers in the system:

- Each layer has its own protocol and protocol conventions. Communications occur between *peer entities* within a layer. For example, a wide area network's Network Layer has a set of protocols specific to the Network Layer.

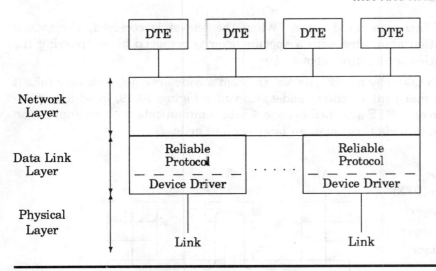

Figure 10.17 Node layering

These protocols deal with the creation, maintenance, and termination of virtual circuits (or perhaps simply the routing of datagrams). Whereas in the Data Link Layer, protocols might exist for the reliable transfer of information between nodes.

■ Although communications occur within a layer between peer-entities, the entities within a layer use the *communication services* offered by the underlying layer. At a minimum, the services associated with a layer consist of the transmission and reception of information. The communication system may offer features that permit a lower layer to return error-status information to the higher layer.

■ Because each layer has its own protocol and uses the services of the underlying layer, it is necessary to *encapsulate* one layer's packet structure in the packet stucture of the underlying layer. The encapsulation involves adding control information specific to a layer (such as sequence-numbering and error-checking information). For example, a packet sent by a DTE in this layered system could proceed through the sequence of encapsulation steps found in Figure 10.18.

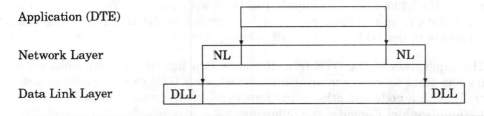

Figure 10.18 An example of encapsulation

Finally, the data within the packet is subject to the rules associated with transmitting information in the Physical Layer. For example, bit-stuffing or *DLE* insertion could occur. When the packet is received, the control information associated with a specific layer is removed before passing the information to the layer above.

■ The path taken by a DTE's packet through a wide area network may take it through many intermediate nodes. Consider Figure 10.19, in which an application on a DTE attached to node *A* is to communicate with an application attached to node *C* through an intermediate node, *B*.

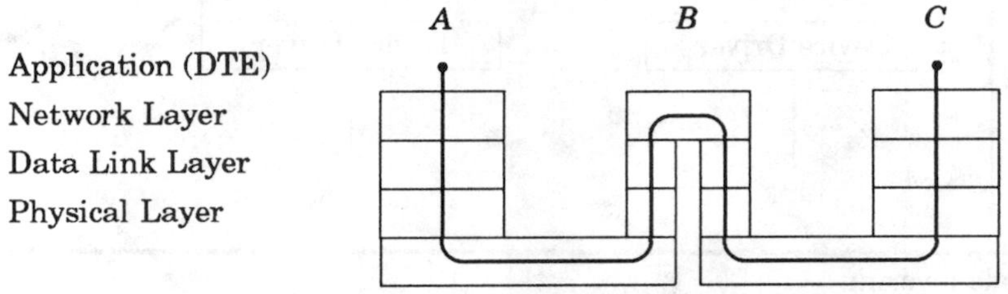

Application (DTE)
Network Layer
Data Link Layer
Physical Layer

Figure 10.19   The path taken by a packet from node *A* to node *C* via node *B*

A packet sent by the application attached to node *A* is encapsulated by each layer on node *A* and eventually sent to node *B*. The packet arrives at node *B*'s Network Layer, which is responsible for routing the packet (by consulting either a routing table or a virtual-circuit table). In either event, the packet is re-encapsulated and sent out the link attached to node *C*. At node *C*, the Network Layer supplies the packet to the destination application.

The node-DTE interface   The node and its DTEs must interact when communications across the wide area network are to take place. The concept of layering still applies between each DTE and the node. In this case, the DTE must inform the Network Layer of the action to be taken with the information supplied, for example:

DTE to Node. The DTE can request a call to be made to another DTE on the network, data can be sent and received from a remote DTE, and the DTE can request that the call be cleared.

Node to DTE. The node can supply the DTE with requests for setting up a call, data from a remote node can be supplied to the DTE, the node can indicate to the DTE that the call is being cleared.

The separation of the DTE from the node is a logical but somewhat arbitrary one since there are many situations where a DTE cannot communicate directly with a node and other situations in which the node and the DTE are indistinguishable. Consider the following:

DTE and Node Combined. In an attempt to reduce costs, many networks have node software that is intended to function on interconnected DTEs (i.e., the DTEs themselves are the nodes). The DTEs communicate via leased lines or, in some cases, dial-out facilities. Packets are formatted by software (typically within the operating system) and forwarded to the Network Layer software.

In this network design not only are costs reduced, but the features offered by the operating system (for example, file storage for messaging), can simplify the design of node software.

DTE and Node Separate. In most commercial wide area networks, the node and the DTE are separate and distinct. If the DTE is programmable, packets can be formatted by the DTE according to the Network Layer's requirements and sent to the node for transmission. However, if the DTE is simply an interactive terminal (or a computer emulating a terminal), a number of problems arise. For example, where is the data to be formatted into a packet, and how does the node determine the intended destination of a packet?

The solution adopted by many wide area networks is to develop a software package known as a *Packet Assembler/Disassembler* (PAD) that on the DTE-side emulates a host to which the DTE communicates and on the node-side generates packets based upon the Network Layer's requirements (the node can be connected to other DTEs and PADs).

For example, an asynchronous terminal could communicate with a PAD, which encodes and decodes Network Layer packets (Figure 10.20).

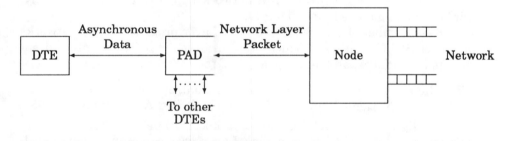

Figure 10.20   Packet Assembler/Disassembler connections

An alternative to having a separate PAD is to have the PAD as part of the node. The number of DTEs that could connect to an individual PAD would be implementation dependent (Figure 10.21). PADs are not restricted to asynchronous DTE communications, PADs are available to support Bisync and other such protocols.

10.4   WIDE AREA NETWORK PROTOCOLS

From the discussion in the previous section it should be apparent that there is no single wide area network protocol: each layer is associated its own set of rules, standards, and protocols. In some cases, there can be numerous choices of protocol within a single layer.

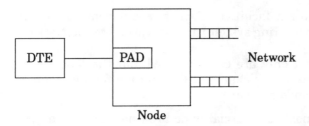

Figure 10.21   A PAD can be part of the node

10.4.1 Physical Layer Standards

The Physical Layer connects pairs of nodes through a communication channel. Physical Layer standards define the mechanical, electrical, functional, and procedural rules associated with the communication channel. Examples of Physical Layer standards include RS-232-C, RS-449 (RS-423-A and RS-422-A), X.21, and X.21*bis*.

10.4.2 Data Link Layer Protocols

The Data Link Layer is responsible for the formatting of information for transmission across the underlying Physical Layer. Typically, the Data Link Layer offers a reliable communication service to the higher layers, by maintaining error detection and flow control. In a network supporting datagrams only, there is not the same need for reliability.

There are a number of different Data Link Layer protocols: some networks use bisync or SDLC, neither of which are considered standards. Internationally adopted standards, all based upon SDLC (see Chapter 6), include:

ADCCP. The Advanced Data Communication Control Protocol, developed by the American National Standards Institute (ANSI) as ANSI standard X.366.

HDLC. The High-Level Data Link Control protocol is a point-to-point synchronous protocol intended for Data Link Layer peer communications developed by the International Organization for Standardization (ISO). HDLC is defined in ISO documents DIS 3309 and DIS 4335.

LAP-B. The Link Access Procedure-Balanced protocol is defined by CCITT as part of the X.25 protocol (see next section). LAP-B is a subset of HDLC.

10.4.3 Network Layer Protocols

Probably the best known Network Layer protocol is *X.25*, a CCITT standard developed to handle virtual circuits between DTEs and a wide area network. In X.25, the node is referred to as the *DSE* (or data-switching exchange) and the connection between a DTE and a DSE is the *data circuit terminating equipment* (DCE); the protocols used within the network are not defined by X.25.

X.25 is actually a CCITT *recommendation* as opposed to a specific protocol, consisting of a detailed description of the Physical, Data Link, and Network Layers:

Level 1. The physical, electrical, functional, and procedural characteristics needed to establish, maintain and disconnect the physical link between the DTE and the DCE. The DTE/DCE interface characteristics are defined in recommendations X.21 and X.21*bis.*

Level 2. The link-access procedure for data interchange across the link between the DTE and the DCE. Level 2 access is defined by the LAP-B protocol.

Level 3. The packet format and control procedures for the exchange of packets containing control information and user data between the DTE and the DCE. Level 3 is also referred to as the *Packet Level DTE/DCE Interface* and describes X.25 virtual circuits. Many public data networks have adopted the X.25 Level 3 protocol for network access.

Structurally, X.25 is organized as depicted in Figure 10.22.

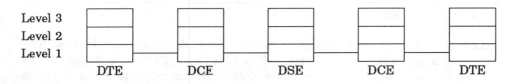

Level 3
Level 2
Level 1
          DTE   DCE   DSE   DCE   DTE

Figure 10.22   The structure of X.25

Level 3 of X.25 defines two types of virtual circuit: a *virtual call* (also known as a *switched-virtual circuit*, SVC) and *permanent-virtual circuit* (PVC). Switched-virtual circuits are those described in previous sections, while permanent-virtual circuits are those in which the virtual circuit is always available for data transfer. There is no call establishment nor call-clearing phase associated with a permanent-virtual circuit.

The three phases associated with an X.25 virtual circuit are as follows:

Call establishment.   A call can be established by any DTE that has an available virtual-circuit number. The call must be sent in a Call-Request packet (note, CCITT labels its bits from left to right, with bit 7 being the low-order bit; an 8-bit quantity is referred to as an *octet*). See Figure 10.23.

The various fields in the Call-Request packet are defined as follows:

MOD. MOD informs the called DTE which Data packet sequence numbering scheme the calling DTE is using: either 8 or 128 (see Data Transfer, below). If the two bits are 01, then modulus-8 is used; however, if the value of MOD is 10, modulus-128 is used. The two other possible bit patterns are not defined. All packets are sent with the MOD identifier.

Group/Channel. A 12-bit virtual-circuit number made from a 4-bit **Group** number and an 8-bit **Channel** number. All packets are sent with the 12-bit virtual-circuit number.

Calling-Len and **Called-Len.** The calling DTE's address length (**Calling-Len**) and called DTE's address length (**Called-Len**). Addresses can be up to 14 digits in length.

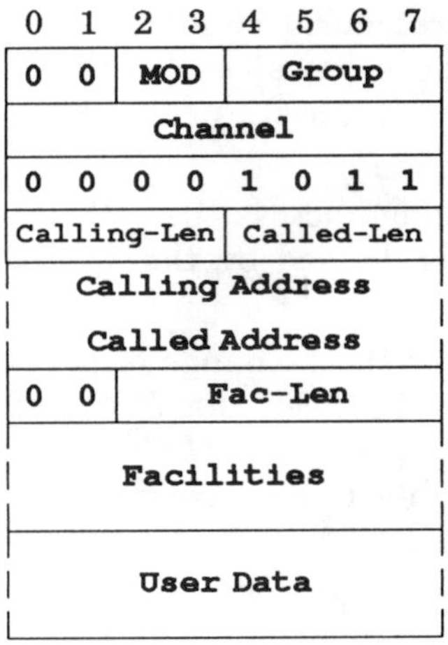

```
 0  1  2  3  4  5  6  7
┌──┬──┬─────┬──────────┐
│0 │0 │ MOD │  Group   │
├──┴──┴─────┴──────────┤
│      Channel         │
├──┬──┬──┬──┬──┬──┬──┬─┤
│0 │0 │0 │0 │1 │0 │1 │1│
├──────────┬───────────┤
│Calling-Len│Called-Len │
├──────────┴───────────┤
│   Calling Address    │
│                      │
│   Called Address     │
├──┬──┬────────────────┤
│0 │0 │   Fac-Len      │
├──┴──┴────────────────┤
│                      │
│     Facilities       │
│                      │
├──────────────────────┤
│                      │
│     User Data        │
│                      │
└──────────────────────┘
```

Figure 10.23   The X.25 Call-Request packet

Calling and **Called Address**. The source and destination addresses. The network address format is defined by CCITT X.121: three digits for the country, one digit for the network within the country, and ten digits to identify the DTE. Each digit is 4-bits long (i.e., a binary-coded decimal digit). Within a network, the organization of the ten digits is defined by the network administration. If the final octet contains a single digit (four-bits), the remaining four bits are zero filled.

Fac-Len. The length, in octets, of the **Facilities** field.

Facilities. The **Facilities** field allows the calling DTE to either indicate or request one or more facilities. The exact facilities supported can vary from network to network, but some of the more common ones include reverse charging (the calling DTE wants the called DTE to accept the network charges for this call), use of a nonstandard window or message size, and restriction of communication to a specific group of DTEs when the calling DTE is a member of a specific *closed-user group* (CUG). Facilities are sent as sequences of octet pairs: the first octet, the facility code, indicates the facility requested; and the second octet, the facility parameter, is the value associated with the requested code. For example, to request reverse charging, the facility code is 00000001, while the parameter is either 00000000 (no reverse charging requested) or 00000001 (reverse charging requested). A specific CUG can be requested by supplying a facility code of 00000011 followed by the 8-bit closed-user group number.

User Data. Data supplied by the calling DTE that is passed, unchanged, to the called DTE.

The Call-Request packet arrives at the called DTE as an Incoming-Call packet. If the called DTE can accept the call, it returns a Call-Accepted packet, which is received by the calling DTE as a Call-Connected packet. The Call-Accepted/Connected packet format is shown in Figure 10.24.

```
 0  1  2  3  4  5  6  7
┌──┬──┬─────┬──────────┐
│0 │0 │ MOD │  Group   │
├──┴──┴─────┴──────────┤
│       Channel        │
├──┬──┬──┬──┬──┬──┬──┬──┤
│0 │0 │0 │0 │1 │1 │1 │1 │
└──┴──┴──┴──┴──┴──┴──┴──┘
```

Figure 10.24 The X.25 Call-Accepted/Connected packet

The overall flow of information in the X.25 call establishment phase is represented in Figure 10.25.

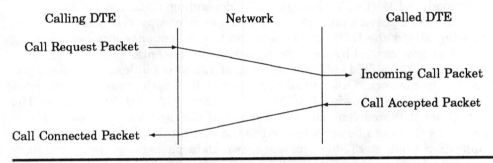

Figure 10.25 The steps in the call establishment phase

At this point, data transfer may commence. However, if the call cannot be accepted, the called DTE responds with a Call-Clearing packet (see Call-Clearing section). Possible reasons for the call not being accepted include the refusal of the called DTE to accept reverse charging or that the called DTE itself was in the process of making a call.

Data Transfer.   Once the virtual circuit is established, data transfer can take place. Unless otherwise specified, the virtual circuit is full duplex, meaning that the DTEs may transmit at any time, as long as their transmit window is open. To ensure that packets are not lost and to permit flow control, X.25 implements a go-back-N sliding window protocol for level-3 Data packets. Each Data packet is sent with both its sequence number and the sequence number of the next expected packet (Figure 10.26).

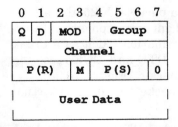

Figure 10.26 The X.25 Data packet

The Q-bit is the *data qualifier bit* and when cleared, signals the DTE to forward the `User Data` to the application associated with the virtual circuit number. However, when set, the Q-bit allows the DTEs to exchange DTE-specific control data; in these situations, the `User Data` is not supplied to the application associated with the virtual-circuit number. The D-bit, when set, requests an end-to-end acknowledgement for this packet *after* is has been successfully delivered to the application by the DTE (X.25 acknowledgements are discussed below).

`P(R)`, the packet-receive sequence number, and `P(S)`, the packet-sent sequence number, are the next-expected and the current-packet sequence numbers, respectively. Sequence numbering is performed modulo-8 (i.e., 0 through 7) or modulo-128 (i.e., 0 through 127), depending upon the value of MOD. Modulo-128 requires that `P(R)` and `P(S)` each occupy one octet. The sequencing allows the DTEs to perform end-to-end sequence number checking as well as flow control by withholding acknowledgements.

The `User Data` field holds a maximum of 128 octets unless otherwise specified by the network. Other valid maximum data lengths must be a power of 2 taken from the following list: 16, 32, 64, 256, 512, and 1024 octets. The M-bit is set if the current Data packet is full and a subsequent packet contains data that is to be concatenated to the current data. For example, if an application sends a 132-byte message, two Data packets are sent: the first, a packet of 128 octets (with the M-bit set), followed by a second packet of 4 octets (with the M-bit cleared). The remote DTE the assembles the 132 bytes before forwarding them to the remote application.

There are three end-to-end acknowledgement packets which correspond to the SDLC/HDLC go-back-N protocol acknowledgement frames: RR, RNR, and REJ. The packet formats are as shown in Figure 10.27 (`P(R)` denotes the sequence number of the next expected packet).

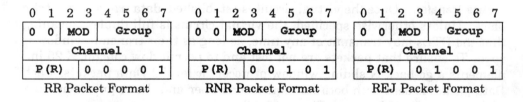

RR Packet Format   RNR Packet Format   REJ Packet Format

Figure 10.27   X.25 end-to-end acknowledgement packet formats

In addition to sending and receiving sequenced Data packets, X.25 also allows for the transmission and reception of unsequenced Interrupt packets. Interrupt packets are intended to convey signalling information (such as a break signal) on a virtual circuit. The response from the DTE and DCE receiving the Interrupt packet is an Interrupt-Confirmation packet (Figure 10.28).

The exchange of data takes place through Data packets across the virtual circuit (Figure 10.29).

Call clearing.   Call clearing can be initialized by either DTE issuing a Clear-Request packet. The DCE connected to the DTE issuing the Clear Request re-

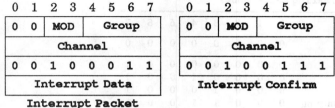

Figure 10.28   The X.25 Interrupt and Interrupt-Confirm packets

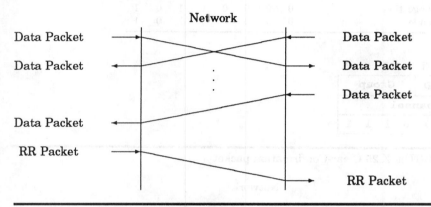

Figure 10.29   Data transfer using X.25

sponds with Clear Confirmation, freeing the virtual circuit. When the packet arrives at the remote DCE, the DCE issues a Clear Indication packet to the remote DTE. The remote DTE then frees its virtual circuit and responds to its DCE with a Clear Confirmation. The format of the Clear Request/Indication packets is shown in Figure 10.30.

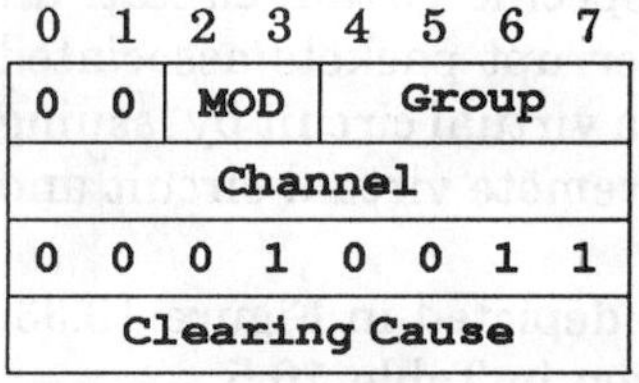

0	1	2	3	4	5	6	7
0	0	MOD		Group			
Channel							
0	0	0	1	0	0	1	1
Clearing Cause							

Figure 10.30   The X.25 Clear Request/Indication packet

The codes for the **Clearing Cause** field are given in Table 10.4.

The format of the DTE and DCE Clear-Confirmation packet is shown in Figure 10.31.

The flow of packets for an X.25 call clearing is as follows (note that the Clear-Confirmation packets are *local* rather than end-to-end). See Figure 10.32.

In addition to the three phases just described, X.25 also defines two other phases, *Reset* and *Restart*.

TABLE 10.4 Clear Request Clearing Cause Values

Code	0	1	2	3	4	5	6	7
DTE Clearing	0	0	0	0	0	0	0	0
Number Busy	0	0	0	0	0	0	0	1
Out of Order	0	0	0	0	1	0	0	1
Remote Procedure Error	0	0	0	1	0	0	0	1
Number Refuses Reverse Charging	0	0	0	1	1	0	0	1
Invalid Call	0	0	0	0	0	0	1	1
Access Barred	0	0	0	0	1	0	1	1
Local Procedure Error	0	0	0	1	0	0	1	1
Network Congestion	0	0	0	0	0	1	0	1
Not Obtainable	0	0	0	0	1	1	0	1

```
0  1  2  3  4  5  6  7
+--+--+-----+-----------+
| 0  0 | MOD |  Group    |
+------+-----+-----------+
|      Channel           |
+------+-----+-----------+
| 0  0  0  1  0  1  1  1 |
+-----------------------+
```

Figure 10.31 The X.25 Clear-Confirmation packet

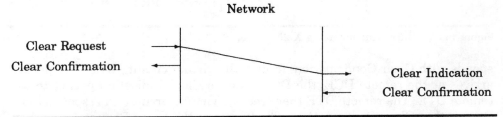

Figure 10.32 The steps in the Call-Clearing phase

Reset. The reset phase allows a DTE to reset a specific virtual circuit: all sequence numbers are cleared and any Data or Interrupt packets associated with the circuit are discarded. Either DTE can reset a virtual circuit by issuing a Reset-Request packet; the remote DTE resets the remote virtual circuit and responds with a Reset Confirm.

The Reset-Request/Indication packet format is as depicted in Figure 10.33. The codes for the **Resetting Cause** field are given in Table 10.5.

TABLE 10.5 Call Reset Resetting Cause Values

Code	0	1	2	3	4	5	6	7
DTE Reset	0	0	0	0	0	0	0	0
Out of Order	0	0	0	0	0	0	0	1
Remote Procedure Error	0	0	0	0	0	0	1	1
Local Procedure Error	0	0	0	0	0	1	0	1
Network Congestion	0	0	0	0	0	1	1	1

```
 0  1  2  3  4  5  6  7
┌──┬──┬─────┬──────────┐
│0 │0 │ MOD │  Group   │
├──┴──┴─────┴──────────┤
│      Channel         │
├──┬──┬──┬──┬──┬──┬──┬──┤
│0 │0 │0 │1 │1 │0 │1 │1 │
├──┴──┴──┴──┴──┴──┴──┴──┤
│   Resetting Cause    │
├──────────────────────┤
│   Diagnostic Code    │
└──────────────────────┘
```

Figure 10.33 The X.25 Reset-Request/Indication packet

The **Diagnostic Code** has a value of zero.

The format of the DTE and DCE Reset Confirmation packet is shown in Figure 10.34.

```
 0  1  2  3  4  5  6  7
┌──┬──┬─────┬──────────┐
│0 │0 │ MOD │  Group   │
├──┴──┴─────┴──────────┤
│      Channel         │
├──┬──┬──┬──┬──┬──┬──┬──┤
│0 │0 │0 │1 │1 │1 │1 │1 │
└──┴──┴──┴──┴──┴──┴──┴──┘
```

Figure 10.34 The X.25 Reset Confirmation packet

Restart. The restart phase allows a DTE to clear *all* of its switched-virtual circuits and to reset its permanent-virtual circuits. Either the DTE or the DCE can request a restart by issuing a Restart-Request packet; the response is a Restart Confirm. Any switched-virtual circuits must be re-established after a restart.

The format of the Restart-Request/Indication packet is as shown in Figure 10.35.

```
 0  1  2  3  4  5  6  7
┌──┬──┬─────┬──────────┐
│0 │0 │ MOD │  Group   │
├──┴──┴─────┴──────────┤
│      Channel         │
├──┬──┬──┬──┬──┬──┬──┬──┤
│1 │1 │1 │1 │1 │1 │1 │1 │
├──┴──┴──┴──┴──┴──┴──┴──┤
│   Restarting Cause   │
└──────────────────────┘
```

Figure 10.35 The X.25 Restart-Request/Indication packet

The codes for the **Restarting Cause** field in the Restart-Request/Indication packet are as given in Table 10.6.

TABLE 10.6 **Call Restart** Restarting Cause **Values**

Code	0	1	2	3	4	5	6	7
Local Procedure Error	0	0	0	0	0	0	0	1
Network Congestion	0	0	0	0	0	0	1	1

The format of the DTE and DCE Restart Confirmation packet is shown in Figure 10.36.

```
0  1  2  3  4  5  6  7
+--+--+-----+-----------+
|0 |0 | MOD |   Group   |
+--+--+-----+-----------+
|      Channel          |
+-----------------------+
|1 |1 |1 |1 |1 |1 |1 |1 |
+--+--+--+--+--+--+--+--+
```

Figure 10.36 The X.25 Restart Confirmation packet

10.4.4 Network-Access Protocols

From the above discussion on X.25, it is apparent that network access is handled by DTEs that support X.25. The various X.25 levels can be embedded in a DTE's operating system and users or applications requiring network access can follow the steps required by the specific operating system. Clearly, without some means of generating and recognizing X.25 packets, DTEs such as asynchronous terminals are unable to access an X.25 network.

Fortunately, CCITT has also developed a series of PAD (Packet Assembler/Disassembler) protocols that permit non-X.25 DTEs access to wide area networks. These standards, *X.3* (PAD parameters), *X.28* (terminal-PAD interface) and *X.29* (PAD DTE interface) define how an asynchronous DTE (i.e., a terminal) can access a remote X.25 DTE through a packet switched network using a PAD.

Since different terminals and their users will have different requirements, X.3 specifies a number of features that can be tailored to a specific terminal. (These features are maintained in a *profile* which is associated with the terminal for as long as it is connected to the network.) For example, the X.3 PAD parameters allow either the remote DTE or the local terminal to modify things such as:

- Whether the terminal can communicate with the PAD to change PAD parameters (PAD parameter 1).

- Whether the PAD is responsible for echoing characters to the terminal (PAD parameter 2). If the terminal expects remote echoing but the DTE does not support remote echo, the PAD can be requested to echo each character entered.

- Which character(s) may be used to signal the PAD that a packet is to be forwarded (PAD parameter 3). Packets can be forwarded when "full" (i.e., after 128 or 256 characters are entered) when a specific character is detected (such as a carriage return), or on each character (useful when working with a full-duplex screen editor).

- Whether the PAD recognizes the flow control characters X-ON and X-OFF; allowing the user to suspend output to the terminal (PAD parameter 12).

- If the PAD supports line-at-a-time input (that is, the end-of-line character causes the line to be forwarded in a packet), the user should be allowed to make changes to the line before the line is sent. X.3 defines editing character selection, in which the character delete, line delete, and line redraw keys can all be defined (PAD parameters 15, 16, 17, and 18).

A terminal connected to a PAD operates in one of two modes: either the terminal is communicating with the PAD (for example, for call setup or call clearing) or the terminal is communicating with the remote DTE (for data transfer). When communication with the PAD is required (for example, to change one or more X.3 parameters), the user issues an escape sequence which is recognized by the PAD, data transfer then ceases while the user communicates with the PAD. The commands and associated responses are defined in X.28 and permit the user to establish a call, clear a call, query PAD parameters, and change PAD parameters. When data is to be sent to the DTE, the PAD is responsible for formatting the data in an X.25 packet.

The DTE can also communicate with the PAD through the X.29 protocol which defines a series of messages intended for use between the DTE and the PAD. These messages allow the DTE to query and select different PAD parameters as well as signalling that the call is to be cleared. The ability to change PAD parameters is useful when, for example, the user activates a full-screen editor. At this time, the DTE can request that the PAD forward every character while the editor is in use.

The Q-bit in the X.25 packet allows the PAD to determine which packets are intended for the terminal (Q-bit is cleared) and which packets are intended for the PAD (Q-bit is set). X.29 packets are sent with the Q-bit set.

10.5   EXAMPLES OF WIDE AREA NETWORKS

Wide area networks fall into two broad categories:

- Those that have been developed by a company and that are intended to work with the company's equipment.

    A good example of this is *Systems Network Architecture* (SNA), developed by IBM, which consists of both hardware and software. SNA is a layered-network architecture consisting of a Physical Layer (Physical Control); a Data Link Layer (Data Link Control) which supports SDLC; and a Network Layer (Path Control). The Path-Control Layer is responsible for packet routing and flow control.

    DECNET is another example of hardware and software products developed by a manufacturer (Digital Equipment Corporation) specifically for their own equipment. DECNET is part of Digital's DNA *(Digital Network Architecture)*, a layered-network architecture. DECNET has a number of objectives, including: to connect Digital computers and operating systems, to support "any" Physical Layer (i.e., full duplex, half duplex, synchronous, asynchronous, serial, parallel, and so on), and to offer facilities to support interprocess communications and file transfer. The Data Link Layer is supported by DDCMP *(Digital Data Communication Message Protocol)*, a sliding-window protocol with a window size of up to 127.

- Those that conform to international standards, such as X.25.

Most public-packet switching networks, such as *Datapac* (Canada), *Transpac* (France), and *Tymnet* (U.S.A.), support networking standards such as X.3, X.25, X.28, and X.29. There are a number of arguments for supporting international standards, rather than the products of a single vendor; the most compelling being that supporting international standards permits the interconnection of equipment from different manufacturers. Another argument, to be pursued in later chapters, is that network interconnection can be an easier task if common protocols are adopted.

10.6   THE COMMKIT WIDE AREA NETWORK

Commkit is supplied with a layered model of a wide area network that demonstrates the functions of a Network Layer supporting virtual circuits, notably: call establishment, data transfer, and call clearing. In addition, a sliding-window procotol is implemented in the Data Link Layer. The wide area network allows communication between PCs connected by null-modem RS-232-C cables. Each PC is treated as an individual node and access to the network is accomplished through an application that allows the explicit testing of the Network Layer protocol.

The wide area network software consists of the following files:

wanlow.c The Physical and Data Link Layers. The Data Link Layer software supports a go-back-N protocol similar to SDLC/HDLC.

wannet.c The Network Layer; responsible for call establishment, data transfer, and call clearing.

wanex.c The application, an interactive message-entry layer that allows the testing of virtual circuits.

wanstrct.h Structures and state information specific to the Physical and Data Link Layer software found in wanlow.c.

wandef.h Definitions and constants specific to the Network Layer, wannet.c.

wancodes.h Definitions and constants used by both the Network Layer and the test software.

Internally, the software uses the send() and recv() primitives to support layering. The Data Link Layer, the Network Layer, and the application are all considered processes and hence are associated with unique queues.

10.6.1   Hardware Requirements

The Commkit wide area network software requires a minimum of two PCs, each with one (preferably two) serial ports, and sufficient null-modem cables to allow the PCs to be linked in a bus-like fashion (Figure 10.37).

To facilitate routing, the wide area network software supplied with the Commkit diskette requires a specific ordering of port connections: serial port 1 must connect to serial port 2 (and vice versa); and a specific ordering of

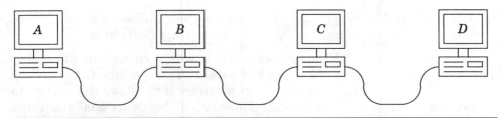

Figure 10.37   A four-node Commkit wide area network

addresses: packets sent out port 1 are intended for PCs with lower-valued addresses, while packets sent out port 2 are intended for PCs with higher-valued addresses. For example, in the network in Figure 10.37, PC D transmits to PC C through port 1, while PC C receives from PC D on port 2. The reasons for this are discussed in the next section and possible alternatives are left as exercises.

10.6.2   Commkit Virtual Circuits

The Commkit wide area network consists of several interconnected PCs. Each PC acts as a network node, while simultaneously permitting processes to communicate using virtual circuits. A Commkit virtual circuit is made from two distinct simplex paths through the network, connecting a process on either end (Figure 10.38).

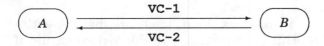

Figure 10.38   Two Commkit virtual circuits (each is simplex)

To create one half of the virtual circuit, a process issues a Call-Request packet addressed to the foreground process on a destination node. As the Call-Request packet moves through the network, the Network Layer on each node creates a pointer to the entity that sent the packet (either a node or the original process). When the Call-Request packet reaches the destination node, the packet is forwarded to the node's foreground process. At this point, a simplex *reverse-path* has been established: from the process that received the Call-Request packet, through the Network Layers on the intervening nodes, then back to the process that originally sent the packet.

Since there can be a number of virtual circuits in operation at any time, each Network Layer maintains an array, vcn_table, of virtual circuits. An entry in vcn_table consists of three fields described in the next sections.

dst_id.   The identifier of the queue associated with the source of the Call-Request packet received by the Network Layer, one of: SP1IH, SP2IH, or the calling process (typically APPLICATION). This identifier is stored since it is this Network Layer's path *back* to the entity that transmitted the Call-Request packet.

Data and Call-Clearing packets put onto the queue indicated by dst_id are on the path back to the process that sent the original Call packet.

dst_vcn.   Each Call-Request packet is sent with a virtual-circuit number determined by the entity that sent the packet. If the entity is the calling process, the virtual-circuit number is an identifier that allows the process to determine the source of the packet. However, if the entity that transmits the Call-Request packet is a Network Layer, the virtual-circuit number is the *subscript* of the Network Layer's vcn_table associated with this particular virtual circuit.

When the Network Layer receives a Call-Request packet, the next available space in its vcn_table is found, and the virtual-circuit number is extracted from the Call-Request packet and stored in the dst_vcn field. The value of the subscript is then placed in the Call-Request packet as this particular Network Layer's virtual-circuit number and sent to the next entity enroute to the destination process.

When the Network Layer receives a Data or Call-Clearing packet, the virtual-circuit number is extracted from the packet and used as a subscript into the vcn_table. The entry in vcn_table specifies the queue onto which the packet is to be placed (dst_id) and the packet's new virtual-circuit number (dst_vcn). This cycle is repeated by each Network Layer.

owner.   The destination entity of the Call-Request packet as determined by the current Network Layer. The destination is one of: SP1IH, SP2IH, or the called process (by default, APPLICATION). The destination is determined by the Network Layer's routing algorithm.

The owner field is used in two situations. First, to ensure that the entity transmitting a Data packet is actually associated with this virtual circuit; if not, an Error packet is returned. Second, it is used to verify that the entity attempting to clear a call is allowed to do so.

For example, assume that process A on DTE x is to call process B on DTE z and the route takes it through DTE y. Initially there is no path through the network from A to B (Figure 10.39).

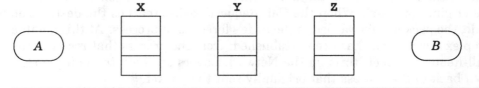

Figure 10.39   Initial network configuration; no path from process A to process B

Process A requests a path to process B by putting B's DTE address, z, in a Call-Request packet. The Call-Request packet also contains a virtual-circuit number generated by A. In this case the virtual circuit number is 0. The Call-Request packet is then sent by A to its Network Layer.

Upon receipt of the Call-Request packet, the Network Layer on DTE x determines that the route to z is the link to Y (one of the serial ports). The

Network Layer then finds the first free entry in its virtual circuit table (in this example, the last, location 2), and in this location stores *A* as dst_id, 0 as dst_vcn, and X as the owner. The virtual-circuit number in the Call-Request packet is changed to 2, the location of the entry in X's virtual circuit table. The first link in the virtual circuit has been established (Figure 10.40).

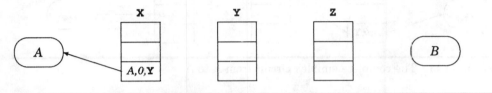

Figure 10.40 First virtual circuit, X to *A*

The Network Layer on DTE X then supplies the Call-Request packet to the Data Link Layer for transmission to DTE Y.

When the Network Layer on DTE Y receives the Call-Request packet, the route is determined (out the link to Z) and the first free entry in DTE Y's virtual-circuit table is found (in this example, location 0). The Network Layer stores X as dst_id, the virtual-circuit number from the packet, 2, as dst_vcn, and Z as the owner in location 0 of its virtual-circuit table. The path now reaches to Y from *A* (Figure 10.41).

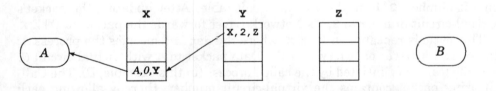

Figure 10.41 Second virtual circuit, Y to X

The virtual-circuit number in the Call-Request packet is changed to 0 and the packet sent from DTE Y to DTE Z. Since the destination address in the Call-Request packet is Z, the Call-Request packet can be supplied to process *B* after the virtual-circuit table is updated: dst_id is set to Y, dst_vcn to 0, and the owner is process *B* (in this example, location 1 is the next available entry in Z's virtual circuit table). See Figure 10.42.

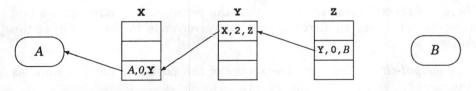

Figure 10.42 Third virtual circuit, Z to Y

The Network Layer supplies the Call-Request packet to process B with the virtual-circuit number of **1**. At this point a simplex circuit exists from process B to process A through the network (Figure 10.43).

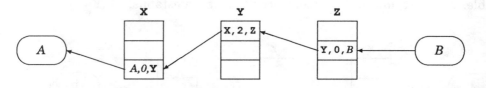

Figure 10.43   The complete simplex circuit from B to A

Process B can now decide whether to accept or clear the call. If the call is accepted, process B issues a Call-Request packet back to process A, creating a second path through the network.

Assuming that the call is accepted, if process B sends a message to process A, B must supply the virtual-circuit number, **1**, and the message in a Data packet to its Network Layer on DTE **z**. The virtual-circuit number, **1**, is used as a subscript into **z**'s virtual-circuit table; since the `owner` field specifies B, the transmission can take place. The virtual-circuit number is changed to **0** and the Data packet is forwarded to the Data Link Layer that connects to **Y**.

When the Data packet arrives at **Y**'s Network Layer, the virtual-circuit number is extracted and, once again used as a subscript. The Network Layer then checks the ownership of the entry and then extracts the link, **x**, and the virtual circuit-number, **2**, from the virtual circuit-table. After updating the packet's virtual-circuit number to **2**, **Y**'s Network Layer forwards the packet to DTE **x**.

This cycle is repeated on DTE **x**, where the `dst_id` specifies the process A; the Network Layer on **x** forwards the Data packet to A with virtual circuit *0*.

Call clearing is initiated by the called process (in this example, B). The Call-Clearing packet contains the virtual-circuit number, thereby allowing each Network Layer on the reverse path to remove the information from its virtual-circuit table. For example, to clear the virtual-circuit, process B sends a Call-Clearing packet with virtual-circuit number **1**; **z**'s Network Layer ensures that B can clear this virtual circuit by checking the `owner` field associated with location **1** in its `vcn_table`. The Network Layer proceeds to remove the virtual-circuit information from the table and forwards the Call-Clearing packet to **Y** with virtual-circuit number **0**. The cycle is repeated by each Network Layer all the way back to process A.

Process A is then expected to issue a Call-Clearing packet for its circuit to process B.

There are several error situations that the Network Layer recognizes and handles by returning an Error packet and error code to the source of the packet:

Invalid virtual-circuit number. The source of the packet is not the same as the `owner`.

Unknown destination. The destination node does not exist.

Network congestion. A virtual circuit cannot be created because a virtual-circuit table on one of the nodes is full.

10.6.3 Layers

The Commkit wide area network is implemented as a series of four distinct layers:

Application Layer
Network Layer
Data Link Layer
Physical Layer

Application Layer The Application Layer consists of a foreground process (do_wan_ex() in wanex.c) that allows the establishment and testing of virtual circuits. The process receives messages sent by either the Network Layer (NETWORK), the keyboard (KEYIH), or the clock (CLKIH), to the APPLICATION queue.

Keyboard characters are displayed on line 1 of the PC's screen and stored in the array buffer. The contents of the buffer are sent to the Network Layer when a carriage return is detected. The virtual-circuit testing software recognizes five commands (the command is a single character stored in buffer[0]):

R   Send a call-request frame. R is followed by a virtual-circuit number, the destination node address, and the source node address.

D   Send a data transfer frame. D is followed by a virtual-circuit number and the message.

C   Send a call-clearing frame. C is followed by a virtual-circuit number.

T   Enter test mode. T is followed by a virtual-circuit number.

S   Stop test mode.

When test mode is entered, a data frame, test_str, containing the letters of the alphabet is sent by the test software to the specified virtual circuit. The virtual circuit must already be established. Packets are sent once a second if x_count is nonzero (x_count is the local process's transmit window used only in test mode). X_count is initialized to 5 when test mode is entered and is decremented each time a Data packet is sent, which eventually closes the transmit window. The transmit window is reopened, by incrementing x_count, each time a packet is received.

The second byte entered after the command byte is the virtual-circuit number (except in the case of S which does not specify a virtual-circuit). The virtual circuit number is entered as an ASCII character (assumed to be in the range 0 through 9); internally, this byte is stored in buffer[1] as the binary equivalent of the ASCII character (i.e., 0x00 through 0x09). This allows the Network Layer to access its virtual-circuit table without requiring special code for packets from the test process.

All messages are displayed in an output region, lines 5 through 23. Messages from the Network Layer are displayed in inverse video in the output region in the order they are received. Error codes are extracted from Error packets and displayed textually in the output region. As soon as a keyboard message is sent, it is displayed in normal video on the next available line in the output region. `Update_line()` updates the line counter (`line`), and clears the next available line of the screen.

Network Layer   The Network Layer is a background process (`network_layer()`, found in `wannet.c`) associated with the queue `NETWORK` (a redefinition of `BACKGROUND_1`) that is responsible for the establishment and maintance of virtual circuits.

`Network_layer()` is called when a packet is available on queue `NETWORK`. Packets are received from either of the serial ports (`SP1IH` or `SP2IH`) or from a process. The packet format (Figure 10.44) is the same in all cases (defined in `wandef.h`).

code	Packet code.
vcn	The virtual circuit number.
msg[0]	The called DTE address (call request only), data, or an error code.
msg[1]	The calling DTE address (call request only), otherwise data.
msg[2] through msg[126]	Up to 128 bytes of data.

Figure 10.44   Commkit Network Layer packet structure

Four different packet `codes` are recognized: Call-Request (R), Data (D), Call-Clearing (C), and Error (E). The virtual-circuit number, `vcn`, is a binary digit used as a subscript into the virtual circuit table, `vcn_table`. The contents of `msg` are ignored by the Network Layer except when the packet is a Call-Request packet: `msg[P_DST]` and `msg[P_SRC]` denote the destination and source addresses respectively. If the packet is an Error packet, `msg[ERR_CODE]` contains the error code.

Once the packet is obtained (using `recv()`), the `code` is inspected and one of the following three functions are called (a packet with an unknown `code` is returned to its source as an Error packet with an error code of `UNKNOWN_CMD`).

handle_call_request().   `Handle_call_request()` is called whenever a Call-Request packet is received (a `code` of D). `Handle_call_request()` is responsible for obtaining a virtual-circuit number and routing the Call-Request packet to the next destination (either the link to the next DTE or the destination process, by default, the process `APPLICATION`). `Get_vcn_tbl()` returns the new virtual-circuit number, which is stored in `vcn_tbl`. If there are no virtual circuits available, an error of `NETWORK_CONGESTION` is returned to the `src` of the message.

The routing algorithm, when combined with the ordering of port connections described above, ensures that Call-Request packets with unknown addresses will not circulate forever:

1. If the destination address is equal to the node's address, the destination of the packet is APPLICATION.
2. If the destination address is greater than the node's address and the packet is received from SP1IH or APPLICATION, the packet's destination is SP2IH.
3. If the destination address is less than the node's address and the message is received from SP2IH or APPLICATION, the packet's destination is SP1IH.
4. If the address does not exist, the call request is aborted and an Error packet is returned to the source of the packet, src, with an error of UNKNOWN_DST.

If the packet can be forwarded, the virtual-circuit number in the packet is changed to vcn_tbl and the packet is sent to the destination determined by the routing algorithm.

handle_data_transfer(). Network_layer() calls handle_data_transfer() when a packet with a code of D is received. The packet's vcn is used as a subscript into vcn_table; if the source of the message is the owner specified in vcn_table, the packet's vcn is changed to dst_vcn and the next destination is taken from dst_id. An error code of INVALID_VCN is returned to the source of the message if the source is not the owner of this circuit.

handle_call_clearing(). Handle_call_clearing() is called when a Call-Clearing packet is received (a code of C). The Call-Clearing packet is forwarded to the next destination and owner is set to −1 to signal that this circuit is now free. An error code of INVALID_VCN is returned to the source if the source is not the owner of this circuit.

Data Link Layer   The Data Link Layer is responsible for the orderly transmission and reception of messages and acknowledgements across a link connecting two nodes. Reliable communications are achieved through the use of a sliding-window protocol.

A single-frame structure is supported by the Data Link Layer, consisting of a series of bytes enclosed by *STX–ETX*. The frame format is given in Figure 10.45 (the size of each field in bytes is listed to the right of each field name).

STX	Control (1)	Information (up to 128 bytes)	CRC (2)	*ETX*

Figure 10.45   The Commkit Data Link Layer frame format

The individual fields are as follows:

Control. The Control field is a single byte indicating the type of frame. Two frame types are supported: supervisory and information. Frames are distinguished by the contents of the Control field:

Supervisory. A supervisory frame is one that contains an acknowledgement (RR). The **Information** field is not sent in a Supervisory frame. The format of the Supervisory **Control** field is shown in Figure 10.46.

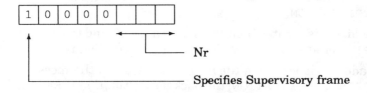

Figure 10.46   The Supervisory **Control** field format

Information. The Information frame **Control** byte indicates the sequence number of this packet (Ns) and the sequence number of the next expected packet (Nr). Information frames contain the **Information** field. The format of the Information frame **Control** field is shown in Figure 10.47.

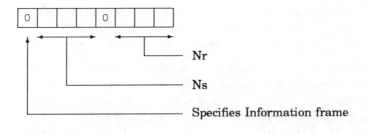

Figure 10.47   The Information frame **Control** field format

Information. Any message of up to 128 bytes in length. Transparency is supported by prefixing any *ETX* bytes or *DLE* bytes with a *DLE* byte. The **Information** field is not sent in supervisory frames.

   Information frames are sent with a 3-bit sequence number (0 through 7), to which the receiving node responds with the *next* expected sequence number. Each frame sent is associated with a timer; if an acknowledgement is not received before the clock expires, the frame and all other pending frames are retransmitted. A transmitted **Information** frame is deemed received by the transmitting node when a **Control** field (either Supervisory or Information) is received with a sequence number greater than the frame's sequence number.

CRC. A 16-bit CRC, calculated using the cyclic redundancy check software in crcsr.c. The **CRC** includes the entire frame except for the leading *STX*, the trailing *ETX*, and any *DLE* prefix characters. The **CRC** is sent with *all* frames and is calculated by the Physical Layer (see the following discussion).

The Data Link Layer is implemented as a series of procedures, the entry point being `data_link_layer()`. `Data_link_layer()` takes two arguments: `device` and `action`, and is activated by one of three conditions:

- A complete frame (either supervisory or information) is received by the Physical Layer (`device` is either `SP1IH` or `SP2IH`); indicated by the parameter `action` having a value of `MSGRECD`. Control is passed to procedure `dl_r_done()`.

- The completion of a frame transmission (either supervisory or information) by the Physical Layer (`device` is either `SP1IH` or `SP2IH`); indicated by the value of `action` being `MSGSENT`. Control is passed to procedure `dl_x_done()`.

- The reception of a one-second clock pulse (from `low_level()`); indicated by the parameter `device` having a value of `CLKIH`. Control is passed to procedure `dl_clock()`.

  One-second clock messages are also sent from `low_level()` to the foreground process, `APPLICATION`.

The remaining three procedures used by the Data Link Layer are:

`dl_clock()`. The clock procedure `dl_clock()` is called once a second to determine:

- If the time limit associated with the message currently awaiting an acknowledgement has been exceeded. When a message's time limit is exceeded, the message and all other messages awaiting acknowledgement are retransmitted. The variable `wan.current_frame` is assigned the index of the message awaiting acknowledgement; transmission resumes from that message via a call to `dl_x_done()`.

- If there are any messages supplied from the Network Layer awaiting transmission.
  `Dl_x_done()` is called if a message is on the device's queue (determined by examining the queue head of the device rather than issuing a `recv()`), and the transmission window is open.

`dl_r_done()`. `Dl_r_done()` is called whenever a frame is received from either port. Supervisory frames are assumed to contain acknowledgements; the acknowledgement sequence number (Nr) is extracted from the control byte, `wan.r_ctrl`. Procedure `update_ack()` determines the amount the window should be opened and updates `wan.awaiting_ack`.

Information frames contain both a sequence number and a piggybacked acknowledgement. If the frame sequence number is equal to `wan.expected`, the message part of the frame is sent to the Network Layer and the acknowledgements are updated. The flag `wan.pending_ack` is assigned `TRUE` to ensure that if no information frames are to be transmitted, at least a supervisory frame will be sent, thereby maintaining throughput.

Pending frames awaiting acknowledgement are *not* retransmitted simply because they are still awaiting acknowledgement. Instead, the `wan.cur-`

rent_frame index is only updated if the frame awaiting an acknowledgement has been waiting for at least one second.

dl_x_done(). Procedure dl_x_done() is called whenever a frame has been sent *or* a condition arises that allows a frame to be sent. Frames (information or supervisory) are transmitted only if one of the following conditions hold (in order of priority):

1. Messages are in the process of being retransmitted.
2. A new message is available for transmission and the window is open.
3. A pending acknowledgement is awaiting transmission.

Since entry to these procedures occurs when interrupts are disabled, mutual exclusion is guaranteed.

Physical Layer The Physical Layer is a device driver and is responsible for the transmission and reception of frames. The Physical Layer recognizes the Data Link Layer frame format and is responsible for calculating the CRC associated with each frame. The entry point to the Physical Layer is the procedure physical_layer(), which is called by low_level() and takes three parameters:

port   The port (either SP1IH or SP2IH), associated with the action.

action   A code indicating the result of the function just completed by the serial port, either XMITDONE or RECVDONE.

in_ch   The character just received (if action is RECVDONE), otherwise zero.

Each port is associated with its own data structure in the array wan (wan[0] for SP1IH and wan[1] for SP2IH, defined in wanstrct.h).

The Physical Layer is full duplex and can be sending and receiving out both ports at any particular moment. This layer can be described in terms of its two primary functions, the transmission and reception of frames:

Transmission (action == XMITDONE). A transmission is initiated by the Data Link Layer sending an *STX* out one of the ports and supplying the Physical Layer with the following information (note that wan refers to either wan[0] or wan[1], depending upon the value of port):

1. The frame's control byte, wan.x_ctrl, indicates whether the frame is a supervisory or information frame. The control byte is included in the CRC.

2. The size of the message to be transmitted, wan.x_size. A size of zero indicates that there is no message (i.e., this is a supervisory frame). Any other value is taken to mean that there is a message to be sent. wan.x_count, initially zero, is incremented as each byte is sent and compared to wan.x_size.

3. A pointer to the message, wan.msgptr.

The transmission part of the Physical Layer is implemented as a state machine consisting of eight states (the current state is indicated by wan.x_state):

SEND_CTRL. This state entered after the transmission of the *STX* has been signalled. The control byte, wan.x_ctrl, is sent and included in the CRC. The next state depends upon the message size; if wan.x_size is zero, wan.x_state changes to SEND_CRC1, otherwise to SEND_DATA.

SEND_DATA. The next byte in the message (pointed to by wan.msgptr) is to be sent and included in the CRC. The byte count, wan.x_count, is incremented as each byte is sent. When the count is equal to the wan.x_size, the state changes to SEND_CRC1.

If the byte's value is either *DLE* or *ETX*, the byte is saved in wan.next_ch, the next state (either SEND_DATA or SEND_CRC1) is saved in wan.next_x_state, and the state changes to SEND_NEXT.

SEND_NEXT. An inserted *DLE* has just been sent. The byte to be sent in this state is taken from wan.next_ch and the value of the state changes to the value in wan.next_x_state.

SEND_CRC1. The lower eight bits of the CRC is to be sent. If the CRC byte is neither *DLE* nor *ETX*, the next state is set to SEND_CRC2. However, if the byte's value is either *DLE* or *ETX*, the byte is saved in wan.next_ch, SEND_CRC2 is saved in wan.next_x_state, and the state changes to SEND_NEXT.

SEND_CRC2. Is identical to SEND_CRC1, with the exception that the upper eight bits of the CRC is to be sent. The next state is SEND_ETX, unless the byte has a value of *DLE* or *ETX*, in which case, the state changes to SEND_NEXT.

SEND_ETX. The frame-ending *ETX* is sent. The state changes to SEND_DONE.

SEND_DONE. Entered after the final *ETX* has been sent, indicated by the UART signalling XMITDONE after the *ETX* is sent. The Data Link Layer is called to signal that the transmission has completed. The state changes to SEND_IDLE.

SEND_IDLE. Indicates that the transmitter is idle.

DLE insertion occurs whenever an *ETX* or *DLE* is found in the message *or* in the pair of CRC bytes. The inserted *DLE* is not included in the CRC; however, the byte following the *DLE* is part of the CRC.

Reception (action == RECVDONE). The receive-state machine is entered whenever data is received from either of the serial ports. Initially, the state machine is searching for an *STX*, denoting the start of frame. Once the frame-ending *ETX* is found, the message part of the frame and the control byte are returned to the Data Link Layer for processing.

The different receive states (indicated by wan.r_state) are as follows:

WAIT_STX. The reception idle state, entered initially and thereafter, whenever a frame has been received. If an *STX* is found, both the receive CRC (wan.r_crc) and the receive data count (wan.r_count) are cleared. The state changes to WAIT_CTRL.

WAIT_CTRL. The byte following the *STX* is assumed to be the control byte; the byte is stored in wan.r_ctrl and included in the receive CRC. The state changes to WAIT_DATA.

WAIT_DATA. In WAIT_DATA, all incoming bytes except *ETX* and *DLE* are included in the incoming CRC, and stored in the receive-message buffer (wan.r_msg). The detection of a *DLE* causes a state change to WAIT_NEXT; the *DLE* is not included in the CRC.

When the frame-ending *ETX* is found, the number of bytes in the message is decreased by two (since the last two bytes are the CRC). The calculated value of the CRC should be zero if no errors were detected. The reception of an error-free packet causes control to pass to the Data Link Layer, otherwise the packet is discarded. The receive state then returns to WAIT_STX.

WAIT_NEXT. Entered after a *DLE* is detected in the WAIT_DATA state. The byte received in this state is included in the CRC and stored as part of the message. Control returns to WAIT_DATA.

If, for some reason, the frame-ending *ETX* is lost, the receive state machine will stay in either the WAIT_DATA or the WAIT_NEXT state. Subsequent frames will be included in the incoming message buffer and hence will be lost. More seriously, a subscripting error will occur if the incoming data is simply copied into the message buffer. To avoid this situation, before a byte is written to the message buffer, the current receive count is checked: if the value exceeds the maximum message size, the receive state is returned to WAIT_STX.

10.7   USING THE COMMKIT WIDE AREA NETWORK

The Commkit wide area network software is supplied on the Commkit diskette, both as source listings and as the executable, wanex.exe.

10.7.1   Creating the Wide Area Network Software

The Commkit diskette is supplied with both a source and executable version of the wide area network software that allows keyboard data entry. If any of the wide area network modules (wanex.c, wannet.c, or wanlow.c) are changed, the modules should be recompiled to make a new executable, wanex.exe.

The executable is created using the make utility:

```
C:\> make wanex.exe
```

10.7.2   Running the Wide Area Network

Once an executable is obtained (either from the diskette or by recompiling), it can be run by typing wanex after the MS-DOS prompt, and specifying the line speed, the address of the node, and the transmit window size used by the Data Link Layer. For example, to set the PC up as node S on a 1200-bps network with a window size of 3, type:

```
C:\> wanex 1200 S 3
```

At this point, the screen is cleared and communications can proceed. Data entered by the user is displayed on line 1 of the screen; all or part of a line can be erased using the backspace key. When the carriage return is pressed, line 1 is erased, but the line is displayed on the next available line in the output region (lines 5 and 23) in normal video. As well as displaying keyboard input, the output region displays all messages and diagnostics from the Network Layer in inverse video. The output region "wraps-around" when the next line to be displayed exceeds the last line in the output region. Control can be returned to MS-DOS at any time by using CTRL-C or CTRL-ALT-DEL.

If several PCs are to be connected to form a wide area network, the cables should be connected from port 1 to port 2. Remember that the address assigned to each station depends upon its position with respect to other stations:

$$\boxed{PC_{n-1}} \vdash \text{port 2} \iff \text{port 1} \dashv \boxed{PC_n} \vdash \text{port 2} \iff \text{port 1} \dashv \boxed{PC_{n+1}}$$

10.7.3 Testing Virtual Circuits

Wanex.exe allows the testing of virtual circuits across the Commkit wide area network. Three different virtual-circuit phases and related packet structures are supported:

Call setup A test process on one node can attempt to establish a virtual circuit with another test process on another node. Calls can be established at any time (for example, during the data transfer phase) as long as there are virtual circuits available. Data transfer can only take place once a Call-Request packet is received.

Half of a virtual circuit is established by a user explicitly creating a Call-Request packet. The format of the Call-Request packet is as follows:

$$\boxed{\text{R} \mid VCN \mid DST \mid SRC}$$

where:

R. The code used to indicate a Call-Request packet;

VCN. The virtual-circuit number assigned by the user for this particular virtual circuit. The VCN can be any keyboard character.

DST. The address of the destination PC, a single character. The address need not be of an existing node (this will be discussed further).

SRC. the address of the source PC, a single character. This should be the address of this station, to allow the remote to respond.

A Call-Request packet establishes one half of a virtual circuit, the called node must respond with another Call-Request packet to the calling node if a full-duplex virtual circuit is to be set up.

Consider, for example, a wide area network consisting of two PCs, one with address 7, the other with address 3. If a virtual circuit is to be established between these two nodes, one node (in this example, 7) issues a Call-Request packet. The virtual-circuit number chosen is the symbol *, meaning that all subsequent packets *received* for this virtual circuit will contain * as the virtual-circuit number. The user on node 7 therefore types R*37 as the Call-Request packet.

After a moment, the Call-Request packet appears on node 3 in inverse video on the output region as $\boxed{\text{R037}}$. This is interpreted as a Call-Request packet from the user on node 7 with the virtual-circuit number 0; all packets sent with this virtual-circuit number will appear on node 7 with the virtual-circuit number replaced by '*'.

To make a full-duplex circuit, the user on node 3 responds R#73; a Call-Request packet to node 7 from node 3, all packets received on this half of the virtual-circuit will contain the virtual-circuit number #. The Call-Request packet arrives at node 7 and is displayed in inverse video as $\boxed{\text{R173}}$. A full-duplex virtual circuit is now established, the user on node 7 must transmit to virtual circuit 1.

The pair of (simplex) virtual circuits can be represented diagramatically as in Figure 10.48.

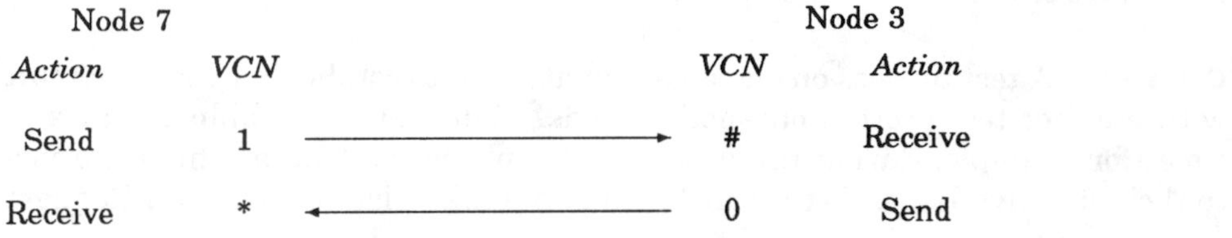

Node 7				Node 3	
Action	*VCN*			*VCN*	*Action*
Send	1	$\longrightarrow$		#	Receive
Receive	*	$\longleftarrow$		0	Send

Figure 10.48   A pair of simplex virtual circuits between nodes 3 and 7

If the destination address supplied does not exist between the two nodes, an error of $\boxed{\text{Unknown DST}}$ is returned. If the virtual circuit table is full on one of the nodes, the call request will be blocked and an error message $\boxed{\text{Network Congestion}}$ is returned.

Data transfer   Once a call has been established and a virtual-circuit number returned, data can be transferred between the two processes at either end of the circuit. A Data packet consists of the character D (denoting a Data packet), a virtual-circuit number (a character), and a string of characters making up the message, terminated by a carriage return:

D	*VCN*	Message

Data is displayed in the output area of the destination node in inverse video. The virtual-circuit number is the value specified by the user when the call request is established.

Continuing with the example begun in the call-request phase, if the user on node 3 is to send a message to the user on node 7, the message must be sent in a packet with virtual-circuit number 0. The message arrives at node 7 and is displayed in inverse video with the virtual-circuit number specified by the user; in this example, the message would appear with virtual-circuit number *.

If the virtual-circuit number in the Data packet is not associated with the process, an error message of $\boxed{\texttt{Invalid VCN}}$, followed by the virtual-circuit number, appears in the output area.

Once a virtual-circuit is established, the test software can be made to send a stream of Data packets to the process at the other end of the virtual-circuit. This is known as test mode and is initiated by typing T followed by the virtual-circuit number over which the transmissions are to occur. Each packet contains the lowercase letters of the alphabet (a through z).

To avoid flooding the node's queues, the test-mode packets have a window size of 5; if a Data packet is not received after five packets have been sent, the window closes. Transmissions resume as Data packets are received, opening the window. Both nodes can be in test mode simultaneously.

For example, if node 3 is to enter test mode and send packets across the virtual circuit, the user types T0. After a moment, the Data packets will start to appear on node 7.

Test mode is disabled by typing S followed by a carriage return.

Call clearing   A call can be cleared by either end of the virtual circuit issuing a Call-Clearing packet along with the number of the virtual circuit to be cleared. The format of the Call-Clearing packet is as follows:

C	*VCN*

The virtual-circuit number to be used is the one in which all Data packets have been sent. In this example, if the user on node 7 is to clear the call, the virtual-circuit number to be specified is 1. This appears on node 3's screen as $\boxed{\texttt{C\#}}$; indicating that no further data will be received from virtual circuit #.

Upon receipt of a Call-Clearing packet, the user should respond with a Call-Clearing packet, thereby freeing up the virtual circuits making up the other half of its virtual circuit.

If the virtual-circuit number is not in use by this process, the request is aborted by the Network Layer and a diagnostic of $\boxed{\texttt{Invalid VCN}}$, followed by the virtual-circuit number, is displayed.

10.7.4   Low-level Testing

The virtual circuits requested by the user and established by the Network Layer are supported by the Data Link and Physical Layers. Communications between each pair of nodes is supported by the sliding-window protocol discussed in Section 10.6.3. This protocol is hidden by the Network Layer; therefore, to examine the actions associated with the protocol it is necessary to use the line analyser.

By placing the line analyser between two PCs running the wide area network software, the different data link frame structures can be seen. All frames have the same format, an *STX* followed by a number of bytes (two of which are the CRC) and finally, an *ETX*.

There are two frame types:

Supervisory frame. These are short, consisting of a single control field containing the value of N(R), and they will appear on the line analyser as one of the following given in Table 10.7.

TABLE 10.7   **Supervisory Frame Values**

N(R)	Internal value	Displayed as
0	10000000	Ç
1	10000001	ü
2	10000010	é
3	10000011	â
4	10000100	ä
5	10000101	à
6	10000110	á
7	10000111	ç

Information frames. These are strings of bytes sent across the channel. The second byte (after the *STX*) is the control field and contains the value of N(S) and N(R). The line analyser permits the decoding of the control field. For example, a ♣ (0x05) indicates an N(R) value of 5 and an N(S) of 0.

The packet's code byte is the third byte to be transmitted (after the *STX* and control field) and has one of the following values: R (call request), D (data), C (call clearing), and E (error). The remaining bytes in the frame depend upon the type of packet. The two bytes prior to the *ETX* are the CRC (more bytes may appear if the CRC contains a *DLE* or *ETX*).

The piggybacking of acknowledgements is best illustrated by putting both nodes into test mode. Once the screen is filled, stop the output using CTRL-S.

10.8   SUMMARY

A wide area network is a collection of nodes interconnected by a series of links; there is no single wide area network topology, although most are partially connected meshes. The purpose behind a wide area network is to offer users a shared communication facility, which is made available "on demand." This is different from the telephone system which must devote an entire circuit to a pair of DTEs for the duration of their communication.

Wide area networks achieve shared communication through the use of packet switching, a technique whereby information is transmitted in a data structure known as a packet that is routed through the network from node to node.

Routing can be achieved through any number of techniques, although most commercial wide area networks use some form of routing table.

There are three types of packet service that a wide area network can offer:

- Datagrams—in which the packet is put onto the network and the various nodes make a "best effort" attempt at having the packet reach the intended destination. There is no guarantee that the datagrams will reach their intended destination in the order they are sent or even if they will reach the destination.

- Messaging—in which a single message is broken into a series of packets and transmitted between nodes. A message, unlike a datagram, is reassembled at each node at which it arrives; the node is responsible for determining the next leg in the route and scheduling a time for the transmission of the message.

- Virtual circuits—which closely resemble a telephone call, consisting of a number of distinct steps. The first, call establishment, sees a Call-Request packet moving from node to node, defining a path (the virtual circuit) through the network. Once the path is established and both ends agree to communicate, the second step can be instituted: the transfer of data across the route defined by the Call-Request packet. When either or both DTEs agree to terminate the call, a Call-Clearing packet can be sent across the network, freeing the different stages across the network.

Wide area networks have also illustrated two important concepts in data communications: layering, in which software is divided into discrete parts, each performing a specific task; and standards, which ensures that DTEs from different manufacturers can communicate. A good example of a layered wide area network standard is CCITT's X.25, a three-layer architecture, which defines a Physical Layer, a Data Link Layer, and a Network Layer.

10.9 EXERCISES

1. Why is it not necessary for the Data Link Layer protocol to be reliable in a datagram network?

2. How does X.25 distinguish Data packets from other packets?

3. Show the layers necessary for a messaging system and for a virtual circuit.

4. The description of how a simplex channel is established on Commkit showed one half of the connection (from A to B). Complete the virtual circuit by making the connection from B to A and showing the virtual circuit tables in nodes x, y, and z.

5. Connect two PCs running the wide area network software via a third, running the analyser. Send nine messages from one station to the other, recording the responses. Explain why the control field in the supervisory frames appear as follows:

ü é â ä à á ç Ç ü

The frame delimiters are displayed on the line analyser as ☺ (*STX*) and ♡ (*ETX*). The CRC bytes are within the frame (i.e., before the final *ETX*).

6. The control field of an information frame can also be represented using the PC's character set. Using the same hardware configuration as above, complete the following table for the control fields of an information frame:

			Ns				
	≻		0	@		'	p
		!	1		Q	a	
		$					
♣	§	%					
♠							
							w

7. Show, by means of a diagram, that the routing algorithm used by the Commkit wide area network actually works. Specifically, set up a network of two stations, *A* and *C*, show what happens when *A* attempts to send a message to *B*. Repeat the exercise for *C* sending a message to *B*.

8. Connect two PCs: one running the line analyser, the other running the wide area network. Send a message from the wide area network PC, making sure that the cables are connected so that the message appears on the line analyser. What is the maximum number of messages that can be sent? Explain the limit: how can it be changed? Why are the messages sent in order?

9. The previous exercise highlights a limitation of the wide area network software: it doesn't know when to give up. Modify the software so that if a response it not detected after ten retransmissions of the same message, the remote node is assumed to be dead and the communication is abandoned.

10. The wide area network supplied with Commkit requires that the stations be arranged in an order that ensures all stations "downstream" of a station's secondary port have addresses greater than that of the station, while stations "upstream" of a station's primary port have addresses less than those of the station. This will clearly lead to a number of annoying problems should someone try to add a new station between two existing stations with consecutive station numbers. For example, how could a third station be added between a station with address A and a second station with address B? The answer is, not surprisingly, it can't: not without reordering the addresses associated with one or more existing stations.

It is not advisable to change the addresses associated with stations within any type of network (including a wide area network), since the address may be "known" by any number of other stations. Can you suggest a reason as to why this is so?

11. The protocol used by the Data Link Layer is a partial implementation of the SDLC protocol, information frames are supported and so are receive ready (RR) frames, however reject (REJ) and receive not ready (RNR) are not. Similarly, if a packet is received correctly but is out-of-sequence, the software does not respond; rather, it waits for the transmitter to send the entire sequence of messages again.

    Modify the protocol to support the following:

    a) Reject (REJ) control frames. REJ frames are typically sent when a packet has been received with a CRC error. The value of *ns* indicates the next valid frame number.

    b) Receive not ready (RNR) frames. RNR frames should be sent when the receive cannot accept packets.

    c) Send a receive ready (RR) frame if an information frame has been received correctly, but out-of-sequence. The value of *ns* indicates the next valid frame number.

12. The Physical Layer is written assuming that once a reception starts, there will always be an *ETX* somewhere in the incoming data stream, allowing the reception to conclude. If an *ETX* is lost, it is also assumed that another frame will be sent, causing the message buffer to reach its limit; forcing the reception state machine back to the WAIT_STX state.

    However, if the transmitting station should cease transmission (i.e., someone turns it off, or the cable is pulled), the reception software will hang, waiting for an *ETX* that will never appear.

    Redesign the reception part of the Physical Layer to ensure that if a byte is not received within five seconds, the reception software is to "assume" that the transmitter is no longer transmitting. A message code should be returned by the Physical Layer to the Data Link Layer to the Network Layer, and finally to the Process Layer, informing the user of the problem.

    Once implemented, how will you test the changes? Does the software support temporary loss of transmission (for example, a loss of less than five seconds)?

13. The previous exercise has other ramifications: how does the Data Link Layer inform the Network Layer than an error has occurred? Once the Network Layer has been informed, it should cease all communications out that link. Modify the software to support this feature.

    This fixes another problem with the software; it means that calls to nonexistent nodes that are not between a pair of nodes will be caught and aborted. Show that your software handles this situation.

14. If a station has several processes, how could a Call-Request packet be routed to the correct process?

4

Local Area Networks

Prior to the development of the microprocessor, most processing was centralized in nature, requiring users to communicate with a single mainframe to which all equipment was attached and upon which their information was stored. The obvious advantage of having a single, centralized computer is that the sharing of resources (such as equipment or information) is a relatively simple procedure controlled by the operating system. For example, a laser printer on a single, centralized computer is accessible to all users through a series of commands, which place the object to be printed on the computer's laser printer queue. However, the one great disadvantage of having a single, centralized computer is that should the central computer fail, it is impossible for a user to access any of the resources associated with the computer.

The microprocessor has changed the way in which the computer can be used. Now, instead of having all resources available to all users on a single computer, the resources necessary to perform certain tasks may reside on one or more distinct computers. One clear advantage in using a number of computers to perform the tasks that were originally performed by a single, centralized computer is that should one of the computers fail, users on the other computers may continue their processing.

However, in a decentralized system consisting of many small, independent computers, it may not be cost effective to supply each computer with the same set of devices (such as laser printers), since the device may remain idle for long periods. Instead, only a handful of computers may be connected to certain costly devices. For example, a problem clearly arises when people whose computers are not connected to a laser printer want to print information on a laser printer. One solution is to have the users carry their information on a diskette to a computer attached to a laser printer, or to wheel the laser printer on a cart from office to office as and when it is required. Of course, neither of these approaches are completely satisfactory since they can result in a great deal of wasted time on the part of the user.

A similar problem arises when users want to share information. If the information resides on one computer, "sharing" may be reduced to copying and distributing a diskette. This, in turn, leads to other problems—such as which user will manage the information and how will changes to the information be handled.

Ideally, what is needed is a mechanism that allows individual computers to communicate with other computers (such as those attached to the laser printers or those with information to be shared).

Although a wide area network (as discussed in Chapter 10) could be used, the cost and speeds associated with wide area networks usually make them a poor choice for exchanging information between a proliferation of computers within a single organization. This limitation stems from the desire to transfer information between computers at disk (or near disk) speeds: thereby giving the same "speed" of service that would be found in a single, centralized system.

To achieve these speeds, *local-computer networks* are often used to interconnect locally-distributed computers. A local-computer network (or more commonly, *local area network*) is similar to a wide area network in that messages are still sent in packets and the stations on the network are identified by using an address; however, a general definition of a local area network requires that the network conform to a broad set of requirements. It must:

- have relatively high data rates (typically 1 to 10 megabits per second)
- span a distance of, at most, 1 kilometer (typically within a single organization)
- support several hundred independent devices
- offer simplicity of functionality and performance
- have low error rates, high reliability, and the minimum of dependence upon any centralized components or control
- permit efficient use of shared resources (including the network itself)
- maintain stability under high load
- allow fair access to the system by all devices
- permit ease of reconfiguration and maintenance
- be low cost

Local area networks (or LANs), like wide area networks, can be discussed from a variety of different angles, such as topologies, access methods, packet formats, and performance. However, unlike most wide area networks which exhibit similar characteristics, there is no single "generic" local area network.

For example, the most popular LAN topologies are the bus, ring, and star; while accessing methods are dictated, in part, by topology; and the performance of different LANs vary greatly depending upon the amount of traffic on the network (the *network load*).

The remainder of this part of the book is devoted to the most widespread local area network technologies, notably bus and ring local area networks in Chapters 11 and 12, respectively. In both cases, both design issues and existing networks are discussed. The Commkit local area network emulators are also examined in detail as a means of showing how the hardware functions.

Chapter

11

Bus Local Area Networks

11.1 INTRODUCTION

A bus local area network is a network in which all computing devices (or *stations*) share a single common communications channel. Stations communicate by passing messages in *packets* across the network. To distinguish between the different stations, each station on the bus is assigned a unique address. In Figure 11.1, a bus network interconnects five stations.

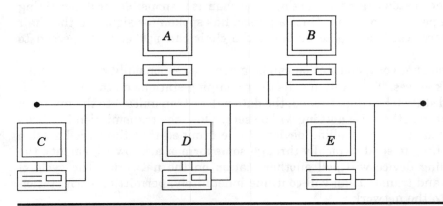

Figure 11.1   A five station bus network

A typical transmission scenario involves one station transmitting a packet (consisting of at least a message *and* a destination address) one bit at a time onto the network. The bits propagate past all stations; the stations are responsible for reassembling the bits into packets. The packet's destination address is examined by each station. The station with the address that matches the destination address in the packet keeps a copy of the packet. Those stations with addresses that do not match the packet's destination address ignore (discard) their copy of the packet. A bus network is also known as a *broadcast* network since each packet that is transmitted is received by all stations on the network. Packets are not physically removed from the network by any of the stations; instead, each end of the bus has a *terminator* which, using resistors, electrically removes the packet.

The bus is a resource that is shared by all stations on the network, and as such, must support mechanisms which:

- prevent one station from monopolizing the network by, for example, transmitting a packet of a size that prevents other stations from transmitting messages,

- resolve conflicts should two (or more) stations attempt to access the network simultaneously

The first of these mechanisms (preventing a station from monopolizing the network) is usually achieved by restricting the maximum size of the packet and enforcing this limit through hardware. However, controlling network access is a somewhat more complex issue and has resulted in a number of solutions.

11.1.1 Controlling Network Access

Controlling access to a bus network is analagous to controlling a group of people, all of whom wish to speak at a meeting. A number of different approaches are possible, including:

- Have one person chair the meeting. The chair is responsible for determining when a person can speak. Once a person has spoken (or signalled the chair that there was nothing to be said), the chair can ask another person to speak.

  In a bus network, one station can be given the responsibility of controlling network access. This station polls the remaining stations on the network. If a polled station has data to send, the data will be transmitted to the intended destination, otherwise nothing will be sent. Once the transmission has been completed or the controlling device has determined that the polled station has nothing to send (typically through some form of acknowledgement), the controlling device will poll another station on the network. The cycle of polling and transmitting will continue indefinitely, permitting each station access to the network.

  There are a number of limitations associated with using a single device to control access to the network. First, should the controlling device fail, none of the other stations could then access the network since the polling cycle has stopped. Second, although polling ensures that all stations have equal access to the network, it can result in poor throughput when one station has a large amount of data to send and the other stations have none (as each station must be polled, regardless of the amount of data to be sent). Third, a change in the status of the network (such as an existing station leaving the network or a new station joining), would require a mechanism allowing the polling device to determine that a change had occurred.

■ An alternative to having a person act as the chair is to allocate a limited speaking time to each person. For example, each person could be permitted to speak for one minute, the first "on-the-hour," the second at "one-minute-past," the third at "two-minutes-past," and so on. The cycle could be repeated once the last speaker has finished. A clock that could be seen by all possible speakers would be essential.

A similar approach could be taken to control access to the network, with the exception that each station could only transmit during specific time periods, as dictated by a global clock (as opposed to a centralized device indicating which station could transmit). The underlying assumption is that all stations could synchronize their clocks. For example, at clock tick 1, station 1 would transmit, at clock tick 2, station 2 would transmit, and so on, until all stations had transmitted, at which point the cycle would repeat.

Many of the problems associated with device polling also occur when using synchronized clocks. For example, should a clock on one of the stations fail, the station may start to transmit out of turn; similarly, should one station have a large number of messages to transmit, while others do not, the network would remain idle unnecessarily.

■ If the money is available, each person can be given a radio that can be tuned to different frequencies. By assigning each person a frequency on which to transmit, anyone could transmit whenever they felt the need, and those people interested in hearing what someone else had to say could tune into that person's frequency.

Assigning each station a unique frequency band ensures that all stations have simultaneous access to the network. Protocols, such as those used in wide area networks, are required to permit the initial establishment of the call between two stations (using one frequency), and then proceeding with the call (possibly on another frequency).

A number of networks have been implemented using this approach, but this type of network is costly because it requires that each station accessing the network use hardware which can switch between a number of different frequencies. Networks which support multiple frequencies (and multiple simultaneous transmissions) are known as *broadband* networks, while networks supporting a single frequency (and hence one transmitting station at a time) are known as *baseband* networks.

Although each of the networks just described have been implemented in both commercial and experimental situations, the underlying requirement of having some form of centralized control (in the first two networks) and attention to the costs involved (in the third), do not make them attractive as bus local area networks.

An alternate approach is to resolve the conflict in much the same way humans do, should two (or more) people attempt to talk simultaneously: everyone stops and (ideally) one person is then allowed to proceed. In the case of humans, if a person is talking and simultaneously hears someone else talking, both should stop in order to determine who should proceed. This is resolved in a number of ways (the bigger person can win, the person with the louder voice can win, or more fairly, the person who has remained silent for the longest is allowed to talk first).

A similar algorithm can be applied to stations on the bus network: any station can transmit whenever it has a packet to send and the network is *idle* (that is, the network is not already in use: an idle network is indicated by the absence of a *carrier signal*). Should two stations simultaneously detect that the network is idle, they can both start transmitting, which will result in a *collision*. Collisions can be detected by the station transmitting its packet and simultaneously "listening" to the channel; if the same data is received as is transmitted, there has not been a collision. However, if the data transmitted is not the same as what is received, a collision has been detected. The transmit-and-listen approach is used by many bus networks and is given the name *collision detection* (often abbreviated to CD).

A collision, once detected, must be resolved as quickly as possible since no useful information is transmitted during a collision. Collision resolution, whether between people talking simultaneously or between stations on a bus network, is not an instantaneous operation. Because of this, there are two main issues to be considered when attempting to minimize the time wasted resolving a collision:

1. how to avoid collisions in the first place
2. how to determine which station is to transmit next, once a collision occurs

Once the network becomes idle, one or more stations may be waiting to transmit their messages. If all of the waiting stations transmit simultaneously (assuming that they all have detected the network being idle), their packets will become garbled, resulting in a collision. In an effort to minimize the possibility of collisions when the network becomes idle, while also attempting to diminish the length of time the network is idle, there are three classes of algorithm used to determine a station's action when the network is *busy* and the station has a packet to transmit:

Non-persistent. The station senses the network: if the network is busy, the station waits a random time period before sensing the network again. The assumption being that it is unlikely that two stations will wait the same random period, with the result that when the network becomes idle, only one of the stations will detect the idle state and start to transmit. However, the non-persistent algorithm can result in wasted bandwidth if a transmission stops and the network returns to the idle state while the stations with packets to transmit continue waiting for their random time period to expire (Figure 11.2).

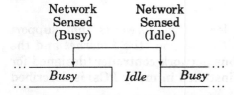

Figure 11.2   The non-persistent algorithm can result in unnecessary idle periods

In Figure 11.2, when the station samples the network, the network is found to be busy; this requires that the station wait for a certain period of time. Meanwhile, the network becomes idle and remains so until the station senses the network again, at which point the network is found to be idle and the station can transmit.

1-persistent. A station with a message to transmit senses that the network is busy and continues to sense the network until the network is idle, at which point the station starts to transmit its message. 1-persistent attempts to ensure that the time the network remains idle is as short as possible.

p-persistent. As with the 1-persistent algorithm, the *p*-persistent algorithm requires that the station continues sensing the network until it becomes idle. Once idle, the station will transmit with a probability of *p*, otherwise it waits a predetermined length of time before sensing the line again. The *p*-persistent algorithm attempts to minimize the network's idle time, while, at the same time trying to minimize the chances of stations transmitting simultaneously.

Although all of these three algorithms require that the station sense the bus before transmitting, collisions can still occur should one or more stations detect an idle network and start to transmit. A common form of collision resolution is to have each station "back off" for a random period of time before attempting to transmit again (somewhat like the non-persistent algorithm).

Bus networks that require their stations to sense the network before transmitting are commonly known as *carrier-sense multiple access* (CSMA) networks. The abbreviations CSMA and CD are usually combined to CSMA/CD when referring to networks that are carrier sensed, support multiple access and collision detection. There are a number of features that make CSMA/CD bus networks attractive as local area networks, including:

- The bus is *passive*. This means that control information such as polling packets are not present on the network; the only network traffic is the data packets sent between stations, and stations are only required to transmit their own packets.

- Control on the bus is *distributed* among all the stations. This means that the failure of one station does not cause all communications to cease.

11.2   EXAMPLES

At present, there are a number of bus local area networks that support CSMA/CD, two of which are discussed in this section: the *Ethernet* and the *IEEE 802.3 bus*. An example of a typical bus network controller (designed for both the Ethernet and the 802.3 bus and installed in many PCs) is described at the end of this section.

11.2.1   The Ethernet

Probably the best known CSMA/CD bus network is the Ethernet, a 1-persistent baseband network developed by Xerox in the mid-1970's. The Ethernet is based upon the research performed on the Aloha system at the University of Hawaii: a broadcast network consisting of various stations scattered throughout Hawaii communicating by radio with the University's central computer facilities.

The Ethernet has the following characteristics:

- A maximum of 1024 stations can be connected over a distance of up to 2.5 kilometers

- Signals are Manchester (phase) encoded (see Section 6.2.2)

- The bus is a coaxial cable

- A data rate of 10 Mbits per second is supported.

Physical organization   An Ethernet consists of a cable interconnecting a series of stations (devices which contain processors such as PCs, workstations, printers, or disks). Stations connect to the Ethernet by means of a *transceiver* cable attached to a *tap*. In its simplest form, the Ethernet consists of a single *segment*; however, more complex layouts consisting of multiple segments are possible, as illustrated by Figure 11.3.

The transceiver cable allows stations to be placed up to 50 meters away from the Ethernet. To avoid interference between station taps, stations must be a minimum of 2.5 meters apart (hence the maximum distance of 2.5 kilometers for 1024 stations). The maximum recommended segment length is 500 meters. The 50-ohm coaxial cable has a diameter of 0.4 inches.

The Ethernet topology is considered a loopless "unrooted tree," which means that a packet traverses the entire tree and that individual branches cannot be used independently.

The Ethernet packet   All data is sent across the Ethernet in an *Ethernet packet*. The start-of-packet is indicated by a synchronizing pattern of 64-bits of alternating 1s and 0s; ending with two consecutive 1s. All bits are Manchester encoded. The packet itself consists of five fields (the numbers in parentheses indicate the size of a field, expressed in bytes). See Figure 11.4 and the following field descriptions.

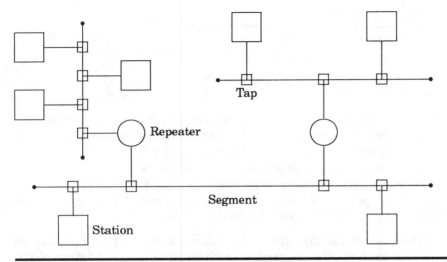

Figure 11.3 Physical organization of an Ethernet

Preamble	DST (6)	SRC (6)	Type (2)	User Data (46 to 1500)	FCS (4)

Figure 11.4 Ethernet packet structure (all sizes in bytes)

The DST and SRC fields. The fields DST and SRC are the destination (i.e., the station for which the packet is intended) and source (i.e., the station sending the packet) addresses of the packet, respectively. All stations on the network are assigned a globally unique 48-bit station address (supplied by Xerox, thereby ensuring the uniqueness of the address). This address is inserted into the Ethernet packet as the source address (SRC).

The destination address (DST) is also 48-bits long and can be:

- A *unicast* address, identifying a single destination on the network. This address is unique to the station. A packet sent with a unicast address is discarded by all stations except the one with the address that matches that in the DST field. The source address (SRC) is a unicast address.

- A *broadcast* address, identifying all stations on the network. All stations on the network share the broadcast address. A packet sent with a broadcast address is kept by all stations.

- A *multicast* address, identifying a group of stations on the network. The number of stations sharing a multicast address is typically determined by the application and can vary over time. A packet sent with a multicast address is kept by those stations sharing the address.

Addresses are distinguished by their high-order bit as shown in Table 11.1.

All commercially available Ethernet hardware supports at least the station's unicast address and the broadcast address. Multicast addresses are also supported to a limited degree by some Ethernet hardware. For example, Digital's DEUNA (Digital Equipment UNIBUS Network Adaptor) hardware

TABLE 11.1   Ethernet Addresses

Identifier	High-order Bit	Remaining 47 Bits
Unicast	Zero	Zeros and ones
Broadcast	One	All ones
Multicast	One	Zeros and ones

can identify up to 10 distinct multicast addresses, while the Intel 82586 can filter up to 64 multicast addresses; however, the multicast address recognition algorithm used in the 82586 can result in multicast addresses that are not supported by the station being accepted by the hardware.

Finally, some Ethernet hardware permits stations to enter *promiscuous mode*, whereby all packets on the network, regardless of the value of the destination address, are made available to the station.

The Type field.   By itself, the Ethernet only offers a point-to-point datagram service between *stations*; the destination address offers no indication of the intended destination process, application, or protocol. The two-byte **Type** field overcomes this limitation by allowing the Ethernet software to route the **User Data** to a specific higher-layer protocol, application, or process. For example, a station may support two services, each associated with its own **Type** value. An incoming packet would be routed to the service indicated by the value of the **Type** field.

The User Data field.   The **User Data** field contains the data sent from one station to the station(s) specified by the destination address. The **User Data** field cannot contain less than 46 bytes, or more than 1500 bytes. All data is transmitted transparently; that is, all possible byte values are considered valid.

The minimum packet size has been chosen to ensure that all collisions will be detected, regardless of the length of the Ethernet (i.e., up to its physical maximum of 2.5 kilometers). For example, if stations A and B each simultaneously transmit a short packet, a collision may go undetected by the transmitting stations (Figure 11.5).

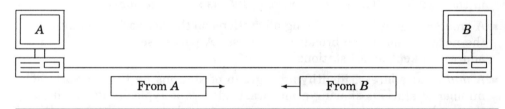

Figure 11.5   A collision of short packets would go undetected

Similarly, a station will miss the collision if its transmission stops before receiving a bit from any other packet (Figure 11.6).

From Figure 11.6, one can conclude that a collision will be detected only if a station remains transmitting for the length of time it takes for a bit to traverse *twice* the length of the Ethernet. The Ethernet transmits 10^7 bps

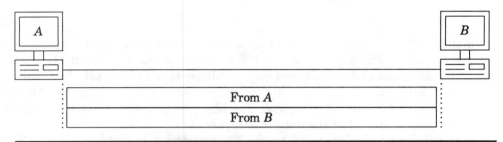

Figure 11.6 The minimum packet length is dependent upon the size of the network

(i.e., 10 megabits a second), or one bit every 10^{-7} of a second. Since the information travels at the speed of light (i.e., 10^8 meters a second), then the "length" of 1 bit is 10 meters. Therefore, 500 bits fill twice the maximum length of an Ethernet (5 kilometers or 5000 meters). By rounding the number of bits to 512 (a power of 2), the minimum number of bytes in a packet would be $512 \div 8$ or 64. Four fields within the packet (the DST, SRC, Type, and the FCS) have fixed sizes amounting to 18 bytes, meaning that the minimum size of the User Data field is $64 - 18$ or 46 bytes!

The maximum User Data field length ensures that a transmitting station does not monopolize the Ethernet for an undue period of time. Most Ethernet hardware supports *anti-jabber* features which cut off the transmitter if the packet's length exceeds the maximum number of bytes permitted (i.e., the total number of bytes from all fields).

The FCS field. The *frame check sequence* (FCS) field is a 32-bit CRC value covering all bits in the packet (excluding the preamble). The transmitted FCS is included in the FCS received by each station once the Ethernet has gone idle. If the calculated FCS is equal to a predefined value, the packet is assumed to be correct.

The end-of-packet is determined when no traffic is detected on the Ethernet. To ensure that each station's receiving hardware has time to examine the packet and supply it to a higher level of software, there is a minimum packet spacing of 9.6 microseconds (μs).

When collisions occur, the stations involved in the collision are expected to wait random time periods before attempting to send their packets again. The use of a random delay is based upon the assumption that if the stations don't pick the same random value, the collision should be avoided. The Ethernet implements a *truncated binary exponential backoff* algorithm that each station uses if a collision occurs. The algorithm works as follows: each time a collision occurs, the station must wait a time period based upon a random number multiplied by the length of time it takes for a bit to travel from one end of the network to the other (51.2 μs) before attempting to transmit again. The random number is chosen as an integer in the range $0 \leq r \leq 2^k$, where r is the random number and k is the number of attempted transmissions or 10, whichever is less; the growth is *truncated* at $k = 10$ (hence the name of the algorithm). The station aborts its transmission after 16 collisions.

11.2.2   IEEE 802.3

In the early 1980's, the IEEE set up a local area network standards committee known as *IEEE 802*. Part of the mandate of the 802 committee has been the definition of data-link and physical-layer specifications for local area networks. All networks are uniquely defined in terms of a physical layer and a *Media-Access Control* (MAC) layer. The MAC layer definition overlays the physical layer and part of the data-link layer.

One of the networks proposed by the 802 committee is 802.3, a CSMA/CD bus network based upon the Ethernet. The 802.3 standard differs from the Ethernet standard in three main areas: electrical connections, addressing, and the **Type** field.

802.3 allows both 16- and 48-bit addresses (the 10 Mbps standard requires 48-bit addresses). Unicast, multicast, and broadcast addresses are all supported. IEEE also assigns each station its own unique *global* address, which allows the station to be uniquely identified anywhere in the world.

The 802.3 packet structure is essentially the same as the Ethernet packet structure with the exception of the **Type** field (all sizes are expressed in bytes):

Preamble	DST (6)	SRC (6)	Length (2)	User Data (46 – 1500)	FCS (4)

In 802.3, the **Type** field is replaced by a two-byte **Length** field. The **Length** field indicates the length of the **User Data** field, expressed in bytes. The **User Data** field can be from 46 to 1500 bytes long, although the **Length** field can have values less than 46. (If the message is less than 46 bytes long, it must be padded to the minimum length.)

Note that it is possible for both Ethernet and 802.3 packets to coexist on either network. For example, Ethernet packets can be transmitted on an 802.3 network as long as the value in the **Type** field does not fall in the range of possible **Length** values. This is achieved by setting the value of the **Type** field to anything greater than the maximum **Length** value (i.e., greater than 1500).

The 802.3 protocol has a number of variants that are expressed in the form *xyz*, where *x* is the line speed expressed in megabits per second, *y* indicates the type of physical medium, and *z* is the maximum length of a segment, expressed in hundreds of meters. The original 10-megabit baseband 802.3 implementation on thick-wire coaxial cable (500-meter segments) is written as 10*Base*5. Other variants include 10*Base*2 (thin-wire coaxial cable, more commonly known as *Cheapernet*), 1*Base*5 (1 megabit over twisted pair), and 10*Base*T (10 megabit over twisted-pair).

The 802.3 CSMA/CD network also implements the truncated binary exponential backoff algorithm to handle collisions.

The 802 protocols will be discussed further in subsequent chapters.

11.2.3   Network-access Hardware

Commercially available network-access hardware for the Ethernet and 802.3, typically consists of three distinct chips as depicted in Figure 11.7.

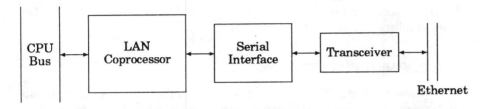

Figure 11.7   Typical Ethernet network-access hardware

The *transceiver* chip is responsible for transmitting and receiving the bits on and off the Ethernet. A transceiver such as the Intel 82502 performs additional functions, including:

- Monitoring the number of bits the station has transmitted and cutting off access to the Ethernet if the number exceeds the maximum allowed in a packet (this is the anti-jabber function). The station is barred from transmitting for about 420 milliseconds; after which the transceiver again permits access to the network.

- Comparing the bits read off the network with those that are being transmitted. Should it occur that the bit sent does not equal the bit received, a collision has been detected. This information is relayed back to the serial interface.

All signals received by the transceiver are Manchester encoded; these signals are not decoded, but rather passed directly to the *serial interface*. The serial interface, such as the Intel 82501, extracts the clocking signal from the incoming data stream and generates the equivalent internal bit value. The serial interface is also responsible for encoding the outgoing data with a 10-MHz Manchester signal supplied to the transceiver. If a collision is detected by the transceiver, the condition is forwarded to the *LAN Coprocessor*. The LAN Coprocessor is a separate processor that implements the Ethernet protocol and performs the following functions:

- Calculates the frame-check sequence (FCS) for outgoing and incoming frames.
- Supports unicast, broadcast, and up to 64 multicast addresses.
- Transmits Ethernet packets supplied from the CPU.
- Filters and supplies Ethernet packets to the CPU.

In the Ethernet (802.3 10*Base*5) the LAN Coprocessor and Serial Interface can be on the DTE itself, connected to the Transceiver by a transceiver cable. The Transceiver physically taps the LAN. In the Cheapernet (802.3 10*Base*2), the three chips are typically on a single board with the Transceiver attached to a coaxial cable connector. The LAN connects to the Transceiver via a bayonet or BNC T-connector (BNC is an acronym of the device and its inventor: *Bayonet, Neil-Concelman*).

The Intel chipset just described supports the entire 802.3 CSMA/CD Media-Access Control functions. There are many other Ethernet/IEEE 802.3 chipsets available from manufacturers, including Advanced Micro Devices (AMD), National Semiconductor, and Seeq Technology.

11.3 THE COMMKIT BUS NETWORK

The communication hardware available with a standard PC does not support any type of bus network. Ethernet cards (using controller chips such as the Intel 82586) are commercially available and can cost upwards of several hundred dollars. However, it is possible to write software that emulates a CSMA/CD bus network by using the PC's serial ports. For example, Commkit is supplied with the following bus network software:

buslow.c	the C routines that allow the PC to emulate a bus network
busdefs.h	the header file containing the various data structures used by buslow.c
busex.c	a set of processes that allow messages to be entered onto the network from the keyboard
busex.h	the bus network packet structure and return codes used by busex.c

11.3.1 Hardware Requirements

The Commkit bus network software requires a minimum of two PCs, each with two serial ports (assumed to be SP1IH and SP2IH) and sufficient null-modem cables to allow the PCs to be linked together in a bus-like fashion (Figure 11.8).

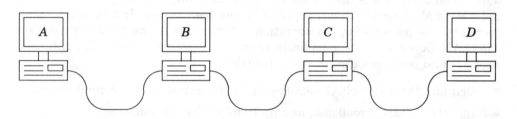

Figure 11.8 Commkit bus network consisting of four PCs

The above network consists four PCs, each supporting two serial ports, with an RS-232 null-modem cable connecting pairs of ports (except the outermost two, which must *not* be connected). There is no prescribed ordering of serial ports (that is, any port can connect to any other; for example: 1 to 1, 1 to 2, or 2 to 2).

11.3.2 Design

The bus network supplied with Commkit is a true CSMA/CD bus network, because before a packet is transmitted, the network is first "sensed," and if it is idle, the packet is then transmitted. Bytes within a packet are sent one at a time out of each of the PC's serial ports. In Figure 11.9, station *B* transmits a packet *N* bytes in length across a four-station Commkit bus network.

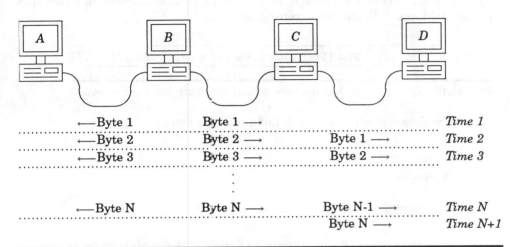

Figure 11.9   The transmission of an *N*-byte packet by station *B*

When a nontransmitting station receives a byte on a serial port, a copy of the byte is taken and then the byte is forwarded out the "other" serial port. The bytes are assembled into packets for subsequent processing.

A collision is detected by the transmitting station receiving a byte. Similarly, a receiving station can detect a collision if it receives bytes on both ports. As in a true CSMA/CD bus network, transmissions are aborted if a collision is detected.

The packet structure   Each message that is transmitted on the network is sent in a packet. In addition to the message, the packet also contains the address of the intended destination station, the address of the transmitting station, and two CRC bytes.

Packets are transmitted transparently; that is, the message portion of the packet can contain any byte value (i.e., from 0 through 255). When transmitted, the packet is delimited by the packet-framing characters *STX* and *ETX*. Any bytes within the message having values *ETX* or *DLE* are prefixed by *DLE* when the packet is transmitted. The *DLE* prefix bytes are removed as the packet is received. The prefix bytes are not included in the total message size nor are they made available to the destination process. Neither the destination address, DST, nor the source address, SRC, are prefixed by *DLE*; since the position of these bytes are "well-known," there is no chance of confusing these bytes for the trailing *ETX*.

Each byte in the packet (excluding the packet-framing bytes, *STX* and *ETX*, and any prefix *DLE* bytes) is included in the 16-bit CRC. The CRC is sent as part of the packet. Should either of the CRC bytes be an *ETX* or a *DLE*, the byte is also prefixed by a *DLE*. The CRC bytes are removed from the packet and are not made available to the destination process. A received packet is assumed to be error free if the receiving station's calculated CRC has a value of zero when the end-of-packet *ETX* is found.

The overall packet structure is in Figure 11.10 (the number of bytes in a specific field are indicated in parentheses).

STX (1)	DST (1)	SRC (1)	User Data (5 to 64)	CRC (2)	*ETX* (1)

Figure 11.10   The Commkit bus network packet structure (all sizes in bytes)

The internal packet structure is defined in busex.h as:

```
struct packet
{
char net_dst;
char net_src;
char message[PKT_MAX + 2];        /* Includes two CRC bytes */
};
```

The maximum size of the message is defined by PKT_MAX in busex.h. PKT_MAX can be changed, but should not be allowed to exceed the size of a Commkit message (128 bytes), nor should it be less than the minimum packet size.

To ensure that all stations have received at least one byte while the transmitting station is still transmitting, there is a minimum packet size defined by MIN_LEN in buslow.h. The choice of minimum packet length is determined by the number of cables connecting the stations on the network. For example, if the network consists of N cables, the minimum packet length is $2 \times N$. By choosing $2 \times N$ as the minimum packet size, collisions can be detected by all stations on the network.

The emulator states   At any moment, the emulator can be in one of three different states: idle, transmitting, or receiving:

The idle state.   If the station has not detected any traffic on the network and there are no packets to be transmitted, the station is in the idle state. When the station is first initialized, it enters the idle state. The idle state is also entered after a packet has been transmitted, received, or after a collision has been detected.

Either of the following conditions will cause the station to leave the idle state:

1. A packet is made available for transmission (the station's state is changed to transmitting).
2. A byte is received on either of the serial ports (the station's state is changed to receiving).

The transmitting state is entered only after the time delay associated with accessing the network has expired. There are two sources of time delay: first, each time the transmitting station sends a packet which collides with another, access is denied for progressively longer and longer periods; and second, once a packet has been received or transmitted, access to the network is delayed by PKT_DELAY clock ticks in order to allow other stations access to the network. As soon as the time delay reaches zero, the station can resume sensing the network.

The transmitting state. The transmitting state is entered from the idle state (i.e., no traffic has been detected on the network) and either of the following conditions arise:

1. A pending packet (i.e., a packet whose transmission was aborted because of a collision) is available for transmission

2. A new packet is available for transmission.

To ensure that the packets are transmitted in the same order that they are supplied to the bus-network emulator, any packet that has been delayed by a collision has priority over new messages. This priority is achieved by having the message queue associated with the bus network read *after* the transmission of a packet.

Message transmission begins in the idle state with the transmission of two *STX* bytes; one out each serial port. The contents of the packet data structure are then sent one byte at a time out each of the serial ports. Each byte from the packet is included in the CRC prior to being transmitted; *DLE* insertion also takes place at this point. Once the message bytes have been transmitted, the two CRC bytes are sent (with *DLE* insertion if necessary) followed by an *ETX*. The transmitting station then returns to the idle state.

The state diagram for a transmitting station is shown in Figure 11.11 (the term send() refers to putting bytes onto the network).

Ideally, only one station at a time will be transmitting on the network. However, on occasion, two (or more) stations may be in the idle state when a packet is ready to be transmitted, resulting in a number of stations commencing a transmission at the same time. The stations will continue to transmit until they *receive* a byte, at which point, a collision is detected. A station can both receive and transmit through the same port because the channels are physically separate. Figure 11.12 shows the effect on the sample bus network if stations *A* and *D* are to transmit simultaneously (* denotes that the collision has been detected and ⇔ indicates that two bytes are on the cable simultaneously).

Upon detection of an incoming byte, the transmitting station immediately aborts its transmission and sends out an *ETX* on both ports. If a *DLE* is the last byte sent, another byte is sent prior to the transmission of the *ETX*, thereby avoiding the possibility of generating a *DLE-ETX* sequence rather than simply an *ETX*. Each transmitting station then "backs off" for a period of time determined by its station identifier and the number of collisions associated with the message.

The station then reenters the idle state and cannot transmit until the back off period has expired. When the station detects that the delay has ended, the pending message can be sent as soon as the network becomes idle.

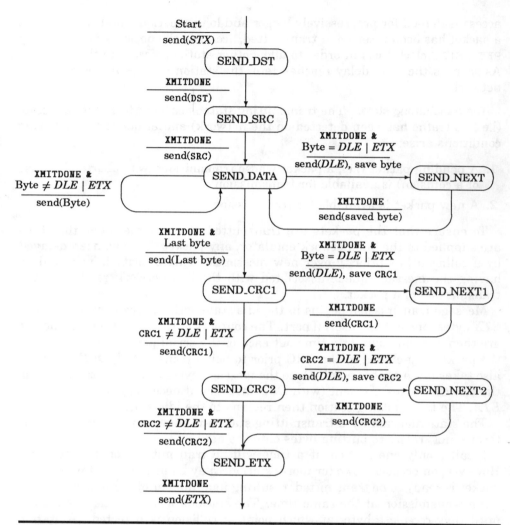

Figure 11.11   The Commkit bus network transmit state machine

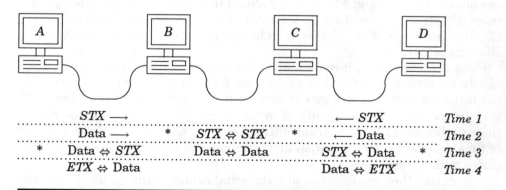

Figure 11.12   Collision detection and resolution

The receive state. The receive state is entered when an *STX* has been detected on either of the serial ports and the station is in the idle state. The receive software forwards the *STX* out the serial port that did not receive the byte: all subsequent bytes associated with this packet are expected to be received on the same serial port (i.e., port 1 or port 2, *not* both). See Figure 11.13.

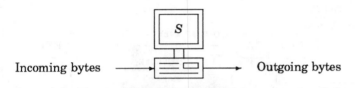

Incoming bytes ———————→   Outgoing bytes

Figure 11.13   Packet flow through a receiving station

All bytes following the *STX* are copied into the `packet` data structure as well as being forwarded through the outgoing port. The first two bytes following the *STX* are treated as the destination and source address bytes respectively. Subsequent bytes are stored in the next available location in the `packet` data structure. *DLE* prefix bytes are also forwarded, but are not kept in the message buffer. All bytes stored in the packet are included in the CRC calculation. Upon reception of the end-of-packet indicator (*ETX*), the CRC is checked. If the CRC value is zero and the destination address byte matches that of the station, the packet is sent to the process responsible for handling incoming messages. In all other cases, the message is discarded and the bus network then returns to the idle state.

Figure 11.14 depicts the state machine for a station receiving a packet. Normally, all incoming bytes are received on the same port. However, should a byte be received on the outgoing serial port, then a collision has occurred. Upon detection of a collision, the receiving station no longer stores the incoming bytes in the packet buffer; instead they are discarded. To ensure that all stations on the network can detect the collision, all bytes (received on either port) are forwarded out of the serial port opposite to the one on which they were received (that is: receive on 1, forward on 2; receive on 2, forward on 1.) See Figure 11.15.

The receiving station continues to forward the bytes until an *ETX* is detected on both ports, at which point the station enters the idle state.

It is worth noting that the collision-handling technique described for reception will not necessarily be recorded as a collision on all receiving stations. For example, in the network of four stations depicted in Figure 11.16, if stations *A* and *D* start to transmit simultaneously, then the receiving stations *B* and *C* will both detect a collision, since they receive data on both ports (a * denotes that the collision has been detected).

However, should stations *A* and *C* transmit simultaneously, only station *B* (of the two receiving stations *B* and *D*) will detect the collision as a true collision, since it receives data on both serial ports. Station *D*, on the other hand, only receives bytes from station *C* (since station *C* will not forward

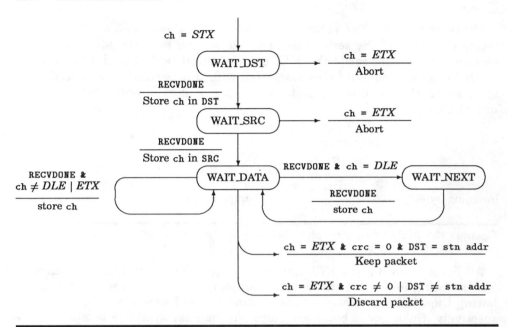

Figure 11.14   The Commkit bus network receive state machine

Figure 11.15   A receiving station must forward a collision

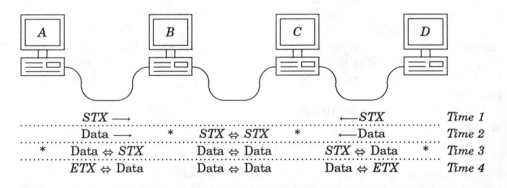

Figure 11.16   Collisions are not detected instantly

the bytes from station A and station D cannot distinguish between the two
station's bytes anyway); with the result being that during a collision, station
D receives a packet with a CRC error from station C. In both situations, the
packet is discarded, but it is recorded as a collision only by stations between

the two transmitters and as a CRC error by all other receiving stations. (A * denotes that the collision has been detected, while the † indicates that the collision is detected as a CRC error.) See Figure 11.17.

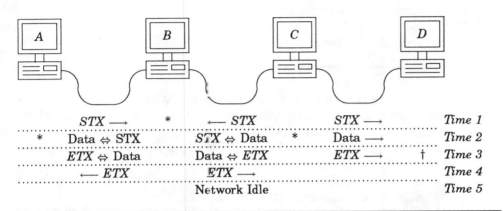

	$STX \longrightarrow$	*	$\longleftarrow STX$	$STX \longrightarrow$	*Time 1*
*	Data $\Leftrightarrow$ STX		$STX \Leftrightarrow$ Data	* Data $\longrightarrow$	*Time 2*
	$ETX \Leftrightarrow$ Data		Data $\Leftrightarrow$ ETX	$ETX \longrightarrow$ †	*Time 3*
	$\longleftarrow ETX$		$ETX \longrightarrow$		*Time 4*
		Network Idle			*Time 5*

Figure 11.17 Receiving station can detect a collision as a CRC error

11.3.3 The Bus Network Implementation

The Commkit bus network software has been written in a layered fashion to allow different high-level applications access to the bus emulation software. The overall structure, shown in Figure 11.18, is for the example presented in this section.

One-Line Messages
Bus Emulation Software
Commkit
Hardware

Figure 11.18 Structure of the Commkit bus network

The processes found in the one-line message-handling software (busex.c) communicate with the bus-emulation software (buslow.c) using send()s and recv()s.

The bus network-emulation software buslow.c requires commkit.obj, intrpt.obj and crc.obj in order to function. Commkit.obj calls the bus emulation software via the low_level() entry point. Low_level(), in turn, calls the bus network software via a common entry-point, bus_emulator(). See Table 11.2.

Network-emulation software The three states described in Section 11.3.2 are implemented directly in bus_emulator().

The idle state. If the station is neither transmitting (i.e., sending a message) nor receiving (i.e., accepting and forwarding a message), it is in the idle state

TABLE 11.2   Bus Emulator States

source	action	ch
CLKIH	Not supplied	Not supplied
SP1IH SP2IH	RECVDONE	Character Received
SP1IH SP2IH	XMITDONE	Not supplied

(indicated by bus.state having a value of IDLE). While in the IDLE state, the bus emulator can be called by one of three interrupt handlers: the clock, CLKIH; serial port 1, SP1IH; or serial port 2, SP2IH.

Interrupts from CLKIH are used for a number of purposes. First, if bus.delay (i.e., the delay required before this station is allowed to transmit) is nonzero, it is decremented on each tick; when zero is reached, the station is allowed to enter the transmission state, TRANSMIT. The transmission state is entered if there is a pending message (indicated by bus.pending) or if there is a message on the BUSNET queue waiting to be sent (the BUSNET queue is actually SP1IH's queue). Procedure send_start() is called when a message is to be sent; send_start() transmits an *STX* is sent out both serial ports.

RECVDONE interrupts from either SP1IH or SP2IH cause the emulator's state to change to RECEIVE if the incoming character is an *STX* (see recv_start()). The emulator remembers the incoming and outgoing ports (for collision detection) by storing the specific port identifiers in bus.inport and bus.outport, respectively. The character is forwarded to the next station by supplying the character to the port on which the character was not received.

The receive state.   The receive state is entered when bus.state has a value of RECEIVE. Recv_byte() is called whenever a character is received on either serial port (SP1IH or SP2IH). Under normal circumstances, the recv_byte() state machine determines what to do next with the incoming character (see Section 11.3.2). Once an entire packet is received and if the CRC is valid, the message is put on the queue BACKGROUND_1. However, if the port on which the incoming character is received is not the same as the original reception port, a collision has occurred, causing the reception to be aborted (signalled by bus.collision set to TRUE). After a collision is detected, reception continues until an *ETX* is received on both ports.

Clock interrupts still occur in the RECEIVE state and are used to ensure that the loss of communications (for example, a missing *ETX* resulting from the crash of the transmitting station does not leave the receiving station waiting "forever" for the missing byte. A watchdog timer, bus.xmit_watchdog, is incremented on each clock tick and reset whenever a byte is received. Should the flow of bytes cease, the timer value increases until it exceeds a maximum, causing recv_abort() to be called. Recv_abort() puts the station back to the idle state and sends a RECV_ABORTED message to APPLICATION.

Each station also supports promiscuous mode, whereby any message received with a valid CRC is accepted, regardless of its destination. Promiscuous mode can be specified by assigning TRUE to the global variable promiscuous after Commkit has been initialized. By default, promiscuous is FALSE.

The transmit state. The transmit state is entered when bus.state has a value of TRANSMIT. An action value of XMITDONE results in the next byte in the packet being sent. Since there is no guarantee that both ports generate interrupts at the same rate, transmissions are controlled separately in procedure send_byte(). When both ports have transmitted the final *ETX*, the message MESSAGE_SENT is sent to the transmitting process and control returns to the idle state.

However, should action have a value of RECVDONE, this indicates that another station is attempting to transmit at the same time as the first station, meaning that a collision is occurring. When a collision is detected, send_collision() is called and bus.collision is set to TRUE. Thereafter, the send_byte() software sends an *ETX* (or a byte followed by *ETX* if a *DLE* was previously sent). Bus.state returns to IDLE when an incoming *ETX* is found.

Collision_action() determines how long the station must wait before attempting to transmit again. A simplified version of binary exponential back off is used: the station identifier, bus.stn_id, is used as the random number between 1 and 4 (stored in bus.backoff), which is then multiplied by the number of times the station has collided when trying to transmit (indicated by bus.backcount) and the packet delay, PKT_DELAY. If the number of collisions exceeds the upper limit (defined in BKOFF_LIMIT), the station gives up trying to transmit this message and informs the transmitting process.

The clock interrupt is used as a watchdog to determine whether the other station involved in the collision has sent an *ETX*. When a collision is detected, bus.delay is set to a nonzero value; if an *ETX* is not found by the time bus.delay reaches zero, the emulator returns to the idle state and a MISSING_ETX message is sent to the transmitting process.

One-line message software   By itself, the bus-emulation software described in the previous section only handles the transmission and reception of packets: packets to be sent are taken off the BUSNET queue and received packets are put onto the BACKGROUND_1 queue. To permit experimentation with the bus network, Commkit includes software that allows the user to enter a packet (destination and source address and data) from the keyboard. Packets are sent by bus-emulation software across the network to the station specified in the destination address. Packets received by emulation software for the user's station are displayed locally.

The one-line message software is supplied in busex.c and consists of the following processes:

do_bus_ex(). This is the foreground process; it accepts data entered from the keyboard by the user (sent from the keyboard-interrupt handler to the APPLICATION queue). Do_bus_ex() also handles the message-response codes returned from the bus network.

Keyboard data is received a byte at a time from KEYIH. All bytes (except CTRL-C and ENTER) are stored in the array buffer and are echoed to the screen (using display()). Receipt of an ENTER causes the buffer to be sent to the BUSNET queue; while a CTRL-C results in the termination of the bus network software (on this station).

Once the bus network has completed the transmission, a message code is returned to the foreground process, indicating the result of the transmission (one of MESSAGE_SENT, COLLISION_LIMIT, or BAD_MSG_SIZE).

do_display(). Messages sent to the BACKGROUND_1 queue are read by the do_display() process and displayed in angle brackets on line 10. The message displayed also includes the destination and source addresses, thereby permitting the verification of any message received.

11.4   USING THE COMMKIT BUS NETWORK

The Commkit distribution diskette is supplied with both source and executable versions of the bus-messaging software.

11.4.1   Creating the Bus Network Software

The Commkit makefile contains instructions to the make utility for the creation of the messaging software, busex.exe. The high-level software is linked with buslow.obj, commkit.obj, crcsr.obj, and intrpt.obj using the make utility. For example, to create busex.exe, type:

```
C:\> make busex.exe
```

The Turbo C compiler includes general.h, ascii.h, and devices.h with busex.c to create busex.obj. Busex.obj is then linked with buslow.obj, commkit.obj, crc.obj, and intrpt.obj, producing busex.exe.

11.4.2   Running the Bus Network Software

Once a compiled version of the bus network emulator is available, it can be run by typing busex after the DOS prompt. The line speed (one of 50, 300, 1200, 2400, 4800, or 9600 bps) and the station identifier (a single character) must be entered on the same line. For example, to run the bus messaging software at 9600 bps and to set the station's identifier to S, type the following:

```
C:\> busex 9600 S
```

If this format is followed and the line speed is acceptable, the screen is cleared and message transfer can commence. Error messages are issued if either the format is incorrect or the line speed is not recognized.

Since the software is running at a low-level, it is necessary to type the destination and source address as part of any message. For example, if the user at station S is to send the message "How are things at your end?" to station L, the following would be typed (note that there is no prompt; ENTER denotes end-of-message):

```
LSHow are things at your end?
```

Packets with destination addresses matching the address of the station are displayed on line 10. For example, at station L, the above packet would be displayed as follows:

```
LSHow are things at your end?
```

To understand what happens during a transmission or a collision, it is best to run the line analyser on a PC connecting two bus-network PCs. Collisions can be caused by typing messages on both PCs (the destinations are not important) and pressing ENTER on both PCs simultaneously. Although the two ENTER keys may be pressed simultaneously and the same algorithm is running on each PC, a collision may not occur, since there is no guarantee that the clocks are synchronized. If collisions seem impossible to achieve, rerun busex.exe at a lower speed.

11.5 SUMMARY

This chapter has examined bus local area networks. Bus networks are named after their topology, in which all stations share a single, common communication channel. There are essentially two problems that the designers of bus networks must overcome: how to control access to the network and how to resolve collisions. Access control is handled by requiring each station to listen to (or sense) the line, prior to transmitting. Collision resolution is handled first by having the stations determine that a collision has occurred and then by ceasing their transmissions. The second step in collision resolution is to attempt to minimize the chances of it happening again. A common solution is have each station back off from transmitting for potentially longer and longer periods by picking random waiting periods. Many bus networks (such as the Ethernet and IEEE 802.3) implement such an algorithm, known as truncated binary exponential backoff. Much of the communication handling is now performed by VLSI chips.

The Ethernet and IEEE 802.3 networks are often referred to as CSMA/CD or Carrier-Sensed Multiple Access with Collision Detection. That is, the network is sensed before transmission and if a collision is detected, transmission is halted.

11.6 EXERCISES

All of the exercises relating to the bus-network software assume that you have access to at least three PCs, each with two serial ports. Some of the questions can be performed without recompiling the bus-network software, since the bus network software and the line analyser are both available on the Commkit diskette. However, others require that modifications be made to the bus-network software (remember to take back-up copies of the originals before making changes).

For those questions where you are expected to modify the bus network software, try testing your software against that of someone else.

1. Set up a three-station bus network, run the bus-network software on the two outermost stations and the line analyser on the middle station. Assign each station on the bus a unique address (such as *A* and *B*).

   Send packets between the two stations. (Remember that at this level you must embed both the destination and source addresses in the packet.) Examine the bus-network protocol using the line analyser by transmitting a packet from one station to the other. Identify the various fields within the packet. (The *STX* character is displayed as ☺, while the *ETX* character is a ♡.)

   What happens if you send a packet to station *C* (i.e., a nonexistent station) from either station *A* or station *B*? Does the packet appear on the line analyser? If so, why?

2. Set up a three-station bus-network, run the bus-network software on two adjacent stations and the line analyser on the third station. Assign each station on the bus a unique address (such as *A* and *B*).

   Now what happens if you send a packet to station *C* from either of the stations? Does the packet appear on the line analyser? If so, why?

3. Configure the network with the line analyser running between two bus-network stations (as in Exercise 1). Type messages on both stations and attempt to transmit them simultaneously (this takes a bit of practice and is usually best achieved by having one person press the ENTER key on both stations).

   If the packets are sent simultaneously, a collision should occur and be displayed on the line analyser. (If, no matter how hard you try, a collision never occurs, rerun busex.exe at a lower line speed.) What happens during the collision? Which station "wins" and is allowed to transmit?

   Start up both stations with the same network address; now, what happens once a collision has been detected? Given the back off algorithm used in the Commkit bus network, what combination of addresses will result in equal back-off time values?

4. As discussed in this chapter, a *broadcast* communication is one in which a single packet is delivered to all possible stations on a network. In a bus network all transmissions are naturally broadcast, since all stations must receive at least the destination address before deciding whether to keep the packet.

   The Commkit bus network is also a broadcast network; however, since a broadcast address is not supported by the network, broadcast messages cannot be sent. Add broadcast addressing to the Commkit bus network. Use 0xF0 as the broadcast address (0xF0 can be generated by typing ALT-P, which echoes as ≡).

   Note that sending a message with a broadcast address is a relatively simple operation. The unicast address is replaced by the broadcast address during the transmission. However, it is during reception that the check must be made.

   Test your software on a three-station network. First, try a broadcast transmission by sending broadcast packets and watching the traffic with a line analyser. Then, test broadcast reception by setting up one (then two) stations to receive and send a broadcast packet from the third.

Are collisions still supported? Does unicast transmission still work? Does the station sending the broadcast packet also receive a copy of the packet?

5. A *multicast* address is one which is *shared* by a number of stations on the network (from none to all possible stations). Implement multicast addressing on the Commkit bus network. Allow a station to belong to a maximum of ten different multicast addresses.

Since multicast addresses can be turned on and off at random, it will be necessary to make some relatively major changes to the bus-emulation software, since, at present, the only reason for communicating with the bus software is for the transmission of a message. You might consider setting up a new data structure (possibly a union), in which the first byte indicates to the bus network the action that is to be taken (i.e., whether the message contains data to be sent, or whether the message contains a new multicast address to be added to the list).

In the Ethernet, a multicast address is distinguished from a unicast by the most significant bit being set to 1. Use a similar scheme for this question: make multicast addresses have a value between 0xE0 (**ALT** ·) and 0xEF (**ALT o**); the multicast addresses are echoed as the symbols: α, β, Γ, π, Σ, σ, μ, τ, Φ, Θ, Ω, δ, ∞, ϕ, $\in$, and $\cap$. Remember, the broadcast address, 0xF0 ($\equiv$), is accepted by all stations.

6. Another type of network-analysis tool that is available to many network managers is the *network analyser*. The network analyser is similar to a line analyser in that data can be captured and displayed; however, most network analysers deal with packets rather than individual bytes. A typical network analyser will allow a network manager to capture packets as they are sent across the bus network, regardless of the destination. Some network analysers allow the user to selectively capture packets; for example, by monitoring a particular source or destination address, or even scanning for certain byte values within the packet. In order to capture data destined to any station on the network, the network analyser operates in promiscuous mode.

Write a network analyser for the Commkit bus network. As packets are received, they are to be displayed on the screen (use printf() to obtain scrolling). Add enhancements to the analyser that allow the user to request a specific source or destination address to be searched for.

7. At present the Commkit bus network has its own packet structure, unlike either the Ethernet or the IEEE 802.3 packet structures. Modify the Commkit bus to support a packet structure similar to that of the Ethernet by adding a one-byte **Type** field to the Commkit bus packet. The new version of the software should route the packet to the process associated with the value supplied in the **Type** field.

Test your software by having two processes on a station, each associated with a different **Type** field. Messages destined to the process associated with **Type** field value 0x45 should be displayed in normal video, while messages sent with a **Type** field value of 0xF4 should be displayed in inverse video. Remember, the destination address takes precedence over the **Type** field (that is, the **Type** field should be considered only if the destination address is the same as that of the station).

Avoid putting the **Type** field check directly into the bus-network driver. Instead, send the message to a background process which forwards the message to the intended-destination process. Consider a number of tests, such as sending a message with a **Type** field value that is not supported on the station to which the message is sent.

8. The Ethernet uses 48-bit addresses to identify a destination host, whereas Commkit uses a single 8-bit address (since, it was assumed no one would attach more than six stations to the network). Modify the Commkit bus emulator so that it supports 48-bit addressing. Consider techniques whereby an address could be checked *on-the-fly*, a byte at a time.

9. Rewrite the bus network's back-off algorithm so that it uses the Ethernet's truncated binary exponential back-off algorithm. In the original implementation of buslow.c, the Ethernet algorithm was used and subsequently abandoned—can you suggest a reason why?

10. Implement the point-to-point telephone utility atop the bus network. Each byte entered will have to be sent in its own packet. Test your software against that of someone else.

11. Develop a testing methodology that can be used to cause each of the bus network error messages to be produced.

12. The minimum packet size of $2 \times N$ based upon the number of cables connecting the PCs in the network is slightly too large. What should the actual minimum size of the packet be? Is it that important?

13. A number of papers have been written which claim that unicast and broadcast addresses are simply special cases of multicast. Explain whether and how this might be true.

12

Ring Local Area Networks

12.1 INTRODUCTION

The CSMA/CD bus local area network, for all of its benefits, is by no means the only, nor necessarily the "best" design for a local area network. In the worst case, it is possible that with the bus local-area network, a station may never be able to transmit its data. Consider the following scenarios:

- Two stations attempt to transmit simultaneously—a collision occurs. By some coincidence, both stations generate the same backoff values, resulting in a continuous series of collisions. Eventually, the collision limit is reached and the transmission of at least one of the packets is aborted.

- A heavily loaded network consisting of several hundred stations are all trying to transmit large volumes of data simultaneously—initially, all transmissions will result in collisions; however, as backoff delays begin to grow longer, some of the transmissions will be successful. Stations that constantly collide might never obtain an opportunity to send their data.

These situations, albeit extremely unlikely on a lightly loaded bus network, have the potential for seriously degrading a heavily loaded network. The source of the problem can be traced to the *nondeterministic* nature of the bus: access to the bus does not guarantee that a station can transmit.

12.2   THE TOKEN BUS

To ensure that every station with data to transmit on a bus network has a guaranteed opportunity to transmit implies some form of *deterministic* access to the network. Deterministic network access requires a certain degree of control that the bus network by itself does not offer. One possible approach is to have a station dedicated to polling all other stations for transmissions, thereby ensuring fair access to the network. However, in Chapter 11 it was shown that centralized polling has its limitations, an important limit being the question of how to allow access to the network should the polling station fail.

A variation on polling is to allow each station to transmit in turn, but instead of having a single, centralized polling station, permission to access the network is passed *between* the stations themselves in the form of a *token*. Stations no longer compete for the network, instead they wait for the token, at which point they can transmit. Once the transmission has been completed, the transmitting station is responsible for forwarding the token to another station to access the network. This cycle continues indefinitely.

At any time, the packet on the network contains either data or a token. Since stations may not transmit unless they have the token, collisions should be rare or nonexistent.

A guarantee that deterministic network access using the token method described above means that after any station has had the opportunity to transmit, it must then wait until all other stations have been given the same opportunity. For example, in a network of four stations (A, B, C, and D), once station A has transmitted, it cannot transmit again until stations B, C, and D have been given permission to transmit. The question is: what type of mechanism is required to enforce this ordering?

As an analogy, consider the path of a memo through an office. The memo originates from the secretary, who passes it to the person first named on the list. The first person passes the memo to the second, the second to the third, and so on until it reaches the last person on the list, who is responsible for returning it to the secretary. The path the memo has taken looks something like that shown in Figure 12.1.

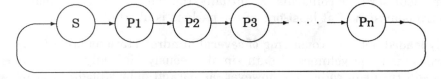

Figure 12.1   The path of a memo through an office

In the case of the memo, the "last" person on the list is expected to return the memo to the first person (the secretary). Similarly, in the network of four stations, the "last" station with the token must forward the token to the "first" station. The path taken by the memo (or the token) is similar to the steps required to traverse a circularly linked list.

The bus network is not a circular list (it is an unrooted tree); however, it is possible, through software, to implement a circular-linked list atop the bus. Quite simply, every station is followed by a unique "downstream" station. For example, Figure 12.2 illustrates how a circular-linked list could be organized on top of a bus network.

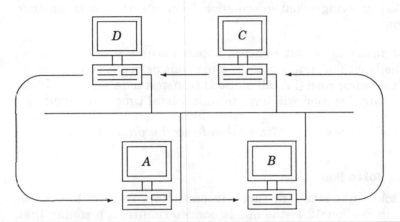

Figure 12.2   A circular-linked list atop a bus network

The stations in Figure 12.2 are linked as outlined in Table 12.1.

TABLE 12.1   Station Successors

Station		Downstream
A	$\longrightarrow$	B
B	$\longrightarrow$	C
C	$\longrightarrow$	D
D	$\longrightarrow$	A

If each station "knows" the station that follows it, then forwarding the token is a simple operation as demonstrated by the following algorithm:

1. Wait for the permission-to-transmit token from the "upstream" station.

2. Upon receipt of the permission token, transmit any pending messages that may exist.

3. Forward (i.e., transmit) the permission-to-transmit token to the "downstream" station.

4. Repeat beginning with Step 1.

Access to the network is now deterministic, a station is guaranteed access to the network once all other stations on the network have had an opportunity to transmit. Note that the underlying bus network remains unchanged; it is still a broadcast network (any packet sent on the network is received by all other stations and discarded if the packet's destination address doesn't match that of the station). The bus now supports two types of packet:

Data packets. Packets containing information sent from one station to any other station or stations. A data packet is simply a bus network packet carrying data.

Token packets. A packet containing an indication that the station specified in the destination address may access the network. A token packet is a bus network packet carrying token information from one station to another specific station.

The use of the token to permit network access ensures that there is an upper limit on the length of time a station must wait before it can transmit. For example, in the worst case (i.e., all stations transmit a data packet when the token is received), a station will have to wait a total time equivalent to:

$$(Number\ of\ stations - 1) \times (Time\ taken\ to\ send\ a\ data\ packet)$$

12.2.1   IEEE 802.4: Token Bus

The push for a token bus standard came, in part, from some of the issues that were raised in Section 12.1: the bus is nondeterministic, meaning that stations on the network may be required to wait unduly long periods before being able to transmit a frame. The 802 standard committee recognized this and set about to develop another standard: IEEE Standard 802.4, Token Bus. Some of the main proponents of the Token Bus were companies such as General Motors and Boeing (both interested in factory and office automation), who were involved in the development of MAP (Manufacturing Automation Protocol) and TOP (Technical and Office Protocols), respectively.

The 802.4 protocol is *not* built atop the 802.3 CSMA/CD MAC layers. Instead, 802.4 defines its own physical and MAC layers. The physical layer uses a *broadband* backbone-coaxial cable and provides three data rates (at separate frequencies): 1 Mbps, 5 Mbps, and 10 Mbps. The separate data rates are intended for equipment that support data, voice, or video. *Physically*, the 802.4 token bus is a broadcast network; *logically*, the stations on the bus are connected as part of a circular-linked list.

The 802.4 frame format is as given in Figure 12.3, and its components are defined as follows.

Preamble	Start Delimiter	Frame Control	Destination Address	Source Address	Data	Checksum	End Delimiter

Figure 12.3   The 802.4 frame format

`Preamble`. A clock-synchronizing sequence; minimum size of 1 byte.

`Start Delimiter` and `End Delimiter`. Marks the start-of-frame (or end-of-frame) by encoding electrically invalid Manchester bit patterns into the byte. The two delimiters are not the same; both are 1 byte long.

Frame Control. Denotes the use of the current frame: the frame is either a data frame or a control frame. When signalling a data frame, the **Frame Control** field indicates the frame's priority and whether an acknowledgement is required by the transmitting station.

Destination and **Source Address**. The 802.4 frame supports an addressing scheme that is identical to that of the 802.3 CSMA/CD bus. Both 16- and 48-bit addresses are supported, although not simultaneously, in the same network.

Data. The message field, up to 8182 bytes (when using 16-bit addresses) or 8174 bytes (when using 48-bit addresses) in length.

Checksum. The **Checksum** uses the 802.3 frame check sequence algorithm and generator polynomial; the **Checksum** includes the entire frame (between frame delimiters).

The Token Bus MAC layer is responsible for two main tasks: data transfer and network maintenance.

Data transfer When a token arrives at a station, the station has a certain amount of time available in which to transmit messages in 802.4 frames; this time is divided between various message queues. The Token Bus defines four levels of message priority (0, 2, 4, and 6, with 0 being the lowest and 6 the highest); each level is associated with its own queue. Messages are transmitted from the highest priority queues first (i.e., from 6 down to 0). Once the messages in a queue have been sent, the queue timer has expired, or if there was nothing in the queue to send, the next lower priority queue is given permission to start its transmissions. If the station has nothing to transmit, the station has finished transmitting, or the station's time limit has expired, the token is forwarded to the station's successor: a control frame with the control frame field set to **TOKEN**. The order of token passing is strictly defined: from high to low addresses. Each station maintains the address of its predecessor and its successor.

Network maintenance Network maintenance covers a wide variety of topics: the addition of new stations to the network, the removal of stations from the network, and the initialization of the network. The maintenance of the network is governed by the stations themselves, through the use of control frames. Some of the conditions that 802.4 can handle are described in the next sections.

Lost token. A token bus cannot function if there is no token on the network. The **CLAIM_TOKEN** control-frame code is used when a station determines that the token is missing and it is necessary to place a new token into the network; for example:

1. When a station is first brought on-line, it monitors the network for traffic; if none is detected within a fixed period of time, the station assumes that it is the first station on the network. However, before putting a token

onto the network, the station first broadcasts a CLAIM_TOKEN frame. If no responses to the frame are received, the station sets up a network of one (itself) and sends frames addressed to itself (thus generating network traffic).

2. All stations contain timers monitoring the network for the token; if a token is not detected within a certain period of time and a station's timer expires, the station broadcasts a CLAIM_TOKEN frame. If collisions occur during the bid for the token, various timers come into play, allowing one station to eventually win the bid. At this point, a new token is placed onto the network.

Adding stations. The physical presence of a station on the network does not necessarily mean that it will receive a token; the station must "join" the network and become a successor of one station and the predecessor of another.

The SOLICIT_SUCCESSOR_1 control frame is sent periodically by any station that happens to have the token, thereby allowing other stations to partake in communications. In order that the strict highest-to-lowest sequencing of stations is maintained, the frame contains the sender's and successor's addresses; only stations waiting to join the network with addresses in that range are allowed to bid. If no bids are received within a certain period of time, the station with the token proceeds with its data transfer. If a bid is received from one station, it becomes the successor of the current station with the token.

Should several stations bid simultaneously, their bids will collide, requiring the use of a RESOLVE_CONTENTION frame to indicate that the bids have failed. The station holding the token then attempts to add a new station by halving the range of possible addresses (i.e., from its address to the mid-point between its address and the address of its successor). This cycle continues until a successor is found.

Stations leaving the network. When a station Q is to leave the network, it sends a SET_SUCCESSOR frame containing the address of Q's successor (say, R) to its predecessor (P). The predecessor, P, makes its new successor R. Q is now removed from the network.

Missing stations. When the station currently holding the token passes the token to its successor, it monitors the bus for subsequent traffic. Ideally, there should be traffic generated by the successor; however, if nothing is heard, the original token holder sends the token again. If no response is heard the second time, the token holder assumes the worst and broadcasts a WHO_FOLLOWS frame, containing the address of the missing station. The missing station's successor is to respond with a SET_SUCCESSOR frame; the token holder updates its successor address and forwards the token to its new successor.

If no responses are forthcoming to the WHO_FOLLOWS, the token-holding station broadcasts a SOLICIT_SUCCESSOR_2 frame. Stations wanting to join the network can bid to become the successor.

One of the reasons behind the topology of the Token Bus is that it lends itself well to automated-factory assembly lines consisting of robots or other computer-controlled equipment. The cabling is laid the length of the factory, and connected to the various pieces of equipment.

By completely changing the topology of the network (that is, by abandoning the bus structure), it is possible to achieve results similar to those of the token bus, with a somewhat less complicated protocol and, potentially higher throughput. The topology in question is the *ring*.

12.3 RING NETWORKS

The topology of a ring network is as the name suggests: the network forms a ring, interconnecting all stations (Figure 12.4).

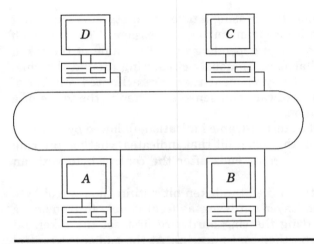

Figure 12.4 The ring network topology

Accessing a ring is similar to accessing a token bus: the station must wait until permission is granted, at which point, transmission can occur. However, there are several notable differences between the ring and the token bus:

Physical Topology. The token bus is a deterministic ring built atop a nondeterministic bus network; all transmissions are broadcast. The token, as it is passed from station to station, follows no particular direction: the physical location of a station has no bearing upon when it receives the token.

A ring network consists of a number of stations connected in a closed loop. In most rings, packets flow in one direction only; that is, out from the transmitting station, past all the other stations and back to the transmitting station, which is responsible for removing the packet.

Successor Identification. The successor station in a token bus must be explicitly identified in the token packet; whereas in a ring, the successor is the next station "downstream" from the current station.

Reliability. Most token bus and ring networks are designed to continue functioning should a station fail. However, should the channel fail, the results can be quite different. The bus can, in theory at least, continue functioning in a degraded fashion as two separate buses.

A channel failure on a ring can result in the total cessation of communications since all information flows in one direction around the ring. Recent developments in ring architecture use *two* separate bidirectional channels: should one channel fail, packets can be routed through the other channel.

There are, broadly speaking, three different types of ring network algorithm: the token ring, the slotted ring, and register insertion.

12.3.1   The Token Ring

Accessing a token ring is similar to accessing a token bus: stations must wait until they receive permission before transmitting a message. The ring itself is in one of two states: *free* or *busy*; depending upon the value of the token in a variable length frame that is continuously circulating around the ring. Frames are made up of bits; at any moment there are a limited number of bits on the ring. The station hardware can sense and change the value of a single bit as it passes the station.

Token ring frames consist of a start-of-frame indication, followed by a control byte that contains a single bit, the token bit that indicates whether the ring is free or busy. The free token frame ends after the control byte with an end-of-frame indication.

A station detecting a free token (i.e., the token bit within the control byte is sensed by the ring Physical-Layer hardware as free) is able to transmit a message. This is done by having the ring hardware first set the token bit within the frame to busy (the bit then continues on). At the end of the control byte, the destination and source addresses are sent. Each bit in the message is then transmitted, followed by a CRC and the end-of-frame indication. The frame circulates around the ring (typically only a few bits are on the ring at any one time) and passes each station.

Upon detection of a busy token, each station takes a copy of the frame, assembling the frame out of the sequence of incoming bits. When the end-of-frame is detected, the receiving station can examine the destination address of the packet to determine if the packet should be kept or discarded.

The transmitting station is responsible for removing the bits off the ring (since only a few bits are on the ring at any one moment, if the bits aren't removed, they will interfere with the transmission of the remaining bits). When the transmitting station has completed its transmission, a new free token (consisting of the start-of-frame, control byte, and end-of-frame indication) must be put onto the ring.

The following series of illustrations show the cycle of events as station D transmits a message to station B. First, in Figure 12.5, station D waits for a free token.

Once the free token is detected, station D sets the token to busy and starts to transmit the remainder of the frame (i.e., the destination address, the source address, the message, and any checksum). See Figure 12.6. Note that during part of the transmission, some of the bits of the free token are still being removed from the ring by station D.

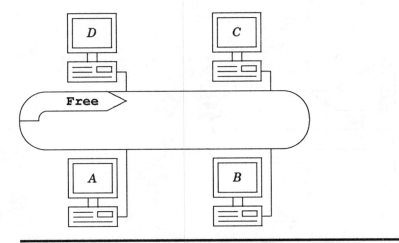

Figure 12.5   Before station D can transmit, it must wait for the free token

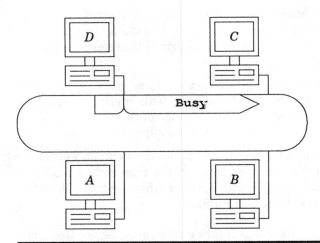

Figure 12.6   Station D transmits, the token now signals **Busy**

The packet circulates past each station on the network; since the token bit indicates **Busy**, each station proceeds to assemble the remainder of the frame. When the destination addess has been assembled, the station compares the frame's destination address with its own: if the destination and the station's address are the same, the station continues to accept the bits making up the frame. Upon detection of the end-of-frame indication, the CRC is checked and the message is forwarded to the station. In this example (Figure 12.7), only station B takes a copy of the frame since the destination address indicates B.

If the number of bits in the packet exceed the number of bits that can be circulating at any moment on the ring, the transmitting station (station D in this example) removes the bits at the same time it is transmitting. The transmitting station continues to transmit until the end-of-packet is sent, at which point the transmitting station can apply one of the following algorithms:

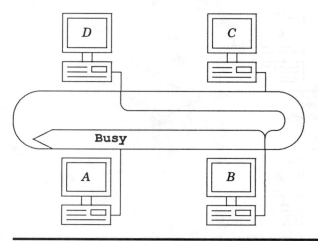

Figure 12.7   The token remains **Busy** as it traverses the ring

- The station can remove the entire packet from the network before reissuing the free token. This is known as *single-frame operation*. Single-frame operation reduces the throughput of the network, since there are periods in which the network is devoid of any frame.

- The station issues a new free token as soon as the busy token is removed from the ring and the end-of-frame has been sent. This method, known as *single-token operation* can be used when the number of bits in the frame is less than the number of bits that can exist on the ring at any time.

- The station can start to transmit a free token as soon as the end-of-frame is sent, implying that several tokens can exist on the ring at any moment; this is known as *multiple-token operation*. This method ensures that the amount of network idle time is kept to a minimum.

In this example (Figure 12.8), station *D* issues a free token *before* the original frame is completely removed from the network (i.e., the network supports single-token operation).

The above algorithm, which requires the transmitting station to remove the frame as it is being transmitted, is known as *source* removal. The alternate approach is to have the destination station remove the frame as it is received (this is known as *destination* removal). Although destination removal would suggest that greater throughput could be achieved, it does suffer a number of drawbacks, such as the following:

- The deterministic nature of the token ring can be lost. That is, instead of ensuring that each station will be able to transmit within a certain number of frame cycles, one station can continue to transmit without giving up the ring. For example, if station *A* transmits frames to station *B* and station *B* issues a free token, then station *A* would receive a free token before any downstream stations (*D*, *C*, or *B*) had a chance to transmit. Station *A* could therefore monopolize the network.

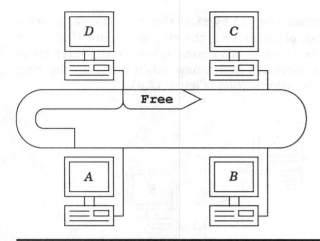

Figure 12.8 Station D frees the token and removes its message

- Support for broadcast and multicast communications would be cumbersome. For example, if the first station to receive a broadcast frame were to release it as a free token, no other stations would receive a copy of the frame. This problem can be overcome by requiring the transmitting station to perform source removal on broadcast and multicast frames only.

    A simpler solution is to use source removal for all transmissions, thereby eliminating these special cases.

Ring errors The objective of a ring network is to ensure that all stations have equal access to the ring. This is achieved using some form of circulating token. Should anything happen to the token to stop it from circulating, network access may become impossible. There are two error situations that can stop network access entirely:

Missing token situation. If the token is removed from the network or becomes so corrupted (through noise) that it is impossible to recognize, then all stations will be left waiting for a free token that never arrives. This is the *missing token* situation.

In addition to being lost because of noise, the missing token situation can arise if a station with a message to transmit removes the free token from the ring and *crashes* before putting the busy token onto the ring. Similarly, the missing token situation can occur if a frame has been sent and the transmitting station crashes after removing the busy token but before the free token is placed back onto the ring.

Circulating busy token situation. The second error situation occurs when the token remains in the busy state. The token can remain busy either through being corrupted (i.e., changed from free to busy, typically because of noise), or by a transmitting station crashing after setting the token to busy, thereby being unable to put a free token back onto the network.

Should either one of these situations occur, the network will cease to function. To avoid the problem, some form of centralized control is needed. Most rings employ a station to *monitor* the network for either of these conditions.

The monitor station   The solution adopted by most ring-network designers is to assign one station the task of monitoring the ring to ensure that if the network enters an error state (such as a missing token or the busy token circulating), the error can be corrected and a new token put onto the ring. This station is known as the *monitor station* (Figure 12.9).

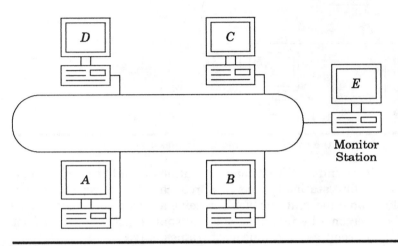

Figure 12.9   The monitor station

Depending upon the network, the monitor can either be a device dedicated to monitoring the ring, or it can be a station that performs monitoring duties in addition to the transmission and reception of frames.

Regardless of how the monitor is implemented, it must still be able handle the two error situations just described. The monitor can detect the missing-token error situation with little difficulty as the network is always being monitored for traffic. Tokens (busy or free) are expected at regular intervals, so that if one does not arrive within the designated period, the monitor can assume the worst and issue a new free token frame.

Detecting the circulating busy token is a somewhat more difficult task, requiring the monitor to determine whether the busy token has just been set to busy or is still busy from a previous cycle around the ring. The approach taken by ring network implementations is to add a bit to the control field which is set by the monitor each time a busy token bit is detected. The bit, often referred to as the *Monitor-Passed* (MP) bit, signals that a busy token frame was detected by the monitor. The transmitting station is responsible for issuing a free token frame with the MP bit cleared. Normally, the monitor will only receive busy token frames with the token bit set to Busy. See Figure 12.10.

There are two conditions that can arise when the monitor detects the busy token: the MP bit is either set or cleared:

Set. If the MP bit is set, it means that the station transmitting the packet did *not* remove the frame from the network. This is an error condition

Figure 12.10   The **MP** bit is set when the monitor detects a **Busy** token

requiring the monitor to remove all bits from the ring and put a new free-token frame onto the ring.

Cleared. If the MP bit is clear, it means that this is the first time the packet has passed the monitor. The MP bit is then set by the monitor.

Rings can be of varying sizes (i.e., total length or number of stations), and this can determine the number of bits that can be on the ring at any one time. In many rings, the monitor is also responsible for maintaining an *elastic buffer* which, acting like a queue, regulates the number of bits on the ring. For example, a free token may require 24 bits; if the ring only has space for 8 bits, then the elastic buffer must be holding a queue of 16 bits.

Other ring errors   Rings that allow at most a single token (free or busy) on the ring at any time (i.e., they operate in single-frame or single-token mode) must be protected from conditions in which more than one token exists on the ring. The *duplicate-token situation* can be caused by noise or some other error, and can result in, for example, two stations attempting to transmit simultaneously.

The solution to the duplicate-token situation requires each transmitting station to examine the source address of the frame *before* removing the frame from the ring. If the frame's source address is not the same as the station's address, then a duplicate-token situation has occurred. Once the duplicate-token situation is detected, there are a number of possible algorithms to handle the error:

- If all stations simply remove frames that do not have the correct source address, and do not place a new free token onto the ring, the monitor station will eventually detect a lost-token situation. Once the lost-token situation is detected, the monitor will reissue a new free token frame.
- The previous solution results in idle periods in which no busy frames can be transmitted until the monitor puts a free-token onto the ring. An alternative solution is to have the stations examine the frame's source address and have the station with the *lower* address value stop its transmission. (This can be achieved by having each station maintain a queue of the incoming bits.) The station with the higher address value continues to transmit its frame.

  The station with the lower address value forwards the bits already in its queue (starting with a start-of-frame indication). Subsequent bits are taken off the ring and stored in the queue for transmission. This ensures that the bits are received in the correct order by the transmitting station.

A second error that must be considered in any ring network that uses a monitor to control network access is: what happens if the monitor fails? Should this occur and an error situation such as the missing token arise, then network access will cease entirely.

Recovery from a monitor failure requires two distinct steps: first, the loss of the monitor must be detected, and second, once detected, the loss must be recovered from. Detection can be achieved in a number of ways, for example:

- The monitor can be required to periodically send monitor-alive messages to all stations on the network; if a monitor-alive message is not detected within an agreed upon time limit, the monitor is assumed to have failed.

- Since access to the ring is deterministic, each station knows that within a certain maximum time, a free token should be available; if the token is not found, the monitor is deemed to have failed.

- All stations can monitor the ring for traffic; if nothing is detected within a given period, the monitor is assumed to have failed.

Once the error has been detected, the remaining stations must then determine which station is to become the new monitor (assuming that a station can become a new monitor); otherwise the error must be signalled to the person managing the network and the monitor repaired manually.

In a typical recovery algorithm, each station that has detected the loss of the monitor announces this discovery (by means of a frame). As the frame circulates around the ring, each station that has discovered and announced the loss of the monitor examines the source address of the incoming frame. If the source address is *less* that the station's address, the frame is discarded: that is, the extra frame is handled as a duplicate-token situation. The station to receive a packet with its own address as the source address becomes the monitor.

The new monitor issues a new free token onto the ring and the network resumes activity.

Connecting to the ring   In most ring networks, the ring does not physically pass through the stations connected to the ring. If the ring were to do so, the failure of a station would cause the entire ring to cease functioning. Instead, each station is connected to the ring through a *bypass relay* (Figure 12.11).

As long as the station is electrically active, the bypass relay remains open, allowing individual bits to be received by the station. Should the station fail, the bypass relay closes and the bits no longer arrive at the station.

Examples   The previous section's description of the token ring can be applied to most existing token rings. However, a number of enhancements and extensions found in several existing ring implementations are now listed.

The IBM Token Ring.   The IBM Token Ring functions, for the most part, as the generic token ring described earlier in this section; however, there are several interesting and notable exceptions:

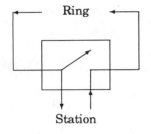

Figure 12.11   Each station connects to the ring using a bypass relay

■ The busy-token frame format is illustrated in Figure 12.12 (sizes are in bytes).

DEL (1)	CTRL (2)	DST (6)	SRC (6)	Data	FCS (4)	DEL (1)	FS (1)

Figure 12.12   The busy-token frame

The frame delimiters **DEL** are bytes containing invalid Manchester bit encodings and different bit values to distinguish between the starting and ending delimiters (X denotes an invalid bit pattern). See Figure 12.13.

Starting delimiter:	0	0	0	X	X	0	X	X
Ending delimiter:	1	1	1	X	X	1	X	X

Figure 12.13   Frame delimiters are signalled by invalid Manchester signals

The control field, **CTRL**, consists of two bytes. The first byte is common to both the free and busy token frames and consists of the following fields (the **Priority** fields are discussed below; **Monitor Count** is simply the MP bit). See Figure 12.14.

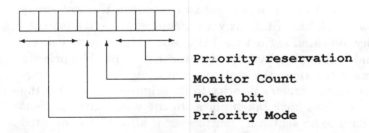

Figure 12.14   The first byte of the **CTRL** field

The second byte of the control field is transmitted only with busy token frames. The **Frame format** field indicates whether the data field contains ring-signalling information or data-link information. If the **Frame format** field indicates ring-signalling information, *all* stations are expected to read the `Control` field. See Figure 12.15.

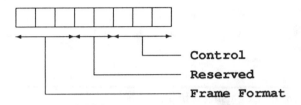

Figure 12.15   The second byte of the `CTRL` field

The destination and source addresses are stored in the `DST` and `SRC` fields respectively. The `Data` field is of variable length, consisting of zero or more bytes. The `FCS` is a 4-byte CRC and covers the entire frame between starting and ending delimiters.

The free token frame consists of the two delimiters and the first byte of the `CTRL` field.

- In the generic token-ring description, all stations have equal opportunity to transmit any frame to any destination. This can mean that priority frames (such as voice or video) are competing with data frames that could potentially be delayed.

To overcome this limitation, busy-token frames are divided into two modes: those that can be transmitted *asynchronously* (periodically) and those that need to be transmitted *synchronously* (on a regular basis). To handle synchronous communications, each busy frame can be associated with one of eight levels of priority, as indicated by the priority bits in the `CTRL` field (zero is the lowest priority, indicating asynchronous mode).

Normally, the ring functions in asynchronous mode, with all stations having access to the ring. Periodically, when a high-priority station requires access to the network, the requested priority can be written into the `Priority Reservation` bits of a passing busy token. The station freeing the token is expected to copy the `Priority Reservation` bits into the `Priority Mode` bits of the new free token. Stations with messages to be transmitted at the level of priority indicated in the `Priority Mode` bits may now do so, thereby ensuring that higher-priority information can be sent. The priority eventually does come down since the station requesting the higher priority is expected to return the token's priority to its original value after the synchronous communications have taken place. In the worst case, stations with asynchronous data to be sent can wait forever if all traffic is devoted to synchronous communications.

- The frame-status byte, `FS`, follows the final delimiter and is used by the destination station to convey status information back to the transmitting station through two status indication bits A (acknowledgement) and C (frame-copied) (R denotes reserved). See Figure 12.16.

R	R	C	A	R	R	C	A

Figure 12.16 The frame-status byte

The interpretation of the A and C bits are given in Table 12.2.

TABLE 12.2 *A* and *C* Bit Interpretation

A	C	Meaning
0	0	Destination not responding.
1	0	Destination present but frame not copied.
1	1	Destination present and frame copied.

The token ring operates at 4 Mbps.

IEEE 802.5 token ring. The IEEE 802 Committee has a token ring network standard: IEEE 802.5, which is compatible with the IBM Token Ring design described above. The addressing scheme follows that of the IEEE 802.3, discussed in the previous chapter.

FDDI (Fiber Distributed Data Interface). FDDI is a 100 megabit per second (Mbps) fiber optic token ring standard developed by the American National Standard Institute (ANSI) committee X3T9.5, based upon the IEEE 802.5 token ring standard. An FDDI ring falls into the category of *Metropolitan Area Network* (MAN) since it can span distances of up to 200 kilometers. Due to its high speed, FDDI can also be used as a *backbone* network, interconnecting smaller, low speed, local area networks (such as Ethernets or 802.5 token rings).

Physically, the FDDI network consists of two rings, one transmitting clockwise, the other counterclockwise. Transmissions can occur on both rings (although the standard recommends that one ring remain in reserve) which gives an FDDI network an effective rate of 200 Mbps. Two classes of stations exist: an A type which connects to both rings, and a B type, which connects to a single ring. Up to 1000 stations can be joined to an FDDI network with a maximum distance of 2 kilometers between class-A stations and 500 meters between class-B stations; for example see Figure 12.17.

As in 802.5, stations wait for the free token before transmitting. When a station is in possession of the token, it has a finite amount of time in which to transmit one or more packets. FDDI defines two types of packets: synchronous, those which a station is guaranteed to transmit; and asynchronous, those which a station can transmit if there is time available (there are eight levels of priority within asynchronous). Once a station has sent its last packet, it reissues the free token (FDDI operates as a multiple-token ring). The station is responsible for removing its packets from the ring even though it no longer has the token.

One of the arguments for a bidirectional ring is reliability; should both rings be cut for some reason, communications can continue by looping one ring back onto the other in the class A stations nearest the break (Figure 12.18).

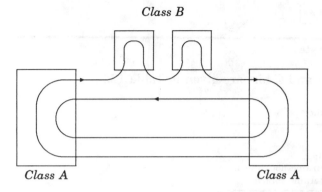

Figure 12.17   An FDDI ring consists of two separate rings

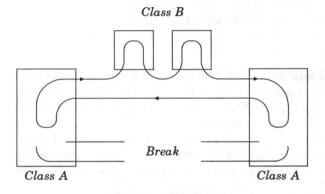

Figure 12.18   How FDDI continues communications in the event of a ring fault

There are presently two FDDI standards: FDDI-1, intended for data traffic; and a new standard, FDDI-2, intended to offer better support for both data and voice.

12.3.2 The Slotted Ring

A slotted ring is similar to the token ring, with the exception that there is a single circulating frame structure that contains space for data (anywhere from 2 to 32 bytes, depending upon the implementation). The frame has two states: free (indicating that a station can send data in this frame) or busy (meaning that this frame has data and should be read). As with the token ring, when the transmitting station receives its busy token frame, it frees the frame to allow another station access to the network.

Slotted rings typically have several circulating frames to help improve throughput. The number of frames on the ring is controlled by the monitor and must be known by all stations to ensure that a transmitting station frees the correct frame.

Example   Probably the best known slotted ring to achieve any degree of commercial success was the Cambridge Ring, developed in the late 1970's at the University of Cambridge. The format of a Cambridge Ring frame (more commonly known as a *minipacket*) is given in Figure 12.19 (note, all sizes are in *bits*).

Start (1)	Full/Empty (1)	Monitor (1)	DST (8)	SRC (8)	User Data (16)	Type (2)	Response (2)	Parity (1)

Figure 12.19   The Cambridge Ring minipacket

The `Start` bit, with a value of 1, preceeds all other bits in the minipacket and is used by the ring hardware as a synchronization bit to signal the start of the minipacket. The status of the packet then follows and indicates whether the packet is in use (`Full`, value 1) or available for use (`Empty`, value 0). The `Monitor` bit is set by the monitor to handle the circulating-busy situation; the bit is set by the monitor when a `Full` token passes the monitor and is cleared by the transmitting station.

The destination, `DST`, and source, `SRC` addresses are both 8-bits long. At most 254 stations are allowed on a single ring, addresses 0x00 and 0xFF are reserved. Two bytes of data are sent in the `User Data` field, while the `Type` field indicates the type of data.

The `Response` bits are sent by the transmitting station with the value 11; they are to be changed by the destination station and are interpreted as follows:

11   The destination has not changed the response bits, implying that the destination does not exist.

01   The destination has accepted the minipacket.

10   The destination has accepted minipackets from another source.

00   The destination is busy and cannot accept the minipacket at this moment.

The monitor station is a separate device; if the monitor fails, the entire ring will shut down.

12.3.3   Register-Insertion Ring

The register-insertion ring doesn't really correspond to any of the ring algorithms that have been discussed so far; instead, it functions more as a ring of store-and-forward stations.

Each station in a register-insertion ring has two registers, each used to hold a variable length frame: one from the upstream station, and the other from the local station. Frames arrive at a local station as a stream of bits, which are copied into the upstream register. When the destination address bits have arrived, the local station compares the address in the register with its own address. If the frame is addressed to the local station, the remainder of the frame is copied to the station, otherwise the frame is forwarded to the downstream station, one bit at a time (the upstream register acts as a queue: with the oldest bits being sent first and the most recent arrivals being stored at the end of the queue).

Before the local station can transmit, the frame must be stored in the station's register. When the upstream register is empty, the station's ring hardware checks the station's register; if there is a frame to be transmitted, the bits in the frame are shifted onto the ring to the downstream station. Should bits arrive from the upstream station, the local station copies the incoming bits into the upstream register while completing the transmission from the station's register.

12.4   THE COMMKIT TOKEN RING

Although IBM manufactures a token ring, few PCs built by IBM (or anyone else for that matter) are supplied with token ring hardware as standard equipment. However, as with the other networks studied in this book, it is possible to write emulation software that illustrates the principles of ring networks.

Commkit is supplied with a token ring emulator, implemented using the following software:

ringlow.c   the low-level token ring emulation software

ringdefs.h   the header file required by ringlow.c and containing the various data structures used by the ring network software

ringex.c   a high-level interface allowing experimentation with the token ring

12.4.1   Hardware Requirements

The Commkit ring network software is written for PCs supporting two serial ports. A typical Commkit ring-network configuration consists of four PCs, each having two serial ports, with null modem cables connecting the ports as shown in Figure 12.20.

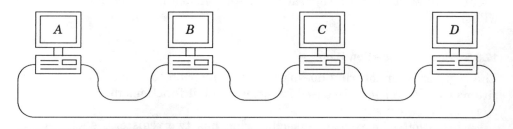

Figure 12.20   A Commkit ring consisting of four PCs

Note that unlike the bus network, serial port 1 *must* connect to serial port 2, since the ring algorithm stipulates that bytes arrive on port 2 and are forwarded on port 1.

12.4.2 Design

The ring network supplied with Commkit is a true token-ring network in that before a message can be transmitted, the station with the message must first wait for the free token to appear before it can transmit. When the free token arrives at a station with a message to transmit, the station sets the token to busy and sends the bytes in the message, one at a time, out serial port 1. All stations receive copies of the bytes making up the message as they circulate around the ring; each byte arrives on serial port 2, a copy of the byte is taken, the byte is then forwarded out serial port 1. The bytes are removed from the ring by the transmitting station, at which point a new free token is issued and allowed to pass to the next station in the ring.

For example, if station B were to transmit a 4-byte message, the flow of information would be illustrated by the sequence of events shown in Figure 12.21 (the flow is counter-clockwise from station B).

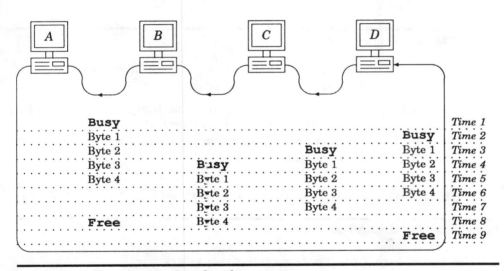

Figure 12.21   The transmission of a 4-byte message

In Figure 12.20, at *Time* 1 station B puts a **Busy** token onto the ring which is received by station A. At *Time* 2 the **Busy** token has reached station D (after being forwarded by station A), and the first byte (Byte 1) arrives at station A. The **Busy** token is removed from the network at *Time* 4, but station B waits until the last byte (Byte 4) is received at *Time* 8 before putting the **Free** token onto the network.

As with most other token rings, the Commkit ring network requires that one station be the monitor to ensure that the token is not lost or damaged. The monitor checks for the missing token and the circulating busy situations.

Frame structure   All information sent on the ring (be it a free token or a busy token and data) is sent in a variable length frame. The general format of a frame is shown in Figure 12.22.

STX	Information	ETX

Figure 12.22   Generalized Commkit ring frame structure

There are two valid frame structures:

Free token. The free token is a 3-byte frame that circulates past each station; indicating that the network can be accessed. A station that has a message to transmit can seize the token, set it to busy and transmit the message. Once the message has been sent, it is the responsibility of the transmitting station to place a new free token onto the ring.

The format of the free token frame is shown in Figure 12.23 (each field is one byte long).

STX	CTRL	ETX

Figure 12.23   The Commkit free token frame

STX and *ETX* delimit the token packet, while CTRL is the control byte. The free token CTRL byte has a value of 0x04.

Busy token. A busy token is a variable length frame that can hold up to 64 bytes of transparent data. The framing characters are *STX* and *ETX*.

The overall frame structure is displayed in Figure 12.24 (all sizes shown in parentheses are expressed in bytes).

STX (1)	CTRL (1)	DST (1)	SRC (1)	User Data (5 to 64)	CRC (2)	ETX (1)

Figure 12.24   The Commkit busy token frame

The control byte, CTRL, contains one of two values:

BUSY. The frame contains data for a specific station (as indicated by the DST field). A CTRL field set to BUSY has a value of 0x08.

MNTR_PASSED. The frame is BUSY (0x08) and has passed the monitor (0x10).

DST and SRC are the destination and source addresses of the frame, respectively; both are 1-byte long.

To avoid confusing data *ETX* with the end-of-frame delimiter, *ETX*, the ring-network software prefixes all *ETX* and *DLE* bytes with a *DLE*. When bytes are removed from the network for local storage by a station, the prefix *DLE* character is discarded. However, the frame contents are not modified as they are forwarded by a station.

The CRC is generated by the transmitting station using the CRC-16 algorithm and covers the entire frame except for the frame delimiters and the control field. The control field is not included because its value changes as it passes the monitor station.

Emulator states A ring station is always in one of three states: idle, transmitting, or receiving. A station is considered to be in the idle state if it has nothing to transmit although a free token has been detected. If the token is found to be busy, the station enters the receive state, and continues to copy and forward each byte until the end-of-frame byte is detected. The station enters the transmit state if the token is free and a message is waiting to be sent. The token is first set to busy and the message is then transmitted, a byte at a time. Upon completion of the transmission, a free token is put back onto the network.

Idle state. A station is in the idle state if it has just forwarded a free token (either because the station has no data to send or because the station has just finished transmitting). All stations enter the idle state as soon as they are initialized. What a station does in the idle state depends upon whether or not it is the monitor.

If the station is the monitor, it is responsible for ensuring that there is always a token on the ring. This is achieved by running a timer in the background which periodically causes the monitor to check whether token frames (free or busy) are still circulating. If none have been detected, a free token is put onto the ring. The ring monitor state machine is illustrated by the state diagram given in Figure 12.25

The monitor initially waits for an *STX*; upon receipt of an *STX*, the byte is forwarded and the monitor waits for the control byte. Anything other than an *STX* causes the monitor to enter the error state, WAIT_CLK.

When the control byte is received, it is examined by the monitor:

- If the byte indicates a FREE token and the monitor has a message to transmit, the control byte is set to BUSY and MTR_PASS (signalling that the monitor has detected a busy token). The monitor enters the transmit state to allow the transmission of the addresses, the message, and the CRC.

- If the token is BUSY, the monitor changes the control byte to include MTR_PASS as well as BUSY. The control byte is then forwarded and the monitor enters the receive state, and waits for the remainder of the busy token frame.

- If the monitor has no messages to transmit and the control byte indicates a FREE token, the control byte is forwarded and the monitor waits for an *ETX*.
  If the next byte is an *ETX*, the monitor forwards the byte and proceeds to wait for an *STX*. Anything other than an *ETX* causes the monitor to enter the error state, WAIT_CLK.

- If the control byte indicates a BUSY token and the token has passed the monitor (MTR_PASS), or if the control byte is unrecognizable, the monitor enters the error state WAIT_CLK.

All monitor-idle states are associated with a timer. Should a byte fail to arrive at the monitor within a prescribed period of time, the monitor assumes the worst and reissues a new free token onto the ring. If a bad or unknown byte is received by the monitor, the monitor enters the WAIT_CLK state; all subsequent bytes are removed from the ring and the monitor then issues a new free token.

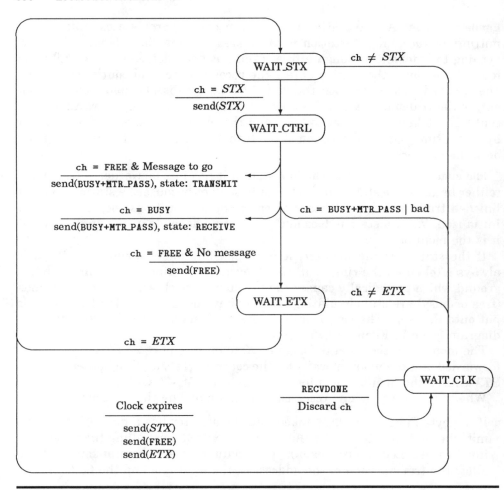

Figure 12.25   The ring monitor idle-state machine

When the monitor is first initialized, a free token frame is sent and the timer is started. If the timer expires before anything is received, another free token frame is issued.

Although all stations support the monitor software, only one station can be the monitor at any moment. If a station is not the monitor, it uses the state machine shown in Figure 12.26 for the idle state.

Except for a number of housekeeping states devised to ensure that the token is circulating, the two state machines are identical. For example, if the monitor has a message to transmit, it must wait for a free token in exactly the same manner as that of a nonmonitor station. The additional monitor states enforce the free token frame structure of *STX*-CTRL-*ETX*. The nonmonitor station leaves the correction of an invalid frame to the monitor.

Transmit state.   The transmit state consists of *two* state machines. The first is for the transmission of data onto the ring, and the second is for the removal of the data from the ring once it has completed the journey around the ring.

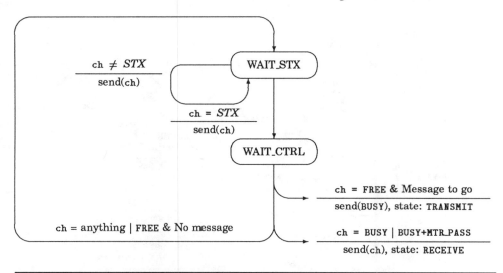

Figure 12.26   The idle-state machine for nonmonitor stations

The transmission state diagram is given in Figure 12.27.

The *STX* and the control field (set to BUSY) are already sent by the time the transmit-state machine is initiated. The transmit-state machine is responsible for sending the destination and source addresses, the bytes in the message, the two CRC bytes, and the final *ETX*. Additionally, *DLE* insertion takes place whenever a *DLE* or an *ETX* is found in the data stream, or as a CRC byte. The CRC includes all transmitted bytes *except* for the control field, any *DLE* prefix bytes, the CRC bytes, and the frame delimiters.

The transmitting station is also responsible for removing its packet from the network. A second state machine runs in parallel with the transmit-state machine, removing the packet from the ring (Figure 12.28).

The removal of a packet from the ring involves taking the remainder of the previous free packet from the ring (an *ETX*) and then waiting for the incoming *STX*. Once the *STX* is detected and removed, all subsequent bytes that make up the packet can be removed. Should an *ETX* be detected in place of the control field, the destination address, or the source address, it is assumed that the transmission has been aborted, probably by the monitor. *DLE* insertion must be recognized to avoid confusing a data *ETX* or a CRC *ETX* with the end-of-packet *ETX*. CRC calculation is not performed.

Receive state.   The receive state is entered after a station receives a packet with the token bit set to BUSY in the control field. The receive state is responsible for copying the message from the network and storing it. Each byte received must be forwarded to allow all the stations on the network access to the packet.

The state machine for a station receiving a packet is as given in Figure 12.29.

Upon detection of a BUSY token, the station waits for the remainder of the frame. Data is removed (and forwarded) in state WAIT_DATA; while *DLE*

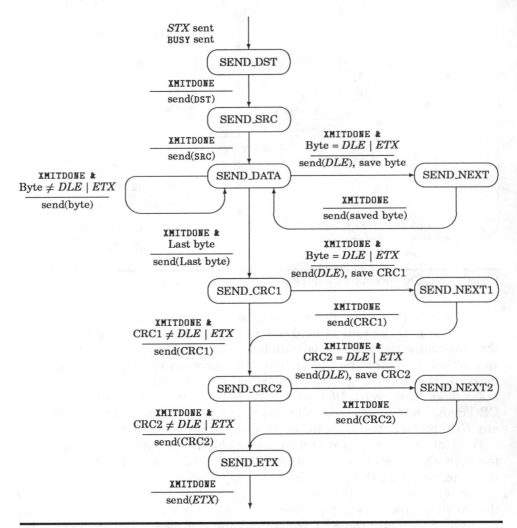

Figure 12.27   The Commkit ring network transmission state machine

removal is handled in state WAIT_NEXT. (Note that *DLE* removal only affects the data to be stored; the *DLE* character is still forwarded.) When the end-of-frame delimiter *ETX* is found, both the CRC and the destination address are examined; if the CRC is zero and the destination address is that of this station, the message is kept, otherwise it is discarded.

12.4.3   The Token Ring Implementation

The Commkit token ring is an implementation of the state machines described in the previous section. The emulator, found in `ringlow.c`, is interrupt driven; serial port and clock interrupts are passed through `low_level()` to `ring_emulator()`. Keyboard interrupts are forwarded to the foreground process (queue: `APPLICATION`), while clock interrupts are forwarded to the

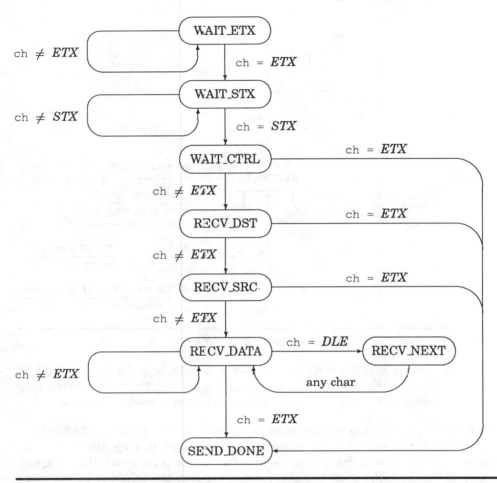

Figure 12.28   The Commkit ring network transmitting station-receive state machine

background process (queue: BACKGROUND_1) HZ times a second. Messages to be sent on the network are supplied by any process to the ring via the queue RINGNET (a redefinition of SP2IH). MSG_AVAIL is ignored since the ring software only checks the RINGNET queue when a free token is received.

Ring_emulator() is called after a serial port interrupt (either XMITDONE or RECVDONE) occurs. Each byte that is received may (or may not) be transmitted to the next station, depending upon the state of the emulator; ring.char_to_go (found in ringdefs.h) indicates whether a character can be transmitted. The fact that the byte just received can be transmitted does not necessarily mean that it will be transmitted immediately. Indeed, there may be other bytes waiting to be transmitted, or a byte may be in the process of being transmitted (indicated by ring.xmit_active). Before attempting to transmit the byte, ring_emulator() checks the queue SP1IH; if the queue is not empty, the byte must be put onto SP1IH (the SP1IH queue acts as an *elastic buffer*, holding those characters that are waiting to be transmitted).

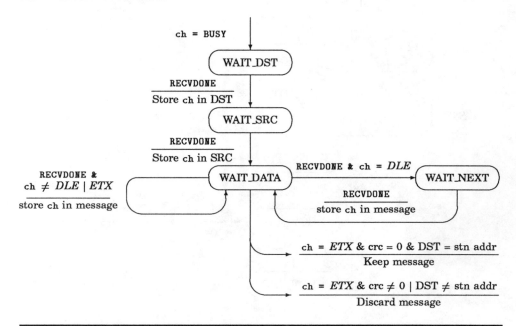

Figure 12.29   The Commkit ring network receive state machine

In the various emulator states, whenever a byte is to be transmitted, it is stored in ring.to_go and ring.char_to_go is set TRUE. The three ring states (indicated by ring.state), and their related procedures follow.

Idle state   The idle state is entered when ring.state is equal to IDLE. Ring_idle() implements both the monitor and monitorless ring-idle state machines in a single procedure. Whenever a free token is received, the RINGNET queue is checked, the presence of a message causes the token to be set BUSY (or both BUSY and MONITOR, if the station is the monitor); the ring.state changes to TRANSMIT. If a BUSY or MNTR_PASSED token is received, the token is flagged to be forwarded and the station enters the RECEIVE state. Should the monitor detect anything amiss in any state, the monitor enters the WAIT_TIMER state, removing all data from the ring until the timer, ring.token_timer, expires. (Token_timer is decremented in check_for_token(), which is called once a second after a clock interrupt in low_level().)

The individual state within the Idle state is indicated by ring.r_state.

Transmission state   The transmission state (indicated by ring.state having a value of TRANSMIT) is entered if a free token has been received and a message is to be sent. The transmission state is implemented as two different procedures: send_byte() (called after an XMITDONE interrupt) and clear_line() (called after a RECVDONE interrupt).

Send_byte() transmits the various characters making up the packet: the destination address, the source addresses, and the bytes in the message (the overall message structure is defined in ring.x_msg). Send_byte() implements the transmit-state machine described in the previous section; the specific transmission state within `send_byte()` is maintained in `ring.x_state`. If a byte requires a *DLE* prefix, `send_byte()` calls `send_dle()`, which "remembers" the byte to be sent as well as the next state.

Bytes are removed from the ring by calls to `clear_line()` after each RECVDONE interrupt. `Clear_line()` implements the byte-removal state machine described in the previous section (the current state is indicated by `ring.r_state`); the incoming bytes are not checked, nor is the value of the CRC. When `ring.x_state` is equal to `ring.r_state` (i.e., they both have the value SEND_DONE) a free token is put onto the ring (by a call to `send_token()`).

Reception state Whenever a BUSY or MNTR_PASSED token is received, `ring.state` changes to RECEIVE. The receive-state machine described in the previous section is implemented in `recv_byte()`. `Recv_byte()` accepts bytes from the ring whenever a RECVDONE interrupt is signalled. The first two bytes are taken to be the destination and source addresses, respectively. The remaining bytes are read from the ring, stored in `ring.r_msg`, and marked for transmission. The specific receiving state is indicated by `ring.r_state`. Upon detection of the end-of-frame *ETX*, the destination address and the CRC are inspected: if the local station is the intended destination, the message is sent to queue BACKGROUND_1; control then returns to the Idle state. If the global variable `promiscuous` is TRUE, all valid frames are accepted and sent to queue BACKGROUND_1, regardless of destination.

Errors such as the packet being too long or a bad CRC cause the reception to be aborted and `ring.state` is changed to IDLE.

All of the routines described are common to both monitor and nonmonitor stations; they are distinguished by the value of `bus.monitor` (TRUE if the station is the monitor, FALSE otherwise).

12.4.4 High-Level Software

The token-ring software performs two basic operations: (1) it takes messages off the RINGNET queue, turns them into packets and transmits them when the opportunity arises, and (2) it copies messages from the network, forwarding them to the BACKGROUND_1 queue. To facilitate ring network experimentation, `ringex.c` contains a number of processes through which the user can communicate with the ring network:

`do_display()`. This is responsible for displaying messages sent by the token-ring emulator to queue BACKGROUND_1. When a message from RINGNET is available, `do_display()` takes the message from the queue and displays it on line 10 enclosed in angle brackets. Messages from the clock interrupt handler are read but ignored.

`do_ring_ex()`. This is the foreground process, accepting characters sent by the keyboard interrupt handler, displaying and storing them in array `buffer`; it is assumed that the data is entered as a valid ring packet (i.e., the destination address, the source address, and up to 64 bytes of data). Upon receipt of a carriage return, `buffer` is forwarded to the token-ring queue RINGNET for eventual transmission. A CTRL-C causes control to return to MS-DOS (the ring ceases to function at this point).

12.5   USING THE COMMKIT TOKEN RING

12.5.1   Compiling the Token Ring

The token ring source code `ringex.c`, `ringlow.c`, and `ringdefs.h` can be compiled and linked with `commkit.obj`, `intrpt.obj`, and `crc.obj` to make `ringex.exe`:

```
C:\> make ringex.exe
```

If changes are made to `ringex.c`, the `make` utility only recompiles `ringex.c`; relinking to the existing object modules.

The Commkit diskette is supplied with an executable version of `ringex.exe`.

12.5.2   Running the Token Ring

To run a compiled version of the token ring, type `ringex`, followed by the line speed (one of 50, 300, 1200, 2400, 4800, or 9600 bps), and the station identifier (any character) after the DOS prompt. For example, to have the network run at 1200 bps and make this station have station address E, type the following:

```
C:\> ringex 1200 E
```

The ring network differs from the bus network in that one station must be the monitor; the monitor station is identified by typing a capital M after the station identifier. The token ring will not function if there is not a monitor station. For example, to make station S the monitor station, type:

```
C:\> ringex 1200 S M
```

If the station is not the monitor station, simply ignore the M or type any other character. As with the other Commkit modules, if the line speed is not recognized or the format of the command line is not adhered to, an error message is generated.

Each PC on the ring must have two serial ports. The PCs are connected by null modem-cables linking serial port 1 with serial port 2. The ring will not function if the ports are not connected in this manner.

Once `ringex.exe` is running, a message can be passed between stations by typing the destination station's address, the source station's address, and then the message. For example, to enquire what the weather is like over by station S, you could type:

```
SEWhat's the weather like over there?
```

At station E, the message would appear part way down the screen enclosed in angle brackets:

```
<SEWhat's the weather like over there?>
```

Any station, including the monitor, can transmit and receive messages. To get a better understanding of how a ring network functions, place a line analyser between two of the stations.

Control can be returned to MS-DOS by typing CTRL-C or CTRL-ALT-DEL. Unlike the other networks examined in the book, once a station is removed from the ring, all communications cease.

12.6 SUMMARY

Local area networks area allow device sharing among all stations on the network. Networks such as the CSMA/CD bus can potentially restrict access to the network (for example, because of exceptionally heavy network traffic) since access is nondeterministic. By changing the topology (either logically or physically) to a ring, it is possible to develop a local area network that permits deterministic access. In other words, there is an upper bound on the length of time a station must wait before accessing the network.

The solution adopted by both the token bus and the token ring is to permit network access only when the station is in possession of the "free" token. When a station receives the free token (from its predecessor, that is either logically or physically upstream from the station), and the station has a message to be sent, a transmission can take place. Once the station has finished transmitting, a new free token is placed onto the network, thereby permitting network access to the downstream stations.

The token bus differs from the token ring in a number of areas; the most obvious being the topology: one is a bus, the other is a ring. Another difference involves network error-recovery methods: in the token bus, recovery from network errors is distributed among all machines; while in the token ring, the monitor station maintains control over the ring.

The token ring is by no means the only physical ring structure possible, a variation on the token ring is the slotted ring, in which the network supports a single frame structure consisting of a control field with space for the token and space for the bytes in the message.

12.7 EXERCISES

1. Set up the three-station ring network shown in Figure 12.30.

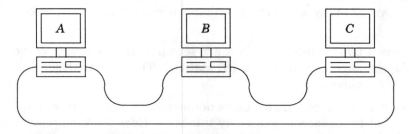

Figure 12.30   A three station ring network

The serial port connections should be as given in Table 12.3. Now, answer the following questions:

TABLE 12.3   Port Connections for Exercise 1

Station	Port 1 (To)	Port 2 (From)
A	C	B
B	A	C
C	B	A

a) If A is the monitor station, B is the analyser and C is inactive, what appears on the line analyser? Why?

b) If C is the monitor station, B is the analyser and A is inactive, what appears on the line analyser? Why?

c) If A is the monitor station, B is the analyser and C is an active ring station; what appears on the line analyser? Send a message from A to C; explain what appears on the analyser. Send a message from C to A; is there a difference in the value of the token? Explain.

d) If C is the monitor station, B is the analyser and A is an active ring station, what appears on the line analyser? Send a message from A to C; explain what appears on the analyser. Send a message from C to A; is there a difference in the value of the token? Explain.

e) If a station sends a message to a nonexistent station (say D), is the message transmitted and carried by the ring network? Explain.

Note that when testing the ring network with the line analyser, the characters given in Table 12.4 appear on the analyser screen.

TABLE 12.4   Line Analyser Representation of Ring Frame

Symbol	Meaning
☺	Beginning of frame.
◇	Free token indication.
↑	Busy token (Passed Monitor bit set).
•	Busy token (Passed Monitor bit cleared).
♡	End of frame.

2. Why do communications cease if a Commkit token-ring station is removed from the network? Why shouldn't this happen on a commercial token ring?

3. What happens if two (or more) stations are set up as the monitor? What happens if a message is sent by a third station? The line analyser can help solve this problem.

4. What happens if all stations are set up as nonmonitor stations? If communications cannot take place, explain why this is so. How can the problem be rectified?

5. Set up the line analyser and a single token-ring station (as the monitor station). Connect the ring network's serial port 1 to the either of the line analyser ports. What happens?

6. Place the line analyser between two stations on the token ring and watch the traffic. How does the ring's traffic differ from that on the bus network? Why is the ring said to be active, while the bus is described as passive?

7. The ring emulator does not handle two (or more) stations transmitting simultaneously; the packet is simply removed by each transmitting station. Modify the ring emulator software to handle multiple tokens.

8. In the introduction to this chapter, the ring network was described as being more efficient than the bus network in some situations. Devise a set of experiments to compare the access times and the various overhead costs of the bus network and the ring network.

9. Modify the Commkit token ring so that the duplicate token situation is handled; that is, two stations on the ring are attempting to transmit simultaneously, the one with the lower address value stops its transmission and allows the other station to proceed.

10. If the monitor station should cease to function, the remaining stations must bid among themselves to determine which station is to become the new monitor. Extend the ring software to allow the remaining stations to bid to become the monitor when the old monitor fails.

    Remember, the Commkit monitor station *cannot* be physically removed from the network, since it is still required to forward each byte on the ring. Therefore, write your software so the monitor station can *logically* be switched out of the ring (for example, reserve a key to signal the monitor software to shut down).

    One straightforward technique is to set `ring.monitor` to FALSE when the user types CTRL-Z (ASCII *SUB*). Then, break the ring by momentarily pulling a null-modem cable out of one of the serial ports. Ideally, the token should have been either damaged or removed entirely from the ring and there is now no monitor.

11. The Commkit ring network is a token ring. Modify the ring software so that it supports a slotted ring.

12. If a channel on a ring network is broken, the circulation of the token stops. Robust ring networks (such as FDDI) allow tokens to circulate in both directions, so that if a break is detected, the loop is still maintained.

    Modify the Commkit token ring so that a cable break can be overcome by circulating the token in the reverse direction when the token arrives at the station where the break has occurred. The design of this is fairly straightforward. Since the RS-232 cable connecting the stations allows full-duplex communications, a backward channel already exists in hardware.

13. When the transmitting station removes the packet from the ring, no CRC calculations are performed. Would CRC calculations be useful when the data is removed from the ring? What benefits, if any, would this give to the transmitting station?

Internetwork Communications

Until now, all network communications have been *intranetwork* communications; that is, the communications take place within a single network. However, there are times when it is necessary for an application on a machine on one network to communicate with a machine on a separate network. Consider the following examples:

- A company consists of a number of separate departments, each with its own local-area network. If electronic information, such as reports or personnel data, is to be exchanged between the various departments, a mechanism is needed to transfer the information between the different networks.

- A group of universities and colleges may all contribute to purchase a "super-computer" which is sited on a local area network at one of the schools. Access to the super-computer from research machines on local area networks at other institutions may require the interconnection of two or more of the various local area networks.

The above are two examples of applications that require *internetwork communications* or communications *between* networks. Internetwork communications take place across a number of interconnected networks. The various networks that make up the internetwork are referred to as an *internet* or *catenet* (short for concatenated network).

Not surprisingly, an internet that spans a region or even a country exhibits many similarities to a wide area network. However, internetwork communications are different from communications on wide area networks for a number of reasons. First, a wide area network is physically a single network, whereas an internet is made up of many distinct networks (it may include wide area networks). Second, the wide area network supports a common set of data-link protocols, shared by the nodes that make up the network; while in an internet, different networks will probably support different data link protocols. Third, a single addressing structure is used within a wide area network, ensuring that each node in the network is uniquely identified; while in an internet, each network supports its own addressing scheme, with no guarantee that the addresses are not duplicated on other networks.

Part 5 examines two issues common to the development and implementation of any internet:

- How does an application on one network identify the intended destination on a remote network?
- How are the various networks involved in the internet interconnected?

Connecting one network to another does not ensure that the two networks can communicate. If nothing else, an application on one network must be able to identify the intended destination service. Chapter 13 examines some of the issues surrounding the development of layered-network architectures to support internetwork communications. Commkit is used to illustrate some of the problems associated with the development of an internetwork architecture.

If all networks making up an internet supported the same protocols and electrical characteristics, interconnecting networks would be a simple task. Since forcing a single network standard on the groups making up the internet may well be impossible (some groups may have already purchased their networks), a mechanism is required to handle protocol-conversion issues when messages flow between the various networks. These mechanisms, known generically as *gateways*, are presented in Chapter 14 and are illustrated by examining the issues surrounding the interconnection of two Commkit networks.

13

Layered Architectures

13.1 INTRODUCTION

With few exceptions, most of the work done thus far on the various Commkit networks has:

- required the user to explicitly build the network packet, identify the destination and source addresses, and, in some cases, enter network-specific control information.

  Although this is useful in teaching the functioning of networks, it is unrealistic to expect the everyday user (other than perhaps someone working on a research project) to perform such tasks. Imagine the user's enthusiasm if every time a message on an 802.5 network is to be sent, the user is required to explicitly type the destination's 48-bit address.

- assumed that the source entity is a process that accepts keyboard characters and forwards them to a remote DTE, where the destination process is responsible for displaying the characters.

  Many operating systems support multiple processes on a single host, meaning that a message arriving at a host for "the process" has little meaning unless the destination process can be explicitly identified.

This chapter considers how communication systems overcome the problems of identifying entities and hiding network-specific features through the use of layered software, producing what is commonly known as a *layered architecture*.

13.2 BACKGROUND

13.2.1 Identifying Remote Entities

Operating systems that support multiple processes require mechanisms whereby individual processes can be identified. For example, in Commkit, each process is associated with a unique identifier (such as APPLICATION, BACKGROUND_1, and so on) and a queue. In Commkit, a source process sends a message to a destination process by supplying the message and the identifier of the destination process to the queue-management software using the send() primitive. Similarly, when a Commkit process is to receive a message, the recv() primitive is invoked, supplying the queue-management software with the process's identifier. The queue associated with the identifier is then accessed and the first available message on the queue is returned to the process.

This model can be extended to the transmission of messages between hosts. That is, a frame containing the process identifier of the destination process could be sent to the destination host. The destination address then consists of two parts: the destination host and the destination process. Upon receipt of the frame, the reception software on the destination host would perform a send() to the destination process specified in the destination address. Overall, the communication software functions like a multiplexer. Messages to various destinations are multiplexed into separate frames and transmitted on the network, while frames are taken from the network and messages demultiplexed using the process identifier (Figure 13.1).

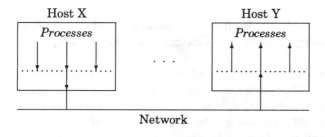

Figure 13.1 Both a process and its host must be identified

Using process identifiers to identify remote processes will work successfully as long as:

- There is a one-to-one mapping between a process and its process identifier.

  In many operating systems supporting multiple processes, a pool of identifiers are recycled among the existing processes. Over a period of time, an identifier may be associated with a number of different processes; as processes terminate, the identifier is freed to be used by a newly created process. Should process identifiers be assigned dynamically, there is no guarantee that the destination process will be associated with the "correct" identifier.

■ All identifiers are the same format.

Different operating systems often use different identifier formats and sizes. This can lead to problems should a network of heterogeneous machines be established. For example, if a 16-bit identifier size is chosen and an operating system that uses 32-bit identifiers is attached to the network, how are 32-bit identifiers to be represented? Similarly, if a 32-bit identifier is taken as the standard, but all identifiers are 16-bits long, space in the frame will be wasted whenever an identifier is transmitted.

From the two situations just described, it should be apparent that process identifiers are not necessarily the best method of identifying a process on a remote host. Ideally, a common process-identifier structure should be agreed upon by all operating systems; however, since this is an unlikely prospect, many communication systems have a second set of identifiers that are used for communications. These identifiers are commonly known as *ports* and have a structure that is agreed upon by all operating systems on the network. A process is associated with its operating system-specific process identifier and is *bound* to as many ports as necessary for the process to perform its communication functions; those processes not involved in network communications are not bound to a port.

For example, in the network depicted in Figure 13.2, processes `Py` and `Pz` are bound to ports 3 and 2 respectively on host E; while on host S, processes `P4`, `P9`, and `P1` are bound to ports 1, 2, and 4, respectively.

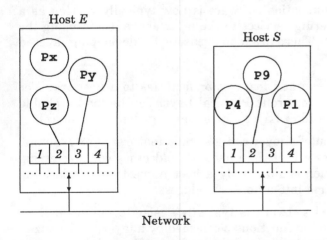

Figure 13.2 Binding processes to ports

The host address and port number are often referred to as a single data structure known as a *socket*; internally, the socket consists of a *host-port* pair. *Host* uniquely identifies the process's host, while *port* identifies the process's port. Should the process number change (for example, the host may crash and reboot, resulting in the software module obtaining a different process number), the system will still function as long as the software module gets the original socket.

Before a process can communicate, it first must bind to a socket. Thereafter, all messages that arrive on the host with the process's port number are returned to the process. When transmitting a message, a process supplies the communication system with the message and the socket of the destination process. The source communication system uses the host identifier to determine the destination host, while the destination communication system uses the port identifier to determine the destination process.

For example, using the Figure 13.2, if process **Py** on host E is to send a message to process **P1** bound to port 4 on host S, the message is sent to socket address $<S,4>$.

Finally, it must be noted that sockets are not the only method of transmitting messages without using explicit process identifiers. For example, a *mailbox* is an intermediate entity that processes can write to and read from. If a process **A** is to send a message to process **B**, the message is written to process **B**'s mailbox. When process **B** reads its mailbox, the message from **A** is returned.

13.2.2 Layering

From the discussion in the previous section, it should be apparent that it is unrealistic to expect each process to support its own version of sockets and the communication software. Instead, most communication software has been developed to offer a range of communication services to processes and their related applications. Communication software is now typically written as a series of *layers*, each one offering services to the layer above it and using the services of the layer below it. There are many reasons for developing layered systems, including:

Enhancing features. Layers can add features or facilities to a network. For example, an unreliable, error-prone Physical Layer can be made reliable through the use of a Data Link Layer supporting a go-back-N protocol.

Hiding features. The addition of a layer can also hide features. For example, it is possible to use names rather than network addresses when referring to a station; an application could supply a host name to an underlying layer which maps the name into a network address.

Ease of modification. Layered software is typically easier to maintain than monolithic software, since the functions performed by a layer are localized to the module associated with the layer in question. Fault detection and subsequent module retesting are also simplified. For example, module testing can be performed in a controlled manner if test software is written that generates the necessary error conditions. This is typically faster than waiting for the error to occur while the module is running.

Portability. Software written in a layered fashion is typically more portable than software that is not. For example, if an application is written for a specific network (say an 802.3 bus) then transferring the application to another network may well require extensive modifications. By writing application software in a *network independent* fashion, moving the application between networks can be a simple task.

Layering has been used extensively in Commkit; for example, the wide area network software consists of four distinct layers:

Physical. The Physical Layer is responsible for the transmission and reception of bytes across the channel.

Data Link. The Data Link Layer defines the channel-packet structure and is responsible for the orderly flow of information between the interconnected DTEs.

Network. The Network Layer is responsible for the establishment, maintenance, and eventual clearing of virtual circuits.

Application. The Application Layer in the wide area network example is a network testing tool that permits the user to establish a number of virtual circuits with various DTEs.

13.3 TERMINOLOGY

Each host attached to the underlying subnet is referred to as a *system*. Within a single subnet, all systems typically support the same layers; the layers themselves are said to form a *layered architecture*. The highest layer of a layered architecture consists of applications and processes using the communication services offered by the underlying layers. The lowest layer deals with the physical connection of the systems making up the subnet.

Although the different layers in a layered architecture perform different functions, there are three underlying similarities:

- Each layer is associated with its own internal protocol. For example, in the Commkit wide area network, the Data Link Layer supports a go-back-N protocol, while the Network Layer has a virtual-circuit protocol.

- Each layer offers services to the layer above it. As an example, the Data Link Layer of Commkit's wide area network offers a reliable point-to-point communication service to the Network Layer.

- Each layer uses the services of the layer below it. For example, the application software in the Commkit wide area network uses the virtual-circuit service offered by the underlying Network Layer.

Because of the widespread use of layering, many layered architectures use a more formal description of each layer and its interactions with its adjacent layers. For example, any layer N offers one or more N-services to the layer above it, layer $N + 1$. Similarly, layer N uses the services offered by the layer below it, layer $N - 1$. Layer $N + 1$ is referred to as the *service user* and layer N, the *service provider*.

Each layer N supports software (or hardware) modules known as *protocol entities* that conform to the N-*protocol* associated with the layer in question.

Protocol entities that exist at the same layer are known as *peer protocol entities*. Peer protocol entities exchange information in *N-protocol data units* *N*-PDUs, using the services of the *N* − 1 layer. The service user that receives information is referred to as the *correspondent user*. This is represented diagramatically in Figure 13.3.

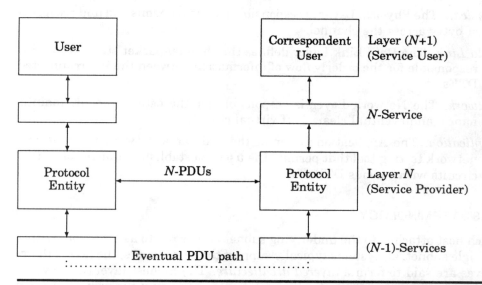

Figure 13.3   Each layer *N* supports a protocol entity that conforms to the *N*-PDU

These definitions are recursive; that is, any layer *N* becomes layer *N* + 1 the further into the architecture one proceeds. At the lowest layer there is no layer *N* − 1; the lowest layer must support the physical interconnection of the systems. Similarly, at the highest layer, there is no layer *N* + 1 other than end users or application processes.

Users at layer *N* + 1 access *N*-services through *service-access point*s (SAPs). Since at any layer *N* + 1 there are potentially multiple users of a particular *N*-service, each service user is assigned a unique SAP address. The boundary between the two layers is known as an *interface* and is crossed through an SAP.

The *N*-layer PDU also contains *N*-layer peer protocol entity control information (such as sequence numbers and checksums) in the *N*-PCI (*N*-protocol control information) as well as the protocol data unit from layer *N* + 1. At layer *N*, the protocol data unit from layer *N* + 1 is referred to as the *N*-SDU (or *N*-service data unit). The *N*-PDU is said to *encapsulate* the (*N* + 1)-PDU. The relationship between the *N* + 1 and *N* layers can be represented as shown in Figure 13.4.

The services offered by any layer fall into two categories: confirmed and unconfirmed (corresponding to the connection-oriented and connectionless services discussed in previous chapters). Support for the transfer of information is described by four primitives (the first two are used by both confirmed and unconfirmed services, while the last two are for confirmed services only).

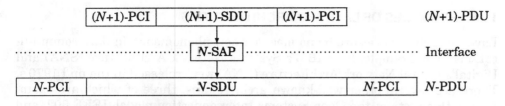

Figure 13.4   The relationship between the $N+1$ and N layers

Request. A service user initiates a transfer to a correspondent user by passing a request primitive to the service provider. The service provider takes this information (an SDU) and encapsulates it into a PDU. The PDU is sent to the correspondent service provider on the remote system using the services provided by the underlying layers.

Indication. Upon reception of the PDU, the correspondent service provider supplies the correspondent user with an indication primitive.

Response. The correspondent user is expected to acknowledge the reception of the indication with a response primitive. The correspondent service provider returns the response to the originating system in a PDU.

Confirm. When the original service provider receives the PDU, a confirm primitive is returned to the user.

The information flow between the $(N+1)$-layer users and the N-layer service is as shown in Figure 13.5 (the response-confirm primitives are only used in confirmed services).

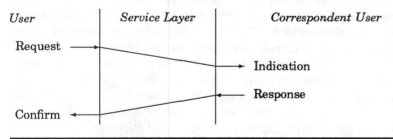

Figure 13.5   Information flow between $(N+1)$-layer users and N-layer service

Many layered architectures have adopted the notation *layer.service.primitive* when referring to the services required by a user at a particular layer. Typical services include *CONNECT* (for establishing a connection), *DATA* (for the transfer of data), *DISCONNECT* or *CLEAR* (for clearing a connection), and *RESET* (for resetting a connection). For example, when establishing a virtual circuit in the Commkit wide area network, the application issues a *CONNECT* request, written as *A.CONNECT.request* and includes the address of the destination application, where *A* denotes application.

13.4   EXAMPLES OF LAYERED ARCHITECTURES

Layered architectures are by no means a new phenomenon in data communications. For example, both IBM's Systems Network Architecture (SNA) and Digital's Digital Network Architecture (DNA) were released in the mid 1970's. There are several other well-known architectures, three of which are examined in this section: the Open Systems Interconnection model, IEEE 802, and the DARPA Protocol Architecture.

13.4.1   The Open Systems Interconnection Reference Model

Proprietary products such as SNA restrict users to a specific manufacturer's line of equipment. When SNA was introduced, both customers and manufacturers alike recognized this problem, and in the late 1970's began pushing for an "open" architecture for which all manufacturers could develop products. The objective of such an architecture was to allow customers with equipment from different manufacturers to communicate on the same subnet, given adherence to a set of agreed-to standards.

Probably the best known example of an open architecture is the *Open Systems Interconnection* (OSI) reference model proposed in the late 1970's by the International Organization for Standardization (ISO). The OSI model consists of seven layers, each of which supports one or more services. Although the OSI model is a standard, it is not an implementation standard. That is, the model explains what each of the seven layers should do; however, the services and protocols associated with each layer are not specified in the model. (Section 13.3 described layering using OSI terminology.)

The main objective of the OSI model is to support communications between end-users on different systems. The end-users are not part of the OSI model, they simply use the facilities offered by the model. The four upper-most layers (*Application, Presentation, Session,* and *Transport*) support end-to-end protocols that are network independent. The lowest three layers (*Network, Data Link,* and *Physical*) support protocols that are network dependent.

Figure 13.6 illustrates the logical and physical flow of information between a pair of end-users on different systems. Messages exchanged between end-users flow vertically through the system until they reach the Physical Layer, at which point the message is transmitted between systems (*xPDU* denotes the PDU used by a specific layer; *Packets, Frames,* and *Bits* normally are not referred to in terms of PDUs).

Network-dependent layers   The lowest three layers of the OSI model (Physical, Data Link, and Network) are network dependent, defining protocols for the transfer of information between systems.

The *Physical Layer* is the lowest layer in the OSI model (layer 1), and is responsible for the transmission of bits over a physical channel. It covers issues such as signalling, modulation, as well, it defines how components are physically interconnected. Examples of standards that are intended for the Physical Layer include RS-232-C, RS-449, and X.21. Physical Layer standards for local area networks include IEEE 802.3 (ISO 8802.3), IEEE 802.4

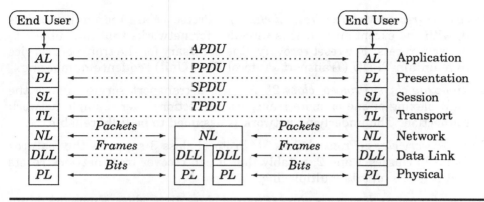

Figure 13.6   The logical and physical flow of information in OSI model

(ISO 8802.4), and IEEE 802.5 (ISO 8802.5). Newer Physical Layer standards include those for ISDN networks, such as I430/1.

The second layer in the OSI model is the *Data Link Layer*. This layer is responsible for the transfer of information in the form of frames across the underlying Physical Layer. The Data Link Layer can be reliable, overcoming Physical Layer errors using go-back-N protocols. Examples of Data Link Layer protocols include HDLC, SDLC, ADCCP, and LAP-B. In some networks, the Data Link Layer is unreliable and each frame is treated as a datagram. Examples of unreliable Data Link Layer protocols are the local area network protocols 802.3 and 802.5.

The *Network Layer* is the third layer of the OSI model and handles the routing of packets across the underlying subnet. In connection-oriented networks, the Network Layer is responsible for call establishment, data transfer, and call clearing. CCITT X.25 is an example of a Network Layer protocol. ISO standards include ISO 8473 and 8348.

Network independent layers   The lower three layers of the OSI model describe point-to-point communications between pairs of nodes on a subnet. The remaining layers assume that the underlying layers can carry information to a given remote system.

The fourth layer, the *Transport Layer*, defines how end-to-end communications can be established and maintained across the subnet. One of the functions of the Transport Layer is to make the network transparent to the remaining upper layers of the OSI model. OSI defines five different classes of connection-oriented transport service. Each class offers a specific quality of service based upon the underlying Network Layer's quality of service:

Simple class (Protocol class 0). The simple class is intended to operate over networks with low failure and error rates. A class 0 Transport Layer service therefore does not enhance the service offered by the Network Layer, since it leaves sequencing and flow control to the Network Layer. In class 0, there is one network connection for each transport connection; should the network connection fail, the transport connection will also fail.

Basic error-recovery class (Protocol class 1). Protocol class 1 is similar to class 0, with the exception that it is intended for networks that are subject to network resets. For reset recovery, it is necessary for the transport service to maintain TPDU (Transport Protocol Data Unit) sequence numbering.

Multiplexing class (Protocol class 2). A class 2 transport service allows the multiplexing of one or more transport connections over a single network connection. The underlying network is assumed to be fully reliable.

Error-recovery class (Protocol class 3). Protocol class 3 supports the features found in classes 1 and 2, notably that it can recover from network resets and it also supports multiplexing.

Error-detection and recovery class (Protocol class 4). A class 4 network is intended to operate atop a datagram network; meaning that extensive error detection and handling features are necessary (i.e., sequence numbering, CRC checking, timeouts, and TPDU retransmission).

Transport Layer protocols include ISO 8072 (OSI transport service), ISO 8073 (OSI transport protocols), and CCITT X.214 and X.224.

The fifth layer of the OSI model is the *Session Layer.* Unlike the lower layers that are concerned with data transportation issues, the Session Layer deals with the management of interactions (or dialogs) of the two end-users. Each session connection has a corresponding transport connection. Should the transport connection fail, the Session Layer can re-establish the connection transparently (i.e., without end-user intervention). Similarly, once an end-user has completed a session, the Session Layer may choose to keep the transport connection active, initiating another session across the same transport connection.

The Session Layer may offer a number of different data-transfer services. The Session Layer supports both full- and half-duplex user dialogs. In half-duplex, the transmitting user is in possession of a permission-to-transmit token; the token can be exchanged by the users. Other data transfer services include *quarantining* and *synchronization.* Quarantining allows the local Session Layer to withhold delivery of a number of messages until explicitly instructed to deliver them by the remote Session Layer. Synchronization is intended to allow a data transfer to "rewind" to a checkpoint specified by end-user application. Both the quarantining and synchronization services are useful in transaction-oriented applications where the loss or retransmission of information may lead to inconsistencies in, for example, a database.

In a truly open system, there is no guarantee that the equipment available to one end-user will be the same as that available to another. If the two end-users are to communicate, it may be necessary to convert the information format used on one system to that used by another. For example, one system may use ASCII and the other EBCDIC; similarly, the internal representation of integer or floating-point numbers may differ, requiring some form of conversion. Layer 6 of the OSI model, the *Presentation Layer*, deals with the representation and transformation of the data between Application Layer entities.

In its simplest form, each system's Presentation Layer could support a translator for every other possible system on the network. If there are N different systems on the network, a total of $N \times (N - 1)$ translators would be needed. However, if a common network-wide information representation is chosen, then only $2 \times N$ translators are needed: one from the machine's internal representation to the network external representation, and the other from the external representation to the internal representation.

Presentation Layer protocols include CCITT X.409, Presentation Transfer Syntax, and GM's MAP Standard Message Format. In GM's Presentation Layer protocol, internal data is converted into a structure consisting of a type identifier (for example, *Boolean*, *Integer*, or *Floating Point*), an optional-length indicator (depending upon the type), and the converted value. For example, Booleans are a single byte (0×00 for true and $0 \times FF$ for false), while a floating-point number is converted into an ASCII string.

The Presentation Layer can also be responsible for the encryption and decryption of information as well as file compression.

The *Application Layer* is the uppermost layer of the OSI reference model, offering application services to the different end-users. Some of the more common application services include file transfer protocols, electronic mail (such as X.400), and virtual terminals (such as X.28 and X.29).

To avoid the duplication of work at the Application Layer, three types of application elements are proposed by the OSI model for use by end-user applications:

- Elements within the end-user application that deals with accessing OSI services (*User Elements—UE*).

- Elements that have capabilities that can be useful to a variety of applications (*Common Application Service Elements—CASE*).

- Elements that have capabilities for specified applications (*Specific Application Service Elements—SASE*).

13.4.2   IEEE 802

The lower three layers of the Open Systems Interconnection model are intended for connection-oriented wide area networks. These networks exhibit a number of common properties, including low speeds (typical maximums of about 56 kbps), high error rates (about 1 bit in 10^5), and the need to perform packet routing from node-to-node. Accordingly, the protocols proposed and developed for the lower levels of the OSI model overcome these limitations.

Since local area networks such as the Ethernet and the IBM Token Ring are faster (speeds of 10 Mbps and up), exhibit lower error rates (about 1 bit in 10^9, and do not require routing), many of the functions provided by the lower OSI layers are redundant or unnecessary in a LAN environment. In short, many of the protocols associated with the lower layers of the OSI model area considered to be too *heavy-weight* for local area networks.

The IEEE recognized these limitations and set about defining the 802 standard, intended for high-speed, low-error rate local area networks. 802 protocols are *light-weight* protocols. As with the OSI model, one of the objectives of the 802 standard is to ensure that equipment from different manufacturers can communicate if the standard is adhered to.

The 802 standard is a three-layer architecture that encompasses the Physical and Data Link Layers of the OSI model. Figure 13.7 shows the overall structure of the 802 protocol family and its relationship to the OSI model.

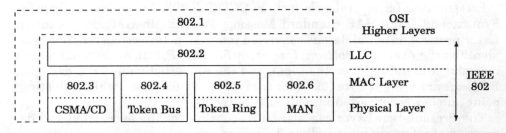

Figure 13.7   Structure of the 802 protocol family and its relationship to the OSI model

The IEEE-802 standard consists of the following parts:

802.1. Overview, internetworking, and systems management; defining the relationship between the various 802 protocols and the ISO higher-layer protcols.

802.2. The Logical Link Control (LLC) sublayer.

802.3. CSMA/CD bus-access method (described in Chapter 11).

802.4. Token-passing bus-access method (described in Chapter 12).

802.5. Token-passing ring-access method (described in Chapter 12).

802.6. Metropolitan-area network (MAN) access method (described in Chapter 12).

The various 802 Physical Layers have been described in Chapters 11 (802.3 CSMA/CD) and 12 (802.4 Token Bus, 802.5 Token Ring, and 802.6 MAN). The OSI Data Link Layer is divided into two parts: the MAC (or Media Access Control) Layer and the LLC (or Logical Link Control) Layer.

Media Access Control (MAC)   The Media Access Control (MAC) sublayer provides three information exchange primitives to the LLC sublayer, regardless of the underlying network. The three service primitives are as follows (note that OSI terminology is used):

MA.DATA.request. The *MA.DATA.request* primitive takes three parameters from the LLC sublayer: the network address of the destination SAP (either a unicast, broadcast, or multicast address), the SDU to be transmitted (i.e., an LLC PDU) and a service class requesting a certain priority level. The SDU is transmitted by the MAC layer using the Physical Layer services of the underlying network.

The service class is used by networks that can support different levels of priority, such as the 802.5 token ring. The MAC sublayer transmits the frame with the specified priority. Networks such as 802.3, which do not support priorities, simply ignore the service class.

MA.DATA.indication. The *MA.DATA.indication* returns the source and destination address as well as the received SDU to the correspondent LLC sublayer. The status of the reception is also returned, indicating whether the frame was received correctly, or the reason the reception failed.

MA.DATA.confirm. The transmission status of the *MA.DATA.request* is returned by *MA.DATA.confirm* to the LLC user, verifying the completion of the transmission or specifying a reason for the failure.

The result returned by *MA.DATA.confirm* only indicates the success of the transmission at the MAC sublayer. In networks such as the 802.5 token ring, the confirmation is extracted from the status bits in the ring frame. However, in the 802.3 CSMA/CD network, the confirmation is generated locally; an example of an 802.3 transmission failure is when the collision limit is reached.

A time-sequence diagram of these primitives and the MAC and LLC sublayers is shown in Figure 13.8.

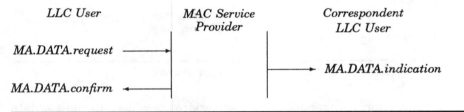

Figure 13.8   MAC services offered to the LLC user

Logical Link Control (LLC)   The Logical Link Control (LLC) sublayer offers three types of service to the upper OSI layers: unacknowledged connectionless; connection-oriented; and acknowledged connectionless. The connectionless services are intended for applications that support their own error checking and recovery schemes.

The unacknowledged connectionless service supports two service primitives: *L.DATA.request*, for the transfer of an SDU to a given remote address; and *L.DATA.indication*, which signals the receipt of an SDU. This service is a datagram service; there are no acknowledgements associated or supported with this service. The time-sequence diagram for the unacknowledged connectionless service is as given in Figure 13.9.

In the acknowledged connectionless service, an *L.DATA_ACK.request* contains an SDU that the delivery of is acknowledged by the remote LLC sublayer (Figure 13.10).

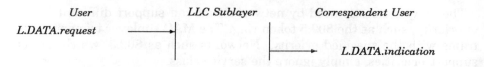

Figure 13.9   Unacknowledged connectionless service

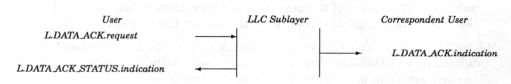

Figure 13.10   Acknowledged connectionless service

The connection-oriented service allows the service user to request the establishment of a connection using *L.CONNECT.request* (note that there is no *L.CONNECT.response* since the response is generated by the correspondent LLC sublayer). See Figure 13.11.

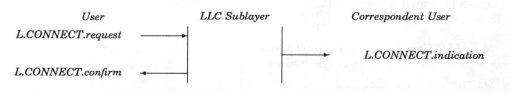

Figure 13.11   Connection-oriented service, connection request

Once the connection is established, either service user may initiate a data transfer using *L.DATA_CONNECT.request* (Figure 13.12).

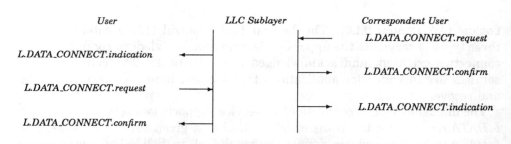

Figure 13.12   Connection-oriented service, data transfer

The connection can be cleared by either user issuing an *L.DISCONNECT.request* (Figure 13.13).

In all three types of service, the addresses supplied to the LLC SAP indicate the destination LLC SAP as well as the destination physical address.

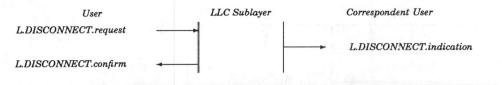

Figure 13.13   Connection-oriented service, connection clearing

Regardless of the type of service, there is a single LLC Protocol Data Unit (LLC PDU) format (all sizes are in bytes). See Figure 13.14. Each field in the LLC PDU is defined as follows:

DST SAP (1)	SRC SAP (1)	Control (1)	Information (M)

Figure 13.14   LLC Protocol Data Unit

DST SAP. The destination LLC service-access point address. One bit indicates whether the SAP is an individual or group address, meaning that any one of 128 individual or 128 group LLC SAPs may be specified.

SRC SAP. The LLC service-access point of the source of the Information.

Control. Each LLC PDU is sent with a control field; the format and contents of which is based upon the HDLC protocol-control field (see Chapters 6 and 10). The connection-oriented service supports both information- and supervisory-control fields. On the other hand, the connectionless services use the unnumbered-information (UI) control field.

Information. A variable length data field, M is a multiple of 8-bits. M can be zero; for example, when sending supervisory PDUs.

There is no LLC checksum, the MAC layer FCS is assumed to offer sufficient error-detection capabilities.

13.4.3   The DARPA Protocol Architecture

The *DARPA Protocol Architecture* (DPA) is an example of an open-system architecture developed for a single (large) customer: the U.S. military. DPA was originally developed in the mid-1970's as part of the U.S. military's DARPA (Defense Advanced Research Project Agency) study of internetwork communications. Earlier research funding from DARPA (or ARPA as it was known in the 1960's) went into the development of the ARPANET packet-switching network.

The DARPA protocol architecture consists of three network-independent layers, built atop the network-access services of any underlying network. The layers and their relationship to the OSI model are as illustrated in Figure 13.15.

The DARPA Protocol Architecture is intended to operate atop almost any type of network, as long as the necessary software exists between the Internet and Network-Access Layers. The underlying network can be connection-oriented or connectionless, a wide area network or a local area network. The

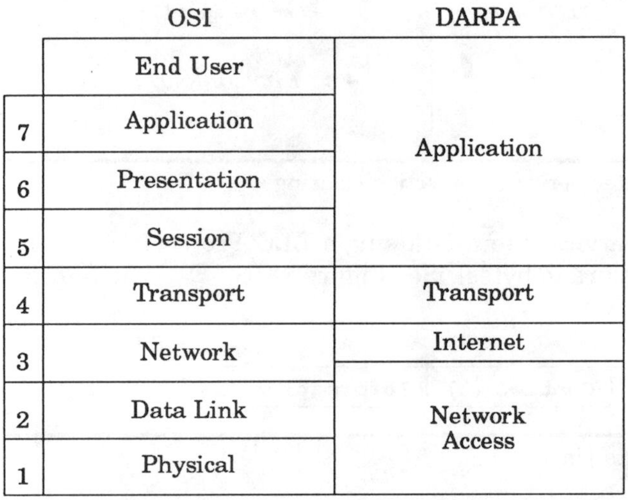

OSI   DARPA

	End User	Application
7	Application	
6	Presentation	
5	Session	
4	Transport	Transport
3	Network	Internet
2	Data Link	Network Access
1	Physical	

Figure 13.15   Relationship between the OSI model and the DARPA architecture

type of service offered by the underlying network is transparent to the top three layers.

In order to achieve this transparency, the designers of the DPA recognized the need to have network independent host addresses. Since different networks support different address structures, each host is assigned a unique 32-bit *Internet address*. When a packet is available for transmission, it is supplied with the destination host's Internet address in an *Internet datagram* to the Internet Layer. The Internet Layer maps the Internet address into a network-specific physical address; this address is then used by the Network Access Layer as the destination address.

Should the Internet Layer not recognize the Internet address, an *Address Resolution Protocol* (ARP) packet containing the unknown Internet address is broadcast on the network. The station with the address in question returns its physical address in an ARP reply packet.

The Internet Layer offers a connectionless datagram service to the Transport Layer (this service is known as *IP* or the *Internet Protocol* (IP)). The Internet datagram contains two parts: a header and a data area. The Internet Layer can fragment datagrams if they are too large for the underlying network. The datagram header contains control information as well as the destination and source Internet addresses.

The Transport Layer offers two levels of service to applications:

- A datagram protocol known as *User Datagram Protocol* (UDP). UDP messages are supplied to the Internet Layer for transmission to a given internet destination. Since a single host may have many processes transmitting and receiving UDP messages, each host has a number of UDP ports to which UDP messages are addressed.

    Upon receipt of a UDP message from the underlying network, the Internet Layer supplies the message to the UDP service, which makes the message available to the process associated with the port specified in the UDP message.

- A reliable full-duplex connection-oriented stream protocol known as *Transmission Control Protocol* (TCP). A message sent by TCP is sent in a *segment*, consisting of a TCP header and a data part. The header contains the source and destination ports as well as a 32-bit sequence number and a 32-bit acknowledgement number. TCP is a sliding-window protocol, the sequence and acknowledgement numbers specify the current byte number and the number of the next expected byte, respectively. The window size is expressed in bytes and each segment is sent with a checksum.

  TCP is usually referred to as TCP/IP since the TCP protocol is interwoven with IP.

Operating systems such as UNIX 4.3BSD support both TCP/IP and UDP. In UNIX 4.3, the combination of the host Internet address and the port number is known as a *socket*.

The Application Layer is the highest layer of DPA; it consists of user and application-specific processes directly accessing TCP/IP and UDP. Some of the better known application services include:

SMTP. Simple Mail Transfer Protocol (SMTP), the DPA electronic mail protocol. SMTP operates atop TCP/IP.

Rlogin. A remote login service offered by UNIX 4.3 BSD, allowing users on one UNIX machine to connect to a remote UNIX machine. Since multiple remote logins are possible, each login, once established, communicates through its own TCP/IP port.

TELNET. TELNET is similar to rlogin, with the exception that TELNET is intended for any remote host supporting the DPA. TELNET operates atop TCP/IP.

FTP. File Transfer Protocol (FTP), is a reliable file transfer protocol that uses both TCP/IP and TELNET. TCP/IP handles the transfer of the file, while TELNET allows the user to signon to the remote host from which the file transfer is to take place.

TFTP. Trivial File Transfer Protocol (TFTP) is a datagram file transfer protocol that uses the UDP protocol.

In all of these examples, each service is associated its own well-known port.

The OSI model, unlike DPA, offers a degree of reliability at each of the lowest four layers. The DPA approach is to have the application service handle reliability on an end-to-end basis.

Although the DARPA Protocol Architecture is used widely for intranetwork communications, it is actually intended for internetwork communications. The internetworking aspects of IP are discussed in more detail in the following chapter.

13.5 COMMKIT SOCKETTES

Commkit supports a simplified version of UNIX UDP sockets, known as *sockettes*. Sockettes offer the foreground process a number of communication primitives that hide the underlying network. The sockette software is designed to work with any of the Commkit networks (i.e., wide area, bus, and ring).

Other than a few lines of specialized code for the calls to the individual networks, the sockette software is identical for all networks; meaning that the replacement of one network by another is transparent to the user software.

Each host in a sockette network is assigned a *name* and a corresponding internal sockette host number. This information is stored in the file `hosts`. The physical station addresses are stored in a separate file, `addrs`, and contain the internal sockette host number along with the associated physical address.

Each foreground process can be associated with up to three sockettes. The sockette itself consists of two parts: a host number and a port number. Host numbers are obtained by the process either from an incoming sockette message or supplying a host name to the `gethostbyname()` primitive (see following discussion). There are ten different port numbers, some of which are "well-known" and are intended for specialized applications. For example, `ECHO_PORT` is port 2 and is intended for a foreground process that echoes each message that it receives.

13.5.1 Sockette Data Structures

The sockette data structures are defined in `sockette.h` and `sockcode.h`. Data structures in `sockette.h` are specific to the primitives found in `sockette.c`, while `sockcode.h` contains sockette return codes and other data structures intended for sockette-application software.

A sockette address (defined in structure `sockaddr`) consists of two fields, a `port` (of type `port_address`, an unsigned character) and a host address, `addr` (of type `host_address`, an unsigned integer). A process *must* be bound to a sockette address if it is to partake in a communication.

Regardless of the network, all sockette messages are sent as part of the `network_msg` structure (Figure 13.16).

net_dst	net_src	sock_dst	sock_src	net_msg

Figure 13.16 The Commkit sockette message structure

The fields in the sockette message are defined as follows:

net_dst   The physical network address of the destination host of the message. This is obtained from file `addrs`.

net_src   The physical network address of the source host of the message. This is obtained from file `addrs`.

sock_dst   The socket address of the destination process, consisting of the destination host and port numbers. **Sock_dst** is generated by the transmitting process.

sock_src   The socket address of the process sending the message and contains the host and port numbers of the transmitting process.

net_msg   An array of up to MAX_NET_SIZE bytes of data.

The network message is transmitted in the underlying network's frame, according to the rules associated with the network in question.

The file hosts consists of one or more host number-host name pairs, entered on separate lines. The host number is any positive integer, while the host name is any name up to nine characters in length. The host number is separated from the host name by one or more spaces. The hosts file is read once, into the data structure host_addrs. The maximum size of host_addrs is set in NUM_HOSTS.

Addresses are kept in the file addrs, in which each entry is a host number followed by the physical address of the station, separated by a single space. The host number is a positive integer, and, in keeping with Commkit's network address structure, the physical address is a single character. Addrs is also read only once into the structure addr_to_physical, the maximum size of which is set in NUM_HOSTS.

13.5.2 Sockette Primitives

The Commkit sockette software supports seven primitives, all of which are found in sockette.c.

int gethostbyname(name, *address)   Gethostbyname() scans the list of host names to find a name that matches the supplied name (a character string). If the supplied name exists, the address of the name is returned in address (a pointer to a host_address structure). If the name is found, SUCCESS is returned, otherwise FAIL.

int getport(*portnum)   Getport() returns the *next* available port in portnum. An explicit port can be requested by entering a positive, nonzero value in portnum (a pointer to a structure of type port_address). If no ports remain or the requested port is already in use, FAIL is returned, otherwise SUCCESS.

int bind(*address)   Bind() attempts to bind the process with the supplied sockette address, address (a pointer to a sockaddr structure). Bind() returns one of the following codes:

- If the port specified in the address is invalid, bind() returns FAIL.

- If the sockette's port address is already in use or all of the sockettes allocated to the process are in use, bind() fails, returning an error code of PORT_IN_USE.

- If the sockette address is acceptable, bind() returns a *sockette number*. The sockette number has a value between 0 and TOTAL_SOCKETTES and must be used by the process whenever the address is to be used as the source address of a message.

int release(sock_no)   Release() attempts to dissociate the process from the specified sockette number, sock_no. The three possible return codes from release() are:

SUCCESS is returned if the sock_no supplied by the process is active.

FAIL is returned if the value of sock_no is outside the range of legal sockette numbers.

NOT_BOUND is returned if the process is not associated with the supplied sockette number.

int get_net_address(sock_host_addr, *phy_host_addr)   Get_net_address() converts the sockette host address pointed to by sock_host_addr to a physical host address, a network address pointed to by phy_host_addr. If the address doesn't exist, FAIL is returned, otherwise SUCCESS.

int sendto(sock_no, *buf, len, *to)   Sendto() sends the message pointed to by buf of length len to the host-port pair specified by the socket address to. If the size of the message is greater than the allowable message length (specified in MAX_NET_SIZE) or the process attempting to transmit is not bound to the sockette number sockette, sendto() fails and returns an error code of BAD_SIZE or NOT_BOUND, respectively. The source socket is obtained by mapping the socket number sock_no into the address supplied to bind().

Note that since the to address can specify any process bound to any sockette (on any machine), it is possible to transmit messages between sockettes on the same machine.

int recvfrom(sock_no, *buf, len, *from)   Recvfrom() returns the first available message that is received for the process's sockette number sock_no (i.e., the address to which the sockette number refers). The message is copied into the memory pointed to by buf. The sockette address of the transmitting process is extracted from the network message and placed into from. The size of the message is returned if a message is available.

If sock_no is outside the range of permissible sockette numbers, FAIL is returned. A length greater than MAX_NET_SIZE results in a return code of BAD_SIZE. If there is no message available, FAIL is returned (i.e., recvfrom() supports asynchronous reception only).

In addition to the above, sockette_init() must be called once, prior to any sockette activity. Sockette_init() initializes the various sockette tables.

13.5.3 Sockette Software Layering

The Commkit sockette software consists of five layers that are depicted in Figure 13.17.

Foreground Process
Sockette Layer
Network Layer
Network-emulation Software
Hardware

Figure 13.17 The Commkit sockette software structure

The tasks associated with each layer are defined as follows:

Foreground Process. All applications using the sockette software must be written as the foreground process (the reason for this is explained later). For communications to take place, the process must first bind to a sockette, thereafter messages can be sent.

Sockette Layer. The Sockette Layer is called by the foreground process whenever a sockette operation is required.

Network Layer. The Network Layer is responsible for determining the destination of any message that is received (either from the network-emulation software or from the foreground process). All messages are network_msgs that are received and forwarded using the recv() and send() primitives, respectively.

Network-emulation Software. The network emulators remain unchanged, all messages that are received are forwarded to the Network Layer through queue BACKGROUND_1.

Hardware. The hardware-interrupt handlers remain unchanged.

13.5.4 Sockette Implementation

The Commkit sockette software is designed to allow sockette communication between foreground processes. The sockette software is divided into two parts: a high-level part consisting of the sockette primitives described in Section 13.5.2, and a low-level part, handling sockette messages from the network and the foreground process.

At any particular moment, the foreground process can be bound to as many as three different sockettes; each active sockette is assigned a sockette number that the process uses when sending and receiving sockette messages. A sockette number is returned after a successful bind() has taken place. The sockette number is an index into the data structure proc_info, an array indicating the status of each sockette (i.e., whether the sockette is in use) and, if the sockette is in use, the sockette's address consisting of a host-port pair.

Whenever a `sendto()` takes place, the sockette number is used as an index into `proc_info` to obtain the sockette address; this address is the source address of the sockette message.

The mapping of textual host names into physical address is a two step operation. First, the array `host_addrs` is used to map the name into the sockette host identifier. Second, the sockette host identifier is mapped into a station's physical address by searching the array `addr_to_physical`.

Each host supports a total of `TOTAL_PORTS` ports; the foreground process can bind to any port that is free. The data structure `port_tbl` contains the status of each port; that is, whether the port is free or has been bound to. If bound, the data structure also contains the queue associated with the port. When the foreground process calls the `recvfrom()` primitive, the port associated with the sockette (obtained by indexing `proc_info` and extracting the port number) is used to index `port_tbl`. If a message is available on the port's queue, it is returned to the foreground process.

Regardless of the source of a sockette message (i.e., either the local foreground process or the network from a remote process), all sockette messages are sent to `network_layer()`. `Network_layer()` compares the physical destination-host address in the network packet with the host's address (`stn_id`). If these two are identical, the destination-port number is used to determine whether the port has been bound to. The message is put onto the destination port's queue if the foreground process is bound to the port in question.

If the packet is not destined for this host, `network_layer()` attempts to forward the packet. The forwarding algorithm is network dependent and selected at compile time in `makefile`:

Wide area network. All messages (from either serial port or the foreground process) are sent to `network_layer()`; Network Layer routes the message by examining the host's identifier and the source of the message (i.e., a serial port or the foreground process). Messages to unknown destinations are discarded.

Ring network. The source of all messages is the foreground process; the message is sent to queue `RINGNET` for subsequent transmission.

Bus network. The source of all messages is the foreground process; the message is sent to queue `BUSNET` for subsequent transmission.

The overall flow of messages is given in Figure 13.18.

The design and final implementation of the sockette software was influenced by the following issues:

- First, since a special initialization call to the Network Layer process is necessary to bind to a sockette, it was decided that only the Commkit foreground process should use sockettes.

- Second, if sockette messages are forwarded by the Network Layer to the foreground process, the sockette primitive `recvfrom()` is not necessary because the message is obtained using a `recv()`.

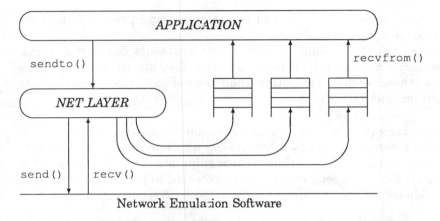

Figure 13.18   Network independent message paths in the sockette software

Fortunately, the second problem is solved by the first. By restricting the use of sockettes to the foreground process, the background queues BACKGROUND_2, BACKGROUND_3, and BACKGROUND_4 can be used to queue sockette messages (queue BACKGROUND_1 is used by the Network Layer). Whenever a successful bind() takes place, the resulting sockette number is used as an index into port_queue_list, a list of the aforementioned background queues. The foreground process is still required to periodically call recv() to ensure that the Network Layer is invoked to handle any sockette messages and to receive any keyboard messages.

Finally, the Network Layer software is required to send a message to the foreground process whenever a sockette message has been queued. This is to ensure that the foreground process (waiting on queue APPLICATION) doesn't wait forever while sockette messages are being queued and not read.

13.5.5 Sockette Example

Three examples of how sockettes function are found in sockex.c:

do_echo()   Do_echo() is a sample echo service; any message that the echo service receives is returned to the sender of the message. Determining the sender of the message is a trivial operation, since the source of the message is supplied in the from address, obtained when recvfrom() is called. The from address is used as the destination address when the message is returned. The echo process binds to port ECHC_PORT.

Echo servers are often used when testing communications software since they have a well-known address and perform the basic server functions of receiving a request and issuing a response.

do_time()   Do_time() is a time server that returns the time of day to any process that requests the time of day. As with the echo process, the source address is available in the frcm address. The time of day is obtained by calling time(), to get the time in seconds, and ctime() to convert the time to ASCII. The time of day is returned to the requesting process. The time server process binds to port TIME_PORT.

Time servers are often found in network environments consisting of machines that do not maintain the time of day when they are shut off. The time server allows these machines to initiate their time of day clock when they are first brought on-line.

do_send_and_recv()   Do_send_and_recv() allows the user to send and receive sockette messages from any other process on the network (including itself). A series of commands allow the user to manipulate the sockette software. The commands that the user can select are processed in process_string() and are as follows (all commands are terminated with a carriage return):

- To bind to a port, the user types CTRL-B NUMBER, where NUMBER is any port number between 0 and 9. If the bind is successful, the sockette number associated with the port is displayed to the user, otherwise an error message is issued.

  Neither the sockette number nor the host-port pair is kept, since the sockette number is supplied to the user for subsequent use.

- To release a sockette (and hence its port), the user types CTRL-R NUMBER, where NUMBER is a sockette number between 0 and 2. If the sockette cannot be released, an error message is issued. The sockette number is obtained from the command CTRL-B.

- Each sockette message must be sent with a source host-port pair. Since the user has three different sockettes from which to choose, the command CTRL-A NUMBER allows the user to select a specific sockette number. The NUMBER must be a valid sockette number (obtained using CTRL-B), otherwise the selection will fail and an error message is issued.

  The sockette number is assigned to active_xmit and is used in all subsequent sendto()s until the next CTRL-A.

- The user can also specify the sockette from which messages are to be received. The command CTRL-W NUMBER causes the software to check for messages sent to the specified sockette NUMBER. If the process has not bound to the specified number, recvfrom() will fail continuously; however, a diagnostic is *not* generated.

  If the NUMBER is valid, waiting_for_message is assigned TRUE and active_recv is assigned the sockette number. Active_recv is used in all subsequent recvfrom()s until it is changed.

- A sockette message requires a destination host-port pair before it can be transmitted. The user can specify the intended destination using CTRL-D HOSTNAME,PORT. If the HOSTNAME and PORT are valid, all subsequent messages are sent to this destination. Error messages are issued if either the HOSTNAME or the PORT are invalid.

  Once the remote sockette host-port pair is determined it is stored in rmt_sock. All subsequent transmissions take place to the socket indicated in rmt_sock.

■ Strings with their first byte other than the control characters specified above are stored in `rmt_sock` and transmitted to the destination (previously specified by CTRL-D), using the active sockette (specified by CTRL-A). If `sendto()` fails, an error message is generated.

13.5.6 Compiling and Running the Sockette Software

The sockette software functions with either of the local area networks and the wide area network. All foreground process software is in `sockex.c`, which requires `sockcode.h` to compile. The Sockette and Network Layer software can be found in `sockette.c`. Both `sockcode.h` and `sockette.h` are needed to compile `sockette.c`. All of the sockette software is network independent except for the code within the Network Layer which conditionally compiles code for whatever network is requested. The specific dependencies are given in `makefile`.

As an example, to make all three different networks, type the following:

```
C:\> make ringsox.exe
C:\> make bussox.exe
C:\> make wansox.exe
```

The resulting executables contain the network-emulation software, the sockette software, and the sockette-demonstration software. Note that the hardware configurations associated with each type of network must still be adhered to.

To run the sockette software, type the name of the executable and the following parameters:

```
C:\> bussox LineSpeed Hostname Option {M or WS}
```

where:

LineSpeed   The line speed (one of 50, 300, 600, 1200, 2400, 4800, or 9600).

Hostname   The name of the local host (as defined in the file `hosts`).

Option   Option specifies the service that the software is to perform. One of:

E or e. Envokes the echo service on this PC. Messages sent to Hostname with port ECHO_PORT are returned.

T or t. Envokes the time service on this PC. Time request messages sent to Hostname with port TIME_PORT result in the current time of day being returned.
Any other character causes the PC to enter send-and-receive mode.

{M or WS}   If the underlying network is the ring network, the character M indicates that the station is the monitor station (there can only be one monitor). If the underlying network is the wide area network, WS is a value between 1 and 7 denoting the station's window size. The field is ignored by the bus network.

When execution begins, the screen is cleared. If either the echo service or the time service has been specified, the sockette address of the source process is displayed. Both of these services can be aborted by typing CTRL-C.

If the PC is in send-and-receive mode, the user can explicitly bind to one or more ports; send messages; receive messages; and release ports. The following is an annotated example of a session between a user on host marvin (host address 12430), the time server on tardis (host address 12345), and the echo server on zaphod (host address 13001). The various PCs are started as listed in Table 13.1.

TABLE 13.1   Host Initializations

Host	Command
marvin	bussox 1200 marvin x
tardis	bussox 1200 tardis T
zaphod	bussox 1200 zaphod E

The example is as follows:

■ First, the user must bind to a port, in this case, port 3 (note, there is no space between CTRL-B and 3):

User:	CTRL-B3
ringsox:	Sockette 0 bound to 12430 3

The response from ringsox indicates that all port 3 communications will take place through sockette number 0.

■ In this example, the user both sends and receives on the same sockette (the time server and echo server return their responses to the source host-port indicated in the request). The test software must be initialized accordingly: the first step sets up sockette 0 for transmission, the second step sets up the same socket for reception:

User:	CTRL-A0
ringsox:	Sockette 0 is the transmission sockette
User:	CTRL-W0
ringsox:	Sockette 0 is the reception sockette

■ The user must also specify a destination; to obtain the current time of day from the time server bound to tardis port 7, the user first indicates the destination and then sends a message to the server. If the server and its host are active, the time should be returned:

User:	CTRL-DTARDIS,7
ringsox:	Remote selected: 12345 7
User:	TIME PLEASE!
ringsox:	Message received: Mon May 06 14:24:37 1991

Each time the user sends a message (i.e., any string without a command prefix), the sockette message is sent across the underlying network to the time server bound to `tardis` port 7. The time server displays the message:

```
Time request from: 12430 3
```

If the user sends several messages before the time server has responded, all messages are forwarded. As the time messages are received, they are displayed.

- By changing the destination, the user can access the echo server, bound to port 2 on host `zaphod`:

User:	**CTRL-DZAPHOD,2**
ringsox:	Remote selected: 13001 2
User:	**HELLO HANDSOME!**
ringsox:	Message received: Hello handsome!

On `zaphod`, the echo server issues the message:

```
Echo request from: 12430 3
```

If `zaphod` is not part of the network, the message will be sent, but a reply will never be received.

- Finally, if the active reception socket is not the same as the transmission socket, the responses from the two servers will not be displayed. For example, consider the effect of binding to port 7 on `marvin` and making the resulting sockette the reception sockette, when sockette 0 is still the transmission sockette:

User:	**CTRL-B7**
ringsox:	Sockette 1 bound to 12430 7
User:	**CTRL-W1**
ringsox:	Sockette 1 is the reception sockette
User:	**PLEASE REPLY**

The echo request is received by the echo server on `zaphod` and echoed, but the returned messages are never displayed. By changing the reception sockette back to sockette 0, the message is displayed:

User:	**CTRL-W0**
ringsox:	Please reply

The DELETE key allows the deletion of any invalid or unwanted characters.

13.6 SUMMARY

This chapter has considered some of the issues surrounding two closely related topics: the identification of entities other than hosts or nodes and the need for layering in communication systems.

Host (and node) identification is achieved by specifying a destination address in the network's frame. By itself, the destination host's unicast address cannot be used to uniquely identify an entity, such as a process, since a host may support tens or hundreds of processes. Instead, when transmitting a message to a remote entity, it is necessary to identify both the entity and its host. In some applications, such as electronic mail, the entity receiving the message may in turn distribute the message to other entities on the host.

Since it is unrealistic to expect a single process to handle functions such as mail distribution, the framing of packets, file transfer, and untold other tasks, many communication systems have been developed in a layered fashion. That is, the communication functions have been divided into a number of well-defined operations and assigned to a layer. Each layer offers the layer above it a number of services, while using the services of the layer below it.

There is another demand for layering: hiding network or manufacturer specific functions, thereby permitting the interconnection of software developed on different machines and on different networks. For layering to work properly, it is necessary to develop standards that are agreed to by the people that use the layers. A number of well-known layered architectures have been proposed and implemented since the late 1970's including the Open Systems Interconnection model, IEEE 802, and the DARPA Protocol Architecture.

13.7 EXERCISES

When testing the various networks using sockettes, remember that the rules governing the physical connections associated with each network still must be applied.

1. Into which OSI layer should the following services be placed? Justify your answers:
    a) A time server.
    b) A service that converts swaps-integer byte from Intel format to Motorola format (see Chapter 1).
    c) The X.25 data-qualifier bit (the Q-bit) (see Chapter 10).
    d) The functions of a ring-network monitor.

2. UNIX sockets reserve a number of ports (typically the first 512) for "well-known" services. Suggest reasons why this approach is taken. When answering this exercise, consider the effect on a Commkit process if the process arbitrarily bound to a reserved-port number (such as the ECHO_PORT). What would happen if echo messages started arriving at the process?

3. Set up a network (bus, ring, or wide area) consisting of two stations and the line analyser. Run the echo process on one station and the send-receive process on the other. Transmit a message to the echo process. What appears on the line analyser? Identify each field in the frame; remember, the host numbers are 2-bytes long while the ports numbers are 1-byte long.

4. Set up a network (bus, ring, or wide area) consisting of three stations (and the line analyser if possible). Run the echo process on one station and the send-receive process on the other two stations. Transmit a message to the echo process from each station. How does the echo process "know" which station is to receive the message?

5. Set up a network (bus, ring, or wide area) consisting of two stations and the line analyser. Run the network test software (i.e., `ringex` or `busex`) on one station and the send_and_receive process on the other. Is it possible to transmit a message from the send_and_receive process to the station running the network test software? What appears on the test station when a frame finally does arrive?

   Can a message be sent from the test station to the station running the send_and_receive process? Does the send_and_receive process receive the message?

6. Compare the connection-oriented wide area network software (`wannet.c` and `wanex.c`) with the connectionless sockette software (`sockette.c` and `sockex.c`). What are the differences between the connection-oriented and connectionless software? How can `wanlow.c` support both connection-oriented and connectionless communications?

7. If a process never reads its sockettes and messages keep arriving, the station eventually runs out of buffer space and crashes. Modify `sockette.c` to handle the situation in which a process never reads a socket. Put a threshold of 10 on the number of messages that will be held before the oldest message is discarded.

8. A *name server* is a service that maps names into addresses, somewhat analagous to a telephone company's directory assistance. For example, a person can ask the operator for someone's telephone number; the operator attempts to find the number and, once found, gives it to the person.

   Implement a name server using sockettes. The name server should support three activities:

   ■ A process can register its name and sockette address with the name server.
   ■ Any process can query the server for the address of a given name. If the name exists, the address is returned, otherwise an error indication is returned.
   ■ A process can remove its own name and address from the name server's list.

9. In IP, the Internet address to physical address-mapping table (`addr_to_physical` in sockettes) is updated dynamically by the Internet Layer broadcasting an ARP packet whenever confronted by an unknown Internet address. Modify `sockette.c` so that unknown host addresses are resolved and the `addr_to_physical` table is updated.

10. Many programmers feel that using message passing is an unnatural programming paradigm, preferring instead to use procedure calls. A programming paradigm known as *remote procedure calls* (RPC) has been developed that permits programs on one machine to call a subroutine on a separate machine.

    The RPC is implemented as a local-procedure call to a *stub* procedure that creates a message containing the parameters and sends the message to a remote-stub procedure. The remote stub unpacks the parameters and makes a local-procedure call to the called (remote) procedure. Once the target procedure has completed its task, the results of the procedure are returned by the remote stub in a message to the local stub. The local stub unpacks the message, updates the necessary parameters and returns to the calling procedure.

Implement RPCs using Commkit's `send()`s and `recv()`s. Issues you should consider include how is call-by-value supported, how is call-by-address supported, and what happens if the remote procedure's host should fail.

To test your software, write a remote procedure that accepts two numbers, adds them and returns the answer in a third number.

14

Interconnecting Networks

14.1 INTRODUCTION

One of the biggest criticisms of the explosive spread and popularity of the PC is that the growth and choice of equipment is very often uncontrolled. For example, upper levels of management within a company may decide that all its employees will use specific machines, operating systems, and software packages. However, as employees learn more about the equipment, they may opt for different operating systems, software packages, or may even change machines entirely.

Although independent thought is admirable, it can lead to problems. For example, what happens if the payroll office manager unilaterally decides to purchase an 802.3 bus network to interconnect all of the stations in the payroll office; while at the same time, the personnel office manager purchases an 802.5 ring network? Sooner or later, someone will want to copy information from a station in the payroll office to a station in the personnel office (for example, from station N to station D). See Figure 14.1.

Since the stations are not on the same type of network, direct interconnection of the networks and subsequent information transfer is not possible because of electrical, packet structure, address, and other protocol differences. Solutions such as physically transferring information on diskettes may be satisfactory on occasion, but if large volumes of information are to be transferred on a regular basis, some other procedure is required.

Similar problems occur should two offices in different cities, each running their own local area networks, need to communicate. If the two cities are

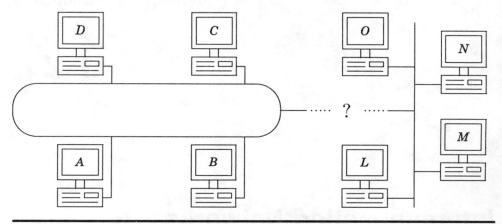

Figure 14.1   How can information be transferred between dissimilar networks?

interconnected by a wide area network, the ideal solution would be to transfer information between the two networks across the intermediate wide area network. However, since the wide area network probably does not support the protocol used by the local area networks nor does the wide area network achieve the speeds of the local area networks, directly connecting these networks is not possible.

Clearly, many of these problems can disappear if the networks are identical, since the packet structures and protocols are the same: simply interconnect the two networks (i.e., make a larger bus or ring). However, there are instances when it may not be physically possible or even advisable to allow all of the traffic on one network to propagate onto another. Consider the following situations:

- Two lightly loaded 802.3 networks are to be interconnected.

  Combining the two lightly loaded networks into a single, larger network may result in a heavily loaded network. The resulting network may offer less than satisfactory performance because of the additional network traffic.

- Two local area networks that are more than one kilometer apart.

  The physical interconnection of the two networks may be impossible because of the maximum physical separation of stations allowed by the network.

- A number of local area networks, each of which supports several hundred stations.

  The interconnection of the networks may be physically possible, but the resulting number of stations may exceed the number allowed on a single network.

- Two local area networks are used within an organization, one with sensitive product information, the other for use by the office staff.

  Combining the two networks and allowing the sensitive information onto the general network may breach company security.

In these examples, the need for network interconnection has been stated, while at the same time, some of the problems associated with network interconnection have been outlined. If networks are to be interconnected, it is necessary to develop facilities that can convert between the different packet structures, addressing schemes, and other network idiosyncrasies; while at the same time they must obey the protocols associated with the individual networks.

14.2 BACKGROUND

Connecting a network to one or more other networks is possible as long as the device(s) supporting the interconnection can handle the various differences between the networks. Although there are many different types and makes of device to support network interconnection, manufacturers and users alike often employ the generic term *gateway* when referring to such devices (Figure 14.2).

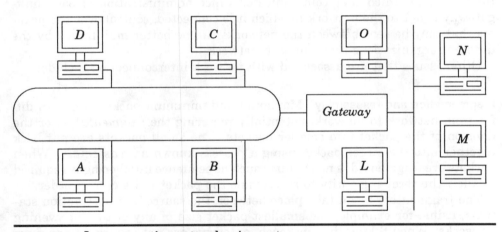

Figure 14.2 Interconnecting networks via a gateway

A gateway connects two or more networks, while obeying the protocols associated with each individual network. For example, the gateway in Figure 14.2 must handle both the bus-network protocol and the ring-network protocol. If the gateway is responsible for changing the packet structure on one network to conform to the rules associated with the other network, it is often referred to as a *protocol converter*.

In some situations it may not be possible to have a single gateway (for example, if the networks are separated beyond the physical limits allowed by the networks or if security reasons dictate which stations are allowed on a network); instead it may be necessary to have a pair of *half-gateways*, each attached to a network and the other half-gateway (Figure 14.3).

Each half-gateway is connected to a single network and conforms to the standards associated with that network. To send packets between the networks, it is necessary for the half-gateways to support a third, common pro-

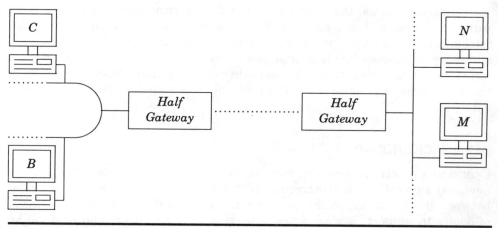

Figure 14.3   Two half-gateways

tocol through which they communicate. Since administration of each half-gateway is left to the network to which it is connected, control over the packets that may be sent between the networks can be better maintained by the different organizations that run each network.

Other issues that are associated with network interconnection include:

Fragmentation and reassembly   Maximum and minimum packet sizes can differ from network to network, potentially requiring the *fragmentation* or the division of the packet into smaller packets. The small packets are put back together into the larger packet using a process known as *reassembly*. When packets are fragmented, a mechanism such as sequence numbering is required to allow the receiving entity to reassemble the packet in its correct order.

The fragmentation can take place between the source and destination stations, using, for example, the smallest packet size of any of the intervening networks. When taking this approach, gateways are not required to perform any fragmentation or reassembly.

Alternatively, the gateways themselves can perform the fragmentation and reassembly. The destination station may still be expected to perform reassembly if the packet is too large for its network.

Connection-oriented vs. connectionless services   Gateways potentially can interconnect networks supporting connection-oriented (i.e., virtual-circuit) services, typically wide area networks, with networks supporting connectionless (i.e., datagram) networks. In these situations, it is necessary to decide upon the level and quality of service required by the applications.

If the communication is to be treated as a virtual circuit, the gateway may be required to support a reliable protocol atop the datagram service. However, an application using datagrams may find many of its packets being sent reliably across a virtual circuit; potentially adding to the cost of the overall communication.

Routing Gateways can be required to perform routing if there are multiple paths through the network between stations. Routing algorithms such as those described for wide area networks in Chapter 10 are often used by gateways.

Other network differences In addition to the issues just outlined, the source network may support features that are not available on the destination network. A good example of this is synchronous mode on ring networks (see Chapter 12): a station transmitting a synchronous packet expects a reply from the destination withi a specific period. If the destination station resides on a separate network, the delays associated with the intermediate gateway(s) forwarding the packet may make a reply within the allotted time period impossible to achieve.

If a gateway acknowledges the packet, this should not be interpreted by the source station as an indication that the destination station has received the packet. In other words, higher-level protocols supporting end-to-end acknowledgements may be required to ensure that packets reach their intended destination.

As already mentioned, the term gateway is a generic term applied to almost all network interconnection devices. However, by examining these devices on a layer-by-layer basis, one finds that there are three types of interconnection device: *repeaters* (Physical Layer), *bridges* (Data Link Layer), and *gateways* (Network Layer). Protocol conversion, another issue in internetwork communication, has been discussed in previous chapters.

14.3 REPEATERS

A repeater is a device that interconnects two *homogeneous* (identical) networks, making a single, larger network. Repeaters are intended to take the traffic from one part of the network and transmit it directly onto the other part without making any changes to the frame structure or the Physical Layer (i.e., OSI layer 1) protocol (Figure 14.4).

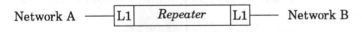

Network A ——|L1| *Repeater* |L1|—— Network B

Figure 14.4 Repeaters function at the Physical Layer

A repeater operates at the Physical Layer, amplifying or regenerating signals. Repeaters can help overcome segment-length limitations and can be used to interconnect networks using different physical media (from coaxial cable to fiber optic cable). A repeater connecting two bus segments passes the collisions between the two segments. A ring repeater extends the size of the ring; the number of repeaters necessary in a ring equals the number of rings being connected. To avoid the situation where two or more stations receive the same packet, all stations must be assigned unique addresses.

Finally, a repeater is not allowed to violate the physical limitations placed upon the network. For example, two maximum-length Ethernets (2.5 kilometers) cannot be joined by a repeater to form a single 5-kilometer Ethernet, since this violates the Ethernet's cable-length restrictions.

14.4   BRIDGES

A bridge is a device or layer of software that allows the interconnection of two or more local area networks at the media-access (MAC) sublayer of the Data Link Layer (OSI layer 2). See Figure 14.5.

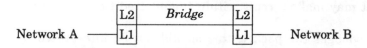

Figure 14.5   Bridges function at the Data Link Layer

The resulting network is referred to as a individual LAN known as a *segment*. Each segment attaches to the bridge through a *port*; a bridge can connect to many segments. Bridges act as store-and-forward devices, taking packets from one segment and forwarding them onto others, following the rules associated with each segment.

  Bridges offer a number of advantages over repeaters:

- Different types of local area networks can be interconnected. For example, a bridge can connect an 802.3 bus to an 802.5 ring. Packets destined for the ring must wait until the bridge is in possession of the token before transmission, while packets intended for the bus are transmitted when the bus is idle.

- Distance limitations can be overcome. Two or more 802.3 bus networks could be connected by a bridge; packets could be sent from one segment to the other through the bridge. The bridge could give the illusion of a single, large network. But since the bridge operates at the Data Link Layer, the Physical Layer requirements (such as distance limitations and electrical requirements) are not violated.

- A single, large local area network can be divided into a number of smaller segments, all interconnected through one or more bridges. The bridge can help overcome the limitations associated with operating a single network that is approaching its physical limitations (i.e., number of stations or maximum length).

The IEEE 802.1 Standard defines two types of bridge: those that are transparent to the stations involved in the communication (*transparent bridges*), and those that require stations involved in the communication to be aware of the existence of the bridges (*source-routing bridges*). Both types are now considered.

14.4.1 Transparent Bridges

To operate transparently, a bridge must function in promiscuous mode, receiving and inspecting all packets sent from each segment to which the bridge is connected. Packets are addressed to the destination station, rather than being addressed to a bridge. All stations must be assigned unique addresses.

In its simplest form, a transparent bridge forwards all packets received from one segment to all those to which it is connected. This approach has a number of limitations, the most serious being flooding: all packets are sent to all segments, regardless of the destination. By allowing all traffic to propagate between the interconnected segments through the bridge, a series of lightly loaded segments can turn into a single, heavily loaded bridged network.

This suggests that there may be a benefit in having the bridge perform some type of *packet filtering*. Ideally, the filtering should allow only packets destined for a remote segment to pass through the bridge, thereby ensuring that the only traffic on a segment is either packets for stations on that segment or packets en route to a remote station being sent via a bridge.

Packet filtering is achieved by having the bridge maintain a list of the addresses of the stations associated with each segment to which it is connected; the bridge can then selectively forward packets between segments by examining the *destination* address of each packet. If the packet's destination address is for a station on a segment other than the one from which the packet is received, the packet can be forwarded to the destination's segment. To allow the station to make these routing decisions, a *forwarding database* is maintained, consisting of each known destination address and the segment from which the packet was received.

Using the example in Figure 14.6, if station S on segment 3 sends a packet to station E on segment 2, the bridge will forward the message onto segment 2 because station E does not exist on segment 3 but it does exist on segment 2 (this is determined by the bridge examining the forwarding database).

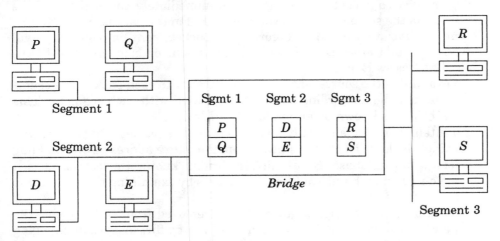

Figure 14.6   The forwarding database for each segment attached to the bridge

Packets sent to stations on the *same* segment are not forwarded even though they are received by the bridge. For example, a packet from station D to station E would not be forwarded by the bridge because station E is on segment 2 (once again, the bridge determines this from the forwarding database).

If the bridge receives a packet with an unknown destination address, the packet is forwarded on all segments except the one on which it was received. For example, if station P sends a packet addressed to station X, the packet will be forwarded on segments 2 and 3, since address X does not exist in the forwarding database. If other bridges are attached to any of these segments, they will continue to forward the packet until it reaches station X. Having the bridge selectively forward packets ensures that the only packets on a segment (other than those en route to another bridge) are those intended for stations on that segment.

The forwarding database can be initialized in one of a number of ways:

- The station addresses can be stored in a file that is read by the bridge when it is brought on-line. The problem with this approach is that the contents of the file are fixed, meaning that changing a station (i.e., removing it or having it change segments) requires that the file be explicitly altered, typically by the network manager.

- Individual stations can explicitly inform the bridge of their existence. When a station joins or leaves a segment, the bridge can be informed, which causes the bridge to update its forwarding database. Although this does eliminate the need for explicit database alteration by the network administrator, special protocols are required to allow the stations to inform the bridge of their status.

- The bridge can determine the locations of the various stations on the segment by examining the *source* address of each packet. That is, whenever the bridge receives a packet from a segment, it immediately knows that there is a station on the segment with the address found in the packet. For example, in the configuration found in Figure 14.7, packets sent on segment 1 will have source addresses D or E, while packets sent on segment 2 will have source addresses R or S.

By examining the source addresses associated with each packet, the bridge can construct the forwarding database associated with each segment. This type of bridge is known as an *intelligent bridge*.

An intelligent bridge initially forwards *all* of the packets that it receives, "learning" the location of each station from the *source* address while building the forwarding database. Eventually, the bridge "knows" the location of each station on a segment and can filter the packets by examining the *destination* address.

Should a station change segments or be removed from its segment, the bridge can also gain this information from the traffic. A station changing segments would have its address appear on both segments; the bridge could then update its forwarding database on the basis of this information. In addition, the bridge determines when a station becomes inactive by periodi-

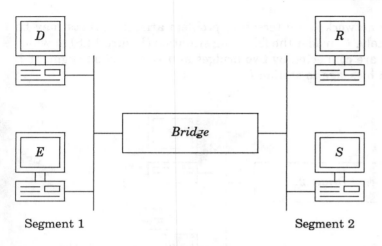

Segment 1   Segment 2

Figure 14.7   A bridge can determine a station's location from a packet's source address

cally purging its forwarding database of stations that have not sent a packet within a fixed period of time (typically every few minutes).

IEEE 802 transparent bridge   The IEEE 802 transparent bridge is an intelligent bridge that performs packet filtering. Each 802 bridge maintains a forwarding database that consists of entries in the form: *port*, the segment from which the packet was received, and *address*, the address of the station.

All packets that are received by the bridge are subject to two separate operations:

Bridge forwarding.   When a packet is received, the bridge examines the forwarding database, comparing the list of station addresses to the destination address in the packet:

- If the address does not exist in the database, the packet is forwarded on all segments to which the bridge is attached, except the one on which the packet was received.

- If the address does exist in the database, the source port is then considered. If the port from which the packet is received is the same as the port in the database, the packet is discarded; otherwise the packet is forwarded to the segment specified.

Bridge learning.   Once bridge forwarding is completed, the packet's address is compared to the list of addresses in the forwarding database. If the address does not exist in the forwarding database, both the source port and the packet's address are recorded in the database.

Inactive stations have their addresses removed from the forwarding database by the bridge. The amount of time an address is left in the database is set by the network administrator.

If reliability is an issue, some network administrators may institute a policy of having two or more bridges connecting a pair of segments. By having two paths through the network, an interesting problem arises: packets may be forwarded indefinitely. Consider the following situation (Figure 14.8) in which segments A and B are connected by two bridges and station S on segment B attempts to send a message to station L.

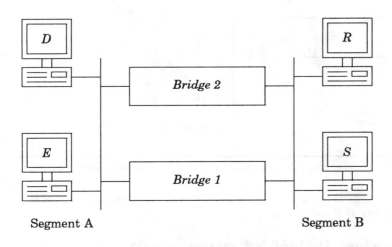

Segment A   Segment B

Figure 14.8   Multiple paths in a network can lead to packets circulating forever

When the packet addressed to station L is received by the bridges, both bridges attempt to forward the packet since (it is assumed) an entry for station L does not exist in either forwarding database (station L does not exist on either segment). Each bridge will then receive the packet forwarded on segment A from the other bridge; and will forward the packet addressed to station L onto segment B. This cycle will continue indefinitely.

If the bridge-learning and forwarding algorithms are to succeed, there can only be a single path between any of the segments making up the bridged network, regardless of the physical topology. Fortunately, it is possible to impose a *spanning tree* onto a bridged network to ensure that there are no loops in the network. A spanning tree is a structure with one bridge as the root of the tree, and other bridges restricting the flow of packets so that no loops exist within the overall network. The 802 transparent bridge uses a *spanning-tree algorithm* to generate spanning trees.

The spanning-tree algorithm operates as follows. One bridge is chosen as the root of the spanning tree, typically the station with the lowest physical address. Then, all bridges determine the shortest path from the segments to which they are connected to the root bridge (i.e., the number of hops required by a packet to reach root bridge). If two or more bridges connected to the same segment require the same number of hops, the bridge with the lower physical address is chosen, the other bridge is *blocked*. (Blocking is a logical operation, the bridge still receives packets, it simply discards those that are not to be forwarded.) The spanning-tree algorithm functions dynamically, with each bridge periodically informing all other bridges of its location, neighboring bridges, and status. Should the status of a bridge or segment change (i.e., fail or become active), the spanning tree can be reconfigured.

For example, consider the following LANs (Figure 14.9) interconnected by bridges; since there are multiple paths through the network, packets can potentially remain cycling "forever."

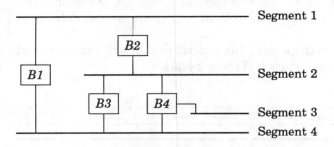

Figure 14.9   A network with multiple paths

If bridge *B1* is taken as the root of the spanning tree, then the other bridges can determine the shortest path to the root bridge. The shortest path from segment 2 to the root bridge can be by bridges *B2*, *B3*, or *B4*; assuming that bridge *B2* has the lowest physical address of the three bridges, bridges *B3* and *B4* block (ignore) all packets sent to and from segment 2. The shortest (and only) path from segment 3 is via bridge *B4*, therefore bridge *B4* will carry all packets destined for and received from segment 3. Bridge *B3* blocks *all* packets and bridge *B4* blocks packets sent across segment 2. The resulting spanning tree is given in Figure 14.10 (the dotted lines denote physical links that are currently blocked).

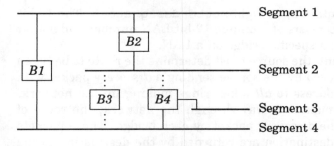

Figure 14.10   A spanning tree routes as bridge *B1*

The bridged network is now free of all loops. Since the bridges are always in communication, a change in topology (for example, a bridge failure) will result in a new spanning tree.

14.4.2 Source-Routing Bridges

Careful observation of the spanning tree in the previous section shows that the resulting bridged network, although free of possible loops, is not necessarily optimal. For example, a transmission from segment 3 to segment 2 results in the packet being sent via bridges *B4, B1,* and *B2*; even though the two segments are physically connected by bridge *B4.*

The designers of the IBM Token Ring recognized this limitation and developed an alternative to the spanning tree for bridged token rings known as *source routing.* Source routing operates as the name implies, the source station specifies the route of the packet rather than letting the bridges determine the route.

Not surprisingly, the route the logical link control packet will take is stored within the frame by the source station (Figure 14.11).

DST Addr	SRC Addr	Routing Info	DSAP	SSAP	Control	Data	FCS

Figure 14.11   A source-routing packet

`Routing Info` is a variable-length field up to 18 bytes in length. The first two bytes are the `routing control` field and contain the following information:

- whether the packet is a broadcast packet, intended for all rings;
- the length of the `Routing Info` field;
- the direction of the packet, either from or to the source station;
- an indication as to the largest frame supported by the bridge for broadcast packets.

The remaining 16 bytes contain up to eight `route-designators`. The 16-bit `route-designator` field consists of a unique 12-bit LAN number and a 4-bit bridge number, identifying a specific bridge on a LAN.

Before a packet can be sent, the source must determine the route to be taken by the packet. This is achieved by the source sending a *discovery* packet with the destination station's address to *all* token rings making up the network. As each discovery packet makes its way through the network, the route of the packet is recorded in the discovery packet by each bridge. Those packets which reach the intended destination are returned by the destination to the source back along the recorded route. The source can then choose which route to use for its communication from the returned discovery packets.

Once the route has been chosen, the source station sends packets with the high-order bit of the address set. This signals the bridge that the packet is intended for a remote token ring rather than the local token ring. The bridge inspects the `Routing Info` field to determine the route.

Source routing has been adopted by the IEEE 802 Committee for routing in interconnected 802.5 token rings. However, the source-routing algorithm is not restricted to ring local area networks, it can be applied to other local area networks as well as to wide area networks.

14.5 GATEWAYS

In many internetworking situations, it is not possible to use a repeater or a bridge because the networks to be connected support different physical properties, addressing schemes, and possibly even owners. A gateway (also known as a *router*) is a device operating at the Network Layer (i.e., OSI layer 3) that is intended to overcome these limitations (Figure 14.12).

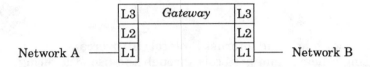

Figure 14.12 Gateways function at the Network Layer

Since gateways are associated with wide area networks, there are, broadly speaking, two types of gateways: those for connection-oriented services and those for connectionless services.

14.5.1 X.75

The same arguments against the direct connection of dissimilar local area networks can also be applied to the direct connection of wide area networks, even if they share a common protocol such as X.25:

- The internal protocols used by the network may differ. Connecting a node on one network to a node on another may not be possible because of physical connection (layer 1) differences or internodal protocol (layer 2) differences.

- Since most public wide area networks are run by different organizations, each party is usually strongly reluctant to permit the "other" organization to connect one of "their" nodes to "our" network.

Instead, most wide area networks allow connection to other wide area networks communicate through a pair of half-gateways using a common gateway protocol. In the case of X.25, the gateway protocol is CCITT X.75.

X.75 is a connection-oriented protocol and is used when an application on an X.25 host (or PAD) specifies an international call in the call-request packet. (The international call is indicated by an X.121 address specifying a network other than the current network.) The node to which the X.25 host is connected then creates a virtual circuit to the half-gateway node. The half-gateway creates another virtual circuit to the half-gateway on the remote wide area network. The remote half-gateway places a virtual circuit to the destination X.25 host (or another half-gateway; repeating the cycle). Once the virtual circuits are established across the various networks, communications may proceed.

The layer 3 protocols between a pair of X.25 hosts (denoted H), between nodes (denoted N), and a pair of half gateways (denoted G) are given in 14.13.

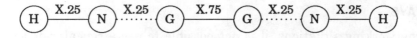

Figure 14.13   The relationship between X.25 and X.75

The X.75 protocol is similar to the X.25 protocol. Additional features in X.75 are needed for routing and accounting.

14.5.2   IP Routing

In Chapter 13, it was shown how the Internet Protocol (IP) overcame different networks, addressing schemes and protocols through the use of layering and by assigning each host a unique Internet address. When sending a message on the Internet, the application supplies a message, the destination IP address and port of the remote entity. The IP software takes the IP address, maps it into a unique physical host address, and then transmits the message, encapsulated in an IP packet, on the local network.

The Internet also supports the routing of messages between hosts on different networks; messages are sent to gateways, which are responsible for the routing of packets between networks. Since each host is assigned a unique IP address, the gateway can determine the route of the packet by comparing the packet's destination address with the addresses in the gateway's routing table. Routing is independent of the high-level protocol in the packet (i.e., TCP/IP or UDP).

The Internet is huge, consisting of thousands of different sites and tens of thousands of hosts. If each packet is routed soley upon the value of the host IP address, the size of the routing table would be enormous and updating the routing tables would be a never-ending task as hosts are added to and removed from the network. To overcome these difficulties, an Internet address is actually a hierarchical address consisting of *two* parts: a *network* identifier and a *host* identifier.

When an application has a message to send to an entity on a remote host, the message and destination IP address are supplied to the IP layer as usual. The packet is encapsulated in a datagram, but since the network identifier indicates a network other than the local network, the datagram is sent to a gateway on the network. The destination IP address is the address of the destination network/host, *not* an intermediate gateway.

When the gateway receives the datagram, the network identifier is extracted from the packet's destination IP address and used to determine the route of the datagram. If the network identifier indicates a network to which the gateway is directly connected, the datagram is forwarded to the destination on that network. However, if the gateway cannot reach the destination network directly, the gateway's routing table is accessed. Each entry in the routing table indicates the address of the *next* gateway on the path to the destination network. Should the specified destination network not exist in the routing table, the datagram is forwarded to a default gateway. This cycle is repeated until the datagram reaches a gateway that is connected to the destination network. Note that the source and destination IP addresses are never altered by the gateways; the IP addresses are used for routing purposes.

The Internet supports *three* different classes of Internet address (Table 14.1), all in the form *net-id*, *host-id*.

TABLE 14.1 Internet Address Classes

Class	Number of hosts
A	more than 65,535
B	256 to 65,535
C	less than 256

Gateways can distinguish between the different address structures by examining the high-order bits of the different IP address classes (Figure 14.14).

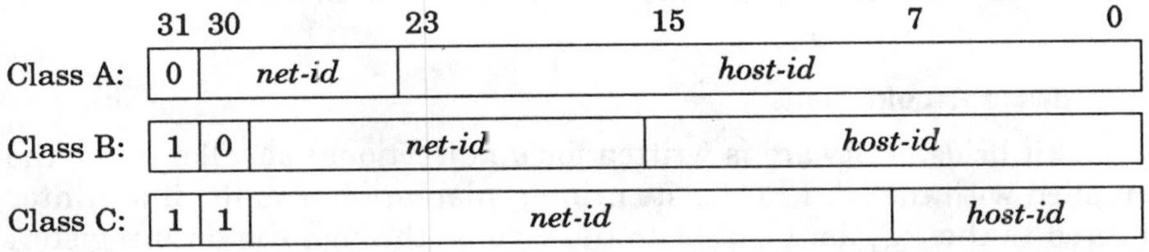

Figure 14.14 Internet address structures

IP addresses are normally written in *dot notation*: each byte making up the 32-bit address is separated by a period, in the format *m.n.o.p*. Using the IP dot notation for address representation, class A networks have values 1.0.0.0 through 127.0.0.0 (the ARPANET is 10.0.0.0); while class B networks are in the range 128.0.0.0 through 191.255.0.0; and class C networks, 192.0.0.0 through 255.255.255.0.

Each IP gateway is responsible for maintaining its own routing table. The routing table can be initialized from static storage or the gateway can communicate with other gateways, dynamically building the routing table. Only a subset of gateways maintain a list of routes to all networks, these gateways are known as *core gateways* and connect directly to the ARPANET. The remaining gateways are known as *non core gateways*. Routing tables are updated by the gateways exchanging routing information consisting of the distances between gateways in terms of hop-counts.

14.6 THE COMMKIT TRANSPARENT BRIDGE

Commkit is supplied with software that emulates a transparent bridge, which allows packets to be sent between two separate local area networks (the bus or the ring) using the PC's parallel port. For example, a pair of two-station networks (one a ring and the other a bus), can be connected by the parallel ports of two of the PCs (Figure 14.15).

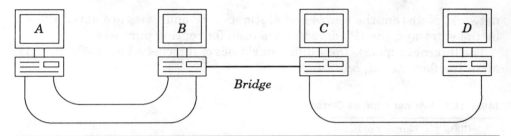

Figure 14.15   The Commkit bridge connecting a Commkit bus and ring

In Figure 14.15, PCs *B* and *C* are connected to the ring and bus network, respectively, as well as being directly connected by a cable through their parallel ports. The bridge is actually a pair of *half-bridges*, which are identical except for the underlying local area network software. A pair of background processes control the routing and formatting of packets. The foreground application allows the user to query the state of each half-bridge.

14.6.1   Hardware Requirements

The Commkit bridge software is written for unidirectional-parallel ports, the type supplied with the IBM PC for its printer adapter. Normally, if a printer is connected to the PC, data is sent to the printer through the data register, port 0x3BC, and the printer status is returned through the status register, port 0x3BD. The control register is port 0x3BE.

Simply connecting the printer ports using a straight-through 25-pin RS-232-C cable and writing data to the data register on either PC will not result in the transfer of data, since the data registers support output only and cannot be read from. Instead, the cable must be rewired so that the output from the data register on one PC appears as input on the other PC's *status* register. The *pins to be exchanged* are as follows: **2** and **15**; **3** and **13**; **4** and **12**; **5** and **10**; and **6** and **11**. The pin swapping should be done on one connector only. Electrically, this should not be a problem, since the data-register pins produce 2.6 mA, while the status register pins can handle up to 7 mA.

The results of these changes mean that data sent to the data register will arrive on the status register (note that the parallel port does not supply data on the lower 3 bits of the status register; these bits are always set). See Figure 14.16.

Data received on pin 11 (bit 7 of the status register) is always the inverted value of what was sent (i.e., a 0 is received as a 1 and a 1 is received as a 0). For example, if a cable is wired according to the above instructions and plugged into the parallel ports on a pair of PCs, then writing 0x1F to the parallel port data register on one PC will result in 0x7F being read from the status register of the other PC.

If parallel port interrupts are to be supported, bit 7 of the 8259 Interrupt Controller mask must be cleared, the parallel-port interrupt vector (number 0x0F) must contain the address of the interrupt handler, and the parallel port control register must be set to 0x10 to enable interrupts. A parallel port

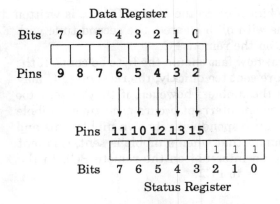

Figure 14.16   The wiring required to connect two parallel ports

interrupt occurs when there is a high-to-low transition on pin 10 (bit 6) of the status register (this is achieved by asserting a low-to-high transition on bit 3; the parallel port inverts the signal).

The parallel port interrupt is *not* the same as the UART's. In the UART, an interrupt will occur after the transmission or reception of a character; whereas in the parallel port, an interrupt will occur only when pin 10 of the status register experiences a high-to-low transition.

14.6.2   Bridge Software

The bridge software consists of two distinct parts: the parallel-port software for the transfer of individual bytes across the cable, `parlport.c`, and the software needed to control the flow of information between the bridges, `bridge.c`

Parallel port protocol   The parallel port protocol software, `parlport.c`, is responsible for the transfer of bytes between two PCs using the parallel port. A quick examination of the connections between the data and status registers reveals that, at most, four bits are available for a data transfer (bits 0, 1, 2, and 4), since the status port will only accept five input bits, one of which must be used to signal an interrupt (bit 3).

Since there are four bits that can be used for data transfer, a byte can be sent from one PC to the other as a pair of nibbles. A total of five bits are sent: four data bits, the nibble; and the fifth bit (bit 3) to signal an interrupt. By sending each 5-bit sequence *twice*, the first time with bit 3 cleared, the second with bit 3 set, an interrupt will occur on the receiving PC. The receiving PC can read the status register to obtain the value of the five bits (bit 3 will be set):

Nibble plus bit 3 (cleared) ───────────→

Nibble plus bit 3 (set) ───────────→ *Interrupt*

This operation must be performed for every nibble sent if an interrupt is to occur on the receiving PC. To send a byte, the cycle must be repeated for both nibbles making up the byte.

Pp_out (ch) sends the lower five bits of ch to the remote PC. Ch is written to port PP_DATA twice, the first time with bit 3 cleared, the second time with it set, thereby causing an interrupt on the remote PC.

This raises an interesting problem: how fast should the byte be sent? If the pair of nibbles making up the byte are sent too quickly, the receiving PC may not have sufficient time to process the nibbles; however, if they're sent too slowly, throughput may suffer. Since an interrupt occurs each time a nibble is sent, the PC receiving the nibble can respond with its own nibble (this and subsequent references to nibble assumes that when a nibble is sent, it is sent as a *5-bit* sequence thereby causing an interrupt on the remote PC). In the following example, PC1 is to send a byte to PC2:

PC1		PC2
Send first nibble	$\longrightarrow$	*Interrupt*
		Save first nibble
Interrupt	$\longleftarrow$	Respond (with a nibble)
Send second nibble	$\longrightarrow$	*Interrupt*
		Make byte from first and second nibble
Interrupt	$\longleftarrow$	Respond (with a nibble)

If full-duplex transfer is to be permitted (that is, both PCs can transmit bytes simultaneously), it is necessary to distinguish between nibbles that make up bytes and nibbles that are for acknowledgements. This can be achieved by sending a special nibble, analogous to the start bit, prior to the transfer of the byte. In this example, PC1 is to send a byte to PC2:

PC1		PC2
Send start signal	$\longrightarrow$	*Interrupt*
		Prepare for incoming byte
Interrupt	$\longleftarrow$	Send acknowledgement signal
Send first nibble	$\longrightarrow$	*Interrupt*
		Save first nibble
Interrupt	$\longleftarrow$	Send acknowledgement signal
Send second nibble	$\longrightarrow$	*Interrupt*
		Make byte from first and second nibble
Interrupt	$\longleftarrow$	Send acknowledgement signal

The byte transmission and reception algorithms are implemented as a pair of finite state machines in parlport.c, one for transmission (pp_xmit ()) and the other for reception (pp_recv ()).

The transmission-state machine consists of four states, indicated by the value of pp_info.xmit_state and is implemented in pp_xmit (). Pp_xmit () is called after pp_recv () has processed the incoming interrupt. Pp_recv () supplies a single parameter, reply_needed, which indicates whether a reply to the remote PC in the form of an acknowledgement is required. The transmission states are as follows:

SEND_IDLE. This is the initial transmission state, which is returned to after a byte has been sent to the remote PC. If there is a byte to be transmitted, pp_info.data_to_go is TRUE, causing a START_SIGNAL to be sent by a call to pp_out(). The byte to be sent is pointed to by pp_info.x_ptr. The state changes to SEND_NIB1.

If pp_info.data_to_go is FALSE, an acknowledgement signal can be transmitted if requested by pp_recv(). The state does not change.

SEND_NIB1. The low-order nibble of the byte pointed to by pp_info.x_ptr is sent in state SEND_NIB1. The 4-bit nibble must be encoded into 5-bits (Figure 14.17).

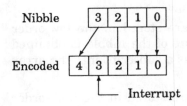

Figure 14.17   Encoding of 4-bit nibble to a 5-bit nibble used by the Data Register

Instead of shifting and masking the various bits, an array, out_nibs, is used. Out_nibs is indexed by the nibble, producing the corresponding bit pattern that would be produced by shifting and masking. In all cases, the resulting bit pattern has bit 3 set. For example, a nibble value of 0x00 produces 0x08, while a value of 0x0E produces 0x1E. The encoded nibbles are transmitted using pp_out().

Once the encoded nibble is sent, the state changes to SEND_NIB2.

SEND_NIB2. SEND_NIB2 is identical to SEND_NIB1 with the following exceptions: the high-order nibble is encoded (using out_nibs) for transmission, and the next state is WAIT_ACK.

WAIT_ACK. After the second nibble is sent and the last acknowledgement is received WAIT_ACK is entered. The receive state changes to SEND_IDLE, and pp_info.xmit_done is set TRUE to indicate that the transmission has completed.

In each of the states that handle the transmission of a byte (all states except WAIT_ACK), a timer is started by calling start_pp_clock(). If a response from the remote PC is not received within two clock interrupts, pp_xmit() is called as if an acknowledgement was received, thereby causing the transmission to continue. If the resulting data value is invalid, higher-level software must resolve the error. The clock is turned *off* in state WAIT_ACK.

A transmission is never started unless the receive state machine is in state WAIT_BYTE. This policy was instituted after a number of tests showed that data could be lost if data transmissions were started while acknowledgements were being returned.

Pp_recv() is called by pp_protocol() whenever a parallel port interrupt occurs; that is, data is received by the parallel port status-register. Pp_recv() shifts the encoded five-bit status-register value right by three, giving it a value between 0 and 31; if no errors have occurred on the channel, this value is the same as the original encoded value. How the encoded value is interpreted depends upon the state of the receive state machine. The receive state machine consists of three states (indicated by the value of pp_info.recv_state):

WAIT_BYTE. The WAIT_BYTE state is the initial receive state and is returned to after a byte is constructed from a pair of nibbles. If the shifted status register has a value of START_SIGNAL, the receive state changes to WAIT_NIB1. Any other value is assumed to be an acknowledgement signal (ACK_SIGNAL) and does not cause a state change.

WAIT_NIB1. The four data bits of the register are stored in the low-order nibble of the byte pp_info.r_data. The value of the nibble is obtained by treating the value of the encoded five-bits as a subscript into the array in_nibs. The state changes to WAIT_NIB2.

WAIT_NIB2. The four data bits of the register are stored in the high-order nibble of byte pp_info.r_data. Once again, the value of the nibble is determined from the array in_nibs. The state returns to WAIT_BYTE.

In all of the states just discussed, once the encoded register value is processed, pp_xmit() is called with a Boolean value indicating whether the transmission state machine is to respond with an acknowledgement (ACK_SIGNAL), start signal (START_SIGNAL), data nibble, or not at all, depending upon the receive state and the transmission state. If a byte is being received, a response is required to ensure that the remote PC can continue to transmit. However, if a byte is not being received, responses may still be required if the local PC is transmitting. Pp_info.ack_count indicates the number of acknowledgements that are expected. If limits were not placed on the number of acknowledgements, a continuous stream of acknowledgements would be exchanged by the PCs, seriously degrading the performance of each machine.

The remaining three parallel-port functions are as follows:

pp_init(). The parallel port software is initialized in pp_init(). If the parallel port software is being used in an application, pp_init() should be declared as an external and called during the initialization phase.

do_pp_protocol(). This function is called by pp_protocol() after each parallel-port interrupt, since it is possible that a byte has been received or transmitted. These conditions are indicated by the Booleans pp_info.recv_data and pp_info.xmit_done, respectively.

If a byte has been received, the value in pp_info.r_data is forwarded to the process associated with queue BACKGROUND_2.

When a byte has been successfully transmitted, a check is made to determine whether there is more to transmit (indicated by pp_info.x_count having a nonzero value). Should there be nothing more to transmit, recv() is called and the queue PPIH is checked. If the queue has a message available for transmission, pp_info.x_count, pp_info.x_buffer and pp_info.x_ptr are updated, otherwise control returns to pp_protocol().

In all cases, if there is a byte to be sent (pointed to by pp_info.x_ptr), pp_info.data_to_go is set to TRUE. If the receive state machine is in the WAIT_BYTE state, the transmission is initiated by a call to pp_xmit().

pp_protocol(code, ch). If parallel port interrupts are to be supported, a call to pp_protocol() should be made whenever a parallel port interrupt occurs. Parallel port interrupts are signalled by a device value of PPIH in low_level(). The code (one of RECVDONE or MSG_AVAIL) and the associated data can be supplied to pp_protocol() by low_level().

The value of the status register is supplied in ch whenever a code value of RECVDONE is received. Ch is then supplied to pp_recv() for processing; once completed, do_pp_protocol() is called.

When a message is available for transmission (signalled by a code of MSG_AVAIL), a check is made to determine whether the transmission can begin immediately by checking pp_info.x_count and pp_info.recv_state. Pp_xmit() is called to start the transmission.

Clock interrupt signals (indicated by a code of CLKIH) are also required to handle the situation when the transmission state machine does not receive an interrupt. Accordingly, clock interrupts must be forwarded from low_level().

Bridge software   Commkit supports a transparent bridge that is designed to connect two local area networks. The bridge is implemented as a pair of half-bridges; each half-bridge is constructed as depicted in Figure 14.18, regardless of the underlying local area network.

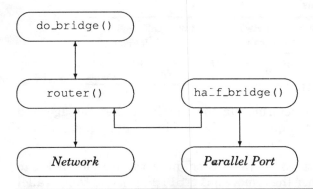

Figure 14.18   The bridge software is network independent

The various components of the bridge software are as follows:

Network. This is either of the local area network emulators, buslow.c or ringlow.c. The network software is identical to the software described in the section on local area networks, with two exceptions: first, the variable promiscuous is set TRUE by the bridge software, thereby ensuring that all network frames are accepted by the station; and second, the token BRIDGE is defined so that parallel port interrupts are routed to the parallel port software.

Parallel Port. The parallel-port software has been described in the previous section. All messages from the half_bridge() are transmitted to the remote PC, while each byte that is received from the remote PC is forwarded to the half_bridge().

router(). Packets received from either the local network (i.e., the network to which the half-bridge is attached) or the remote network are subject to bridge forwarding and bridge learning by router(), found in bridge.c. The incoming packet is taken from queue BACKGROUND_1 and stored in net_msg.

Bridge forwarding involves extracting the destination station identifier from the packet and determining the destination network. Since both local area networks use the same packet structure, access to the packet addresses is network independent (net_msg[0] for the destination address and net_msg[1] for the source address). The destination network is obtained from the array fwding_db, using the destination address as a subscript (fwding_db is an array of 256 elements, sufficient for all possible station addresses). An element in fwding_db has one of three values: the queue number of the local network emulator (NETWORK), the queue number of half_bridge() (BACKGROUND_2), or -1, indicating that the network for this address is as yet unknown.

Since there are only two possible networks, routing decisions are based upon Table 14.2.

TABLE 14.2   Bridge Routing Decisions

Packet Source	Destination network (from fwding_db)		
	NETWORK	BACKGROUND_2	Unknown
NETWORK	*Discard*	*Send to* BACKGROUND_2	*Send to* BACKGROUND_2
BACKGROUND_2	*Send to* NETWORK	*Discard*	*Send to* NETWORK

Bridge learning consists of determining the source of the message and updating fwding_db with the queue number of the process that sent the packet (i.e., either NETWORK or BACKGROUND_2).

half_bridge(). Packets destined for the "other" network are forwarded to the half_bridge from either the remote half_bridge() (via the parallel port software) or the local router() (half_bridge() is also found in bridge.c). Packets sent across the parallel port are enclosed in a frame delimited by the bytes *STX* and *ETX*; *DLE* insertion is required to avoid confusing a data *ETX* with the end-of-frame *ETX*.

Frames from *Parallel Port* are received one byte at a time by half_bridge(). These bytes are assembled into the array remote_msg and forwarded to Router() when the frame delimiting *ETX* is found. All framing bytes and inserted *DLE*s are discarded. If the trailing *ETX* is lost and the number of bytes is about to exceed the limit allowed by remote_msg, the reception is aborted.

Packets from router() are received in their entirety and must be enclosed in a frame prior to transmission. Since *DLE* insertion is also necessary, the packet from router(), bridge_msg, is copied one byte at a time into the array pp_msg. Once the copying is completed, the packet is sent to *Parallel Port* for transmission.

do_bridge(). The do_bridge() function (found in bridge.c), is the foreground process associated with queue APPLICATION, and is intended to allow the user to monitor the state of the local half-bridge. The following commands are recognized by do_bridge():

R or r. Displays the number of bytes sent to each of the active stations by the half-bridge. Each station's total is stored as an element of array r_bytes.

S or s. Displays the port number associated with each active station; the port numbers are the queue numbers of the different networks or the queue number of the half-bridge (BACKGROUND_2). The values are obtained from the forwarding database array fwding_db.

T or t. Displays the number of bytes sent by each of the active stations and forwarded to the remote network. The totals are stored in the array x_bytes.

14.6.3 Compiling the Bridge Software

The Commkit bridge is made by linking the following modules: bridge.obj, parlport.obj, commkit.obj, intrpt.obj, and crc.obj, with one of the local area network modules, buslo.obj or ringlo.obj. Buslo.obj (and ringlo.obj) are versions of buslow.c (and ringlow.c) that have been compiled with the token BRIDGE defined. The two bridges that can be made from these object files are defined in the makefile as busb.exe and ringb.exe.

For example, to make both bridges, (ringb.exe and busb.exe), type the following:

```
C:\> make ringb.exe
C:\> make busb.exe
```

14.6.4 Running the Bridge Software

Both bus and ring bridges are available in executable form on the Commkit diskette; they can also be created using the make utility (see preceding section).

Since the bridge software is independent of any underlying network, it is possible to connect different types of network. For example, the following bridged network could be built out of the ring, bus, and bridge software (the cabling rules discussed in previous chapters and the special parallel port cable connections must still be observed). See Figure 14.19.

The stations would run the software outlined in Table 14.3.

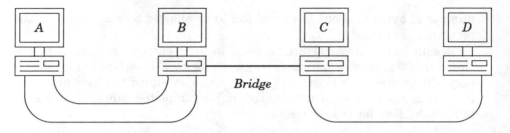

Figure 14.19   The test internetwork

TABLE 14.3   Software for Figure 14.19

PC	Software
A	`ringex 1200 A`
B	`ringb 1200 B M`
C	`busb 2400 C`
D	`busex 2400 D`

Neither `busb.exe` nor `ringb.exe` support transmission on their respective networks, since both are intended to permit the querying of various bridge statistics: R displays the number of bytes sent to each active station; S displays each active station and its network; and T displays the number of bytes received from each active station. **CTRL-C** will abort the execution of a bridge.

It is advisable to run `ringb.exe` as the ring monitor, since this allows one of the remaining ring network stations to be run as a line analyser. For example, in the configuration shown in Table 14.3, PC *A* could be run as a line analyser, showing the traffic on the ring. This permits verification of the forwarding of packets across the bridge. Similarly, a station on the bus network can be run as a line analyser.

Messages can be sent between stations on the same network or between stations on different networks. For example, a user on station *D* could send a message to the user on station *A* by typing:

```
AD Nod your head if you receive this message!
```

Once a message has been sent, the bridges can be queried with regards to the active stations or the number of transmissions. Packet filtering takes place as soon as a station's identifier is entered in the forwarding database. For example, if station *D* sends a message to station *A* and then *D* sends a message to itself, the message is not forwarded, since the bus bridge "knows" that station *D* is on the bus network.

The addresses assigned to the bridges are not used by the bridge, since the bridge only handles the routing of packets and operate in promiscuous mode.

14.7 SUMMARY

Ideally, all the services required by an application should reside on the application's network. However, due to equipment costs, physical distances, and organizational differences, the service required by the application may reside on a different network. In order that the application can access the service on the remote network, facilities must be in place to allow the interconnection of the different networks. Broadly speaking, there are three such approaches, each associated with an OSI layer:

Repeaters. A repeater is a device that allows the connection of homogeneous networks at the Physical Layer. Repeaters are not responsible for routing or fragmentation, nor are they affected by the type of service offered (connection-oriented or connectionless).

Bridges. A bridge operates at the Data Link Layer and permits the interconnection of heterogenous networks. A local area network made from a number of local area networks (known as segments) is called a bridged local area network. Two types of bridges were considered in this chapter: transparent bridges and source-routing bridges. Transparent bridges require less processing on the part of the stations, but often result in the use of a nonoptimal spanning tree to ensure that packets do not circulate forever; whereas source-routing bridges require the active involvement of the source station in the establishment of a potentially optimal route through the network.

Gateways. Like bridges, gateways also permit the interconnection of heterogeneous networks, but operate at the Network Layer. Taking this approach, a network operated by different organizations supporting different protocols and addressing schemes can be interconnected. Since gateways operate at the Network Layer, gateways exist for both connection-oriented and connectionless networks. Gateways are also referred to as routers.

14.8 EXERCISES

1. Explain both how and why a repeater connecting two bus networks permits collisions to be forwarded.

2. Show, by means of examples, the difficulties in making synchronous mode work when connecting a pair of rings by a bridge.

3. The chapter described one possible type of transparent bridge in which all packets are forwarded, and which resulted in flooding and, potentially, packets cycling forever. If a hop-count is included in each packet, would this help? How would this compare with the spanning-tree and source-routing algorithms? Remember, in the spanning-tree algorithm the bridges are in constant communication with one another.

4. An alternative method of routing is known as *reverse-path forwarding* in which packets are forwarded only if they are received on a link with the shortest path back to the source of the packet. Packets are forwarded on all links except the one on which it was received.

    Consider how reverse-path forwarding could be implemented. How would each gateway "know" whether one link was a shorter path back to the source than another? Suggest a structure for the routing table. Could the reverse path ever be changed—how?

5. Suggest methods whereby multicast could be supported on a bridged local area network. Your solution(s) should avoid simply broadcasting each multicast message on all networks, ideally each multicast packet should be transmitted only on those networks were a member of the multicast set exists.

    Can multicast be supported by the spanning-tree algorithm? The source-routing algorithm?

6. Three approaches to initializing an intelligent bridge were suggested in this chapter. Describe the methods needed to update the station address tables if:

    a) a station was removed entirely from the network.
    b) a station was removed from one network and placed on the other (keeping its physical address).

7. Show the resulting spanning tree if bridge *B1* were to fail.

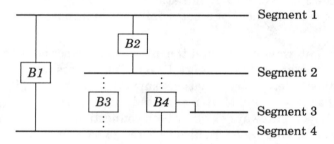

8. Set up two Commkit local area networks and connect them by the bridge. Prove to yourself that the bridge actually works by transmitting packets from a station on one network to a station on the other network. The state of each half-bridge can be determined by querying the bridge.

    Now, consider the following questions:

    ▪ How long does it take for the bridge to "learn" about all the stations on the different networks?

    ▪ What happens to packets that are addressed to stations that do not exist on either network?

    ▪ What happens if two stations on different networks have the same address?

    The minimum number of PCs required for this exercise is four. By alternating the non-bridge PCs on a network between the line analyser and a network station, the traffic on the network can be monitored and traffic can be generated. It is not necessary to take the entire network down, just restart one of the nonbridge PCs with the line analyser.

9. Run a pair of networks at different speeds, one at 300 bps and the other at 9600 bps. Does everything flow smoothly? If one of the bridges crashes, explain why this has occurred.

10. The protocol used by the Half-Bridge does not handle lost or damaged packets. Modify the Half-Bridge software so that a stop-and-wait protocol handles errors in transmission.

11. The routing algorithm used in router() works fine for a bridge connecting two networks; however, it is not general-purpose and could not be used to support more than two links. Redesign the routing algorithm so that it is general-purpose and can function with anywhere from 2 to 16 different links. Implement your algorithm and use the bridge keyboard to generate packets from fictitious remote networks.

12. Modify the bridge software so that the Commkit wide area network can be connected to another Commkit wide area network.

13. Modify the bridge software so that the Commkit wide area network can be connected to a Commkit local area network.

14. What changes to the bridge software are necessary if the two interconnected local area networks support different packet sizes?

15. Try running Commkit sockettes on the separate networks. If the source and destination hosts are on separate networks, is the sockette packet forwarded correctly? Are changes necessary to the networks or the bridges? Explain.

16. Modify the bridge software so that Commkit sockettes will be supported using a form of IP gateway. That is, when a packet is supplied for transmission, if the destination does not exist on the local network, the packet is forwarded to the gateway.

    How will each host know the address of the gateway? What other changes will be required?

An Introduction to C

This appendix offers a brief overview of C for those readers unfamiliar with the language. The description of C covers only those language constructs used by Commkit; additional details can be found in any number of books written on C or in the Turbo C manuals.

A.1 COMMENTS

A comment begins with /* and ends with */. Everything within the comment is ignored by the compiler, including any code or data structures. Comments cannot be nested but can span multiple lines.

A.2 BASE TYPES

C supports three base types from which all other structures can be derived: integers, characters, and floating point. Only integers and characters are considered in this appendix, since Commkit does not use floating point. Any character can be used as either a character or an integer, depending upon the context.

A.3 UNNAMED CONSTANTS

Commkit uses five different unnamed constants:

Decimal constants. A decimal constant is any integer that is acceptable to the machine, such as –17, 0, or 1027. C allows decimals to be either signed or unsigned (Table A.1).

TABLE A.1   The Range of Decimal Constants

signed		unsigned	
Minimum	Maximum	Minimum	Maximum
-2^{n-1}	$+2^{n-1} - 1$	0	$+2^n - 1$

The value of n depends upon the context, and is one of 8 (byte), 16 (word), or 32 (double word or long).

Character constants. Character constants are any alphanumeric characters enclosed in *single quotes*, for example $'A'$, $'1'$, and $'\%'$. Control characters can be declared as character constants using: $'\backslash ch'$, where *'ch'* is a lower case alphabetic character (for example, the end-of-line is delimited by $'\backslash n'$). A backslash is represented as two backslashes in a row ($'\backslash\backslash'$), while a single quote is a quote mark following a backslash ($'\backslash''$).

Octal constants. Octal constants are written with the prefix 0 (zero). All digits following the zero *must* be in the range 0 through 7. For example, 0377, is either -128 (if treated as a signed constant) or 255 (if treated as an unsigned constant).

Hexadecimal constants. Hexadecimal constants are written with the prefix 0xhh (where h denotes a hexadecimal digit, four bits long: 0 through 9, A, B, C, D, E, and F). For example, -1 can be written as 0xFFFF (16-bit) or 0xFFFFFFFF (32-bit).

String constants. String constants are collections of one or more characters enclosed in *double quotes*—"Dusty" is an example of a string. Internally, C appends a null character ($'\backslash 0'$) to the end of each string, thereby allowing an easy way to determine the end of a string. It also increases the size of the string by one byte (this is important when defining arrays of characters, as seen later).

A.4   IDENTIFIERS AND VARIABLES

An identifier is any collection of alphanumeric characters that starts with an alphabetic character. Spaces, tabs, and carriage returns are not allowed within an identifier; however, underscores (_) are allowed.

A.4.1   Variables

A variable is simply an identifier declared to be of a specific type. It is common practice to write all C variables in lowercase. A declaration is written as the type followed by one or more variable names (separated by commas). The declaration is terminated by a semicolon.

Integer variables are declared as either a short (16-bit), int (16-bit), or long (32-bit). By default, all variables are signed, however, the prefix unsigned allows the declaration of unsigned variables:

```
int alpha;
unsigned long beta;
short gamma, delta;
```

Character variables will hold one byte (8 bits) and can be used for either characters or as 8-bit integers. Characters are declared as type char; by default, characters are signed, although they can be explicitly declared unsigned:

```
char ch, data;
unsigned char subscript;
```

A.4.2 Initialization

Variables can be initialized when they are declared. For example:

```
char ch = 'X';
int data = 3;
```

Variables that are not initialized have undefined values until an assignment takes place (see the next section).

A.4.3 Reserved Words

The following reserved words cannot be used as identifiers (and hence variables):

```
auto      break     case      char      continue  default   do
double    else      extern    float     for       goto      if
int       long      register  return    short     sizeof    static
struct    switch    typedef   union     unsigned  void      while
```

The Turbo C User's Guide lists an additional set of reserved words used by Turbo C.

A.5 EXPRESSIONS

C supports a number of different expressions and operators:

Arithmetic The arithmetic operators found in most languages are supported by C, notably: + (addition), – (subtraction), * (multiplication), and / (integer division, the decimal and fraction are discarded). The percent sign % is for integer modulus (i.e., the remainder after division). The normal precedence rules apply (i.e., multiplication, division, and modulus have higher priority than addition and subtraction). Parentheses can be used to change the order of evaluation, for example:

```
2 + 3 * 4      /* = 14 */
(2 + 3) * 4    /* = 20 */
```

Note that arithmetic operations *can* be applied to characters. For example, 'A' + 1 gives 'B' (since the character after 'A' in the ASCII collating sequence is 'B').

Relational   Relational operators allow the comparison of two expressions. There are six relational operators (Table A.2).

TABLE A.2   **Relational Operators**

Symbol	Operation
ex1 == *ex2*	equals
ex1 != *ex2*	not equals
ex1 < *ex2*	less than
ex1 > *ex2*	greater than
ex1 <= *ex2*	less than or equal
ex1 >= *ex2*	greater than or equal

All relational expressions evaluate to either 0 (False) or 1 (True). There are no built-in constants TRUE or FALSE (as in Pascal).

Booleans are built out of integers (or characters). Zero is false, while anything else (typically 1) is taken as true.

Shift   There are two shift operators: << for left shift and >> for right shift. The left-hand expression is the variable (or expression) to be shifted, while the right-hand expression is the amount by which the left-hand expression is to be shifted. For example, x << 3 shifts the variable x to the left by 3 (this is equivalent to multiplying by 8).

Bit-wise   Bits can be set and cleared using the bit operators given in Table A.3.

TABLE A.3   **Bit-wise Operators**

Symbol	Operation
&	bit-wise 'and'
|	bit-wise 'or'
^	exclusive-or

For example, to mask the lower eight bits of an integer i, the bit-wise "and" operator could be used: i & 0xff.

Logical   There are two logical operators, && (*and*) and || (*or*). The logical operators have the lowest precedence and are evaluated from left-to-right. A zero-valued expression is interpreted as false, while all other values are taken as true.

Logical expressions are evaluated from left-to-right until there is no longer any need to continue evaluating. For example, a logical expression consisting of *or* operators (||) is evaluated until the first true (i.e., nonzero) expression is found, at which point the entire logical expression is taken to be true.

Similarly, an expression using the *and* operator (&&) is evaluated until the end of expression is reached *or* one of the expressions is found to be false.

Conditional operator   The conditional operator ? allows an if-then-else like construct to be embedded within an expression:

(expression) ? *true-part* : *false-part*

For example, a problem may require 6 to be added to x if total equals 3, otherwise 4 is to be added to x; this can be written as follows:

```
x + (total == 3) ? 6 : 4
```

A.6   THE ASSIGNMENT STATEMENT

The assignment statement is defined as a left-value (*lvalue*) being assigned the result of a right-value (*rvalue*). It is written as *lvalue = rvalue*. The *lvalue* is always a memory location and the *rvalue* an expression. Unless otherwise indicated, the statement is terminated with a semicolon (;). C supports little or no checking when dealing with variables of the base type, for example:

```
int a;
char b;

a = 'X';        /* Assigning a character to an integer */
b = a + 1;      /* Storing an integer into a character variable */
```

Multiple assignments are allowed:

```
a = b = c = 10;
```

Beware of seemingly innocent typos such as:

```
a = b == c = 10;
```

In this case c is assigned the value 10, then b is compared with c and the result of the comparison (0 or 1) is assigned to a.

A.6.1   Variations

C offers a number of shorthand notations for the assignment statement:

- Statements such as: x = x *<op>* y can be abbreviated to: x *<op>*= y. The *<op>* can be one of: +, -, *, /, %, <<, >>, &, |, or ^ . For example, the statement a = a + b can be abbreviated to a += b.
- Increments (such as a = a + 1), can be abbreviated to a++ or ++a. There *is* a difference between a++ and ++a; a++ indicates that the value of a is to be used in the expression, and once used, a is to be incremented. On the other hand, ++a indicates that a is to be incremented, then its value is to be used in the expression. Similarly, decrements can be abbreviated to a-- or --a. The same rules apply to the positioning of the -- signs.

- It is important to note that an assignment can take place *anywhere*. For example, the following statement:

```
a = (b = 3) * 2;
```

results in b being assigned the value 3, while a is assigned the value 6 (i.e., the value of b after the assignment times 2).

A.7 SELECTION

C supports two selection statements, one conditional and the other a multiway branch.

A.7.1 Compound Statements

Compound statements are groups of zero or more statements enclosed in "curly" brackets (note that *all* statements must be ended with a semicolon):

```
{
Statement1;
/* More statements */
StatementN;
}
```

The compound statement is *not* ended with a semicolon.

A.7.2 The if Statement

The if statement is written as:

```
if ( Expression )
Statement1;
else
Statement2;
```

The *Expression* is evaluated; a nonzero result causes *Statement1* to be executed, otherwise *Statement2* is executed. If the else–*Statement2* construct is omitted, the result is an if-then statement. Note that *Statement1* and *Statement2* can both be compound statements (remember that compound statements cannot be followed by a semicolon).

The following code fragment illustrates an *if* statement: should a equal 'X' or c be less than 2, data is assigned the value five; otherwise data is cleared and a is assigned 'Z'.

```
if (a == 'X' || c < 2)
    data = 5;
else
{
    /* a != 'X' and c >= 2 */
    data = 0;
    a = 'Z';
}
```

A.7.3 The switch Statement

The multiway branch is known as the *switch* statement, it is normally written in the following form:

```
switch( Expression )
{
case Constant:
Statement(s);
break;

case Constant:
Statement(s);
break;

/* Other statements */

default:
Statement(s);
}
```

The *Expression* is evaluated to an integer value; control is passed to the *case* label (a constant) which matches the value of the *Expression*. The *Statement(s)* following the label are then executed. If a section of code is to be associated with a number of different values of the *Expression*, each *Constant* must be associated with its own case label; for example:

```
switch (ch)
{
case 'A':
case 'a':
    /* Statements */
    break;

case 'B':
case 'b':
    /* Statements */
    break;

/* Other 'case' labels and statements */
}
```

Once the set of statements associated with the *Expression* has been evaluated, control can be passed outside of the switch statement using the break statement. It is possible to branch into the middle of a series of statements simply by placing the case label above the first statement associated with the case label:

```
switch(ch)
{
case 'A':
    ch = 'a';
case 'a':
```

```
        /* Statements */
        break;

        /* Other 'case' labels and statements */
    }
```

If the value of the *Expression* does not match any of the case labels, control passes to the statements that follow the label default:. If there is no default, control passes to the first statement following the closing curly bracket of the switch.

A.8   ITERATION

C supports three-structured iteration statements as well as a goto statement.

A.8.1   The while Statement

The while statement is a pre-test, nondeterministic-loop structure, written in the form:

```
    while ( Expression )
    Statement;
```

The *Expression* is evaluated, if it is nonzero, the *Statement* is executed. The cycle is repeated as long as the result of the expression is nonzero. The *Statement* can be a compound statement. For example,

```
    count = 0;
    while (count < 10)
    {
        /* Other statements */
        count++;
    }
```

Often the loop can proceed backwards, producing some interesting software:

```
    count = 10;
    while (count--)
    {
        /* Statements */
    }
```

The loop will be entered with the final value of count being zero; the next iteration will determine that count has a zero value and the loop will terminate.

An infinite loop can be written by setting the *Expression* to 1: while(1).

A.8.2   The do..while Statement

The do..while statement is a post-test, nondeterministic loop, written in the form:

```
do
    Statement;
while ( Expression );
```

The *Statement* (which can be a compound statement) is executed before the *Expression* is evaluated. The cycle continues as long as the *Expression* produces a nonzero result. Multiple statements must be written as a compound statement.

A.8.3 The for Statement

The for statement allows the construction of deterministic loops (i.e., loops with a known initial condition, final condition, and increment). The format of the for statement is as follows:

```
for ( Expression1; Expression2; Expression3 )
    Statement;
```

where *Expression1* is the initial condition (typically an assignment), *Expression2* is the termination condition, and *Expression3* is the increment. For example, to count from 0 to 10, a for loop could be written as:

```
for (i=0; i<=10; i++)
{
    /* Statements */
}
```

Note that the for loop is equivalent to:

```
expression1;
while (expression2)
{
    /* Statements */
    expression3;
}
```

Finally, any or all of the *expression*s may be omitted. For example, the following set of statements are performed "forever":

```
for(;;)
{
    /* Statements */
}
```

A.8.4 The goto Statement

An unconditional transfer of control can be achieved using the goto statement. The goto statement is written with an identifier (a *label*), for example:

```
goto done;
```

The label must be within the same function (see Section A.10) as the goto, is terminated with a colon (not a semicolon) and can branch forward or backward over any number of nested loops:

```
while(1)
{
     /* Statements */
     if (data == 'X') goto done;
     /* Statements */
}
done:
/* Statements */
```

Note that `goto` is different from `break` in that `goto` can branch to anywhere within a function. However, `break` is more structured since control passes to the first statement beyond the end of the block in which the `break` is written. The `continue` statement passes control to the end of the block in which the `continue` is written.

For example, if the statement `goto done` were replaced by `break`, execution would resume with the first statement outside the `while` loop. However, if `continue` replaced `goto done`, the statements between the `continue` and the closing curly bracket would be ignored, with execution resuming at the start of the loop (i.e., the `while`).

A.9   AGGREGATE DATA TYPES

C allows complex data types (notably arrays, structures, and unions) to be constructed out of the three base types. Additionally, pointers to the base types or aggregate types can be constructed.

A.9.1   Arrays

An array is a data structure consisting of one of more elements sharing a common type and name (an identifier). Arrays are declared by specifying the array's type, its name, and dimension. For example, to declare an array of 10 integers, the following declaration could be used:

```
int data[10];
```

An individual element in the array is accessed using a subscript enclosed in square brackets. Subscripts are integers (or characters) and must be in the range 0 through N-1 (where N is the size of the array). For example, the array `data` could be set to zero using a `for` loop:

```
for (i=0; i<10; i++)
    data[i] = 0;
```

Arrays can also be initialized when they are declared:

```
int data[10] = {0, 0, 0, 0, 0, 0, 0, 0, 0, 0};
```

An array can have a maximum of two dimensions, where each dimension is separated by a comma.

A string is simply an array of `char`s. For example:

```
char name[10];
```

Text strings cannot be assigned directly to string variables in an assignment statement, although individual characters may be assigned to each array element. However, C has many string manipulation routines that can be used to access, compare, and manipulate strings.

Strings can be initialized at compile time in much the same way integer arrays are handled (note that the curly brackets are omitted):

```
char name[10] = "Your name";
```

In the above example, the array name is assigned the nine characters of the string "Your name". A tenth character (the null character) is added at the end of the string. To avoid counting each character in a string, C allows a shorthand notation for character string initialization:

```
char name[] = "Your name";
```

A.9.2 Structures

Separate data structures that are related can be placed in a single, larger data structure known as a struct. The basic format of a structure is:

```
struct
{
field(s);
}
```

The structure consists of one or more *field(s)*; where a *field* is a data-structure declaration. For example, a person's birthday consisting of a day, month, and year are all related items that can be grouped into a struct:

```
struct
{
int day;
int month;
int year;
}
```

A structure can be used to declare a new data structure or a new data type (or both); the previous example is incorrect in that the structure has not declared a new data structure or a new data type.

Data structures are declared with the name of the data structure following the closing curly bracket. For example, a data structure, my_birthday, with the fields day, month, and year, could be declared as follows (note that the structure ends with a semicolon):

```
struct
{
int day;
int month;
int year;
} my_birthday;
```

To declare a new data type, the name of the new type is entered after the word struct and before the '{', (note that the structure must be terminated with a semicolon after the closing bracket), for example:

```
struct birthday
{
int day;
int month;
int year;
};
```

Structures can be declared within other structures.

The rules for declaring a data structure of type struct are the same as any other declaration: the name of the type (for example, struct birthday) must be followed by one or more *identifiers*, separated by commas and terminated with a semicolon:

```
struct birthday evans_birthday;
struct birthday the_cats_birthday;
```

The individual fields within the structure are accessed by specifying the name of the structure (i.e., the *identifier*), followed by a ".", followed by the name of the field (note, this can be recursive if structures within structures are declared). Structures can also be initialized at compile time. For example:

```
struct birthday evans_birthday = {18, 5, 1978};
struct birthday the_cats_birthday;

the_cats_birthday . day   = 1;
the_cats_birthday . month = 4;
the_cats_birthday . year  = 1990;
```

The individual fields within the structure can be manipulated based upon their type.

Structures can be declared as arrays and accessed using subscripts:

```
struct birthday cat_family[5];
int i;

for (i=0; i<5; i++)
{
    cat_family[i] . day   = 0;
    cat_family[i] . month = 0;
    cat_family[i] . year  = 0;
}
```

A.9.3 Unions

Data structures can share the same memory locations using a union. A union is declared and accessed in the same way as a structure, with the difference being that each *field* entry in a union refers to the same memory location.

For example, the following union declaration allows a 32-bit location to be accessed as four bytes, two words, or one long word:

```
union memloc
{
char byte[4];
int word[2];
long double_word;
};


union memloc x;
```

The variable x refers to a single 32-bit location, and can be visualized as follows:

x.byte[0]	x.byte[1]	x.byte[2]	x.byte[3]
x.word[0]		x.word[1]	
x.double_word			

A.9.4 Pointers

All data structures are associated with an address. C allows the program to access a data structure through the name of the data structure or its address. The address of a data structure is obtained by placing an & before the name of the data structure. For example, the address of an integer x can be obtained by writing & before the x.

A pointer is declared as a pointer to a specific type. For example, a pointer to an integer is declared as:

```
int *ptr;
```

Pointers are assigned values (usually addresses, although this is not a necessity due to C's lax type checking) using an assignment statement. To refer to the location indicated by the pointer requires placing an * in front of the pointer's name.

A typical, contrived, example of how a pointer functions is as follows:

```
int *ptr;        /* A pointer to an integer */
int data, ans;   /* Two integers */

ptr = &data;     /* 'ptr' now contains the address of 'data' */
*ptr = 7;        /* 'data' now has a value of 7 */
ans = *ptr;      /* 'ans' takes the value of the location */
                 /*  pointed to by 'ptr' (i.e. 7)         */
```

Pointers can point to array elements as long as the types agree, for example:

```
char *cptr;       /* A pointer to a character */
char array[10];   /* A string of 10 characters */

cptr = &array[2]; /* 'cptr' points to the 3rd element in 'array' */
*cptr = 'S';      /* 'array[2]' now contains 'S' */
```

Pointers can be incremented and decremented. For example, to initialize `array` to `'?'`, one could write:

```
cptr = &array[0];  /* or simply `cptr = &array' */
i = 0;
while (i < 10)
{
    *cptr++ = '?'; /* Assign '?' then increment `cptr' */
    i++;
}
```

Pointers can also point to structures and unions. A structure (or union) pointer is declared to be a pointer to the specific structure. When referring to a *field* within the structure, the pointer name is followed by ->, and finally the field name:

```
struct birthday evans;
struct birthday *guess; /* Pointer to struct `birthday' */

evans . day = 18;
evans . month = 5;
evans . year = 1978;

guess = &evans;               /* Address of struct `evans' */
guess -> day -= 5;            /* Decrement `day' by 5 */
guess -> month = 2;          /* Change `month' to 2 */

if (guess -> year > 1950)
    guess -> year = 1949;  /* Change year to 1949 */

/* `evans' now contains 13 (day), 2 (month), 1949 (year) */
```

A.10 FUNCTIONS

A C program consists of one or more functions. All functions have the same format, notably:

Result-Type Function-Name (*Parameter-Declarations*)
{
Function-Body
}

The *Result-Type* can be any type: a base type (`int`, `char`, `long`, `unsigned`, etc.) or an aggregate type. However, if an aggregate type is being returned, it should be returned as an address since the function returns at most a 16- or 32-bit integer value. A *Result-Type* of `void` indicates that nothing is to be returned, meaning that the function is essentially a procedure. The *Function-Name* is a valid identifier name, while the *Function-Body* is enclosed in curly brackets: {...}. The *Function-Body* consists of (local) variable declarations as well as executable statements.

If the *Result-Type* is omitted, the function is assumed to return an integer. The *Parameter-Declarations* are optional: if they are omitted, the parenthesis must follow the *Function-Name*. For example, the function ex1() is an integer function:

```
ex1()
{
/* Statements */
}
```

All parameters are considered local to the function and when listed, must be separated by commas. For example, the following function is of type int with three parameters (arg1 is an integer, arg2 is a character, and arg3 is a pointer to an integer):

```
int example(int arg1, char arg2, int *arg3);
{
/* Statements */
}
```

A value can be returned from a function using the return statement. For example, the following function returns the larger of two integers:

```
int largest(int data1, data2)
{
return (data1 > data2) ? data1 : data2;
}
```

A function is called by writing the *Function-Name*, followed by the arguments associated with the function. For example, to find the largest of two numbers num1 and num2, one could write:

```
answer = largest(num1, num2);
```

It is possible to ignore the return value by *casting* the function to void:

```
(void) largest(num1, num2);
```

Unless otherwise specified, all parameters are *call by value*; meaning that whatever changes take place to the parameter in the function, the corresponding argument remains unchanged. Should it be necessary to have the function change the value of the argument, C allows the arguments to be passed *by reference*.

A call by reference parameter requires the *address* of the data structure to be the argument; the corresponding parameter in the *Parameter-Declarations* must be a pointer to the specified type. Structures *must* be passed by reference. Consider the following example:

```
void ex2(struct birthday *bptr, int *iptr)
{
bptr -> day = 26;
bptr -> month = 8;
bptr -> year = 1954;
```

```
*iptr = 123;
}

void call_ex()
{
struct birthday jaws;
int dusty;

ex2(&jaws, &dusty);

/* jaws: 26 (day), 8 (month), 1954 (year), and dusty: 123 */
}
```

All variables declared within a function are local to the function. Global variables are those variables declared outside of functions and which are global to all functions. Aggregate types can be declared globally as well. Since C programs can be developed in a number of different files, global data structures (common to a number of separately compiled functions) can be declared as externals using the extern type. For example, assuming a number of separately compiled functions shared a common data structure cookie of type struct birthday, one file would require the declaration: struct birthday cookie (to reserve the memory location); while the other files would contain the declaration extern struct birthday cookie. The linker resolves any addressing problems.

An alternative to declaring a global variable that is used by a single function is to declare a local static variable. The static variable retains its value between calls of the function, whereas all other local variables are *automatic* in that they are created on the stack for the duration of the function's call. A static variable can be initialized at its declaration:

```
int example()
{
static char data = 'X';
/* Statements */
}
```

The entry point from the operating system into the program must be a function with the name main(). This function can have two parameters, the first indicating the number of items entered on the command line when the program is loaded, and the second, an array of pointers pointing to each word (assumed to be a character string) entered on the command line. These two parameters are given the names argc and argv respectively:

```
main(int argc, char *argv[])
{
/* Statements */
}
```

For example, if an executable program example has three arguments entered on the command line as follows:

```
C:\> example cricket dusty 1200
```

Then the value of `argc` is 4 (there are four "words" entered on the command line), and `argv` is an array of string pointers (Figure A.1).

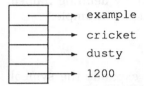
example
cricket
dusty
1200

Figure A.1   `argv` is a list of pointers

Any of the strings can be accessed; for example, to access `dusty`, one would refer to the third element of `argv`, notably `argv[2]`.

Some general points about functions:

- Functions cannot be local to other functions; that is, all functions are global.

- Forward references to functions are allowed, however, the functions are assumed to return integers. Function headers (i.e., the *Result-Type*, the *Function-Name*, and the *Parameter-Declaration*) can be defined as global statements at the start of the file or even external.

- By default, the compiler passes all strings *by reference*.

- Unless the *Result-Type* is specified, the function is assumed to be of type `int` (returning an integer value).

A.11 COMPILER DIRECTIVES

C supports a number of compiler directives that instruct the compiler to perform an action that need not result in the generation of code. Two compiler directives that are used by Commkit are `#define` and `#ifdef`.

The `#define` compiler directive instructs the compiler to store a symbol and a value in the symbol table. A common use of `#define` is to declare *named constants*, for example:

```
#define TRUE      1
#define FALSE     0
#define LIMIT     25
#define MASK      0xff
#define VALUE     'w'

main()
{
char data[LIMIT];   /* 'data' is an array of size LIMIT */

if (data[3] & MASK == VALUE)
    then data[3] = 0;
}
```

It is common to write all defined symbols in UPPER case to distinguish them from other data structures. Defined symbols are *not* variables, they cannot be an *lvalue* nor are they associated with an address.

The #define directive can be used for more than simply defining named constants—it can define entire expressions or statements, for example:

```
#define FOREVER      for(;;)
#define DOUBLE_X     x *= 2;
```

Whenever a defined symbol is written, the compiler expands the symbol into whatever the symbol is defined as. For example, whenever FOREVER is encountered, the compiler actually compiles for(;;).

Arguments can be passed to compiler directives as well. For example, to allow any value to be doubled (instead of x as in the previous example):

```
#define DOUBLE(value) value *= 2;

main()
{
int x, count;

DOUBLE(x)        /* Compiler produces x *= 2;     */
DOUBLE(count)    /* Compiler produces count *= 2; */
}
```

Multiple arguments are allowed, although the exact number depends upon the compiler.

Conditional compilation is possible using the #ifdef compiler directive in conjunction with the #define directive. Conditional compilation permits the programmer to instruct the compiler to generate code under certain conditions (for example, when searching for an error).

For example, to track down an error, it is possible to plant diagnostic statements throughout a program. Once the error is found, all the diagnostic statements may be removed (although existing code may potentially be damaged). An alternative is to leave the diagnostic software in the program, but to associate the diagnostic statements with directives that instruct the compiler when to include the diagnostics:

```
void a_procedure()
{
     /* Statements */
#ifdef DEBUG
     /* Diagnostic statements */
#endif
     /* Statements */
}
```

The compiler will include the diagnostic statements between the #ifdef and #endif if DEBUG has been defined; otherwise the diagnostic statements are left out of the compilation. DEBUG can be defined simply by writing #define DEBUG (there is no need to associate a value with DEBUG, the compiler simply marks it as defined).

A.12 SOFTWARE MANAGEMENT

There are two types of source code files: *source* files (with a .c extension), that is, C programs that can be compiled; and *header* files (indicated by the .h extension), containing definitions and data structures. All of the source files have an equivalent *object* version (each with an extension .obj), consisting of executable software that must be linked (with other object files) to create an executable file (with an .exe extension).

To minimize the amount of compiling required each time a change is made to a source file, a software management tool known as make is supplied with Turbo C. The make utility controls the recompilation of files by reading the commands specified in the makefile. The makefile contains a list of *dependencies*, which specify the source files that must be recompiled and relinked after a change is made. For example, the file ipc.obj is dependent upon ipc.c: should a change occur to ipc.c (i.e., if the time and date of ipc.obj is earlier than that of ipc.c), ipc.c is recompiled using tcc, the Turbo C compiler, a new copy of ipc.obj is produced. The executable version of ipc.c (ipc.exe) is also specified as a dependency, this time the Turbo linker tlink is called to link the object files ipc.obj, commkit.obj, and intrpt.obj to create ipc.exe.

The instructions in the makefile are processed by the make utility by typing:

```
C:\> make
```

When the make utility finds a file that must be recompiled or relinked, the specific line in the makefile is displayed. If all files are found to be up-to-date, make returns to the MS-DOS prompt.

A specific file can be processed by the make utility by typing the file name after make. For example, to check whether ipc.exe is up-to-date, one could type:

```
C:\> make ipc.exe
```

B

Running and Testing Commkit

One of the biggest sources of frustration for any programmer is to be stuck with software that doesn't function as expected. This is as true for communications software as it is for any other type of software. This appendix is intended to suggest a number of techniques that can be used to help find and correct errors.

B.1 GENERAL HINTS

There are no hard and fast rules that can be used when modifying software and checking for errors. However, the following points may help reduce some of the frustration that can accompany working with communication software developed by someone else:

- Use the line analyser to monitor the communication channel.

  The line analyser is intended to remove as much of the guesswork as possible with respect to what is occurring on the channel. Knowing what is happening "down there" often makes it easier to determine what is happening "up top."

- Timing is often critical when testing communication software: avoid writing software that "assumes" a specific line speed.

  Software that is hard-coded to work at one line speed can break down at different speeds. A good example of this can be found in ring-network software: the ring monitor is designed to wait five seconds without sensing a token, after this time all traffic is removed from the network and a new token is placed on the ring. The software works correctly at all speeds except

50 bps. Since 50 bps is roughly 5 characters per second, a message of more than about 25 characters will cause the monitor to reset the network. (There is an exercise in Chapter 12 which expects you to correct this problem!)

■ Don't make too many changes at once: make a limited number of changes and then exercise the software. If an error occurs after a limited set of changes have been made, you can be rather confident that the error has been caused by the new software.

It is also wise to avoid making changes to the line analyser at the same time as other software is being changed. For example, an error occurring after modifying both the line analyser and the point-to-point software can lead to untold hours of frustration since there are two possible sources of the error.

■ Check the wiring that interconnects the various PCs before blaming the software. A good example is the ring network that requires a specific ordering of connections (i.e., serial port 1 to serial port 2). If the wiring is wrong, the software can't be expected to function properly.

■ The message buffer queue can suddenly empty if messages are being sent but never received. This causes the queue of pending messages to be displayed on the PC and the software to terminate. The first byte displayed after dump is the process (queue) number: this will give you an indication of which process is not reading its queue.

■ Remember, the background processes are only envoked when the foreground process performs a `recv()`. The foreground process can cause the message buffer queue to empty if it sends vast numbers of messages to a background process while never pausing to perform a `recv()`.

■ When testing network software, put sequence numbers into the messages being sent, the sequence numbers allow you to determine whether messages have been lost, corrupted, or are simply hiding somewhere waiting to be transmitted. The line analyser displays all binary information as a byte using the PC's character set; as the sequence number increases, the sequence number displayed by the line analyser will progress through the character set table.

■ If possible, avoid using `printf()` anywhere other than the foreground process. If the implementation of `printf()` is not reentrant, results can be unpredictable, should an interrupt handler access `printf()` at the same time the foreground process does. Use `message()` or `display()` in interrupt handlers.

■ *Always* make backup copies of working software; there's no enjoyment in retyping a set of software from a week-old listing.

■ Although most compiler warning messages can safely be ignored, they often provide useful clues as to why things aren't working.

■ If all else fails, Commkit recognizes CTRL-ALT-DEL as a catastrophic abort and will return control to MS-DOS.

B.2 A FINAL THOUGHT

Remember, testing only indicates the presence of errors, it does not prove their absence. In other words, just because a test has run for an hour and an error hasn't occurred, doesn't mean that the software is error-free. Design your tests to exercise as many parts of the software as practical (i.e., both the true and false parts of an `if` statement and the different `case` options in a `switch` statement).

Character Codes

In its most basic form, all information within a computer is represented as a data structure consisting of one or more bits. The "fundamental" data structure that most computer manufacturers refer to when describing their equipment is the *byte* (for example, many PCs are sold with 640-kilo*bytes* of storage).

The byte itself can be interpreted in a number of different ways; for example, as an integer or as a character. Various *character codes* have been developed over the past century that specify a standard to which various manufacturers conform when mapping the bits making up the byte into a 'character'. The character need not be printable; some characters are treated as control codes that are used in the transmission of information.

This appendix considers three such character codes: Baudot, ASCII, and EBCDIC.

C.1 5-BIT BAUDOT

The Baudot code is a *5-bit* code, in which five bits represent a single character (in many documents, the word *unit* replaces the word *bit*). The code is named after a Frenchman, Emile Baudot, an early pioneer in telegraphy who developed the code in the 1870s. Teletypewriter services such as those offered by Western Union use equipment that recognizes the Baudot code for the transmission and reception of Telex messages. The 8250 UART, used by the PC, can be configured to accept 5-bit data.

At first it may appear that a 5-bit code is of little use since a maximum of only 32 (i.e., 2^5), different character-code values are possible. However, by defining "shift" characters, the number of possible character values *doubles* to 64. There are two shift characters:

LTRS, the incoming data are to be interpreted as letters; and

FIGS, the incoming data are to be interpreted as figures.

Although there are many different implementations of the Baudot code, all characters received as LTRS are interpreted in the same way; however, FIGS may be unique to a specific application. The CCITT International Alphabet Number 2 (or IA2) is a 5-bit Baudot code used for telex communications.

Table C.1 shows the Western Union Telex 5-bit code (the Letters column is common to *all* five-bit Baudot codes, not only Western Union).

TABLE C.1   The Western Union 5-bit Telex Code

	Letters	Figures		Letters	Figures
00000	Blank	Blank	10000	T	5
00001	E	3	10001	Z	"
00010	LF	LF	10010	L	)
00011	A	-	10011	W	2
00100	Space	Space	10100	H	#
00101	S	'	10101	Y	6
00110	I	8	10110	P	0
00111	U	7	10111	Q	1
01000	CR	CR	11000	O	9
01001	D	WRU	11001	B	?
01010	R	4	11010	G	&
01011	J	BELL	11011	FIGS	FIGS
01100	N	,	11100	M	.
01101	F	$	11101	X	/
01110	C	:	11110	V	;
01111	K	(	11111	LTRS	LTRS

There are four special characters:

WRU, is a shorthand notation for 'who are you',

BELL, causes a bell to ring on the receiving teletype,

CR, a carriage return, and

LF, a line feed.

As an example, if the bit pattern 01110 is received, it is taken as either a C in LTRS mode, or a ":" in FIGS mode. The LTRS and FIGS characters are only transmitted when the user shifts from letters to figures or vice-versa.

C.2   7-BIT ASCII

Five-bit codes, such as the Baudot code, are restrictive in that only uppercase characters are handled, the interpretation of each character depends upon whether a shift character is properly received, and there is no room for control characters.

In light of these limitations, a number of organizations worked together and developed the 7-bit ASCII (American Standard Code for Information Interchange) code, formally known as ANSI (American National Standards Institute) standard X3.4-1977. ASCII supports 128 possible characters (i.e., 2^7): uppercase and lowercase character, numbers, special symbols, and control characters. The CCITT equivalent of ASCII is known as CCITT International Alphabet Number 5 (or IA5).

Table C.2 is the 7-bit ASCII table. To read the bit pattern associated with a specific character, find the character in the table, concatenate the three bits at the top of the character's column with the four bits to the left of the character. For example, the letter S is the bit pattern 101 concatenated with 0011, or 1010011.

TABLE C.2   The 7-bit ASCII Code

	000	001	010	011	100	101	110	111
0000	NUL	DLE	SP	0	@	P	`	p
0001	SOH	DC1	!	1	A	Q	a	q
0010	STX	DC2	"	2	B	R	b	r
0011	ETX	DC3	#	3	C	S	c	s
0100	EOT	DC4	$	4	D	T	d	t
0101	ENQ	NAK	%	5	E	U	e	u
0110	ACK	SYN	&	6	F	V	f	v
0111	BEL	ETB	'	7	G	W	g	w
1000	BS	CAN	(	8	H	X	h	x
1001	HT	EM	)	9	I	Y	i	y
1010	LF	SUB	*	:	J	Z	j	z
1011	VT	ESC	+	;	K	[	k	{
1100	FF	FS	,	<	L	\	l		
1101	CR	GS	–	=	M	]	m	}
1110	SO	RS	.	>	N	^	n	~
1111	SI	US	/	?	O	_	o	DEL

The control characters are defined as follows:

NUL	The null character	DLE	Data Link Escape
SOH	Start of header	DC1	Device Control 1
STX	Start of text	DC2	Device Control 2
ETX	End of text	DC3	Device Control 3
EOT	End of transmission	DC4	Device Control 4
ENQ	Enquiry	NAK	Negative Acknowledgement
ACK	Acknowledgement	SYN	Synchronization
DEL	Bell	ETB	End of transmission block
BS	Backspace	CAN	Cancel
HT	Horizontal tab	EM	End of medium
LF	Line feed	SUB	Substitution
VT	Vertical tab	ESC	Escape
FF	Form feed	FS	File separator
CR	Carriage return	GS	Group separator
SO	Shift out	RS	Record separator
SI	Shift in	US	Unit separator
		DEL	Delete

Originally, 7-bit ASCII was developed for machines supporting 7-bit bytes (actually eight bits in total: the eighth bit of a character was treated as a parity bit). However, since most bytes occupy eight bits within the machine, many manufacturers have extended the 7-bit ASCII character set to support a further 128 characters. For example, the PC treats bytes with values greater than 127 as special graphic characters, generated using the ALTMODE key.

C.3   8-BIT EBCDIC

In recognition of the limitations associated with 5-bit codes, a number of 6-bit codes were developed, including the 6-bit Transcode from IBM. The 6-bit Transcode supports all upper case English characters, numbers, symbols, and sixteen control characters.

When IBM adopted the 8-bit byte for their large mainframes, they also developed a new character code, known as EBCDIC (Extended Binary Coded Decimal Interchange Code). EBCDIC is *extended* in that it was introduced to replace the older 6-bit codes (sometimes known as binary coded decimal codes). EBCDIC supports 256 different character codes (i.e., 2^8); including all upper and lowercase English characters, numbers, symbols, and control characters. There are many gaps in the EBCDIC table where no specific character translation is defined.

EBCDIC is found primarily in large-scale IBM and IBM-compatible computers as well as support equipment, such as terminals and printers. The EBCDIC character assignments are as follows (two eight character tables Table C.3a and C.3b are used because of space restrictions):

TABLE C.3a The EBCDIC Character Set (0–127)

	0000	0001	0010	0011	0100	0101	0110	0111
0000	NUL	DLE	DS		SP	&	-	
0001	SOH	DC1	SOS					
0010	STX	DC2	FS	SYN				
0011	ETX	DC3						
0100	PF	RES	BYP	PN				
0101	HT	NL	LF	RS				
0110	LC	BS	ETB	UC				
0111	DEL	IL	ESC	EOT				
1000		CAN						
1001	RLF	EM						
1010	SMM	CC	SM		¢	!	|	:
1011	VT				.	$	,	#
1100	FF	IFS		DC4	<	*	%	@
1101	CR	IGS	ENQ	NAK	(	)	_	'
1110	SO	IRS	ACK		+	;	>	=
1111	SI	IUS	BEL	SUB	|	¬	?	"

TABLE C.3b The EBCDIC Character Set (128–255)

	1000	1001	1010	1011	1100	1101	1110	1111
0000					{	}	\	0
0001	a	j	~		A	J		1
0010	b	k	s		B	K	S	2
0011	c	l	t		C	L	T	3
0100	d	m	u		D	M	U	4
0101	e	n	v		E	N	V	5
0110	f	o	w		F	O	W	6
0111	g	p	x		G	P	X	7
1000	h	q	y		H	Q	Y	8
1001	i	r	z		I	R	Z	9
1010								
1011								
1100								
1101								
1110								
1111								

Single-Port Operations

Much of the Commkit software has been written for PCs that support two serial communication ports. In certain situations it may be financially impossible to purchase an additional serial port for your PCs. This may potentially render many of the experiments described in the book unworkable. Fortunately, much of the software can be rewritten to work with either a single serial port, the parallel port, or both. In all cases, it is necessary to have a copy of Turbo C to recompile the changes.

The Commkit software unaffected by the use of a single port includes: the interprocess communication software, the point-to-point telephone utility, the modem-control software, and all of the stop-and-wait protocol. In addition, the wide area network software can be made to function with only two stations; however, routing is still an issue.

Suggestions as to how the remaining software (the line analyser, the bus network, the ring network, and the bridge) can be modified are discussed in this appendix.

D.1   BASIC CONCEPTS

There are two problems associated with the execution of software that requires two serial ports:

- waiting for data on a nonexistent serial port.
  Not surprisingly, if the serial port does not exist, it is impossible for the software to receive data from the serial port.

- waiting for an indication that a transmission has completed.

Software can write to a nonexistent serial port, but a transmission completion indication will never be returned. Should the software require a transmission completion indication before sending the next character, a deadlock condition will be reached.

The objective of any software modification is to ensure that neither of the above conditions are encountered.

D.2   THE PARALLEL PORT

The parallel port can be used in place of a serial port. For example, instead of communicating through serial port 1 (SP1IH), the software can be written to communicate through the parallel port, PPIH.

Using the parallel port requires the use of special cabling and the parallel-port software, parlport.c. A complete description of the necessary cabling and how the parallel-port software functions can be found in Chapter 14.

In all situations, the parallel port must connect to another parallel port.

D.3   THE LINE ANALYSER

The line analyser should have two serial ports in order to function. If only one additional serial port card is available, it should be used in a PC as a line analyser. This will allow the monitoring of network traffic, thereby facilitating error detection and correction.

However, the parallel port can be used in place of one of the serial ports. Bytes are received from and sent to PPIH. Sanity checks are still required.

D.4   THE BUS NETWORK

The bus-network software requires the use of two serial ports: when transmitting, bytes are sent out both ports; and when receiving the byte received is forwarded out the other port.

Single port operation can be achieved by ensuring that only one port is accessed (i.e., transmission occurs out a single port only and bytes are never forwarded during a reception). For example, by setting bus.x_state to SEND_DONE for serial port 2, transmissions should never occur through serial port 2. Similarly, if bus.etxfnd is set to TRUE for serial port 2, collisions can be handled when they occur on serial port 1.

Forcing collisions in a single port configuration may best be achieved if the PCs operate at a very slow line-speed. If the line analyser is available, it should be used: first to allow the collision to be monitored, and second, to help slow down the rate of transmission.

The parallel-port software can be used in the bus network. It may be necessary to modify pp_protocol() so that it returns XMITDONE and RECVDONE status codes before calling the bus emulator. Additional changes to the transmission software are also necessary for the transmission of bytes out the parallel port. It may be necessary to use the send() primitive in order to supply bytes to the parallel port.

D.5   THE RING NETWORK

The ring network software receives bytes from serial port 2 (SP2IH) and forwards them on serial port 1 (SP1IH). By sending and receiving through the same serial port, the ring network can be made to function between a pair of PCs. The changes required are minimal, since all transmissions are sent via serial port 1 and input can occur on either port (the source of the receive completion interrupt is not checked).

The parallel port software can also be used as part of the ring network. Although most of the ideas discussed with respect to the bus network are applicable to the ring, *two* distinct sets of software must be produced:

- One set must be able to transmit on the serial port and receive on the parallel port.

- The other must be able to receive on the serial port and transmit on the parallel port.

In addition, an even number of PCs are required (see Figure D.1).

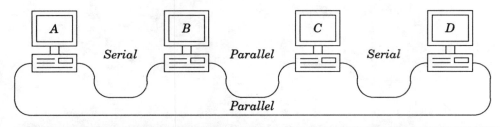

Figure D.1   A ring of serial and parallel ports

D.6   THE COMMKIT BRIDGE

Since the Commkit bridge already supports the serial ports and the parallel port, only the Network Layer software using the single port software described above is necessary. Messages can be sent from station to station across the network and the bridge statistics can still be obtained.

D.7   A FINAL WORD

Before proceeding with the suggested changes described in this appendix, check your PCs again—sometimes the serial ports are not labelled as such.

Also, many PCs are now supplied with "multi-function enhancement peripheral cards" (especially PC/ATs). These cards have a parallel-printer port, a game port, and *two* serial ports. In some cases, only one serial ports is connected—check whether your PC is supplied with such a card.

And finally, remember to make copies of any software before modifying it!

Suggested Readings

PART 1 BACKGROUND

- Lipschutz, Seymour, *Essential Computer Mathematics*, Schaum's Outline Series, McGraw-Hill, New York, 1982.
- Sarch, Ray, ed., *Basic Guide to Data Communications*, McGraw-Hill, New York, 1985.
- *Turbo C Reference Guide, Version 2.0*, Borland International, Scotts Valley, Calif., 1988.

PART 2 POINT-TO-POINT COMMUNICATIONS

- *Data Communications, Local Area Networks, UARTs Handbook*, National Semiconductor, Santa Clara, Calif., 1990.
- McNamara, John E., *Technical Aspects of Data Communications*, Digital Press, Digital Equipment Corporation, Bedford, Mass. Second Edition, 1982.
- *Technical Reference Manual for the IBM Personal Computer*, IBM Corporation, Boca Raton, Fla., 1983.
- Thorne, Michael, *Programming the 8086/8088*, Benjamin/Cummings, Menlo Park, Calif., 1985.

PART 3   LONGER DISTANCE COMMUNICATIONS

- Martin, James, *Security, Accuracy, and Privacy in Computer Systems*, Prentice-Hall, Englewood Cliffs, NJ, 1973.
- Schwaderer, David, *C Programmers Guide to NETBIOS*, SAMS, Indianapolis, 1988.
- Sharma, Roshan, Paulo de Sousa, Ashok Ingle, *Network Systems*, van Nostrand Reinhold, New York, 1982.
- Moshos, George, *Data Communications: Principles and Problems*, West Publishing Company, St. Paul, 1989.
- *Datapac: Standard Network Access Protocol Specification*, Trans-Canada Telephone System (now Telecom Canada), Ottawa, Canada, 1976.
- Tanenbaum, Andrew, *Computer Networks*, 2nd ed., Prentice-Hall, Englewood Cliffs, NJ, 1988.
- *IBM Synchronous Data Link Control: General Information*, IBM Corporation, Research Triangle Park, NC, GA27-3093-2, 1979.
- *General Information—Binary Synchronous Communications*, IBM Corporation, Research Triangle Park, NC, GA27-3004-2, 1970.

PART 4   LOCAL AREA NETWORKS

- *Microcommunications Handbook*, Intel Corporation, Santa Clara, Calif., 1985.
- Keiser, Gerd, *Local Area Networks*, McGraw-Hill, New York, 1989.
- *Local Area Networks: An Advanced Course*, Lecture Notes in Computer Science 184, Huchinson, D., Mariani, J., and Shepherd, D., eds., Springer-Verlag, Berlin, 1985.
- *Carrier Sense Multiple Access with Collision Detection (CSMA/CD) Access Method and Physical Layer Specifications*, ANSI/IEEE Standard 802.3-1985.
- *Token-Passing Bus Access Method and Physical Layer Specifications*, ANSI/IEEE Standard 802.4-1985.
- *Token Ring Access Method and Physical Layer Specifications*, ANSI/IEEE Standard 802.5-1985.

PART 5   INTERNETWORK COMMUNICATIONS

- Comer, Douglas, *Internetworking with TCP/IP*, Prentice Hall, Englewood Cliffs, NJ, 1988.
- *Local Area Networks: An Advanced Course*, Lecture Notes in Computer Science 184, Huchinson, D., Mariani, J., and Shepherd, D., eds., Springer-Verlag, Berlin 1985.
- Keiser, Gerd, *Local Area Networks*, McGraw-Hill, New York, 1989.
- Sloman, Morris, Jeff Kramer, *Distributed Systems and Computer Networks*, Prentice-Hall, Englewood Cliffs, NJ, 1987.

Index

About the Author

Larry Hughes is an Associate Professor of Computing Science at Saint Mary's University in Halifax, Nova Scotia, where he is currently teaches introductory and advanced-level courses in data communications, operating systems, and distributed systems. Dr. Hughes earned his doctorate in Computing Science at the University of Newcastle upon Tyne. His experience in data communications derives in part from a number of years with Bell Northern Research as project leader for several Datapac projects. He has used the Commkit approach to teaching data communications in both community college and university settings. Dr. Hughes' research interests include multicast communications, distributed systems, and hypermedia.